EASTERN

EXPERIENCES

EASTERN EXPERIENCES.

BY

L. BOWRING, C.S.I.

GYAN

Published by

Gyan Publishing House
5, Ansari Road
Daryaganj, New Delhi-110002
Phone: 011-47034999, 9811692060
E-mail: books@gyanbooks.com

Distribution Network
gyanbooks.com
India, USA, Canada, UK, Australia

ISBN: 978-93-6208-595-5 (PB)
First Published, 1858

2nd Impression 2024

Printed at: Gyan Press, Delhi.

EASTERN EXPERIENCES
Author: L. BOWRING

EASTERN EXPERIENCES.

EASTERN

EXPERIENCES.

BY

L. BOWRING, C.S.I.

LATE

CHIEF COMMISSIONER OF MYSORE AND COORG.

SECOND EDITION.

LONDON:

HENRY S. KING & Co., 65 CORNHILL.

1872.

PREFACE.

THE FOLLOWING sketches of Mysore and Coorg are based upon notes made during the course of several tours through those provinces, to which has been added such information from published official reports, and other sources, as could be comprised within moderate limits. The other papers contain observations recorded at the time, and old reminiscences.

The letters from my wife to her friends at home will perhaps afford a lively idea of first impressions in India, and, although placed at the end of the book, as sweets come after solids, many may think that, being more digestible, they should take precedence of the heavier articles.

For the sake of uniformity, the scientific system of spelling oriental names has been generally followed, but it has not been thought necessary to alter the old familiar mode of writing in the case of such well-known names as Mysore, Seringapatam, Coorg, Bangalore, &c.

L. BOWRING.

TORQUAY: *May* 1871.

CONTENTS.

MAPS AND DIAGRAMS.

ERRATA.

Page 51, line 5, *for* 'Nílgeri' *read* Nilgiri.

„ 62, „ 6 from bottom, *for* 1016 A.D. *read* 1116 A.D.

„ 76, „ 9 *for* 1265 *read* 1275.

London, Henry S. King & Co. 65 Cornhill.

MYSORE,

HISTORICAL AND DESCRIPTIVE.

About four years ago, a more animated discussion than usually arises on Indian subjects took place in Parliament regarding the future of the Mysore province, and an announcement by the Secretary of State that Her Majesty's Government had recognised, on certain conditions, the adoption of a son made by the sovereign of the territory, was received with satisfaction.

It is proposed in this paper to give some account of a country which is the second in rank of the Queen's feudatory provinces in India, and which, in many other respects, is not devoid of interest.

Mysore has an area of about 28,000 square miles, a population of four millions, and a revenue of more than one million sterling. It is greater in extent than some European kingdoms; and although the population is only 143 to a square mile, and is therefore much less than that of most European States, or than that of Bengal and the North-west Provinces, it is nearly the same as that of the Punjab and the Madras Presidency. The taxation falls at the rate of about five shillings per head, while of the total income nearly four-fifths are realised from land revenue.

The tables at foot [1] give the details of the population in 1869–70, and of the government revenue and charges from all sources in 1868–69.[2]

Few parts of India have a more diversified surface than Mysore. An orographical map of the country

[1] 1. *Population.*

1. Hindus	3,839,679
2. Jains	12,623
3. Native Christians[a]	8,186
4. Musalmans	189,272
5. Eurasians.	2,855
6. Europeans[b]	4,151
Total	4,056,766

[a] It is believed that a considerable number of Caste Christians are comprised in this total.

[b] Includes European soldiers.

2. *Revenue.*

	Rupees
1. Land Revenue	77,53,672
2. Forests	3,51,476
3. Excise	9,56,510
4. Customs	7,19,157
5. Assessed Taxes (Moturfa)	3,79,425
6. Salt	14,429
7. Stamps	3,40,131
8. Post Office	37,620
9. Law and Justice	1,15,348
10. Police	7,545
11. Education	20,171
12. Miscellaneous	1,00,147
13. Military Local Force	7,921
14. Public Works	74,726
Total Rupees	108,78,278
Equal to	£1,087,827

3. *Charges.*

	Rupees
1. Refunds	15,142
2. Land Revenue	9,90,769
3. Forests	1,19,950
4. Excise	20,165
5. Assessed Taxes	844
6. Stamps	18,153
7. Mint	320
8. Post Office	1,28,316
9. Palace Charges and Public offices	14,88,137
10. Law and Justice	10,81,959
11. Police	5,15,817
12. Education, Science and Art	1,81,280
Carried forward	
Brought forward	
13. Medical Services	1,08,214
14. Stationery and Printing	54,648
15. Treaty Assignments and Allowances	25,71,155
16. Miscellaneous	82,904
17. Charitable Institutions and Pensions	3,66,988
18. Mysore Local Force	11,18,324
19. Public Works Department	15,49,856
Total Rupees	104,12,941
Equal to	£1,041,294

[2] This year is taken in preference to 1869-70, as in that year some of the instalments of revenue were postponed till 1870–71, thereby affecting the receipts.

would exhibit an immense plateau, studded, either with bold isolated hills, called drugs (droogs), or with ranges, some of which attain, on the western frontier, an altitude of nearly 7,000 feet above the sea. Scarcely a single square mile of level ground can be found on the plateau, the surface being everywhere undulating. The great station of Bangalore has an elevation of 3,031 feet, but, from this point, excepting a few other places in its vicinity, the general level of the country falls away on all sides, the southern part of the province, under the Nilgiri hills, being less than 2,000 feet, while the northern frontier at Harihar shows a height of only 1,800 above the sea. The same tendency is observable towards the east, as also on the western border, till one reaches the stupendous mountain ranges which separate Mysore from the districts of Canara on the coast.

The height of the Mysore plateau, in a latitude where the continent of India is only 350 miles across, gives it the full benefit of both the north-east monsoon in the beginning of winter, and the south-west in the rainy season.

The average rainfall yearly at Bangalore is about 35 inches, but there is a striking difference between the fall on the east and the west sides of the province, the yearly average in some of the eastern subdivisions being only 15 to 20 inches, while on the western gh́ats it frequently amounts to more than 100 inches.

The country is well watered, both by streams and artificial means, and is therefore productive; but, with the exception of a few favoured localities, it is very feverish, owing partly to the great alternations of temperature to which it is subject, and also to the malaria produced by the decomposition of the sienite rock which covers the province. The dense jungles on the borders have also a prejudicial effect on health.

Mysore is divided into three divisions, and eight districts, as follows :—

1. *Nandidroog.*	2. *Ashtagram.*	3. *Nagar.*
Bangalore (Bengalúr)	Mysore (Maisúr)	Shimoga
Toomkoor (Tumkúr)	Hásan	Kadoor (Kadúr)
Kólár		Chitaldroog (Chitaldrug)

This division was made a few years ago for purposes of administrative convenience, but the nature of the country and the habits of the people differ widely in the several districts, and it is therefore proposed to give such details of the peculiarities of each as may be comprised within the moderate limits of this paper.

NANDIDROOG DIVISION.—BANGALORE.

Bangalore being the present head-quarters of the Mysore administration, the district of that name first deserves mention. It has an area of 2,586 square miles, a population of 659,000, and yields a revenue from all sources of 180,000*l.*

The foundation of the town of Bangalore is attributed to a prince who arrived in the country in a starving state, and was entertained, somewhat after the fashion of King Alfred, by a woman who gave him some beans called 'Bengalu' to eat, in commemoration of which, the grateful chief, when he succeeded in establishing his sway, called the scene of his adventure Bengaluru, or the City of Beans, corrupted in English to Bangalore. Another tale relates that the first ruler of note was one Vira Gauda, who, to preserve the fair fame of his daughter, who was persecuted by an importunate suitor of rank, fled from Kánjeveram, in the Madras presidency, and established himself at Bangalore, of which he after some time obtained possession. Little interest attaches to the history of this family till the time of Kempe Gauda, or the Red Chief, who having discovered some hidden treasure at Alsúr, in the neighbourhood of the town, proceeded at once to strengthen his position by building a fort, within which he erected a temple dedicated to his family gods.

About this time the authority of the kings of the Anagundi family, who, for several centuries, had reigned at Vijayanagar on the Tungábhadra river, was waxing faint, and a host of small barons called Pálegárs (from páliam, a subdivision of a country) sprang up, each helping himself to as much territory as he could seize and hold. Among these, Kempe Gauda occupied a conspicuous place; but not content with fortifying his abode in the plains, he, like the other Pálegárs, sought for a stronghold to which he might betake himself in troublous times. Twenty-eight miles from Bangalore, in the heart of a rugged hill country, is a superb granite rock, 4,024 feet above the sea, called Sávandrug. It has bold precipitous sides, and can only be approached by a narrow and steep ascent up the face of the hill, which is covered with thick jungle, and in its numerous sharp turns offers formidable obstacles to an attacking force.

The most singular feature in the hill fortresses called Drugs, or droogs (from a Sanskrit word signifying inaccessible), of which there are more than twenty in Mysore ranging from 3,000 to 5,000 feet in height, is that water, generally of good quality, is almost invariably found on the summit of these mountains. This circumstance naturally led to these precipitous fortresses being selected as strongholds for offensive and defensive purposes, and, as all the easier approaches were strengthened by double walls, bastions, and gateways, the reduction of such forts was, in olden time, only to be accomplished by treachery.[1]

Having selected Sávandrug as his place of refuge, Kempe Gauda added to the natural strength of the rock by throwing up stone walls wherever the sides of the hill were not inaccessible, and so formidable was the fortress deemed to be, that it was never captured by any native commander, the solid walls remaining to this day to attest the excellence of the materials employed in building them.

The arduous task of reducing this stronghold was, however, successfully accomplished by Lord Cornwallis' army in the first war with Tippu Sultán, notwithstanding the extreme difficulty of dragging artillery over the

[1] An interesting account might be written of the more remarkable forts in India, such as Deogiri in the Deccan, which is scarped all round perpendicularly to a height of 150 feet; Bandogarh in the Réwa territory, which is surrounded by a morass well-nigh impassable; the famous fortress of Chitór, celebrated in the annals of Rájput chivalry; Singgarh, the scene of Sivaji's principal exploit; the vast stronghold of Rothás on the river Són, in Behár; Kalinjar, the key of Bundelkhand; Rintimbór, Riyási, and many others noted in past times, not to speak of those which have acquired historical renown in our own days, such as Trichinopoly, Seringapatam, Delhi, Lucknow, &c.

rugged stony country beneath it, the formidable nature of the defences, and the number of guns placed in position. The garrison lost heart and fled, although, if defended by men of resolution, the fort might long have held out against the British force.

During the feeble rule of Kempe Gauda's successors, Bangalore fell successively into the hands of the Musalman sovereigns of Vijayapur or Beejapoor, and the Mahrattas, and was finally sold by Kásim Khán, a general of the Emperor Aurangzeb, to the Mysore Raja, then rapidly rising in importance.

When Haidar Ali had usurped power in Mysore, he strengthened the fortifications of Bangalore, while the town itself was protected by a deep ditch and a dense thicket, so that, on the place being stormed in 1791 by Lord Cornwallis' army, the loss of the British was rather heavy.

After the capture of Seringapatam in 1799, English troops were stationed at that place for many years, but, on fever of a virulent type breaking out and continuing persistently, it was determined to select a more salubrious locality. The elevation of Bangalore, and its position on the high road from Madras to Mysore, pointed it out as a fitting place for the new headquarters, and the troops were accordingly removed thither. It has many advantages in regard to climate and situation, but there is a great deficiency of water, and in seeking sites for new barracks, an egregious error has been committed in building them on an exposed site, without a drop of water, and in close proximity to the drainage of the station. Little attention seems to have been paid to the opinion of those best qualified to advise on so important a question, for a far better site, with an ample water supply, and removed from the noxious influences of foul drainage, was available to the eastward of the Alsúr reservoir.

To add to the blunders about the site, the arsenal was left in the fort, several miles off, on the further side of the native town, while thousands of pounds have been spent on palatial barracks, indifferently built, and standing on a plateau where nothing will vegetate, and where there is not space for a single officer's house.

The presence of a large British force speedily attracted to Bangalore the usual surrounding of traders, and a further impetus was given to its growing prosperity by the transfer to it of the civil administration of the province when the government was taken out of the hands of the late Mahárája Krishnaráj in 1831. Again, on the opening of the railway in 1864, the town became the nucleus of the trade of the whole country, and the population has increased so largely that it now ranks next to Madras among the cities of Southern India. According to a census taken two years ago, the population amounted to 132,000, of which the cantonment contained 79,000, and the old town 53,000 inhabitants. The bulk of the population is Hindu, there being only 11,000 Musalmans, 3,900 Europeans (including English soldiers), and 2,500 Eurasians.

According to popular tradition, the city is destined to still further expansion. On some of the eminences in the vicinity are picturesque little temples, called 'Mantapams,' which are assigned as the future limits of the place, two of them being far beyond the inhabited quarters.

The climate seems to be equally suited to Europeans and natives, epidemics being of rare occurrence, and other diseases of a mild character. In proof of its salubrity, it may be observed that, although it is situated in the 13th degree of north latitude, and therefore exposed to a tropical sun, the English soldiers are in the habit of playing cricket on the parade-ground for eight months of the year without any ill effects.

If well watered, and if partially protected from the sun, European fruits and vegetables attain a perfection which is rare in India, and at the monthly shows, held in the neat market-place in the cantonment, a stranger will be surprised to see the interest taken by the native gardeners in the improvement of their stock, and the intelligent competition to which these periodical exhibitions have given rise. Both fruits and vegetables, however, rapidly deteriorate in the absence of a fresh supply of seeds yearly. In the Public Garden, called the Làl Bágh, the formation of which is attributed to Haidar Ali, the visitor might at first imagine himself transferred to a purely European pleasure-ground, till, advancing, he sees the gorgeous creepers, the wide-spreading mangos, and the graceful betel-nut trees which characterise the east. The garden is a beautiful retreat, and is frequented by all classes, the natives being attracted to it mainly by the menagerie attached to it. Of late years, the Government of India have shown a laudable desire to encourage, on the part of the people of the country, an interest in all that humanises and refines the mind, instead of treating them like an inexhaustible milch-cow; and the formation at great stations of horticultural gardens, menageries, and museums has been productive of the best effects.

Owing to its superior climate, and to its being within easy reach of Madras, Bangalore has acquired an importance which would never have been anticipated. The non-official European population is large, and yearly increasing, while property is beginning to acquire a great value, land already selling for building purposes at a high rate. The commercial interests which have grown up during a long and settled rule demand attention, while the British Government has spent large sums on military buildings. The sovereignty of the soil is, however, vested in the Maharaja, and it therefore will be a question for anxious consideration how to secure best the interests of all parties when the young chief attains his majority. It is extremely improbable, on the one hand, that his officials would efficiently administer civil and criminal justice, and supervise municipal matters in a large station full of Europeans; while, on the other, the interests of the non-military population are far too weighty to be made over to ordinary military tribunals.

The only solution which will avert serious complications hereafter, appears to be the surrender by the Maharaja to the British Government of the town and station of Bangalore, together with such portion of the entourage as may be essential for public purposes, the jurisdiction being placed in the hands of a civil officer instead of the military authorities. The time has gone by when military tribunals could deal properly with all the litigation that may arise in great stations in India, as cases of a complicated nature which demand experienced judges frequently arise, while house property is far too valuable to be dealt with summarily. All power of appropriating private houses for military purposes ought to be put an end to, it being the duty of the English Government to provide residences for their officers, should they not be able to do so themselves. The former custom of reserving certain houses within particular limits for military occupation, tends to deteriorate the value of the property, and is neither necessary nor excusable at the present time.

The Mysore State pays to the British Government 250,000*l.* yearly for the protection afforded by the troops quartered in the territory; but those troops now cost about 360,000*l.*, owing to the great rise in prices, and the enhanced cost of maintaining the various military departments since the treaty was originally made with the Raja. It would, therefore, appear fair to assume the latter sum as the basis of calculation, and to purchase from His Highness the sovereignty of Bangalore, and of a sufficient circle of jurisdiction around it, ceding to him the island of Seringapatam, which belongs to the British Government, although it is rented by the Raja at a valuation of double its present income.

It is to be observed, however, that Bangalore is now of great value, not so much from its yearly receipts, as from the circumstance that the British

Government has expended there a large capital on military buildings. Again, the Raja may urge that he does not require in these peaceful times so large a force as is now stationed at Bangalore,[1] and that it is a mere matter of convenience to the British Government to retain so many European troops at so salubrious a station. Should circumstances render necessary a fresh treaty, he will be able to obtain more favorable terms than might at first sight be imagined. The former treaties being still in force, and actually adhered to in judicial questions, not without occasional inconvenience, his sovereignty cannot be challenged, and he appears to have a vantage ground, which he may fairly employ in demurring to any enhancement of the subsidy now paid by him, unless an equivalent abatement is made for any territory ceded by him.

Assuming the income of Seringapatam at 2,500*l.* yearly, its value at twenty years' purchase would be 50,000*l.*; whereas, the value of Bangalore, exclusive of all municipal income, would be at least four times as great. Seringapatam would, however, be specially important to the Raja, as being the seat of his ancestors, and invested with a sacred character, so that a mere money payment would not represent its value accurately. If ceded to the Raja, it would be necessary to stipulate against the fortress being further strengthened.

[1] It consists of 1 Regt. of European Cavalry; 1 Regt. of European Infantry; 3 Batteries of European Artillery; 2 Regts. of Native Infantry; and 3 Companies of Sappers.

The administration of the province was for thirty-seven years carried on in an ancient palace in the Bangalore fort, which was built by Haidar Ali, and was, according to a pompous inscription let into the wall, the admiration of the heavens. It is in some respects interesting, as connected with the history of the usurper and his son, but is architecturally insignificant and in a dilapidated state, while the fort itself, though noteworthy as the place of captivity of many Englishmen, and, among others, of Sir David Baird, during the war with Tippu Sultán, is no longer formidable.

Within the last few years, a fine range of public offices has been erected close to the military station. Should the Raja, on attaining his majority, reside permanently at Mysore, like his predecessor, this building would be useful to the British Government.

Like all great military stations in India, the cantonment of Bangalore is a heterogeneous assemblage of people of various nationalities and speaking several languages. In its bazars and streets are to be seen the enterprising Tamilian merchant, employé, or servant; Telugu-speaking Brahmans, gardeners and sepoys; Kanarese agriculturists, shepherds, and bullock-drivers; the proud and dignified Musalman, despising his Hindu compatriot, and disliking though fearing the foreigner; stray Arabs, Afghans, and Parsis, slender and dark Eurasians, and sturdy and fair Englishmen. It is hard to say what particular race predominates, or in what city of India one finds oneself, for there is a general resemblance in all military stations, though few wear so European a guise as Bangalore, with its many churches and its numerous attractive gardens.

Passing from the cantonment to the town hard by, there is no mistaking the fact that one is in the centre of a population which is almost exclusively Kanarese in origin and in language. Intrusive Europeans are rarely met with, and even the Musalmans are so few in number as scarcely to attract attention, save in particular localities where a small mosque denotes their presence. Hindu life is here seen in its native simplicity, everything conveying the impression of that unchanging oriental type which has characterised for thousands of years the Indian existence, and which lies deep below the surface of western refinement. The tinkling of small bells, morning and evening, in the heavy and quaintly-carved temples, betokens the offering up of the daily sacrifice according to the primitive Hindu custom, strings of white jasmins being thrown at the feet of the idols, or the lingam, by devout worshippers, who creep into the narrow doorway which leads into the mystical and dark sanctum, where is placed some personification of the deity. When the sun first shows himself above the horizon, high-caste Brahmans are to be seen resorting to the city tank, where they pour water over their heads and shoulders, and recite silently the sacred Gáyatri verse, as they make their ablutions. As the day advances, the petty shopkeepers, who do not seem in Mysore to be such early risers as in other parts of India, display their wares, whether for food or for dress, in the most tempting manner, those of the same trade having their shops in close proximity to one another in a rivalry which would seem to be injurious. Baskets full of the various grains of the country, or of betel leaves tied up in bundles of one hundred leaves, garlands of white and yellow flowers tastefully tied together with threads, small platters of betel nut chopped into four pieces, heaps of cotton and silk goods, piled one on the top of another, and trays of sweetmeats of every kind, melting in the sun and swarming with flies, meet the eye, everything being exposed in open shops.

There is little of the brilliancy which attracts in European shops, or even of the show in some of the great towns of Northern India, nor is Bangalore remarkable for any manufactures, except carpets of rare quality, rugs, and articles of mixed silk and cotton. Nevertheless, some of the leading merchants are men of substance, and bear the honourable appellation of Shetti, which entitles them to wear a gold signet-ring, to be accompanied in processions by smaller city functionaries, and to immunity from certain taxation. They trade largely in grain, exporting the millets and pulses of the province, and importing rice from the low country. Their greed is sometimes complained of, and in a time of famine it is difficult to resist the clamor of the poorer classes, and to refuse to interfere arbitrarily with prices as the ancient rulers did under similar circumstances. It is doubtful, however, whether Indian traders are more rapacious than those of other countries, and, although they rarely bestow money, they readily give grain to the needy, while the more wealthy have founded resting-places, called chhatrams, where travellers put up, and where food is distributed gratis to the higher castes. The character of the native bankers stands as high as that of any bankers in the world, breach of commercial honesty, as regards the due acceptance and payment of bills, being almost unknown among them.

There are no native merchants, however, in Southern India to rival the millionaires of Amritsar, Agra, or Bombay, so that the trading classes, keen as they are about their own affairs, exercise no influence whatever over the administration of the country. Again, the landed aristocracy, which existed prior to the ascendancy of the Mysore Rajas and the usurpation of Haidar Ali, is absolutely extinct, so that neither land nor money conveys that right which should give importance to the possessor. The result is that both the commercial and agricultural communities are as a bundle of sticks, the whole of the authority of the province being in the hands of the officials, nine-tenths of whom are Brahmans. Many of these are men of great ability, and some bear a very high reputation for integrity and zeal in the service of Government, but, as they all, to a man, hold land, it is obviously difficult to carry out any measures of reform which may affect their interests in the soil. In many parts of India, native officials are prohibited from holding land in the districts where they serve, but such a prohibition is impossible in Mysore, where the practice is universal, and a declaration only of the fact is therefore exacted.

Owing to the numerical strength, the superior talents,

and the landed influence of the Brahman servants of Government, and moreover to the fact that the chief of the State has richly endowed and supported the Hindu temples of the province, it is not surprising that Mysore should be a superstitious priest-ridden country. In fact, the Brahmans are all-powerful, and, although some of them are excellent men, it is natural that they should be tenacious of the authority so long wielded by themselves and their predecessors.

Let no one suppose that a missionary has only to show his face and conquer in Southern India, and that native superstitions and false creeds will vanish like a mist before the rising sun. The Indian mind is now passing through a period of unbelief, despising secretly what it professes openly, but as far as ever from adopting Christianity in lieu of the old faith of the Hindus.

The influence of Brahmans being still paramount, it is extremely unlikely, humanly speaking, that they should, of their own accord, open a flood-gate which would sweep them away into the open ocean of no-caste, where they would be lost amidst the myriads of their inferiors. The secular education taught in government schools seems but to have the effect of sharpening their wits, and of supplying them with ready and derisive sarcasms on the religion of Europeans. Nor is it an easy matter for the ablest missionary to contend with and vanquish the astute Brahman of the South, who, by equivocation or silence, can effectually baffle his adversary, or, by complimenting him on his learning, adroitly change the subject.

According to a Kanarese proverb, 'Hennu, mannu,

hana,' that is, 'Woman, land, and money,' are the principal objects of desire to man, and it is certain that the Brahmans have acquired their full share of the last two. In an agricultural country like Mysore, where so large a proportion of the revenue comes from the land, the local influence of individuals of course depends upon the extent of their possessions, and the desire to hold land may be said to extend to all classes, far more than is the case in Europe. The poor, as well as the rich, endeavour to secure land for cultivation, and in former days it was even the custom to pay the police and the rural levies, either wholly or partially, by assignments of land. In times of scarcity, such as periodically visit India, when the month's pay of a needy official will purchase only a few pounds of grain, scarcely sufficient to support the lives of himself and his family, the possession of an acre or two of land is a valuable addition to his income.

In the vicinity of Bangalore, owing to the rapid increase in the population and consequent wealth of the place, land, whether for agricultural or building purposes, has acquired an enhanced value. The soil is mostly of a rich red colour, like that of Devonshire, and when the rainfall is abundant, is very productive, while the tillage is carefully attended to by the ryots, who are skilful cultivators, ploughing their lands three or four times over, and using manure extensively. It is their custom to sow two or three kinds of seed in parallel rows in the same field, and one consequently sees, growing together, the five-headed rági, a small species of millet, which, when made into pudding, is the staple food of the people; ballar, a creeping bean with a sweet-scented white flower; and jólá, a large kind of millet, which grows to a height of several feet. In dry, that is, unirrigated land, are also grown various kinds of pulses—the castor-oil plant, sesamum, and horse gram, which, unlike the gram used in the north of India, is a bean and not a pea. A little cotton sufficient for household consumption is also grown, but the people do not appreciate the foreign species, alleging that they are not so hardy as the indigenous kind.

As the several crops that are grown in the same field ripen at various periods, a difficulty at once presents itself to the introduction of English reaping machines, nor are the holdings of the ryots sufficiently large to admit of their growing the different crops in separate fields. They prefer to have, if possible, a little of everything, and cling fondly to the methods of cultivation pursued by their forefathers, whose prejudices they hold in the utmost respect. The most splendid shower of rain at the driest season of the year, when it is urgently wanted for ploughing purposes, will not induce the ryot to take his bullocks to the field on a Monday.

At a trial made some years ago of English reaping instruments, ploughs, and threshing machines, the natives objected to both the former, the reaping machines being useless for the reason above given, while the ploughs were not considered light enough for the bullocks of the Mysore cultivators. The objection to the threshing machines, which were, in other respects, admired, was the heavy cost, and, unless they can be made at an outlay to the ryot of 2*l.* or 3*l.*; it is unlikely that they will ever be extensively used in India.

In land irrigated by tanks, or artificial reservoirs, with which Bangalore is abundantly supplied, and which number more than 20,000 in the whole province, paddy of several kinds,[1] sugar-cane, and mulberry are grown, together with betel-leaf, cocoa-nuts, plantains, and the betel-nut tree, the fruit of which, however, is of inferior quality, compared with that of the western districts.

Wells are abundant round Bangalore, water being near the surface in all the valleys, and a great variety of vegetables is raised in the land thus irrigated. The well chiefly used is the rude Yátam or Pekotta, consisting simply of a fulcrum stem, with a cross stem, and a drawing rod. The water is raised from the well by one person standing on the cross stem, and emptied into the field by another. Vegetables are brought to the markets daily for sale, as also strawberries and apples, which, at certain seasons, are of excellent quality, and yield a handsome profit to the gardeners.

A great proportion of the Bangalore ryots are by caste Wokkaligaru, Kunbis, Reddis, and Tigalaru, the last being gardeners of Tamil origin. It may be remarked, however, that all classes hold land, and know something of agriculture.

The cultivators, as a body, in the neighbourhood of Bangalore, are well off, and both they and their wives, when they visit the city on fair-days, make a show

[1] More than twenty varieties exist.

of their wealth, in truly oriental style, by wearing jewellery and bangles. There is a good deal of sturdiness in the Mysore ryot, who is not slow to speak his mind, if his interests are affected, presenting in this respect a remarkable contrast to the subservient and cringing Bengáli. Some attempts have been made to impart a little education to him by the formation of schools within small circles, but he is not fond of learning, and thinks that his children will neglect the plough for their books. If his crops are good, and the government officials keep aloof, he is perfectly happy, nor has the spread of education as yet affected greatly the original constitution of the village communities, which are complete little worlds in themselves.

In the phrase 'bárá balóti,' or the twelve professions, is comprised all that is essential to village life; but although twelve is the recognised number, the details vary occasionally,[1] while the Government takes no note of any of the village officials, except the following:—1. Gauda or Patél; 2. Shánabhóg; 3. Tóti; 4. Talári; 5. Nirganti. Of these the Gauda is the head-man of the community, and the channel of communication with Government, being responsible for the collection of the revenue. The Gaudas are of various castes, but are scarcely ever Brahmans, except where the

[1] Ordinarily the following comprise the Barabaloti:—

1. Gauda.	7. Carpenter.
2. Shánabhóg.	8. Potter.
3. Tóti.	9. Currier.
4. Talári.	10. Barber.
5. Nirganti.	11. Washerman.
6. Ironsmith.	12. Priest.

original head-men have disappeared, and their authority has been usurped by the Shánabhógs. The latter are always Brahmans, and as they keep the village accounts, and have much influence in assessing the land, they often fleece the people and defraud the Government, being alike avaricious and untrustworthy. Although nominally holding their land and perquisites at the pleasure of the State, it is no uncommon circumstance for a Shánabhóg to partition by will among his family his official emoluments, and the disputes that arise about the succession to this lucrative post give more trouble to the revenue officers than any other class of cases.

The Tóti is a village servant who performs various menial offices. The Talári is the watchman, who guards the crops, conveys messages for the head-man and accountant, and assists them in carrying the revenue collections to the Government treasury. The Nirganti (from 'niru,' water, and 'gante,' to measure) distributes to the cultivators the water of the tanks, it being his special duty to work the sluices, and to provide against mishap to these important means of irrigation. In the case of large tanks, there are three or four of these useful functionaries, on whose efficient discharge of their work much of the prosperity of a village depends.

Some of the Mysore tanks are of great age and of considerable size, that is, probably 300 years old, and 10 miles round. As the country is generally undulating, and intersected by numerous valleys, threaded by natural watercourses, it occurred to the natives, many centuries ago, to dam up the supply thus furnished, in order to irrigate their fields in the dry season, and, in this way, as population increased, and additional land was brought under the plough, a chain of such tanks was formed, gradually increasing in size and capacity as the line was prolonged. In many instances, advantage has been taken of gorges in the hills, to throw up colossal embankments, which have withstood, with fair success, the floods of centuries; but, as a general rule, the tanks of Mysore are mutually dependent works, situated in the same catchment basin. This close dependence upon one another admits of every reservoir in the chain receiving the surplus escape water of the work immediately above it, so that there is no wastage; but, on the other hand, should the annual upkeep be neglected, the larger tanks are subject to great risk from the sudden breaching, during high floods, of those higher up in the line.

From the same cause the railway, which forms, as it were, a vast embankment over the face of the country, and which, if not amply furnished with sufficient water-way at numerous points, has the effect of arresting the free discharge of the accumulated surface drainage, is much endangered in the event of great tanks in its neighbourhood giving way after continuous and heavy rain.

The embankments of first-class tanks are more than a mile in length, fifty feet wide, and as much in height, with sluices at either end, and immense escape-weirs, solidly constructed of large stones. The embankment is pierced by a culvert, which in some instances, is of such a size as to admit of a man creeping through it, and on either side of the embankment is a sluice, that in the water being worked with a plug which regulates the discharge, while from that on the other side the irrigation channels are taken which supply water to the fields. A tank, when full, is said to contain six months' supply, and, taking this as a maximum, the people reckon the water stored after each fall of rain at one, two, or three months' supply, as the case may be, fifteen days being the minimum. When the smaller tanks, either from want of rain, or from some defect, temporarily run dry, Bengal gram is commonly planted in the bed, Government taking a share of the produce. It often happens, however, that so much silt has been deposited in the tanks, that their repair is impracticable.

At Hosakóté, in the Bangalore district, is one of the largest reservoirs in the province, receiving the drainage of many square miles of country, and having below it many hundred kandies of rice-land. A kandy of irrigated land is about two acres in extent, twenty kudus (koodoos), of 500 square yards each, making a kandy. In dry or unirrigated land the kandy is also divided into twenty kudus, but each kudu contains 3,200 square yards, or about two-thirds of an acre. The term kandi, or khanduga in Kanarese, signifies the extent of ground requiring a kandy-weight of seed to sow it.

On land paying a fixed money assessment the Government demand is called the Kandáyam, and is roughly estimated at one-third of the gross produce; but the greatest inequalities now exist, owing to the roguery and favouritism practised by the minor government officials. These are in course of rectification by the survey department now at work in the district according to the Bombay system, the only settlement in India of which it can be said that the Government revenue always increases under it, that waste land is invariably taken up for cultivation, and that the assessments never break down. The average rental payable to Government on irrigated land of good quality near Bangalore may be said to be twelve shillings an acre. Deducting the cost of ploughs, cattle, and labor, a handsome profit remains on the cultivation of irrigated land;[1] but this varies greatly in all parts of the country, with reference to the quantity of water available, the price of labour and stock, and the proximity of markets. Land under irrigation channels taken from rivers is, of course, more remunerative than that under tanks, the water supply being more certain; but all wet land, as it is called, is coveted, and its possession is frequently a bone of contention.

As in other parts of India, no proprietory right was understood to be vested in the holders of unirrigated land. This may appear strange, as tank or garden land was acknowledged to be saleable by the person in

[1] The value of the out-turn of a kandi, or two acres, of irrigated land, is, on an average, from £8 to £12, from which, deducting the rental at £1 4*s.*, and the cost of labour, cattle, and manure at £2 6*s.*, or a total of £3 10*s.*, there remains a profit of from £4 10*s.* to £8 10*s.*, or from £2 5*s.* to £4 5*s.* an acre.

The value of the out-turn of a kandi, or thirteen acres, of unirrigated land, in a good season, may be estimated at from £15 to £20, the expenditure being about £3 10*s.*, leaving a profit of from £11 10*s.* to £16 10*s.*, or from 18*s.* to £1 5*s.* an acre; but if the rainfall is irregular or deficient, little remains to the cultivator's credit.

possession; but in the case of the former, the State itself was regarded as the proprietor, and the occupants as yearly tenants-at-will. Acting on this principle, the Government leased out whole villages to favoured individuals, either officials, or courtiers, or influential head-men. The Mahrattas, during their ascendancy in Mysore, appointed Désmukhs and Déspándes, who were answerable for the revenue of certain limited tracts of country; but these were swept away during Musalmán rule, and Faujdars, or divisional officers, took their place.

The late Mahárájá revived the evil practice of leasing out circles of country to the highest bidder, and in so doing ruined the province, and brought about his own downfall. Since 1831, every cultivator has had his lease, which for many years was annually renewed; but of late, leases have been confirmed for five years. The Bombay system of settlement, now being carried out in Mysore, gives leases of thirty years' duration, so that, while the ryot acquires a proprietory right, and a wide margin of profit, on payment of an easy rent, the State, on the expiry of the term of the lease, is entitled to raise the rent, should increased prices and the enhanced value of land warrant this being done.

Under the Bombay system of settlement, the Government receives only the value of from one quarter to one-sixth of the gross produce, and the assessments are therefore lighter than those of Upper India, where one-third of the gross produce is usually paid; but, on the other hand, the Bombay settlement-officer assesses all the culturable waste land of a village, and leaves but a limited area free for grazing purposes.

Among the more profitable crops grown under tanks is mulberry. The introduction of silkworms into Mysore is attributed to Tippu Sultán, and is one of the few benevolent measures for which he can take credit. During the last eighty years considerable attention has been paid to rearing silkworms by the Musalmán population of the Bangalore and Mysore districts, this branch of industry being very remunerative till recently, when the same disease which attacked the silkworms of Europe showed itself in those of Mysore, and the out-turn of silk began to decline sensibly. Several attempts to resuscitate it were made by an enterprising Italian firm, who received every encouragement from the State; but, although cartoons of Japanese and Chinese silkworms' eggs were twice imported at considerable cost, and distributed gratis to various localities, these efforts did not meet with success, and the silk trade still languishes. The Bangalore district used to produce 4,000 maunds (24 pounds = 1 maund), but the out-turn is now much smaller, nor will the trade revive till a change occurs in those climatic causes which seem to affect the vitality of the silkworm.

The central and eastern portions of the Bangalore district do not contain any hills of magnitude, and though the surface is undulating, the country is generally open; but in the sub-division of Kánákanhalli to the south, rugged hills and deep jungle mark the course of the river Kaveri, where it forms the boundary of the district. The western sub-divisions are covered with hills, extending north and south of Sávandrug, presenting highly picturesque scenery.

The most remarkable of these mountains is a hill called Sivagangá, about thirty miles from Bangalore, sacred in the eyes of Hindus who profess the Saiva faith, the reverence paid to it being probably due to its peculiar form, which, when viewed from the north, resembles the 'lingam,' or emblem of the god Siva. The hill is 4,400 feet above the sea, and is capped by a summit which, on one side, overhangs the rock below in the shape of a pent-roof. Many years ago, five silver bells were, at great risk, suspended under this projecting point, in honor of the god; but it is said that they were adroitly stolen afterwards by the man who hung them up, iron bells being substituted for them. There is a fine view from the top of Sivagangá, which is frequented by crowds of pilgrims at certain periods of the year.

The only towns of interest in the Bangalore district, besides Bangalore itself, are Devanhalli, where Haidar Ali first distinguished himself as a soldier, and where his son, Tippu Sultán, was born, and Chennapatam. At the latter place are two tombs of some elegance, one erected in memory of Ákil Sháh Kádiri, the religious preceptor of the usurper; and the other in honour of Sayad Ibrahim, the Commandant of Bangalore, who obtained from the British Government signal marks of favour, owing to the humanity shown by him to English prisoners who fell into his hands during the wars with his master Tippu.

There are no temples of special beauty in the district, though those at Alsúr, Mágadi, Sivagangá, and Bégúr are not without interest. In all of these, however, the carvings are inferior to those in the temples of the western districts, and no ancient inscriptions have been found, except at Bégúr, whence a valuable stone slab has been transferred to the museum at Bangalore.

The language spoken by the vast majority of the people of Bangalore, as well as of the other districts of the province, is Kanarese, and Mysore is emphatically the Karnatic in an etymological sense. Kanarese is spoken with the greatest purity at Mysore, the capital. In the hill districts to the west, the dialect contains many words and phrases peculiar to the Halé Kannadi, or old Kanarese, while the writing differs slightly from that in common use. Twenty miles eastward of Bangalore, Telugu begins to prevail in lieu of Kanarese, and is generally spoken in the Kólár district.

Musalmáns ordinarily converse in Hindusthání, and the various Hindu sects, in their domestic privacy, make use of their mother tongue—that is, the language spoken by their ancestors, whether the latter were natives of Mysore, or emigrants from countries where Tamil, Telugu, or Mahratta is the vernacular.

Kanarese is the official language of the province, and is therefore used in all public documents, though at one time Mahratta took its place; and in the days of the Musalmán usurpers, Persian prevailed.

TOOMKOOR (*Tumkúr*).

The district of Toomkoor contains an area of 2,766 square miles, a population of 492,000, and yields a revenue of 115,000*l.* It forms the watershed between the Mysore affluents of the river Krishna on the north, and those of the Kaveri on the south, the chief town, of the same name, being on the high road from Bangalore to Bombay. Parts of the district are highly picturesque, having a park-like appearance, wooded glades and gently sloping hills being characteristic of some of the sub-divisions. In its agricultural features it does not differ generally from the Bangalore district, but cocoa-nut trees are grown in a peculiar manner in dry land. The trees are planted ten or twelve yards apart, and are watered till they are four years old, when they are left to depend upon the rainfall, and produce excellent fruit up to the tenth year of growth. Notwithstanding the height of the trees, the shade renders it impossible to grow any cereals beneath them.

There are two drugs of some celebrity in this district, namely, Devaraidrug, which, being only ten miles from Toomkoor, forms a readily accessible sanatarium for the residents of that station, its elevation of 4,000 feet making it a most agreeable place of retreat in the summer months. The other drug is called Madagiri, and is one of the most difficult of ascent of all the strongholds in the country. This is owing to the slippery surface of the rock and its great steepness, while to the natural difficulties have been added several fortified gateways and high walls, stretching over the side of the mountain, so that, if defended by a resolute garrison, the position must, in former days, have been impregnable. On the top of the drug, at an altitude of 3,900 feet, there is a good supply of water. Many of these hill forts were furnished with cannon, which have now, however, been burst by an officer of the ordnance department, specially deputed for the purpose. Some of the smaller guns were found to be loaded, and owing to the dryness of the climate, the powder was still serviceable. Indeed, a small brass gun, which was not known to be loaded, suddenly burst when preparations were being made to melt it, and the discharge killed a man. This gun was supposed to have been loaded more than sixty years ago, in the time of Tippu Sultán. It was also found, on experiment, that rockets of the same period, which were discovered in another fort, were quite serviceable.

There are only a few places of note in the district besides Toomkoor. Of these, Sírá was formerly a place of importance, and the head-quarters of the Musalman Subadár; but, although occupied for some time by British troops after the fall of Seringapatam, it was found necessary to abandon it, owing to the prevalence of fever, which, in this part of the country, is of a serious type. In its fine mosques, and its numerous ruins, it shows signs of its former prestige.

Tipatúr is of some note as one of the chief depôts to which is brought the betel-nut raised in the hill districts of the west, to be mentioned hereafter. This traffic is one of the most lucrative of the country, the agriculturists being entirely in the hands of the traders, who hire gangs of Lambádís and Korchars, wandering tribes, who, at the proper season, take their cattle and donkies into the hills, and carry the betel-nut to Tipatúr and other emporiums, whence it is despatched to Arcot,

Madras, and other places, where this luxury is highly prized.

Kunigal was formerly the remount depôt of the Madras Government, and has capital paddocks and abundant grass, owing to the proximity of a tank of the first class, but the place is unhealthy, and, since its abandonment as a depôt, has dwindled in importance, though it is now the breeding-place of the Mysore Horse, and is also one of the principal spots where silkworms are reared. It has been supposed that the carelessness of those who tend the worms in disposing of the refuse has generated sickness, but the necessity of cleanliness is not more apparent to the people of this town than to those of an adjoining one, who, being interdicted by the local board from making a *cloaca maxima* of the fort ditch, resented this invasion of their former privileges, and sent in a petition to the highest authority requesting that traditionary usage might be respected.

A considerable portion of Toomkoor is covered with hills, sienite, composed of quartz, felspar, hornblende, and mica, being the main formation. In some parts of the district iron is worked extensively in a rude fashion, but the most curious mineral product is a fine black hornblende, hewn out of a rock called the Karikal Gudda, or Blackstone Hill, whence were conveyed to Seringapatam the beautiful polished pillars which adorned Tippu's palace and Haidar Ali's tomb, and from which also was extracted the material of many of the works of art to be seen in the numerous Hindu temples of the country.

KÓLÁR.

The Kólár district has an area of 2,281 square miles, a population of 479,000, and a revenue of 121,000*l.* It is noted for the number of its tanks, there being 4,274 of these useful reservoirs, some of them of large size.[1] The country is in parts very fertile, producing, besides sugar-cane, rice, and other ordinary crops, good potatoes, and opium to a small extent. The high road to Madras formerly ran through the district, the southern portion of which is now intersected by the railway as a substitute, but the old route is still much used by pilgrims proceeding to the famous shrine of Tirupati in North Arcot, a spot held so sacred that it is said never to have been desecrated by the steps of Europeans, in which respect it is perhaps unique among the places of pilgrimage of India, while the fact evidences the great toleration and consideration towards the Hindus of the British Government.

Kólár is still a town of importance, having a population of more than 10,000, and is said to have been named after a hind named Kollá, who discovered a large hidden treasure, which his master made use of to ingratiate himself with the Pennakonda Rajas, by whose permission he founded the town. Another tradition asserts that it was founded during the reign of the Chóla kings, in the first century A.D.

The legend of a buried treasure giving wealth and

[1] The cultivated area under the 4,274 tanks comprises 107,382 acres, yielding a revenue of £83,629 yearly. In many cases the irrigated area exceeds 1,000 acres.

status to the lucky finder is, not unnaturally, frequently found connected with the history of Oriental places, but another kind of tradition is less common. The latter is to the effect that a certain prince was out hunting, when his dogs pursued a hare, which turned upon its enemies and chased them instead. The construction put upon so strange a circumstance by the prince was that the soil where it took place must be male soil (gand bhúmi), that is, land of peculiar virtue, and therefore well fitted for building a fort on, and the tradition invariably ends by the hunter prince at once setting to work in erecting a stronghold, by means of which he succeeds in subduing all the country around. This legend is often met with in Mysore, and always in nearly the same words.

Three miles from Kólár is the Satsringa, or Hundred-headed hill, a fine mountain 4,000 feet high, of somewhat fantastic shape, on the summit of which are four or five villages with fertile land attached. The fine spring which is seen issuing from the Antra-Gangá temple is reputed to be the real Gangá, brought to the place by the deity to save a favored devotee from the trouble of proceeding to bathe in the genuine sacred stream. On the lofty hill dwelt the famous Rishi, or ascetic Jamadagni, who fell desperately in love with Renuka, daughter of a Raja and mother of the celebrated Parsurám, by which connection the Rishi lost all the merit of his previous devotions. His chaste wife, being unjustly suspected of infidelity, was slain by one of her sons, at the instigation of his father, who, in his turn, was murdered by the Kshatriyas for this foul deed. Parsurám avenged his father's death by exterminating all the warrior tribe of Kshatriyas.

At Kólár is the mausoleum of Fateh Muhammad, father of Haidar Ali, who was born at Búdikóte, seven miles off, that place and the vicinity having been held by Fateh Muhammad on a service tenure. Muhammad Ali, grandfather of Haidar Ali, with other members of the family, was buried in the same tomb, which is kept in repair at the cost of Government, and is a rather handsome structure.

A considerable portion of the Kólár district was, prior to the usurpation of Haidar Ali, held by petty chiefs called Pálegárs (from Páliam, a subdivision of territory), who, in course of time, contrived to seize tracts of country yielding a revenue of from 5,000*l.* to 30,000*l.*, according to their respective prowess and daring. These small barons generally bore the title of Naik or Náyaka, and were mostly of Telugu origin, having settled in Mysore within the last 4 or 500 years, after the downfall of the Vijayanagar and Pennakonda dynasties. They placed their main reliance upon the strong hill fortresses which stud the country, but frequently preferred residing in the more civilised places adjacent to the drugs.

Among the most noted of the hill fastnesses is Nandidrug, a grand mountain 4,800 feet above the sea, and about thirty-five miles due north of Bangalore; from the top of which 300 of the tanks of the country are visible. This celebrated rock is nearly precipitous on all sides except the west, from which direction it was assaulted in 1791 by Lord Cornwallis's army, and captured, after a gallant defence by the commandant, Lutf Ali Beg, one of Tippu's officers. Numerous marks of the round shot fired from the English guns are still to be seen in the walls. The residence of the Killadar, or commandant, is still preserved, and as the summit of the hill offered good sites for building, several houses have been erected, the place affording an agreeable sanitarium during the hot months of March, April, and May. There is a fine reservoir of water, and a good deal of wood on the hill, which is crowned by a temple sacred to Nandi. The bold bluff side of the mountain on this face is terminated by an overhanging mass, commonly called Tippu's Rock, from a tradition (of which, however, there is no proof) that he used to order prisoners to be hurled over it. There are two steep ascents from the plains, formed of flagged pathways, to the main gateways, besides a more difficult climb from the east to a small postern, but these were commanded by the guns of the fort, and were virtually impracticable, and the assault of the English force took place therefore on the western side, notwithstanding that this was protected by a double line of fortifications. The country around is covered by hills to the east and the north, in which latter direction there is a fine range extending to the frontier of the provinces, but pierced at intervals by narrow gorges, called locally Kanivés, through which, prior to the formation of roads by British officers, the trade of the country found outlets from the westward. One of the Madras regiments, the 36th Native Infantry, was raised near Nandidrug in 1800, and bears the name of the Nandi

Battalion, while one still sees, at the foot of the hill, the square where the corps was located, remains of houses, and a graveyard.

The adjacent town of Chikka Bálápur is probably the healthiest place in the whole Mysore country, and, had it not been in a somewhat difficult country, and too far off the main road from Madras to Mysore, it would probably have been selected, in preference to Bangalore, as the most fitting station for European troops. It is a large town with a thriving trade, and an abundant supply of water. Indeed, it was at one time contemplated to furnish Bangalore with water from the neighbourhood of Nandidrug, the foot of the hill being 200 feet higher than Bangalore, but the project fell to the ground, as the contour line would have doubled the direct distance from that station, and the undertaking would have been costly, while a closer investigation showed the practicability of providing the water required from elevated ground adjacent to the town.

The fief of Chikka Bálápur was founded by Maré Gauda, son of Male Bhaira Gauda, about the year 1447, and seems to have been a dependency of the Pennakonda Rajas, who were overthrown by the Mahrattas. Ninth in descent from the founder was Chikkappa Gauda, in whose time Haidar Ali reduced the Páliam, and took possession of Nandidrug, the stronghold of the Pálegár. The chief is said to have held a tract yielding an income of 30,000*l.*, but the family were reduced to the position of pensioners, in which they still remain. Rámaswámi Naik rendered aid to the

British Government during the wars with Tippu Sultán in 1792 and 1799, and seems in consequence to have expected his restoration to his hereditary possessions, an anticipation which was however never realised.

Another chiefship of local importance was that of Gúmanaik Páliam, founded by Gúma Naik and Láka Naik about the year 1400. These Pálegárs were by caste Yadikal, and belonged to the Kumbi race, in which tribe they exercised sacerdotal functions, which gave them considerable influence. Narsimma Naik, ninth in descent from Gúma Naik, was, however, dispossessed by Haidar Ali, and the chiefs, who formerly held a territory yielding 10,000*l.*, sank into the comparative insignificance of stipendiaries. They are still much respected by the people of the country, which is a hilly and difficult tract, affording a refuge to gang-robbers, who infest the borders of Mysore and the adjoining district of Kadapa in the Madras presidency.

The greater portion of the population of the Kólár district speak Telugu, which has, however, of late years been invaded by Kanarese, the language in general use in Mysore territory. Both are written in the same character, though a few letters differ in the two tongues, which diverge, however, radically more than Italian from Spanish. Telugu is far more melodious than Kanarese, and is probably spoken by three times as many people. In great stations, such as Bangalore, both languages are currently spoken, as well as Tamil, the speech of the people of Madras, who, either as officials, or as menial servants, are found in Mysore in great numbers. When to these tongues are added Hindusthání, the favourite colloquial of all Muṣalmáns, and English, which is now spoken by many educated persons, and by most of the official community, it will be apparent how wide a linguistic knowledge is needed to comprehend the speech and habits of a population comprising such various elements. In this respect, native officials have a great advantage, as it rarely happens that Europeans are sufficiently conversant with the vernacular languages to speak and understand more than a little Kanarese and Hindusthání.

Within the last few years the study of Kanarese has been greatly facilitated by the Mysore state, educational works having been printed and circulated in large numbers throughout the province. To the Wesleyan community much credit is due for their exertions in type-founding and printing useful books, while the press of the Catholic mission has also produced several elementary books, as well as treatises of a religious character. As it is hopeless to substitute English for the languages of the country, it is evidently desirable to foster as far as practicable the latter, and to supersede indigenous works of an objectionable character by others in which all the best features of modern civilisation and science are preserved.

More than one-quarter of the population of the Kólár district are Vokkaligaru, a caste exclusively employed in agriculture, and numbering many branches, the most remarkable of which are the Marasu Vokkaligaru, who have the strange custom of amputating the first joint of the ring-finger of their daughters in honour of their deity.

The shepherd caste, called Kurubaru, worship the god Birappa, of whose feast the following amusing account is given by a native writer.

'Eight days before the feast, the priest must get his head shaved, bathe himself, and take but one meal a day for eight days. On the feast day, he worships the god in the temple, and then comes out. In the court, there is a stone pillar, like a temple lamp-post. Coming to this, he kneels down before the idol, shuts his eyes, and rests on his hands and knees. Then all the ryots who have come to the festival bring cocoa-nuts, and going up to the pillar where the priest is kneeling, press one upon another, crying, "I am first, I am first." Then ten of the most respectable people come out, and take the cocoa-nuts which the people have brought into their own hands. Four others, strong men, stand near the priest, to whom the elders hand the cocoa-nuts, which they break on the head of the priest, who sits on his hands and knees before Birappa, with his eyes shut, holding out his shaven head, his body being naked, except a cloth round the waist. There he sits, till great heaps of cocoa-nut fragments are piled up as high as an elephant on both sides of him. Though so many nuts are dashed upon his bare skull, the priest feels no pain, does not utter a sound, and never cries "ap-pap-pa! ay-yo! Kuy-yo! morro!" but sits kneeling, with his hands before him, holding out his head for the nuts to be broken upon.'

Among a people where such rude customs prevail, it may easily be supposed that superstition is rife, and that Brahmans are held in great respect. As in other parts of the province, they are numerous, forming probably nearly a tenth of the whole population. They are divided into the indigenous Kanarese Brahmans, and those of Mahratta, Tamil, or Telugu origin.

In respect to religious tenets, most Brahmans belong to one or other of three schools, namely, Smárta, Mádwa, and Sri Vaishnava. The Smártas maintain the inseparability of the creature from the creator, wear cross marks on the forehead, and follow the teaching of the Sringiri Swàmi, the successor of Shankaráchári. Mádwas hold that the creature is separate from the creator, wear a vertical mark on the forehead, and revere the high priests at Narsipur in the Hásan district, and Sosilé in Mysore. The Sri Vaishnavas consider that the creature is finally absorbed into the divine essence. They wear the trident, or device of Vishnu on their forehead, but dispute among themselves whether this mark should be furnished with a base or not. Their great apostle, Rámánujáchári, was a native of Sriparambatur, near Madras, but for many years preached his doctrines in the Kanarese country, where the Sri Vaishnava tenets have many adherents. The high priests of the sect reside at Kambakōnam and Tinnevelly, but the Raja's family priest, Parakálaswami, who lives near Mysore, is considered to be the chief exponent of Sri Vaishnava doctrines in the province.

The Bedars, who are supposed by some people to

represent the former rulers of the country, are a sturdy active race, much addicted to sport, and good cragsmen and soldiers. To this caste belonged many of the Pálegárs, or petty barons, who, after the fall of the Vijayanagar dynasty, carved out for themselves independent principalities, which, however, were swept away by Haidar Ali and Tippu. They number in the Kólár district about 40,000 souls.

The crops raised in Kólár are the same as those grown in the Bangalore and Toomkoor districts, but owing to the abundance of tanks, the proportion of irrigated land is far greater, and the crops are finer. Betel leaf is one of the most remunerative crops. The vine is planted in holes, in furrows, which are manured and well watered for several months. The cuttings are shaded from the sun by branches of trees, quick-growing plants being sown in the intervening ridges to support the creepers of the vine when they commence to climb. The leaves are of very slow growth, but are gathered every two or three months, and fetch high prices, while betel-leaf gardens last about twenty years.

In the Bétmangalam sub-division of the district, gold is found to a limited extent, by washing the alluvial soil, in a small range of hills running north and south; but the quantity extracted scarcely repays the labour entailed, though at one time it was supposed that the field was very productive. A full account of the process followed was given by Lieut. Warren, of the Survey Department, so far back as the year 1803.

ASHTAGRÂM DIVISION.—MYSORE (*Maisúr*).

The district of Mysore has an area of 3,091 square miles, a population of 763,000, and a revenue of 157,000*l.*

It is perhaps the most interesting part of the province, as it contains the ancient capital of the present Mysore family, the seats of most of the members of royal stock, and some of the finest shrines in the country. It is also the most fertile part of the territory, owing chiefly to the numerous irrigation channels which are taken from the river Kávéri. This celebrated stream, which is, with some reason, held in veneration from its size and fertilising qualities, rises in Coorg, Tala Kávéri, its source, being a place of great sanctity in the eyes of all the Hindus of Southern India. The river enters Mysore at Frazerpett, called by Tippu Khóshálnagar, but more anciently Nanjrájpatan, whence it takes a westerly course through Mysore, till it leaves the province at the famous falls of Sivasamudram. At convenient intervals, dams, called Anekats (from 'ane,' a dam, and 'katte,' to build), have been thrown across the stream, from which channels are taken on one, or frequently on both banks. Some of these works were carried out more than 300 years ago, during the time of the Anagundi kings, who reigned at Vijayanagar in the Bellári district, and, although of ancient date, and liable to be occasionally breached by floods, they are still magnificent specimens of native engineering. The contour lines which the channels follow have been conducted with much ingenuity, considering the imperfect implements used, at the highest possible level over considerable distances—sometimes seventy miles[1]—and all the land lying between them and the river benefits by their fertilising properties. It has been supposed by some talented engineers that, instead of many such dams at short intervals, it would be feasible to substitute one first-class work, with channels of great length, at a somewhat higher level than the existing channels, so as to irrigate all the land which is now watered by the latter; but to this is opposed the circumstance that, at many points along the river, hills intervene, and would obstruct the prolongation of the channels, while, at the same time, small streams and subsidiary surface drainage, which now tend to augment the main stream, would probably remain unutilised. There can be no doubt, however, that, as in the case of the tanks of the country, the irrigation channels were not constructed on any uniform system, and that they owe their existence to various influential persons, who sought to benefit their own lands by constructing them, without much regard for the interests of others above or below them. One of them, near Sálágrám, called the Alal Katté, is 800 yards across, and is so solidly built that it is said never to have needed repair. As it straggles across the stream in a very irregular manner, it would not be regarded by modern engineers as a

[1] The Chikka Devarai Ságar channel is seventy-two miles long, and irrigates more than 10,000 acres of land, paying a revenue of £7,200.

successful work, although it has stood fairly the test of time.

It would be wearisome to give the names and length of all the channels, much as they conduce to the prosperity of the country, and it will suffice to say that they have now been brought under systematic supervision with a view to economise the supply, to effect an equitable distribution of water, and to execute thoroughly the requisite annual repairs. A considerable portion of the best land under them, and particularly of that nearest to the source of water supply, is held by Brahmans on rent-free tenure, owing to the lavish hand with which the late Raja of Mysore alienated the resources of his country in favor of persons who were, but too often, unworthy recipients of his bounty.

The Káveri, a few miles below Sálágrám, precipitates itself over a picturesque fall, called the Dhanuskóti, and, being joined by the Hémávati river from the adjoining district of Hásan, and also by the Lakshmantírth from South Coorg, flows under the walls of the renowned Seringapatam fortress. It is then joined by the Kabani (which rises in the coffee district of Wainád) at Sosilé, where the meeting of their waters is held sacred, and at length reaches the ancient town of Talkád, called in olden time Dalavanpar. A fabulous antiquity is given to this place in the local legends, and it is not improbable that it was a town of note in the days of the Chéra dynasty, as it is known that the kings of this race flourished in the adjacent districts of Koimbatór and Salem; but, in recent times, it has attracted attention, owing to a strange story which connects it with the Mysore royal family, and which is known as the 'curse of Talkád.'

It is stated that when the Mysore chiefs were beginning to subdue the country around them, one of the Rajas, in the year Sálivâhan, 1556, marched against the lord of Talkád, whom he defeated and slew in battle, seizing his territory and despoiling his family of their wealth. His despairing widow, after witnessing the slaughter of her husband and the wreck of their home, drowned herself in the sacred Kávéri, into which she first threw a gold ring, and in doing so pronounced a curse against the Mysore House, prophesying that Talkád should be buried in sand, and that the Raja's dynasty should come to an untimely end by the failure of male heirs. The first part of the curse has been accomplished, for it is a remarkable fact that the river Kávéri has, in the course of years, heaped up immense mounds of sand, fifty and sixty feet high, which have buried many old temples, and encroached so much on the town that it has been found necessary to abandon it as the head-quarters of the sub-division. Whether the second part of the prediction will be verified remains to be seen, but it nearly came to pass a few years ago; and it is not surprising that the people of the country think with superstitious awe of the widow's prophecy, and of her denunciation of the cruelty of the Mysore chief. It is to be hoped, however, that the fulfilment of the curse was enacted when Haidar Ali usurped the sovereignty of the country, and, apparently, extinguished for ever the rule of the Hindu princes of Mysore.

Leaving Talkád, the Kávéri pursues its course till it reaches the romantic island of Sivasamudram, famous for magnificent falls, over which the river precipitates itself on leaving the Mysore country. This picturesque place should be visited in the rainy season, as during the winter months, which are ordinarily the most healthy in India, fever is rife, owing, it is supposed, to the exposure to the sun and air, and the consequent disintegration of the large rocks in the river. Moreover, a better idea of the grandeur of the cataracts can be gained when the stream is in flood, though, on the other hand, a near approach to them is then more difficult. Sivasamudram is said to have been an ancient capital, but there is at present no vestige of former buildings, except a few ruins, and an inscription near a modern temple, which is illegible. It is certain, however, that the island had become a dense jungle, and that the old bridges which connected it with the mainland had become impassable.

Their repair was undertaken fifty years ago by a confidential servant of the Mysore Resident, named Rámáswámi Modeliar, who expended several thousand pounds on the work, for which he received from the British Government the title of 'Janopakár Kám Kartá,' or, the constructor of a work useful to the people, as also an estate of five villages, yielding about 800*l.* yearly. From the Mysore State he received seven villages, yielding 900*l.* yearly, in recognition of his meritorious exertions. The bridges are fine specimens of native workmanship, being composed of hewn stone, supported on colossal pillars twenty feet high, firmly fixed in the rocks of the river, while they are so constructed as to resist the force of the current during high floods, which are truly formidable. The Jágírdár, or proprietor, hospitably entertains all visitors to the spot, where a convenient residence has been built for their accommodation.

The northern cataract, called the Gangana Chuki, is about two miles from the house, and is approached by a steep path, leading down from the tomb of Pír Ghaib, a Musalmán saint, who is supposed to have disappeared mysteriously from view at this place. On reaching a point about half-way down the fall, one sees the stream rushing precipitately over the face of a tremendous abyss, and dashing over vast boulders of rock in a cloud of foam, till it hurls itself into a deep pool below, 300 feet from the summit. The noise made by the roar of the waters is deafening, and as one's ears are stunned by their loud thunder, so one's sight is blinded by the steam of mist which hides from view the sacred stream, as it rushes furiously forward over great rocks to meet the sister fall below. The scenery around is extremely grand, the hills being clothed in dense forest, and the solitude of the spot lending a picturesque charm to its beauties.

The southern cataract, called the Bhar Chuki, is perhaps even finer, as a far greater volume of water is seen from the point of observation, at the foot of a flight of difficult steps, which lead down to the stream facing the cataract. The fall can be approached from the summit, but is difficult of access, and a lady some years ago lost her footing, on incautiously nearing the verge, and was dashed over the cataract. During the rainy season, the river pours over the hill-side in an unbroken volume, a quarter of a mile across; but in the dry months it is divided into several distinct falls of great splendor, which the tourist can contemplate at his ease as he discusses his breakfast on the opposite side of the stream. The Bhar Chuki is of less height than the Gangana Chuki, and therefore perhaps less imposing, but is certainly more lovely, while the whole locality leaves an indelible impression on the mind of the visitor.

The whole of the southern side of the Mysore district is girt round by a dense and unhealthy forest, the level of the country falling rapidly down to the foot of the Nílgiri mountains, which constitute at this point the frontier of the province. It is in fact a Terai, similar to that at the foot of the Himalaya, and equally prejudicial to health, even the wild tribes who reside in the jungles showing, by the prevalence among them of fever and spleen, the insalubrity of the region. It is, however, rich in teak, blackwood, and other valuable forest [1] timber, and is consequently precious in the eyes of the forest conservator and his assistants, whose duty frequently takes them into the most feverish tracts, dwelt in only by half-savage Kurubas and Soligas, two of the aboriginal races whose destiny it seems to be to inhabit a country which is regarded with dread by more civilised people. These unfortunate beings, few

[1] Pterocarpus Marsupium (*Honné*); Terminalia Tomentosa (*Matti*); Hardwickia Binata (*Karáchi*); Bassia Latifolia (*Hippé*); Conocarpus Latifolia (*Dindida*); and many others.

in numbers and uncared-for by their neighbours, are the only workmen who can be obtained to fell trees in the noisome jungles, where they also collect honey, gums, and other forest produce, scared by herds of elephants, who dispute with them the lordship of the woods. Other animals and birds are rare in these dense jungles, although peacocks are occasionally met with in flocks in the wooded glades.

It is not improbable that the skirts of these vast forests had formerly a larger population than is now met with, as in various places near the Coorg frontier curious explorers have discovered remains of the ancient denizens in the shape of numerous cairns, supposed to be the burial-places of their race. They are commonly called 'Pándava Kallu,' or stones of the Pándavas,—everything ancient being connected, in the eyes of Hindus, with these heroes; and in the absence of any authentic account of their origin, this assumption passes muster. They consist of a small chamber, enclosed between three or four stone slabs, with a large slab on the top, and have a general resemblance to the Kistvaens of Europe. The rear slab is generally pierced by a circular hole, rather larger than a man's body, from which it has been inferred that they were dwelt in by the ancient Rishis or Ascetics; but it may be said, in opposition to the theory of their having been inhabited, that there is no trace of smoke on the roof. On the other hand, if they were burial-places, it is remarkable that neither bones, nor jars containing ashes, have been found in them, the only relics discovered having been empty pots, some of quaint design, a few rusty implements, a little rági seed, and, in one instance, a man's jaw. The structures do not face east or west, or north or south, but are seen facing all sides.

About ten miles to the right of the high road from Mysore to the Nílgéri hills, is the sacred hill of Gopálswámi, a picturesque and verdant mountain, 1,500 feet above the plains, on which there are eight springs, to which mysterious virtues are attributed, the locality, in spite of its unhealthiness and the fear of wild beasts, being much frequented by pious Hindus. The upper portion is surrounded by ancient fortifications, built of immense stones, and of great extent, reputed to have been constructed by one Dankana Naik or Dhan Naik, of whose palace a few traces are still to be seen, together with five massive gateways. Tradition is silent as to the history of the chiefs who dwelt here, but it is a curious fact that, in many cases in the jungles in the neighbourhood, tanks long disused are to be seen, while rice, called by the natives kád-akki, or forest rice, grows wild, being no doubt produced from seed, self-planted in land which was once under cultivation. Such decadence of places once of local note is common in India, and everywhere are to be seen the ruins of fortresses which in olden time were the only means of upholding the power of their possessors.

Among the most valuable products of the Mysore forests is sandal wood, which has, from the earliest times, been a royal monopoly, the tree being felled and sold exclusively by government agency. It is of most capricious growth, being found neither in dense forests nor in the open country, but just outside the skirts of the heavier jungles, and only in certain localities, where it is to be seen in clumps like an orchard, or in hedge rows, or growing singly. Attempts to rear it from seed have been unsuccessful, and it refuses to flourish, except over very limited tracts, of which Periapatan is the principal. The tree is of the size of an apple tree, with a delicate small leaf, and a large black berry when ripe.

Of late years an attempt has been made to grow cinchona on the Bilikalrangama, or white stone mountain (so called from the appearance of the hill as approached from the west), a hill about 4,500 feet high, where some of the succirubra species have been planted with fair results. The plantation is, however, exposed to the depredations of wild elephants, which, together with bison and sambre deer, are found in this isolated range of hills, which is a favourite resort of enthusiastic sportsmen.

Among the hills in the Mysore district of historical celebrity is Kabáldrug, a fortified conical hill of considerable height, and with precipitous sides, on the summit of which many Englishmen are said to have sighed away their lives, owing to insufficient food and bad water, while prisoners of the savage Tippu. Long before his time, Kabáldrug was the state prison of offending members of the Mysore family, and it is said that one of the Rajas was sent here by a powerful minister, to expiate by a slow and lingering death his offences against the State. The ascent is somewhat hazardous, unless one's shoes are taken off, or goloshes worn over them, as the rock is extremely slippery, and the steps, which have been rudely cut on the glassy surface at the most perilous points, have been worn away and scarcely afford foothold. Goloshes are very useful for climbing slippery granite rocks, especially when they are covered with dry grass, which, when growing on a precipitous mountain side, is difficult to walk over with safety.

Of all the towns in the Mysore district, the greatest interest attaches to Seringapatam, as the seat of two dynasties, and the scene of combats glorious in the annals of the British army. When the Vijayanagar princes succeeded to the authority formerly wielded by the Jain Rajas of the Belál race, Talkád, which was the ancient capital of the latter, and before them of the Chéra kings, had already been deserted for Dwárasamudram, which was destroyed by the Musalmán invaders. The last of the Rajas took refuge at Tonúr, where there is a strikingly fine reservoir, called the Pearl Tank, constructed several hundred years ago by Rámánujáchárí, the famous Vaishnava teacher. Close by, as if erected in contempt of him, is the tomb of Sháh Sálár Masaúd Ghάzi, a Musalman saint, with the date 760 Hijri on it, from which it may be inferred that he accompanied the bitter foes of the Hindu people who invaded Mysore.

The growing power of the Vijayanagar chiefs soon extinguished the last traces of the Belál race, and Seringapatam was selected as the head-quarters of the viceroys of the new sovereigns. The tract in the vicinity, called the Ashtagrám, or the eight towns, was granted in the twelfth century by the last of the Belál kings to Rámánujáchárí. In 1454 a descendant of one of his disciples, named Timmana, or Dhannaik, was appointed viceroy by the Anagundi sovereign, and erected a fort, and a temple dedicated to Sri Ranga, or Vishnu, to construct which numerous old Jain temples in the neighbourhood were destroyed.

The site was apparently well selected, being on an island, laved on both sides by the sacred Kávéri, a formidable and rocky stream, which, when unbridged, was in itself a natural defence. The ancient Hindus always evinced a predilection for the banks of great rivers as the sites of their capitals, the most conspicuous of these being Srinagar in Kashmír, on the Jhilam, Hastinapura, or Delhi, on the Jamuná, Prayág, or Allahabad, Benares, and Kanauj on the Ganges, Banawási on the Vardá, with many others, some of which remain to this day. To all appearance, Seringapatam, strong by nature and by art, and under the protection of the god Vishnu, who gave his name (Sri Ranga) to the place, was eminently well chosen. Indeed it was for a century the seat of the Anagundi, or Vijayanagar deputies, whose authority was implicitly obeyed by all the country around, till Ráj Wodiar, the Baron of Mysore, raised the standard of revolt in 1609, and seized the famous stronghold.

During the rule of Haidar Ali, this usurper, who was alive to the value of so formidable a fortress, strengthened it considerably, as well as the other principal forts in his country, and his son Tippu Sultan having called in the aid of French engineers, the place was very formidable when besieged by the British army. It could, indeed, be easily shelled now-a-days by guns placed in position on the surrounding hills, and defects may be found in the absence of revêtements, and other details; but the gateways are of great solidity, with complicated approaches, and the walls are mostly still in good preservation. In fact, if it were suddenly seized by a rebel force at the season when the river is in flood, and if the two bridges over it were destroyed, its reduction might entail considerable loss, and it is worthy of consideration whether it would not be advisable to break down the curtain of the walls at intervals for a length of 100 yards. The place where our troops crossed the river on May 4, 1799, is marked by two cannon buried in the ground, and as the breach that was made is still visible, and the walls are for the most part intact, a lively and accurate idea may be formed of the state of things when the memorable assault took place. Inside, nearly every vestige of the Muhammadan rulers has disappeared, their palaces having been levelled to the ground, while the temple of Sri Ranga still stands erect as a memorial of the old Hindu dynasty. The town now contains barely 7,000 inhabitants, and though less unhealthy than it was fifty years ago, is still dreaded for its fever, which deters visitors from sleeping inside the fort, though their fears on this head are somewhat exaggerated. Deserted houses and ruins meet the eye at every step, and the vegetation looks rank and unwholesome. The prevailing sickness has been attributed to the paddy flats in the vicinity of the island, as also to the destruction of the sedge or sweet flag which grew in the river; but it is more probable that the real cause of fever is to be sought in the nature of the rocks, which, being composed of sienite, become disintegrated, and when uncovered by water, and heated by the sun, emit a malarious infection, which produces the fever so much complained of.

At a short distance from the fort is the Daryá Daulat Garden, a pleasure house of Tippu Sultan, which is covered with grotesque frescoes of the battles between him and Colonel Baillie. In the mimic fight, the latter is represented as reclining helplessly in a palankin, while Tippu, on horseback, is serenely smelling a bouquet of flowers amidst the shooting and stabbing which is going on around him. All kinds of strange combats are depicted—headless bodies, with the heads some inches off on the ground, being a favourite item, while the guns which have performed the feat are shown, with a stalwart Mysorean holding the portfire. The French soldiers in Tippu's service are invariably painted with moustaches, while the English have smooth faces, save the traditional mutton-chop whiskers. In order to perpetuate the memory of the Duke of Wellington, who resided for some time in this picturesque abode, Lord Dalhousie, when Governor-General, directed the restoration of the curious paintings which adorn its walls, the arabesque interior also having been re-embellished, at a total outlay of more than 5,000*l.* Unfortunately this garden house partakes of the unhealthiness of the fort, but it is a pleasant place for a mid-day picnic.

At the farther end of the island, in the Lál Bagh, repose the remains of our implacable foe, Tippu Sultán, who was buried in the mausoleum erected in honour of his father, Haidar Ali. It is a handsome structure of white marble, with black hornblende pillars, somewhat in the fashion of the famous Táj at Agra, but less profusely ornamented, and of a poorer design. It is kept up at the cost of the British Government, great attention being paid to the building and the fine garden which surrounds it, whose gloomy cypresses lend a sombre charm to the scene. As one stands in the tomb, words faintly uttered resound in the lofty dome with a mournful sound, attoning the mind to those mixed feelings of pride and sympathy which are called forth by dwelling on the downfall of one of our direst enemies, and by commiseration for his untimely end. Till recently, comparatively little attention was paid to the monuments of the brave men who fell on our side, nor are any of them remarkable. It is a proof of the toleration of the British Government that the Musalmáns of Seringapatam were permitted to place within Tippu's tomb a tablet, which records in glowing and fanatical verses the death of the zealot. By the process called Abjad, according to which every letter of the alphabet has a numerical value, the date of his demise, according to the Muhammadan era, is found in the following expressions:—'The light of Islám and the faith left this world;' 'Tippu became a martyr for the faith of Muhammad;' 'The sword was lost;' 'The offspring of Haidar was a great martyr,' all these phrases producing, on adding up the numerical value of the words composing them, the year 1213, i.e., 1799.

The inscription on the tomb of Haidar Ali is of a

much more modest character. It is a curious fact that, great as was the prestige of the latter, and famous as he was, both in war and as an administrator, he is never spoken of in the same terms of deep veneration as his son Tippu Sultan, shallow and pretentious as was the nature of this sovereign. Tippu, however, was an incarnation of Musalmán bigotry and intolerance, qualities which, though they made him abhorred and feared by those whom he persecuted, won for him unbounded admiration and respect from all true followers of Islam. He was, in fact, in those days, what the Wahàbis are now, a puritanical observer of the letter of the Muhammadan law, and a relentless opponent of those who did not belong to his faith.

The island of Seringapatam belongs to the British Government, but is rented by the Maharaja of Mysore for 5,000*l.* yearly, which is more than double its present income. When this arrangement was made, it was a convenience to the Maharaja to eliminate British jurisdiction from a place only nine miles from his capital, while the administration of a small island far removed from any British District was embarrassing to our Government. There is little object now in retaining Seringapatam, the fortress being no longer required for political purposes, while the island has been for fifty years under Mysore rule. To the Raja, however, at the seat of his ancestors, and as containing a famous shrine of his religion, it is of greater value than would be represented by a mere calculation of the income at so many years' purchase. The English Government would, therefore, do well to dispose of it to him, on the young chief's attaining his majority a few years hence.

Mysore, the head-quarters of the district, and the capital of the province, has a population of 73,000, and is, therefore, a considerable place, but is badly situated, and were it not for its being the seat of the Sovereign, would soon lose the factitious importance that it now possesses. The locality is feverish, and the want of an abundant supply of water is a great defect. In the time of the celebrated minister, Purnia, an attempt was made to bring to the city the water of the Kávéri, but although the requisite channel was excavated at an immense cost, the project failed, as a sufficient flow could not be secured at the only practicable level, and recent enquiry by experienced engineers has demonstrated the impossibility of success. There are few good houses in the town, the majority being constructed of wattle and mud, while the Raja's palace within the fort can scarcely be considered worthy of the name. It is surrounded on all sides by houses, many of them of a mean description, and although there are some fine temples hard by, with summits gaily decorated with gold, and it is itself a somewhat lofty building, it evidences little architectural taste or skill. It is to be observed, however, that when Seringapatam fell, and it was determined to erect a residence for the young Hindu Raja Krishnaráj at Mysore, instead of at the former place, there was no suitable dwelling ready for him, while the minister was compelled, in the financial exigencies of the State, to exercise a close economy. It is not surprising, therefore, that the Raja's palace should be more commodious than elegant, and that, while there appears to be plenty of room for all the household and establishments, the royal apartments are of a somewhat mean character. Notwithstanding that Mysore is a place of no antiquity, and that it is occasionally extremely unhealthy, the circumstance that it became in 1799 the capital of the young Raja led to a petty village growing into a large town, with a considerable population. This is the more remarkable, as it possesses no special trade nor manufacture, its prosperity being almost entirely dependent upon the presence of the Raja and his court.

In the immediate neighbourhood of the town of Mysore is Chámundi, a fine hill, 1,000 feet above the plains, on which is a temple dedicated to the goddess of that name, better known as Káli, the wife of Siva She is the hereditary deity of the Raja's house, and the name of Mysore or Maisur is said to be derived from the circumstance that she destroyed at this place Mahéshásúr, the buffalo-headed demon. The temple built on the summit in her honour is greatly venerated by the Mysore Rajas, who pay it periodical visits, ascending the hill by a flight of rudely-cut steps, two-thirds way up which is a colossal basava or bull, sacred to Siva, carved out of an immense block of black hornblende, by orders of Raja Dodda Deoraj, two hundred years ago.

It is currently asserted that in the temple, as at Kolhapur, and other places where the dark rites of Káli were celebrated, human sacrifices were offered in former days, and there can be little doubt that the belief in their efficacy still lingers in the minds of the people, especially in the more secluded parts of the country.

The temples most revered by the late Maharaja, besides Chámundi, were those at Chámrájnagar and Nanjanagudú. The former town was the birthplace of his father, but the temple, though profusely ornamented with stone carvings, is not otherwise remarkable. In the vicinity of the town, however, there are a few remains of a place called Manipur, which is said to have a high antiquity, having been founded by a son of the Pándava Prince Arjuna, in consequence of the Rishi Rómaharshana having discovered on the site representations of two of the gods of the Hindu mythology. The city was, it is said, several miles round, but nothing is now to be seen, except two or three temples, of which the era is uncertain. The belief that one or more of the Pándava brothers visited Mysore, as well as other parts of Southern India, is universal among all natives, and may perhaps be adduced as circumstantial evidence in favour of the historical truth of the famous epic, the Mahábhárata. It is difficult otherwise to account for the fact that the people are so familiar with the names of the Pándavas, whose exploits and adventures form a favorite subject of conversation with all classes of the community.

Nanjanagudú was named after the god Siva, in commemoration of his having swallowed poison without evil effects arising. The temple is 15 miles from the capital on the river Kabani, and is frequented by crowds of devotees in March, when a great car-festival is held in honour of the god. Though its gold top shines brightly in the sun, and the carvings on it are not devoid of merit, the building has the heavy appearance usually observable in the temples of Southern India. It is handsomely endowed, and when the late Raja was at death's door, consecrated rice was sent to him daily from it, in the hope that, by partaking of it, he might be cured of his malady. His Highness had, however, long suffered from swellings in the neck and legs, accompanied by severe coughing, vomiting, and purging, and the Brahmanical specific was of no avail.

Far more remarkable than Nanajangudi is the ancient temple of Sómnáthpur, said to have been built by Jakanáchári, a celebrated architect of the time of the Belál Rajas. If the name of the builder is correctly given, and, from the near resemblance of the carvings on the structure to those on the famous Halibede temple, in the Hásan District, there is no apparent reason for questioning the fact, the story confirms the tradition that the kings of the Belál race conquered this part of Mysore, and upset the rule of the Chéra sovereigns of Talkád, which is only distant a few miles from Sómnáthpur. Vishnu Vardhana, the first of the Belál chiefs who abandoned the tenets of the Jain faith, previously followed by his forefathers, is asserted to have reigned about the year 1016 A.D., so that the Sómnáthpur temple, which was built in his time, is ancient. The carvings on the outer face are extremely beautiful. The temple stands in the centre of a square courtyard, flanked by fifteen compartments on each side, which are supported by finely-cut pillars, the roofs between each set of pillars and the entrances to the cells being delicately chiselled. At the main entrance there is a very large black stone Shásana, with a long inscription on it in ancient Kanarese characters. The reference in the inscription to Dwárasamudram points clearly to Halibede, the seat of empire of the Belál kings, but it is difficult to identify the name of the bestower of the endowment with that of any of the sovereigns of that House. Narsinha[1] is the name of the royal donor in the inscription.

In former days, when paper was unknown, it was the custom in Southern India to write all manuscripts on palm leaf, but, in the case of grants of land to temples, it was more usual to record the gift on copper plates, or on stone slabs. The former are generally 6 inches by 4, written on both sides, and held together by a copper ring, on which is stamped the seal of the donor, the inscription being either in Sanskrit or ancient Kanarese. The stone slabs vary from 7 to 3 feet in height, and from 3 to 5 feet in width, containing fifty or more lines of writing, and looking like huge gravestones set on end. They are always found inside, or in close proximity to temples, and are religiously preserved as the title deeds, on the strength of which assignments of land or money are held by the shrines.

The inscriptions first note the day of the lunar month, and the year of the gift, and after a preamble, setting forth the glories of the dynasty of the donor, and the virtues of the recipient, mention in detail the nature of the donation, such as the receipts

[1] A king named Narsinha is mentioned in Brown's 'Cyclic Tables,' p. 5, as being a son of Vishnu Vardhana, the date assigned being 1163 A.D.

from irrigated and unirrigated land, hidden treasure, all immovable objects, and all that then existed on the land, or that might be acquired by self-exertion. They invariably end by imprecating curses on those who disturb the charity, alleging that a gift to a Brahman must be as sacred in the eyes of the sovereign as his own sister, and that land given by a stranger for pious purposes should be regarded as a mother is regarded. There are hundreds of such grants in the Mysore country, and though it is supposed that many of those on copper are forgeries, there is little doubt that most of those carved on stone are genuine.

In many cases, the Shásanas are divided into three compartments, the lowest representing a struggle for supremacy between rival princes, who, mounted on elephants and horses, and accompanied by armed hosts, are fighting fiercely; in the centre, the victor is represented in heaven, seated on his throne, and attended by celestial nymphs; while in the upper compartment, he is seen offering sacrifice to the deity. Between the compartments, one generally finds several lines of writing, but the attempts hitherto made to decipher the more ancient inscriptions of this class have not been attended with much success, as the old language of the country is known to few, and the writing is chiefly in the Grantham or ancient Tamil character. It is supposed by some that the Shásanas on which the carved figures are found were put up in memory of the conqueror on his decease, but little is known of them with certainty.

The most ancient inscriptions appear to be of the period of the Kadamba and Haisal or Belál dynasties, and the oldest were perhaps carved one thousand years ago, beyond which time history in Mysore does not reach with precision. One main cause of the difficulty in ascertaining the exact date of any inscription is the practice of the Hindus of reckoning by the cycle of sixty years, so that, though the *name* of the year is always given, the corresponding year of the Sálivâhan era is frequently omitted. Hindus still cling fondly to the cycle, of which the commencing years are deemed auspicious and the closing ones unlucky, as may be supposed from the phrases 'blood-vomiting,' 'bloody-eyed,' 'wrathful,' and 'final,' the names of the 57th, 58th, 59th, and 60th years. The crops are asserted to be always deficient in these latter years, as was certainly the case at the close of the last cycle in 1866–67, and no orthodox Hindu will contract a marriage in the final year.

A few miles from Mysore is one of the largest establishments in India for refining sugar. The cane, of which the jaggory is used for the purpose, is grown chiefly near Seringapatam, and is one of the most profitable crops, though it takes fourteen or sixteen months to attain maturity. The jaggory is boiled in water, in which some lime and animal blood are mixed, and, after being filtered, is passed through charcoal to discolor it. It is then boiled by steam, when crystallisation takes place. After cooling, the crystals are separated from the treacle, and are assorted into three classes, of which the first is of excellent quality. In connection with the sugar refinery is a distillery, where a superior kind of spirits is produced, which has a large sale, both in Mysore and beyond the frontier. An inferior kind of spirits, made of jaggory, taken from the date palm, is also largely consumed in the country.

The high road from Mysore westward leads by Yelwál, a country-house of former Residents, to Hunsúr, at one time a flourishing depôt of the Madras Government, where various useful trades were carried on, which were alike profitable to the people and the State, but which an unwise economy stopped. A great quantity of leather accoutrements, as well as wood and iron implements of all sorts, were made for the army at a minimum of expense, owing to the facility with which hides were procured, and to the vicinity of valuable forests temporarily made over by the Mysore State to the British Government for the construction of gun-carriages.

The principal feature in this establishment, however, was the department for breeding cattle, called the 'Amrit Mahál:' from 'amrit,' milk, and 'mahál,' a department, a phrase apparently coined in the time of Tippu Sultán. The Mysore cattle were famed throughout India for their speed and endurance; and although not so powerful in appearance as the Hissar breed in the north, they were more hardy, and far better adapted to the draught of guns, and were generally employed for this purpose, till the importation of Australian horses led to their being used solely for heavy siege guns. The breed was kept up with great care and at a heavy expense, but it was invaluable to the country, and good bullocks could be purchased at 8*l.* or 10*l.* the pair. After the abolition of the department, when the agriculturists were left to their own resources, the breed of cattle rapidly degenerated throughout the country, and a fair pair of bullocks now costs double what it did fifteen years ago, thus entailing a considerable charge to the Madras Government. The department has, however, been recently revived, with fair prospects of success. The Mysore cattle stand high at the shoulder, have very powerful withers, sinewy but slender fore joints, and long curved horns. They are mostly white, or iron grey, but some are of a bluish-grey colour, and a few black. The best kinds are found in the Mysore district, and the cows are good milkers, but they require a change of pasturage, and for this purpose many grass preserves, called Káwals, some of which are well supplied with water, are reserved for their use in different parts of the province, so as to admit of the transfer of the herds in the dry season from the central grazing grounds to others nearer the hills, where more moisture then prevails.

Leaving Hunsúr, the high road to Coorg passes through Periapatam, formerly the stronghold of a petty Pálegár, and the centre of the track where the sandal-wood tree grows with the greatest luxuriance. It is cut down by contract and carried to the depôt, where it is prepared by hand, and after the bark is stripped off, the wood is assorted according to quality, in logs three feet long, which are piled in heaps, and sold by auction. It sells at the rate of 1*l.* per 56 pounds' weight, if of fine quality, but there are eight or nine divisions made at the periodical sales, according to the fineness of the grain, the absence of flaws and cracks, and the size of the log, which rarely exceeds nine inches in diameter, after it has been prepared in the government timber-yards. There are five distinct qualities of sandal-wood logs, but, besides these, the following classification is made: Jaj Pókal, or logs hollowed inside; Baghair adad, or logs unassorted, as being under four seers' weight; Chilta, or chips; and Ghut jar, or big roots. In fact, every portion of the tree is carefully preserved, while from the smaller cuttings a good deal of oil, faintly resembling atar of roses, is made, and extensively used in Southern India, where the genuine atar is rare.

A considerable revenue is raised from sandal-wood in Mysore, it being exported to Bombay, where it is used for carving, and for funeral pyres by luxurious Hindus, while large quantities are sent to China, the Indian wood being much superior to that of the Feejee Islands, where it is also found. Persons felling sandal-wood without authority are liable to fine, and the conservancy of the trees forms as important a branch of the duties of the forest department as the preservation of the royal forests.

About nine miles north of Periapatam, near the town of Bettadapur, is a very fine peak called Malikárjuna, which is a prominent object throughout the western part of Mysore. There is a wearisome flight of steps to the summit, passing through many gateways, and at the top there is a small temple which has attained some notoriety, owing to its having been struck by lightning, which is regarded by the people as a token of the presence of the Divinity, who, in the shape of the god Siva, honored it by a visit. From this point a splendid view may be had of the Coorg mountains, and of a wide stretch of country on all sides.

Immediately west of Periapatam commences the belt of jungle which encircles the Mysore district throughout its western and southern sides. It is extremely unhealthy, and infested in many places by wild beasts. Although tigers are not generally found in the denser forests, these are the favourite haunts of elephants, which travel long distances, and do immense injury to the rice fields. So great are their ravages, that it is not uncommon for the people to fence in with strong bamboo thickets the whole of the cultivated land of their villages, thus forming an extended cordon which the animals find it difficult to penetrate. They are occasionally caught in pitfalls, and expeditions are sometimes organised to hunt them down, but, unless they are caught when very young, they are not easily domesticated. One, which was captured when three months old, was sent in to the menagerie at Bangalore, where it used at first to lament piteously the absence of its dam, refusing for some time to be consoled.

In the denser forests of the district, the only inhabitants are the wild Kurubas, consisting of the Betta or Hill Kurubas, and the Jénu or honey-collecting Kurubas, of whom the latter are of a very low type of humanity. The Betta Kurubas earn a livelihood by felling trees, and are much employed by the forest officers. Having means of obtaining a regular livelihood, they have fixed habitations, called 'hádis,' and, although totally uneducated, and having no religion except the reverence paid by them to the demons of the woods, they are less savage than might be expected under the circumstances. They are small in stature, like most wild tribes, but have tolerably well-formed conntenances. They will eat or drink almost anything, save beef.

The Jénu Kurubas are very unprepossessing in appearance, particularly the women, their heads being covered with a dense tangled mass of hair, which gives them a wild and brutish aspect. Their occupation is collecting forest produce, especially honey, which they extract in great quantities by putting torches at night-time underneath the combs, which are attached to the trees. They climb up an adjacent tree, from which, by aid of a pole, they manage to draw themselves across to the tree where the bees are, when the insects are easily smoked.

Both these tribes may be placed in the same category at the Sóligas of the Bilirangam Hills, but whereas the former use only bamboos and boughs for the construction of their dwellings, the Sóligas build their huts of mud and grass, owing to the comparatively cold climate in which they live. The Sóligas and Jénu Kurubas are very shy, but are supposed to practise magical arts. The former are good sportsmen and excellent trackers of game.

On the eastern side of the Mysore district is Yelandur, a jágír yielding 4,500*l.* a year, held by the descendants of the celebrated minister Purnia, who, during the late Maharaja's minority, conducted the administration of the province with signal success, in recognition of which service the estate was given to him under the guarantee of the British Government. It is the most fertile tract in Mysore, having first-class tanks, under which are rich gardens of cocoa-nut, betel and pan leaf, besides abundant crops of mulberry and red rice. The jágír has been declared to be indivisible, and as the present proprietor, Krishna Murti, has received an excellent education, he will not only be the foremost of the Raja's subjects, but may fairly aspire to hold the post formerly occupied by his distinguished ancestor.

HÁSAN.

The Hásan district has an area of 1,697 square miles, a population of 592,000, and a revenue of 126,000*l.* Though small in extent, it is better known to Englishmen than any other portion of the province, as the western side of the district is occupied by numerous coffee planters, who have converted a wild and hilly region of jungle into a smiling garden, studded all over with evidence of their industry. With the exception of the three sub-divisions, forming this particular portion of the district, its general features correspond with those of the Mysore and Toomkoor districts, on which it abuts to the south and east.

In ancient days all this part of the Mysore province was ruled over by the kings of the Belál or Haisal race, whose era is said to date from the year 714, this being the earliest epoch which can be traced with any approach to accuracy. They were of the Jain faith, and have left many vestiges of their power and piety. Their capital was for some time at Dwárasamudram, now called Halébidú or Halibede, where a magnificent temple still attests their glory and the skill of their architects. Some of the Jains appear to have come from upper India, but the Belál kings are said to have been natives of the soil, and were probably the representatives of those who still clung to the Buddhistic faith, after its suppression by the Brahmans.

Horrible stories are told of the atrocities committed by the latter in extinguishing the rival beliefs, it being alleged that many Buddhists were brayed alive in large mortars, and tortured in various ways. It is, at any rate, certain that an intense hatred of the Brahmans still prevails in the minds of all Jains, which is the more striking, owing to the gentle and peaceful creed which they profess, the destruction of animal life in any shape being hateful to them. But in the remote places in the hills, to which the persecution of the Brahmans has driven them, and where they are still found exercising influence and cultivating large demesnes, it is their practice to go out into the woods and curse the Brahmans with all their heart and soul.[1]

In most parts of India, the Jains are a trading community, and, being energetic and opulent, they have extensive commercial connections. They have fine temples on Mount Tilla, called Jógi Tilla, in the Punjáb; at Benares; at Párasnáth, in Bengal; on

[1] Orthodox Hindus, on the other hand, aver that to encounter a Jain is worse than to meet a mad elephant, or than to rush into a house on fire.

Mount Abu, in Rájputána; at Palitána, in Guzerát; and many other places; but perhaps none of these is so remarkable as the shrine of Srávan Belgúl, in the Hásan district.

This temple is on the summit of one of the superb granite mountains for which Mysore is remarkable, known by the name of Chandrabetta, or the Mountain of the Moon. It is difficult of ascent, owing to the slippery nature of the rock, but is of no great height. At intervals on the glassy surface are small gateways, which devotees pass under, on their way to the temple at the top, which is reached by several flights of steps near the summit. In the centre of the enclosure forming the sacred precincts, towers up a colossal statue of Gomatéshwara, one of the incarnations of the Jain deity. It is 57 feet high, and faces the north, so that it is visible for many miles around. It was seemingly cut out of some rock which projected high above the general level of the hill, or the hill itself may have been cut away, as in the case of the famous Kailás temple at Ellora. The face has that serene and quiescent look which characterises most Buddhistical statues, and is not devoid of a certain amount of dignity, but the ears are long pendent flaps, and the hair is curled spirally over the head, which detracts considerably from the grace of the god's aspect. The shoulders are immensely broad, and the arms, which hang down the sides of the figure with the thumbs turned outwards, are rather too large and long. The proportions are generally good, however, as far as the thighs, but below this the statue dwarfs suddenly, and the legs, particularly from the knee to the foot, are contracted to about half their proper length. As the god, like other Jain deities, is represented as standing erect, this circumstance deprives the figure of much of its power, but it is nevertheless a majestic work of art. It is probable that in order to preserve the proper proportions throughout, it would have been necessary to cut away an enormous additional quantity of rock, which would have been difficult and expensive.

A symbolical tree issues from between the legs, whence it branches off right and left, with leaves on either side of it, and, twining over the thighs, disappears at the hips of the figure, being, however, again seen winding in a double fold over the arms, where it terminates in a curl, below which are bunches, apparently meant for fruit. The statue is in *puris naturalibus*, but the feet stand on a carved resting-place, fashioned somewhat in the shape of a sandal, but quite flat. On either side of the statue are blocks of stone, over which also creep trees similar to that which issues from between the legs, while there are four inscriptions of a few lines each at the base of the stones. A platform was specially erected to ascertain the exact height of the statue, which was found to be 57 feet, and not 70 feet, as generally supposed.

Within the enclosure ornamented by this grand figure, are seventy-two smaller statues, ranged at intervals in compartments on three sides of the square. These represent the various personifications of the Jain deity, which are twenty-four in number, and there is therefore much repetition among them, nor do the figures, which are almost all in an erect attitude, differ greatly from one another, except that each of the twenty-four personifications has its own váhana, or vehicle, on which it stands. The great statue was erected in the time of the Belál kings, and, it is said, by Jakanáchári, but this is mere surmise, and it is probably anterior to this period; Colonel Mackenzie assigns as early a date to it as 1121.

Adjoining Chandrabetta, is another craggy hill called Indrabetta, where are some pretty temples and a picturesque pillar. The high priest of the Jains resides at Srávan Belgúl, but though reported to be learned, he is not a celibate, and is therefore not much respected by his flock. The town is noted for its brass vessels of all kinds, which are manufactured in thousands, and sent to all parts of the country.

Halibede, or Dwárasamudram, must in former times have been a town of considerable size and importance, for although the Musalmán invaders did their work well, and destroyed ruthlessly whatever offended their iconoclastic eyes, enough still remains to testify to the glories of the past. The country around is fertile, sugar-cane being grown to a great extent in the black soil, as well as til, kusumba, and garden produce, there being a good supply of water in the large tank called Kákánaddi. Dwárásamudram was also called Dwárkáwatipatan, but the origin of both words is unknown, although the former might perhaps indicate an approach to the sea-coast by the old Kudadukal pass, under the Belálraidrug hill.

The town was founded in the twelfth century, and

for 200 years was the capital of the Belál kings, till the subversion of their power by Káfúr, the Musalmán general, in the fourteenth century. It was of great extent, and is said to have contained 725 Bastis, the name given to enclosed Jain temples, of which only a few still exist. The oldest of these is called Ádinátheshwar, or the primæval lord, a small and simple building, at the left entrance of which is a stone tablet, with the date 1197 of the Saliváhan era on it (1265 A.D.) The second, Sántéshwar, or the lord of tranquillity, is somewhat larger and more ornamented, but is still a plain structure. The third, Párasnáthéshwar, one of the principal incarnations of the Jain deity, is a large building, the pillars being of a fine black hornblende, which, when moistened, is of a dark-green color. This stone is found in the Karikal quarries in the Toomkoor district, but the main portion of the temple is built of Balapam, or potstone, found in an adjacent hill, called Pushpagiri, or flower-hill. The temple is richly decorated outside with carvings of Jain deities, and inside is a large statue of black stone, standing erect with the arms at its sides, and having that air of tranquillity and dignity which characterises the great figure at Srávan Belgúl. There is a remarkably fine shásana at the entrance of this temple. These three are the only genuine Jain temples now standing, and the priests are in very indigent circumstances, there being but few Jain families now in the place.

The great Saiva temple of Halibede, called Haisaléshwara, was built, it is said, in the reign of Vishnu

Vardhana, the tenth king of the Belál race, who was persuaded by a favourite mistress to desert the faith of his ancestors, and to adopt the tenets of the followers of Vishnu. The architect was a Brahman, named Jakanáchári, whose celebrity is attested by the numerous temples in the country of which the origin is attributed to him. The Haisaléshwara temple, though much injured by time, is undoubtedly a striking work of art, and the graceful execution of the carvings on the exterior is probably unrivalled in India. The decorations are in layers, the bottom one representing elephants, the second mythical lions, above which are delicate scrolls, then men on horseback, above these another fringe of scrolls, then scenes from the wars of the Mahábhárat, and the story of the Rámáyana. There are eight or ten such layers within a height of eight feet, the number not being uniform throughout, though their general character is the same. Above these are figures of various deities, under beautifully carved canopies, standing on a basement of finely wrought scrolls. Many of the mimic scenes on the layers are gracefully designed, and the scrolls are singularly rich and elegant. In the projecting portions of the building outside, the roof is supported by square-cut pillars, which are not remarkable, but, in the recesses, a finely chiselled fretwork is to be seen, intersected at intervals by handsome black pillars of hornblende of striking design. There are two shrines inside the building, and several smaller altars, the roof being supported by well-wrought pillars of the same fashion. Outside the temple, and facing it, are two structures called mantapams, in which recline bulls of great size, one of hornblende, the other of potstone. There are several stone tablets let into the wall of the temple, but they are not of special interest. A considerable sum of money has of late years been spent in restoring this interesting relic, but the great size of the stones presents difficulties, while it is impossible to reproduce the delicate carvings where they have been wantonly injured by Musalmáns or mischievous boys.

At Jámgal, eight miles distant, in the Kadúr district, is another temple of the same character, but it is of small size and is much worn. So great is the celebrity of the Halibede carvings, that, at the present time, they form the model on which all the workers in sandal-wood fashion the choice designs so often met with, and the name of Jakanáchári is justly famed throughout the province. Of the Aramané, or palace of the old Jain kings, scarcely any traces are to be seen, and excavations have not proved successful; but there are still, on the western side of the town, remains of the wall and ditch which protected it, testifying, by the great size of the stones forming the fortifications, to the importance of the place.

At Bélúr, ten miles east of Halibede, is another temple of singular beauty, dedicated to Késhava or Vishnu. It is entered by a magnificent gateway of great height, near which is a fine quadrangular building, in which is deposited the gigantic car which is used for carrying about the idol at the periodical processions. The temple is of considerable height, and is topped by a large canopy in the shape of an umbrella.

The southern side of the building is of especial beauty, there being some exquisitely-carved shrines on either side of the steps leading to the temple, which is erected on a stone platform five feet above the ground. The general character of the carvings approximates to those on the Halibede building, but the walls are more ornate, and there are several smaller temples in the enclosure which surrounds the main building. An excellent idea of these striking works of art can be obtained from the photographs taken of them by order of the Madras and Mysore Governments.[1] The architect is said to have been Jakanáchári, who built the Halibede temple.

At Nágamangalam, on the eastern side of the district, is another temple of great size, but not otherwise remarkable, also said to have been planned by this famous builder, to whom is assigned the construction of all the most elegant remains of Hindu taste and magnificence to be found in Mysore.

One of the most frequented places of pilgrimage in this part of Mysore is Mélkóté, said to be called Yadugiri in the old Puránas, which assign to it a great antiquity. It is one of the places where Vaishnava Brahmans congregate in great numbers, and constant disputes about precedence arise between them, the Rajas Guru, Parakála Swámi, having vainly tried to assert his pre-eminence, which is strenuously resisted by the other priests. The temples are richly endowed by the Raja, but are not architecturally beautiful,

[1] See notes on photographs taken by Captain Lyon, edited by J. Fergusson, F.R.S. Marion & Co., Soho Square, 1870, pages 72–83.

though the southern gateway of the town, called Rai Gópál Bágalu, is fine. The country around is interesting to the geologist, the formation being sienitic quartz, in which is found talc and the gopichandana white clay, which is used for making sectarian marks on the forehead.

To the north of the district, near Arsikere, is the Tirupati hill, known in the Sthal Purána, or local legend, by the name of Amaragiri, or immortal hill, an appellation given to it by an ancient Muni, who, for some fanciful reason, considered it to be the finest hill between the rivers Krishna and Káyéri. It is ascended by a painful flight of steps, said to be 1,700 in number, it being a religious duty on the part of pilgrims to crack a cocoa-nut on each step. The temple on the summit is dedicated to Janárdan, but is not remarkable, though the hill commands a fine view of the country around. It is the extremity of a range running nearly due north to the frontier of the province. The term Tirupati, or the sacred lord, is applied to Vishnu, who is however generally worshipped in Mysore under the designation of Venkata, and hence this name is constantly met with among the people of the country, as, for instance, Venkatiengár, Venkata Ramana, and other combinations. Of late years, educated natives are prone to bestow long, high-sounding names on their children, generally, however, selecting the appellation of their favourite house-deity, but in former times names were more simple, the higher classes rejoicing in such appellations as Narsappa, Subayyá (appa and ayyá being respectful salutations similar to our word 'sir'), while more unsophisticated agriculturists contented themselves with still shorter names, such as Bomma, Timma, Bhaira, and so forth.

In the Hásan district is found a considerable congregation of native Christians. In the town of Ganjám, near Seringapatam, they are numerous, but belong chiefly to the trading community. At Bangalore and Mysore, they are mostly Tamil employés, menial servants, or soldiers. In the Mysore infantry, called the Bár, from a Kanarese word signifying a line of troops, there are many Christian soldiers, known by the name of Alémán; and in the time of Tippu Sultán there was a whole battalion of them, under an officer named Surappa (Xavier), who, on one occasion, when the tyrant meditated the destruction of the Christian church at Seringapatam, called his fellow believers to arms, and defied his master. In the Hásan district, however, the native Christians are mostly agriculturists, entire villages being found whose ancestors were converted several generations ago.

The Catholic mission in Mysore dates from the time of the Jesuits, who had several stations in the province, nearly all of which were however swept away during the persecutions of Tippu. It is not known whether the Apostle of the East, St. Francis Xavier, ever visited Mysore, though at Mangalore, close by on the western coast, are to be found the descendants of Brahmanical and other families converted by him. John de Britto, who was martyred on the eastern coast, did cross the Ghâts, though it is uncertain whether he entered the Mysore province, owing to the few details given in his letters. During the Portuguese ascendancy, many of their clergy laboured in Mysore, and near the river Kávéri are to be seen the remains of a chapel within an enclosure marked by four stones, on which are inscriptions dated 1704, granting the land to the 'Sanyásis of Rome.' At Heggadévankotta, near the Kabbani, a chapel was also built, but the priest was killed, it is said, by the villagers.

No church, however, worthy of the name appears to have been built till the Abbé Dubois, of the Missions Etrangères, commenced the erection of one at Mysore, and another at Sathalli, in the Hásan district. This zealous missionary resided for a quarter of a century in the province, and was intimately acquainted with the habits of the people of Southern India, of whom he has left an interesting account. Since his time, the Sathalli church has been much enlarged and embellished, and is a fine building with a nave and aisles. A convent is attached to it, where native nuns teach young girls reading, writing, and sewing. The priests have also established a dispensary, from which they supply medicine, not only to their own flock, but to all comers, gratis, and they are consequently frequently applied to. There are twelve villages in the neighbourhood almost entirely inhabited by Christians, numbering, it is said, 1,000 souls, and it is a strange sight in a heathen land to see them trooping to mass on a Sunday at the sound of the church-going bell. Their simple devotion is touching, and though their general education is imperfect, they are well instructed in the tenets of their faith, and are good members of society. Of late years, many Kanarese religious books have been printed at Bangalore and circulated among them.

The majority of the congregation are what is called caste Christians, that is to say, while following the Christian belief in all matters touching their faith and morals, they preserve their ancient social customs in everything which does not trench upon religion, and in respect to degrees of relationship in marriages, and to succession to property, have the same rules as their neighbours of the same caste who are not Christians.

The system of caste is in many points, doubtless, objectionable, and it is somewhat difficult to say where religion begins and social observances end, but the fact remains that those native Christians who have preserved their caste are more moral, and better servants of Government than those who have shaken off the trammels. It is a mortifying admission to make perhaps, but it is undoubtedly true. In the Mysore service, there are several caste Christians, holding high positions, whose character is irreproachable. It may be added that the greater strictness with which they, in common with Hindus of the same caste, adhere to ancient practice in regard to consanguinity, probably tends to preserve purity of blood, although it has a disadvantageous effect in debarring them from raising themselves in the social scale, except so far as government service is concerned. Throwing open the doors of government employment to all comers has not, however, in the opinion of many persons well qualified to judge, produced a higher standard of ability, and men of the best caste are, as a rule, superior to those below them in social status.

The tenacity with which the native Christians cling to their ancient usages induced the Catholic missionaries, at an early period, to concede to their converts the privilege of preserving all their customs appertaining to marriage ceremonies and the division of property, but in the delicate questions which frequently arose on these subjects, the Christians readily submitted to the arbitrament of their clergy, so that disputes rarely came into court. The native Christian congregation under the ecclesiastical jurisdiction of the Missions Etrangères numbers in Mysore nearly 20,000 souls, comprising influential merchants, tradesmen, agriculturists, shepherds, and artisans, besides servants of Government, soldiers, camp followers, and menial attendants.

The various congregations following the Protestant faith number possibly 2,000 souls under all denominations.

The Wesleyan Mission commenced its operations in 1822, among the Tamil people of Bangalore, and subsequently occupied seven or eight other stations among the Kanarese-speaking population of the interior. The London Mission commenced work in 1820, and is chiefly employed in Bangalore, where they have an excellent school for native girls. Both missions have turned their attention to the literature of the country to good purpose. The Catholic Missions have not hitherto succeeded in imparting a first-class secular education in their schools, but the Wesleyan and London Missions have made great efforts in this direction. To the Wesleyans is due the credit of having trained up many of the highest native employés in the province, and the London Mission Schools have, of late years, attained a high standard. The Wesleyans have an excellent press, and print yearly a large number of Kanarese books, both secular and religious, the type being excellent. The Catholic Mission has adopted types, of which the matrices were cut in Paris, but, though clearly incised, they are somewhat too thin to please the eye.

All the missions, now-a-days, appear to devote their efforts principally to printing and circulating books and pamphlets, mainly, of course, of a religious character. These have no doubt the effect of leavening the native mind, and possibly of preparing it for the future reception of the truth, but the immediate effect is scarcely perceptible, and conversions are very few in number. All that even the Catholic Missions can do at present is to preserve what their predecessors won. Natives do not, indeed, object to read the Bible in schools as a class-book, but it leaves no permanent effect apparently, and is regarded by them like any other book in the curriculum. The circumstance that both Protestant and Catholic Missions are in the field, teaching doctrines in many respects opposed to one another, has a prejudicial effect upon the native mind, and until the time comes when a considerable number of the higher classes in India lead the way in adopting Christianity, it is highly improbable that any general movement in this direction will take place. The present state of things is by no means encouraging, notwithstanding what may be asserted in annual reports; indeed, it is thought by many that the distrust shown by natives has increased rather than diminished.

The native Christians are generally looked down upon by the rest of the community, and especially by the Brahmans, who naturally inculcate the highest reverence for their own priestly order, and contemn and despise all beneath them in caste. It is seldom, however, that any acts of open violence are perpetrated, though occasionally such have been committed from superstitious motives, and the following singular instance was brought to light some years ago.

The belief in the efficacy of human sacrifices still lingers in the native mind, and occasionally shows itself in absurd accusations against Christians, to the effect that children are immolated on the threshold of newly-built churches, but the practice is not unknown among the Hindus themselves. In the Hásan district, there was a tank, the embankment of which had been breached unfortunately three or four years in succession. At one end of this embankment was a Christian village, called Gádanhalli, and at the other, a heathen village, called Mallagudda. The head-men of the latter, being greatly discouraged at the repeated injuries to the tank, conceived an idea that, in order to give the embankment stability for the future, an animal sacrifice was necessary, and superstition added that the immolation of a human victim would effectually propitiate the deity. The villagers accordingly clubbed together and bribed, for the sum of 2*l*., a man named Honna to execute the deed. This individual, having proceeded to an adjoining pagoda, in company with other persons, and consulted omens of success, immediately set about the work. In the evening of the day there was in the Christian village of Gádanhalli one of those processions in which the natives of India rejoice, and which seem indispensable to their happiness, whatever faith they may follow. A poor widow had an only son, a boy of six or seven, who, attracted by the spectacle, went to join in the amusement. He never returned, and the next morning his body was found floating in the tank, directly opposite the place where the embankment had been last breached. The whole affair was hushed up, and it was reported that the boy had been accidentally drowned, but with some difficulty a clue was found, and, notwithstanding the efforts of the chief local government officer, a Brahman named Srinivás Ayengár, who was a relation of the accountant of the village (the principal instigator of the tragedy), to screen the criminals, the murder came out. Honna showed the place in the tank where he had thrown the boy's blanket and handkerchief, and in the accounts of the repair of the tank an entry was found of the sum paid to him for committing the foul deed. The accomplices in the murder were brought to trial, and, in spite of sundry efforts made to effect their release, were duly punished.

The malnád (from 'malé,' a hill, and 'nád,' a division of country), or hilly portion of the Hásan district, comprises the whole of the Manjarábád sub-division, and a portion of those of Bélúr and Mahárájdrug, and is a tract full of interest. The general level is about 3,000 feet above the sea, but, though a hill country, it is in reality a depression between the stupendous ghát range of the Kadoor district on the north, and the superb mountains of Coorg on the south, which close it in with seemingly impassable barriers. Its ancient name was Balam, from the Sanskrit 'Bala,' or strength, and it was certainly a strong country, being bounded on the east, first by the river Yagachi, and secondly by the Hémávati (the latter of which is a stream of considerable size), while on the west the only approaches to it were by almost inaccessible passes, the chief of which is called Bisalé. The whole country, being covered by dense forests on its western face, is frequently enveloped in fog, and being thus obscured, when visited by Tippu Sultán, he gave the spot whence he surveyed the region, and where he subsequently built a fort, the name of Manjarábád, or 'the abode of mist,' from 'Manju,' a Kanarese word signifying mist, and 'ábád,' Persian for an abode or dwelling. The hill on which stands the fort that has given its modern name to the country, is 3,400 feet above the sea, and is lower than many other prominent peaks, one of which, Jénkal, is more than 4,000 feet.

Although, as one approaches the frontier between Manjarábád and South Canara, the scenery is strikingly wild, owing to the thick forests which cover the great Ghát ranges, the interior of the country to the south is comparatively open—beautiful clumps of noble trees and grassy hill-sides giving it the appearance of an

English park. In fact, in some places, the observer can scarcely resist the conclusion that art, and not nature, has been at work in laying out this attractive region in the most picturesque way possible. The people take great pride in preserving the sacred groves that surround their favourite temples, showing, in this respect, a feeling akin to that of the Coorgs, who devote to the worship of their special deity Ayappa, or Pan, some of the finest forests in their province. There is little connection, however, between the people of Manjarábád on the one side and the Coorgs on the other; or between the former and the men of the Nagar division—arising, no doubt, from the difficulty of communication in so hilly a region.

Such intercourse as there was with outsiders was carried on by means of the old passes, which, though rugged and dangerous, were traversed by traders, whose pack-bullocks managed with considerable risk to climb these mountain paths, laden with grain and cloths. There was also a thoroughfare for pilgrims proceeding to the famous shrine of Subhramani, below the Ghâts, whither thousands of worshippers, desirous of paying their respects to the snake deity, resorted every year, by way of the Bisalé Ghát. This pass leads down to the low country underneath the precipitous sides of the magnificent Kumár Parvat, or Pushpagiri, in Coorg, and the gradients being one in ten feet, or even one in five, and the narrow way being frequently blocked up by immense boulders and the shattered fragments of ancient steps, the communication is well nigh impracticable.

When Manjarábád became the head-quarters of the

Mysore coffee-planters, attention was naturally directed to the old passes, which offered the only access to the coast, but, as it was found that it would be a waste of time and money to maintain paths which, with such severe gradients, could never be made practicable for cart traffic, it was wisely resolved to seek for more easy descents from the Mysore table-land. Accordingly, two roads have been opened—one, the Manjarábád Ghát, par excellence, in the centre of the sub-division; and the other the Kodekal, or Búnd Ghát, which traverses the northern side of the country. Both these roads have been fairly laid out, and are available for carts, the gradients being easy; but they are liable to be much injured by heavy floods in the monsoon, and their maintenance in proper order is always a matter of anxious consideration. The southern part of the sub-division is still inadequately supplied with communications to the coast, although the Bisalé route is still used by native traders, who are satisfied with the old mode of conveyance by bullocks.

It may be remarked that, although the trade with the coast in miscellaneous articles, such as grain, cloth, fish, and salt, must always be maintained, it is probable that, on the completion of the contemplated railway through Mysore, the course of the coffee trade will be diverted, and that the produce which is now sent for shipment to places in Canara, on the western coast, will be transmitted by rail to Madras, or even to Bombay.

In the Kempu Holé, or Red River, at the foot of the Manjarábád Ghát, garnets are found in great numbers, but they are not sufficiently valuable to become an article of commerce.

The Manjarábád country appears in ancient time to have been an appanage of the Belál Rajas of Halibede, but was an unimportant jungle tract. During the ascendancy of the Vijayanagar princes, some of whom exhibited much energy and enterprise in improving their dominions, attempts were made to reclaim the wild region of Balam; and the leading people of the country claim a descent from the first emigrants who, with little difficulty, overthrew the aborigines, now represented by the agrestic hinds who work on the farms of the lords of the soil. For many ages, and indeed till within the last forty years, the lower castes of Manjarábád were simply slaves living on the estates of the Patéls, or head-men, who clothed and fed them and their families, and regarded them as part of their property. They were generally treated with kindness, and received presents on marriage ceremonies and other festivals, but their bondage was a recognised fact; so much so that they could be legally sold, with or without the estate to which they were attached. Their transfer in this way was, however, of rare occurrence, but, since their manumission, many have left the homes of their masters and entered the service of coffee planters, who pay them double the hire formerly received by them. To the Patéls this is a sore grievance, and it is very difficult to persuade them of the justice of the course prescribed by Government, they being deaf to all suggestions that they have an easy remedy in their hands by doubling the wages of these unfortunate outcasts.

The Patéls are locally of great importance, and the 'Shímé Gauda,' or Lord Lieutenant of the county, holds a large estate, receives sundry emoluments in the shape of land and fees, and is treated with much respect by the whole hill-side. All the Patéls exercise considerable influence within their own villages, and formerly possessed feudal authority, which, under the Jagannath of civilisation, and codes of equal justice to all, has sensibly diminished. In their own homes, which are often strongly fortified, and surrounded by a deep fosse, they still, however, maintain a patriarchal authority, each farm being complete in itself, and, in respect to the requirements of daily life, independent of its neighbours. Cloths, blankets, household utensils, and such other articles as cannot be made up or manufactured in the house, are readily procured at the periodical Santés, or fairs, which are held in different parts of the country.

In the absence of the despotic authority formerly wielded by them, the Patéls cling fondly to the use of the insignia granted to them by the Vijayanagar kings, and value them as much as Europeans do titles, orders, and crosses. One of the Patéls enjoys the following :— 1. A green umbrella borne by an attendant over his head. 2. A swinging sword. 3. A cloth for fanning him in the heat. 4. A caparisoned horse. 5. A Yák fan. 6. A palankeen. 7. A conical cloth on a pole, to keep off the sun. Other chiefs have spears, torches at daytime, Karané horns, drums, lances, silver sticks, &c. Of all these marks of rank the Karané horn is the most curious, it being five feet long, and so heavy that a man can barely raise it at intervals, to bellow forth a thundering blast, when he is forced to drop it again. The use of a curved horn, called a kombu, is common in Mysore. It is carried by a man, whose special duty it is to accompany the Amildár, or officer of the sub-division, when the latter leaves his head-quarters; and when he approaches a village, the hornman sounds a not unmusical blast, winding up with a high note, which has the effect of producing the immediate presence of all the villagers to pay their respects to the Amildár. The Karané is a giant among horns, and is straight. It is rarely met with except in the hill portions of Mysore, or as an appanage of some of the principal temples, which, in the shape of fiddlers, singing and dancing women, and heathenish musical instruments, turn out a deputation to meet distinguished visitors which would astonish Exeter Hall.

Foremost among the chiefs of the country was the Aigúr Pálegár, to whose ancestor, Lingappa Naik, one of the Vijayanaga Rajas—either Bukka Ráya or Harihara Ráya—is said to have granted as a fief, in 1397, not only Manjárábád or Balam, but several other sub-divisions in the plain country, yielding a revenue altogether of between 70,000*l.* and 80,000*l.* It is not known what tribute was fixed as payable to the Vijayanagar kingdom, but it is probable that the Pálegár, and the Patéls under his jurisdiction, yielded only a nominal allegiance to that State, and exercised uncontrolled authority in their own country.

On the dismemberment of the Vijayanagar dominions, and the rise to power of the Mysore Rajas, the

Balam country became a bone of contention between these chiefs and the Naiks of Ikkéri, a territory in the Shimoga district, whose founders also derived their authority from Vijayanagar. The latter, during the rule of Sivappa Naik, a chief of considerable repute, appear to have subjugated all the hill country between the present Bombay frontier and Coorg ; but their sway was evanescent, and the Aigúr Pálegár only paid an occasional tribute to them. Nor did the Mysore State exercise any well-defined authority over Balam till the time of Haidar Ali, who not only subverted the Ikkéri or Bednór dynasty, but annexed Balam permanently to his own dominions. The Pálegárs were, however, refractory, both Krishnappa Naik and his son Venkatádri Naik giving much trouble to Tippu Sultán, while even after the fall of Seringapatam, the latter endeavoured to evade submission to the Mysore Raja, asserting his independence. There was no question, however, that Balam was by conquest an integral part of Mysore, so British troops were despatched against the Pálegár, who, after more than one disastrous check to the English force, was defeated by Colonel Wellesley, taken prisoner, and hanged by orders of the Minister.

The head of the family, the descendant of this Pálegár, is a political detenu, but has still considerable local influence. Attempts have been made to induce the Pálegárs who lost their patrimonial possessions in the time of the Musalmán rulers of Mysore, and who now receive miserable pittances from the State, to take up tracts of waste land for cultivation on favorable terms of rent, but they are generally both proud and indolent, and the measure has met with but partial success. Whenever they are permitted to dwell for a time in the country where their forefathers ruled, they have little difficulty in extorting contributions from the heads of villages, but their prolonged residence proves embarrassing to the people, and it is not without inconvenience to the Government.

Manjarábád is divided locally into six náds, each of which has its own Patél. Every nád is divided into a certain number of mandés, there being thirty-six in all, each, also, having a Patél, while below these again are the head-men of single villages. The nád Patéls are also the head-men of the mandés, or group of villages in which they reside, and have much local weight and importance. In fact, the whole system is purely feudal, and is well suited to a difficult country covered with hills and forest, for, the population being limited and widely scattered, and the natives living on detached farms, and not in villages, it is impossible to carry out any orders of Government without the ready co-operation of the leading men, who, for their service, have small rent-free holdings, called ' umblí.'

Three of the nád Patéls are by caste Lingáyats, who follow the teaching of priests called Jangamas—men of little repute for learning—while the other three Patéls are of the Halé Wokkaligaru, or ancient farmer-caste, a term which seems peculiar to the hill country. Their slaves were styled Halé Makkalu, or ancient children, and are also called Holiaru. There is not so much difference in dress between them and their masters as between the Coorgs and their hinds, a black blanket wrapped tightly round the loins, and thrown over the shoulder, being common to all; but those worn by the head-men are of finer material, while they use waist-cloths and turbans, white or colored. Matchlocks and wood knives are carried by all classes.

Though not, perhaps, so gallant a race as the Coorgs, the head-men are fine fellows, and infinitely superior to their neighbours in the plains. They are, however, very superstitious, and it is said that the immolation of human victims was, in past years, not unknown to them.

Rice is the principal crop grown in the country, the numerous streams that rise in the forest-clad hills affording an abundant supply of water, so that artificial irrigation, whether from tanks or wells, is in consequence seldom resorted to. Of the crops grown in unirrigated land in the adjoining plain districts, few are raised, but, if produced, they are free from extra assessment.

A good deal of grain is sent out of the country in bags made of the bark of a tree called 'gaja mara,' or elephant tree. The trunk is steeped in water, after which the bark is removed entire by threshing it, in which state it is not unlike the leg of an elephant.

Beautiful as it is to the eye, Manjarábád would be an insignificant tract, were it not for the importance which it has derived within the last generation from the production of coffee, which has entirely changed the face of the country, and made its name known in the markets of Europe. The dense jungles which only produced cardamoms, lac, pepper, and other forest produce, have everywhere disappeared under the axe of the planter, smiling gardens taking their place.

The introduction of the coffee plant into Mysore is assigned, with every appearance of truth, to a Musalmán ascetic, who resided on the summit of the magnificent mountain in the Kadoor district, called in ancient time Chandradróna, but more recently Bábá Búdan, after the individual referred to. He is said to have brought the tree from Mecca, whither he had gone on a pilgrimage, and to have planted it in the vicinity of his home, whence its cultivation gradually spread, though only to a limited extent, to the adjoining hills. For many years the Mysore State rented out the produce to a Madras firm, and a long time elapsed before European enterprise conceived the idea of expending capital, and forming regular plantations.

About twenty-five years ago, a successful attempt to grow coffee was made in Wastára, not far from the Bábá Búdan hill, by Mr. Cannon, who gradually extended his operations, and is said to have realised a large fortune. His example was soon followed by others, and as Manjarábád, having fine forests and a good climate, appeared well suited for planting operations, a great many European gentlemen settled there, and obtained grants of lands for coffee cultivation. The produce at first paid one rupee per maund of 28 pounds, which rate was eventually reduced to one quarter, or sixpence, that is, the excise duty is now two shillings per hundredweight. As the selling price of a maund (28 pounds) of coffee in the country is about ten shillings, the government duty falls at 5 per cent. on the out-turn, a demand which may be said to be moderate, especially as an allowance is made for the husks on weighing the coffee.

It was at one time contemplated to substitute an acreage for the present excise duty, on the ground that the latter system operated repressively on the extension of cultivation, and that it was a tax upon industry. Primâ facie, it did seem hard that, if a planter expended large sums and brought his coffee gardens to the highest state of cultivation, he should be taxed according to the amount of his produce, while native proprietors, who cultivated their holdings in a slovenly and imperfect manner, escaped with an easy payment, but, on closely examining the subject, it was found to be impracticable to comply with the wishes of the European planters. In the adjoining province of Coorg, an acreage has been substituted for the previous excise, on the following terms, namely, that for the first four years no rent be charged, that from the fifth to the ninth year two shillings an acre be paid on the whole area of an estate, after deducting grass land, and that after the ninth year the payment be four shillings. It was supposed that the limitation of the demand, and the greater security given by title-deeds issued on behalf of the Secretary of State, would greatly improve the position of the planter, and add considerably to the value of the estate.

In Mysore, however, there were various reasons which made this course unadvisable. In the first place, as the province was administered in trust on account of the Maharaja, it was not in the power of the English officials to give permanent title-deeds, and the grants for coffee-planting are, therefore, necessarily of a temporary nature, although the British Government has expressed an opinion that the engagements will be binding on any future ruler of Mysore. The grants, called puttahs, are however as complete as circumstances will admit. They are signed by the chief official of the province, and are duly numbered and registered, and guarantee the continuance of the grant so long as a prescribed number of coffee trees per acre are planted, and the regulated excise is paid. The area and boundaries are also specified with a fair amount of accuracy, in the absence of a scientific survey. Any transfers made by the original grant-holder can be registered in the local registry offices, and there is, therefore, little essential difference between the validity of the grants and those issued in Coorg.

The second obstacle to fixing an acreage was the extreme difficulty of carrying out a regular survey of coffee holdings. When it is considered that the plant is grown among forests, in a rugged hill country, within ill-defined areas, that the holdings of native proprietors are frequently very small and only occasionally cultivated, and that sometimes only a few hundred trees are planted, or, rather, scattered about, in the heart of dense jungles, it will be apparent what a length of time would elapse, and what a heavy expense would be entailed, before a scientific survey could be effected. Further, it is obvious that the entire work could not possibly have been carried out in one season, so that the imposition of an acreage in some cases and of an excise in others, would have produced much embarrassment and dissatisfaction.

Lastly, to the majority of the native planters an excise is preferable to an acreage. They have little desire to sell their holdings, and rarely bring them into the market, either for sale or mortgage, while an excise duty, which adapts itself to good or bad seasons, and the consequent outturn of the crop, does not press so heavily upon them as an unalterable land-tax, which is collected rigidly at the same rate under all circumstances. Of the whole excise now paid in Mysore, about nine-tenths are paid in the Kadoor and Shimoga districts, and about three-fourths in the Hásan district by natives, so that, on a consideration of the general question, it was necessary to guard carefully their interests before effecting any change.

The produce of a European estate may be estimated at from 140 to 280 lbs. per cultivated acre, or, say, 210 lbs. as an average, whereas on that of a native holder, who is unwilling to lay out large sums in improving his estate, it is rarely more than 42 lbs. The former, therefore, pays on 210 lbs., at sixpence per maund of 28 lbs., 3*s.* 9*d.* per acre, or about what the highest acreage in Coorg reaches on the whole cultivation, whereas the native, under the excise system, on his produce of 42 lbs. per acre, pays only 9*d.*, so that a heavy acreage would have a most disadvantageous effect. Indeed, as the native planters in Hásan contribute yearly to the excise about 2,300*l.* and the European planters only 600*l.*, an acreage would probably have proved detrimental, both to the government revenue and to native industry. The above figures may not be strictly accurate, but they are sufficiently near the mark to illustrate the subject.

It does not appear practicable to reduce the excise, which, as above observed, falls only at the rate of 5 per cent. on the crop, while the Hásan planters are probably better off than their neighbours in Coorg and the Wainád, as their felling and clearing expenses have been smaller, labor is cheaper, and the succession of bad seasons has affected them somewhat less than those who pay an acreage. At the same time, the great stimulus given to the coffee trade in other countries has acted prejudicially to their interests, eagerness to make a fortune has led to much inferior land being occupied, and, above all, the ravages of the insect called the borer have dismayed many a stout heart and able head among them. Owing to the drought which prevailed for several years, the borer beetles, as well as destructive species of moths in the grub state, made their appearance, chiefly in the plantations situated farthest away from the ghâts, where the climate is drier than in the estates to the west, and did incalculable damage. It was found that large sums had been thrown away in felling the finest forest timber, thus inducing dryness in the soil, which had previously consisted of a rich mould. As in Coorg, the surface soil being swept away by the heavy rains, the coffee plants soon began to show signs of decay in withered leaves and swollen trunks. Hundreds of them were cut down and thrown away, being irretrievably ruined by their insect foes, and it became necessary to plant the charcoal tree and other fast-growing plants, to give the protection and secure the moisture formerly yielded by the primæval forest.

In the uncertainty as to the ultimate success of growing only coffee, some of the planters have turned their attention to the possibility of rearing cardamoms, pepper, and cinchona. The first of these is indigenous, the jungles specially devoted to it having hitherto been leased out, and the ordinary mode of procuring the spice being to fell some of the giant trees of the forest on the gháts, when the heads of the cardamom spontaneously appear. It is also sown, but less commonly. The pepper vine grows naturally. Plants from the cinchona nursery on the Bábá Búdan Hill have been distributed in Manjarábád, and if the altitude is sufficient, which seems questionable, they will no doubt be successfully cultivated by the planters, as well as by the villagers. All the latter have small gardens, called Hittalú, attached to their houses, and as fever is frequently prevalent, it is expected that, in the absence of means for extracting the quinine and other essential compounds of the bark, the latter will itself be used in the shape of a decoction, a practice with which, in regard to other trees, Orientals are quite familiar.

According to the latest returns, there are more than 21,000 coffee plantations in Mysore, of which Europeans hold nearly 300; but, whereas the total area of estates occupied by natives is 78,000 acres, that of European estates is 33,000 acres, so that nearly all the larger grants are held by Englishmen, and in many instances several estates are held by the same person.

There is no doubt that the European planters have conferred an immense benefit upon Manjarábád and the adjoining sub-divisions where they have established themselves. The native landholders, averse to the curtailment of their own feudal powers, and fearing the consequences of their agrestic laborers quitting their employ, frequently regard with a jealous eye the colonization of their country by the interlopers. Nevertheless, many of these have won their esteem and confidence. Cases of violence calling for the intervention of the officers of Government rarely occur, and the planters of Manjarábád are, as a body, gentlemanlike and considerate, and in every way entitled to the fullest support which the State can consistently give them. There is little prospect, however, of their ever realising the brilliant fortunes that at one time dazzled their eyes by anticipation.

NAGAR DIVISION.—SHIMOGA.

The Shimoga district contains an area of 4,650 square miles, has a population of 430,000, and a revenue of 167,000*l.* It formed, together with the Kadoor district, which is now separated from it for administrative purposes, the kingdom of Ikkéri or Bednór. It comprises plain country, a submontane tract, and the malnád[1] or purely hill region, the features of all of which differ greatly, as well as the

[1] Kanarese, 'Mala,' a hill, and 'Nád,' a division of hill country.

character of the people who inhabit them. Of its nine sub-divisions, four constitute the malnád proper, namely, Ságar, Nagar, Káulidrug, and Anantpur, while Chennagere and Honáli are mostly open country, and the remaining three partake of the characteristics of the other divisions according to their proximity to or remoteness from the wooded hills of the west or the level plains to the east. The distinction referred to is, however, at best arbitrary, as there is little uniformity in the surface of any portion of the country.

The Chennagere sub-division was formerly in the possession of the Pálegárs of Tarikere, in the Kadoor district, who belong to the Bédar caste, and who built forts here and at Baswapatam, a fertile and picturesque tract adjoining. Their principal temple seems to have been at Santé Bennúr, a town reputed to be the most salubrious place in this part of Mysore. The temple was, however, destroyed by the Musalmáns, who used its stones to construct a handsome mosque of great size on the site. The Pálegár, whose god had been thus insulted, suddenly attacked Santé Bennúr with a force of 1,000 men, massacred all the Muhammadan population, and polluted the mosque with swine's blood, since which desecration it has been abandoned. It was, however, occupied for a time by British troops after the fall of Seringapatam.

In the centre of Chennagere is the Súlékere lake, which, when full, is five miles long and twenty miles round, being probably the finest reservoir in Southern India, except the Kammam tank in the Kadapa district of Madras. It was built, it is said, many hundred years ago by a courtesan ('Súlé,' a courtesan, and 'kere,' a tank, in Kanarese). The local legend asserts that this woman was a king's daughter, who, having formed a connection with some divinity, built, as an expiatory act, the tank, which submerged the town of her father, who cursed her as a prostitute. The work is a very fine one, as the reservoir receives the drainage of twenty square miles, all of which pours into the gorge where it is built. The embankment is of no great length, the defile between the adjacent hills being narrow, but it is of stupendous width, height, and strength, though not quite straight. It has resisted successfully the floods of centuries, but owing to the great pressure of the volume of the water in the tank, the difficulty of properly working with rude plugs the enormous sluices was immense, and the latter in course of time became much injured, and could not be utilised. Of the two sluices, that to the north was called the Siddhana, and that to the south the Basava, and both were in bad order. During the drought, which a few years ago prevailed, advantage was taken of the circumstance to repair the sluices, which a man could pass through with ease, although the first adventurer was encountered by a cobra on entering the northern one. The channels had also fallen into disrepair, and the great extent of land immediately below the tank (reputed to be more than 20,000 acres) was covered by a dense date jungle; so that the vast supply of water afforded by this magnificent reservoir flowed uselessly away to the river Tungábhadra, near Harihar. When the channels, which are now in hand, are fully repaired, hundreds of acres of sugar-cane can be grown under them, and the feverish jungle, which is now dreaded by cultivators, will give place to smiling gardens. It is, in fact, one of the few irrigation projects of modern days in Mysore which is likely to prove highly profitable. It is a remarkable fact that, notwithstanding the damaged state of the sluices, and the great force of the water when escaping through them, the embankment has always remained firm and uninjured, a satisfactory proof of the solidity of the structure.

On the western side of the Chennagere sub-division, the Bél fruit is found growing wild, but though abundant and highly astringent, it does not seem to have the same useful properties, when employed to cure dysentery, as the cultivated species. An osier, called the Ambádi, also grows abundantly, from which ropes are made by steeping the plant in water. The fibre is very strong, and is preferred to coir rope. About two rupees' weight is yielded by each plant, and the manufacture is largely exported.

The Honáli sub-division is also a plain country, having little jungle, save in the vicinity of a small range of hills which separates it from Chennagere, while the crops raised in it are similar to those produced to the eastward. The town of the same name, which is situated on the Tungábhadra river, formerly belonged to an Afghán family, whose representative still resides there. The first Nawáb, a Jamand Afghán by descent, was named Abd ul Nabi Khán, and was an officer of the Court of Delhi. He settled in the Dhárwár district, where he, as well as the Sávánúr Nawáb, with whom he was connected, received an estate from the emperor. The two chiefs, as also the Nawábs of Karnúl and Kadapa, took a prominent part in the struggles for supremacy which characterised the troubled period after the extinction of the Vijayanagar dynasty, but the last two houses are now extinct. The Sávánúr Nawáb has held his own, and is still of some local importance, but the Honáli chiefs, after the death of Nawáb Kutab-ul-Mulk during the siege of Seringapatam, sank into insignificance, and now possess little but a barren title. In fact, the Musalmán families which once played so conspicuous a *rôle* in the history of Southern India, have lost all their former importance, and, with the exception of the Carnatic Princes of Arcot, there are but three Musalmán chiefs of any note in the Madras Presidency, namely, the Raja of Cannanore, the Nawáb of Masulipatam, and the Jágírdár of Bangánpilli.

Shimoga, which gives its name to the whole district, is one of those sub-divisions which partake alike of the features of the open country and of the hills, the western and south-western parts being covered with deep jungle. The town contains 16,000 inhabitants, and is the head-quarters of the Nagar division and of the Shimoga district, which has given it a certain importance, though the unhealthiness of the place and the absence of any thriving trade, militate against its population increasing rapidly. The majority of the people are poor, and are greatly under Brahmanical influence. The town is situated on the Tungá river, a fine stream with a rocky bed, which was successfully bridged about twenty years ago, while, about the same time the sister river, the Bhadra, was bridged at Benkipur, twelve miles distant. The two streams unite at Kúdli, about halfway between Shimoga and Honáli, and previously to their being bridged, the access to Shimoga was very difficult in the rainy season, the rivers being crossed by basket boats, called 'dónis,' a kind of coracle, which is liable to be upset in transit. Although this inaccessibility had a prejudicial effect upon trade, it added, in former days materially to the strength of the Nagar country, while the formidable mountain ranges to the west and the south, were an insurmountable barrier to an invading foe. During the wars with Tippu Sultán, Shimoga was attacked, however, by the Mahrattas, under Parsurám Bhao, who ruthlessly plundered the country, and left marks of devastation from which the people have scarcely yet recovered. The extinction too of the Ikkéri dynasty appears to have operated prejudicially upon the vitality of the whole Nagar territory.

In the eastern parts of the Shimoga sub-division, dry crops are produced, in the centre, both these and rice, and to the west, the latter only. The common Kanarese name for rice land is 'gaddé,' and to this in the central parts, is attached what is called the 'hankal,' on which unirrigated crops are grown, such as various kinds of millet, beans, grain, castor-oil plants, &c. Garden-land, producing cocoa-nuts and betel-nut, is found under tanks, but the latter is of an inferior quality to that grown in the Malnád.

To those who are fond of shooting, Shimoga is a

favourite station, as in the neighbourhood, tigers, leopards, and bears are not uncommon, while bison are sometimes met with; though more rarely than formerly. Spotted deer, jungle sheep, and antelope abound in some places, but the elk does not often come so far to the eastward.

Shikárpur adjoins Shimoga. The northern part borders on Dhárwár and is open, while in the southern part, heavy jungle prevails. It is a fertile sub-division, sugar-cane being grown to a large extent, together with various other crops of a superior kind. In the low jungle, not far from Shikárpur, tigers are common. On the frontier is a magnificent reservoir, called the Másúr Madak tank, the embankment of which forms the boundary between Mysore and Dhárwár. It was constructed by some influential chief, who conceived the idea of storing up the accumulated waters of the Kumadvati river, which, at this point, cut its way through a gorge in a low range of hills. An Arabic inscription records the repairs effected by the Sávánur Nawáb. The embankment is of immense height and strength (a female having, it is said, been immolated to ensure its stability), and the old sluice of colossal size; but, in course of time, the river, when in flood, burst through the barrier, and carried away a portion of it. Ten years ago the Bombay Government undertook the repair of the sluice, though at a lower level than the original design, and a considerable amount of irrigation is now afforded by the tank to the neighbouring villages of Dhárwár. It is believed, however, that it would be quite feasible to restore the whole work, as originally planned, in which case an almost unlimited supply of water would be available, the old sluice being perhaps twenty feet higher than the modern one, so that the storage capacity of the tank would be vastly increased, the only obstacle being the submersion of Mysore villages, which would ensue on raising the level of the water-spread.

In the north of the Shikárpur sub-division, near the thriving mart of Siralkoppa, is the ancient town of Belgámi, which was formerly the seat of a Jain principality. There are three temples, dedicated to Kaitéshwara, Sóméshwara, and Tripurahántéshwara, all of which are richly carved, while in the interior of the latter is some beautiful stone screen-work. The architect is said to have been Jakanáchári. It is probable that these temples, which are now devoted to the worship of the god Siva, as appears from their names, were originally dedicated to the worship of the Jain deities, as in the court-yard of the first there are no less than fifteen slabs, elaborately covered with ancient Kanarese characters, the stones in several instances being headed by groups of figures, which from the circumstance that the principal personage is represented in a sitting attitude, cross-legged, are evidently of Buddhistic or Jain origin. All the temples have met with rough usage, apparently from the Musalmáns; but an attempt has been made to rescue the Shásanas from oblivion by having photographs taken of them. There are so few learned natives, however, who have an intimate acquaintance with the ancient Kanarese language, that it is a matter of great difficulty to secure an accurate translation of these old monuments, and the versions supplied cannot be deemed trustworthy. The ancient inscription discovered in the Bégúr temple, eight miles from Bangalore, was sent to various persons with a reputation for learning; but none of them could decipher it. It was in the ancient Grantham character, and referred, seemingly, to the victories of a Raja who was represented as engaged in a fierce combat with another chief, one being seated on an elephant, and the other on horseback, amidst a cloud of javelins and spears, hurled by themselves and their followers. This curious monument was purchased by Government, and deposited in the Bangalore museum.

Sórab is another sub-division of a mixed character, the southern portion being covered with thick jungle, frequently found in isolated patches. These forests are called káns, and are partially cultivated with sago palms, pepper vines, and other products. They are generally attached to the holdings of the more substantial farmers; but the Government has the exclusive right to all large timber trees in them. The northern portion of Sórab is comparatively open, and is a rich country, producing sugar-cane in abundance, as also betel-nut.

All this portion of the Shimoga district was in ancient days incorporated with the territory of the Kadamba kings, who ruled at Banawási, in the Canara district. This town was called Kaumudi; and near the temple of Madhukéshwara, which is said to be very old, there are eight or ten inscriptions, one of them in the Devanágari character. The Kadamba dynasty appears, in the earlier centuries of the Christian era, to have been one of the most powerful in southern India, and the position of their capital, Banawási, on the Vardá, was well chosen; but they seem to have succumbed to the princes of the Belál race long before any authentic record is available. Their stronghold was, it is said, Chandraguti, or Chandragupti, so called from a legend that from its height it obscured the moon. It is a fine hill, near Sórab, of considerable height, and well fortified. There is a temple on it dedicated to Renuká, mother of Parasurám, which is deemed very sacred, and where at certain times, under a curious overhanging rock, devotees, both male and female, worship naked.

The town of Sórab is insignificant; but it is one of the few places where sandalwood is carved. There are only a limited number of families who practise this art, the designs being mostly taken from the bas-reliefs on the famous Halibede temple, and other well-known sculptures of the same period. They manufacture boxes, boards fitted for albums, walking sticks, and various other fancy articles, the carving being very minute and delicate, and surpassing the workmanship of Bombay or Canton. The wood is, however, difficult to carve, being extremely hard against the grain, and liable to split with the grain, so that great care is requisite in working it, and the labor is so tedious that few persons will engage in it. It is consequently a very expensive manufacture, boxes 18 inches long and 12 wide costing 20*l.* or 30*l.*, and single boards 5*l.*

Ságar is the largest and most interesting sub-division of the district, the scenery being grand, the people peculiar, and the trade considerable; while it contains the birthplace of the Naiks of Kiladi, better known, from their subsequent capital, as the Bednór dynasty. It is, *par excellence*, a hill country; but, whereas there are heavy jungles on its eastern side, as one approaches the frontier, the forest gives place to a beautiful open region with grassy slopes, called 'shólas,' and meadows called 'jaddu,' interspersed with patches of wood, betel-nut gardens, and rice flats. The Gháts which bound Mysore are mostly covered, however, with thick forests, abounding in haiga, wild jack, and poon trees, round some of which twine creepers, larger than a man's arm, coiling round the trees like gigantic Pythons. Splendid góni trees, larger than the largest oak, afford ample shelter to travellers under their dense foliage. The haral gurigé, or gamboge tree, grows luxuriantly, and wild plantains, closely resembling in appearance the cultivated species, offer a feast to the monkies which abound on the hills. In the more open places, one sees the superb crimson flowers of the burga, or cotton tree, the red flowers of the polásha, used by Hindus while offering sacrifice, and the pretty white sítádandehu.

In the thick woods, which abruptly terminate on verdant swards, bison are common, and issue forth in the early morn and the afternoon to browse on the rich herbage, while large herds of elk are occasionally seen, trotting or gallopping along the paths which they have made on the hill-side. Sometimes packs of wild dogs, which are very like the jackal, cross one's path in pursuit of deer, which they hunt down in company. In the highest trees is heard the boom of the great langúr monkey, and, more rarely, one sees the pretty black monkey of Malabar. Elephants traverse the jungles in small herds of ten or twelve, and sometimes do immense damage to the rice plants, which they tear up and devour at night to the dismay of the cultivators, who rarely attempt to snare or kill them. Tigers are not common, as they prefer the more open jungle to the eastward; but they sometimes haunt particular hills, and are supposed to be the representatives of certain much-feared sylvan deities. In such cases, they frequently issue from their lair by day, and daringly carry off the cattle grazing on the hill, attacking or killing any herdsman who may have the courage to attempt to drive them away. Temples to the tiger god are met with in some places on the summits of the principal hills. The beautiful little mouse deer is often captured, and the western side of the Gháts produces many varieties of birds rarely met with elsewhere, such as the large red-headed woodpecker. Jungle fowl abound in all the forests, but are very shy and wary.

The whole of the great Ghát range, of which the Ságar hills form a part, is exposed to the full effects of the south-west monsoon, which rages with fury from June till the middle of August. Its approach is heralded in the early part of April by heavy thunder storms, which burst on the crest of the mountains, and with tremendous roar announce the end of the hot dry months. During April, and part of May, the weather is changeable, being sometimes cool, but more frequently oppressive. At the end of the latter month, the monsoon sets in, and blows nearly uninterruptedly till August, during which period heavy and continuous rain falls, the country being flooded by formidable torrents which cut off communication for days together, interrupt all trade, and isolate the different villages from one another. A perpetual mist hangs over hill and valley, the climate is damp and feverish, and the Malnád is a detestable place of sojourn to those not habituated to it from early childhood.

After a lull in September, the north east monsoon generally brings with it a few heavy showers; but these rarely last long, and when the weather clears up, the climate is delightful.

Ságar is watered by numerous hill streams, the principal of which are the Vardá, and the Sheráwati. The latter, after a course of about sixty miles, precipitates itself over the falls of Gairsoppa, which may truly be called one of the wonders of the world, for, though the volume of water is less than that of the Kávéri, the immense height of the chief fall is almost without a parallel. The country around is singularly wild and beautiful, the solitude adding a charm to the scenery. These celebrated falls are five marches, or sixty miles from Shimoga, there being a good road throughout, and are exactly on the frontier of Mysore and Bombay. The latter Government has built an excellent rest-house for travellers who come to visit the wonderful cataracts. The approach from Ságar is very striking when the vista of hills, through which the Sheráwati winds far below, opens to view. The best season for looking at the falls is the cold weather, when the river has subsided sufficiently to admit of one's crossing the stream to enjoy the view from the Mysore side; but it is at all times a magnificent sight.

On descending the hill on which the rest-house is built, and clambering over about 100 feet of the rocky bed, which, in high floods, is submerged, one arrives at the tremendous abyss down which the river is hurled; and as the nature of the ground admits of one's venturing to the very verge of the gulf, and peering down to its profoundest depths, the scene before one is truly appalling. The chasm forms a semi-circle of no very great width, notwithstanding its immense depth of 830 feet, down which pours the great Raja fall in one unbroken column. Half-way down, it is encountered by the Roarer, another fall, which precipitates itself into a vast cup, and then rushes violently downwards, at an angle of 45°, till it meets its famous compeer. A third fall, called the Rocket, shoots downwards in a series of jets; while the fourth, called the Dame Blanche, is an Undine-like cascade, gliding quietly over the mountain side in a sheet of foam. To the natives of the place these splendid works of nature are known simply as the Jóg, a Kanarese word for a waterfall, coupled sometimes with Kúrkani, the name of the nearest village. Gairsoppa is a dozen miles off; so this name, as applied to the falls, is a misnomer.

The height of the cataract was ascertained in a

manner which evinced much ingenuity and daring. A party of officers of the Bombay navy contrived to fasten a rope to a tree on the further side of the chasm, and, drawing it taut on the Bombay side, launched on it a cradle, in which they placed themselves, and, having hauled themselves out to the centre overhanging the abyss, they ascertained the depth of the fall by letting down a plumb line.

It is possible to gauge the depth by throwing down a stone, and watching till it strikes the pool beneath, about eight seconds being occupied in the fall, but this method is of course uncertain, as it is difficult to fix with precision the exact moment when the bottom is reached. Anyone with a strong head can sit on the edge of the abyss, letting his legs dangle over it, and thus gaze down into the cauldron below; but nervous people throw themselves at full length on the rock, and peep cautiously over the verge.

To amuse visitors, the natives of the place light at night bundles of hay and throw them down the gulf, which is brilliantly lighted up for a time, the flaming mass gradually disappearing from sight till it seems only a small ball of fire in the abyss. Rockets and blue lights are also thrown in, and during their brief transit, illuminate for a few moments the vast depths, scaring, as they burst, the innumerable pigeons that build in the clefts of the rocks.

The Bombay officers having plumbed the gulf, amused themselves by temporarily turning aside the stream above the Roarer fall, and letting themselves down into the cup into which it is precipitated, breakfasted there. They left a modest record of their plucky feat in the visitors' book, with a sketch of their operations, which some subsequent visitor had the bad taste to mutilate and disfigure. There is a charming view of the falls from the opposite side of the stream, at a place called Watkin's platform, and the adventurous visitor can also find his way to the pool at the bottom, but the ascent is extremely laborious, and the impression produced by gazing upwards at the cataracts is not to be compared with the enthralling and terrific view from the verge of the abyss.

A few miles north of the town of Ságar, which is one of the great depôts for betel-nut, the staple product of the Malnád, or hill country, is Kiladi, the ancient homestead of the Bednór family. The founder was a Malava by caste, one of the aboriginal races who are devoted to agriculture, and worship the god Siva, and who are common in this part of the country. This individual, whose name was Bhadrayya or Bhadrappa, is said to have discovered in 1560 A.D. a buried treasure, after having sacrificed, as a propitiatory offering, two slaves to his deity. Having visited Vijayanagar, to the king of which capital the hill country owned allegiance, he obtained from the ruling sovereign, Sadásiva Ráya, a grant of the Malnád and of part of the coast, on a feudal tenure.

It is probable that, at this period, there were many petty Jain rulers of local importance, who had partially resisted, owing to the difficult nature of the country, the pretensions of the Anagundi kings. The chief of these was the ruler of Kárkal below the Gháts. His ancestor Jaindatta is said to have come from Mathura in Upper India, and to have established himself at Kárkal about the year 1300, as an inscription at that place, dated 1333–34, gives his name, his birthplace, and claims for him a Surajbansi descent. His son took the title of Bhairasú Wodiar, a Kanarese appellation, and for some time the family appears to have been feudatory to the Belál sovereigns. But, on the extinction of this dynasty, the Kárkal chiefs, though retaining their Jain faith, were obliged to succumb, nominally at any rate, to the Vijayanagar or Anagundi kings. Thus, an inscription at Bédúr or Háduwalli, in Canara, mentions the name of Dévarasú Wodiar, son of Sangaráya Wodiar, as holding under Krishna Ráya of Vijayanagar in 1522–23. There is circumstantial evidence that this Jain family did come from Mathura, in the fact that their stronghold above the Gháts was called Govardhangiri, on the hill of Govardhan, a place near Mathura, which is well known in Hindu mythology.

Jaindatta, on his first appearance in Mysore, appears to have settled at Hombucha or Húmché, an ancient Jain colony, then at Sisila, and finally at Kárkal. In the fort of Govardhangiri, which is about 1,800 feet above the sea, there is a temple, which was formerly devoted to the Jain worship, in front of which is a curious copper pillar, inscribed on all four sides with Kanarese writing. This, as well as a pair of Dwárpálkás or warders, also in copper, was brought from Gairsoppa, on the downfall of the Jain dynasty which had long ruled there, and deposited at Govardhangiri which was esteemed a place of great strength. It is in the remotest corner of Mysore, and has rarely been visited by Europeans. It stands on a promontory, the rock on all sides being precipitous, save an approach from the south-east, which is limited to a narrow neck of land on which are two causeways called Sárá, strongly fortified by outposts called úkhads, and with tremendous ravines on either side. A difficult path then leads down to a third causeway, above which towers up the fort on one side, while on the other a rugged and devious pass, commanded for some distance by the fortress, leads down to the plain country beneath. The fort is in fair repair, but is now deserted and overgrown with jungle, though the old pass is still used by traders, who carry down to Gairsoppa on pack-bullocks the rice grown in the upper country, which finds a ready sale. The road is frightfully steep and rough, and it is a marvel how any laden animal can traverse it; yet 50,000 bullocks yearly descend and ascend it, carrying down grain and bringing up salt for consumption in the Malnád.

The annexed pedigree gives the succession of the Naiks of Kiladi, down to the time of the subversion of the family by Haidar Ali.

When Bhadrayya had received the investiture above referred to, he took the name of Sadásiva after his royal master, and began to strengthen his position by erecting a fort, but his successor, disliking Kiladi as a residence, transferred his capital to Ikkéri, a town a few miles south of Ságar, where are still to be seen a few traces of the fort and palace built by this chief.

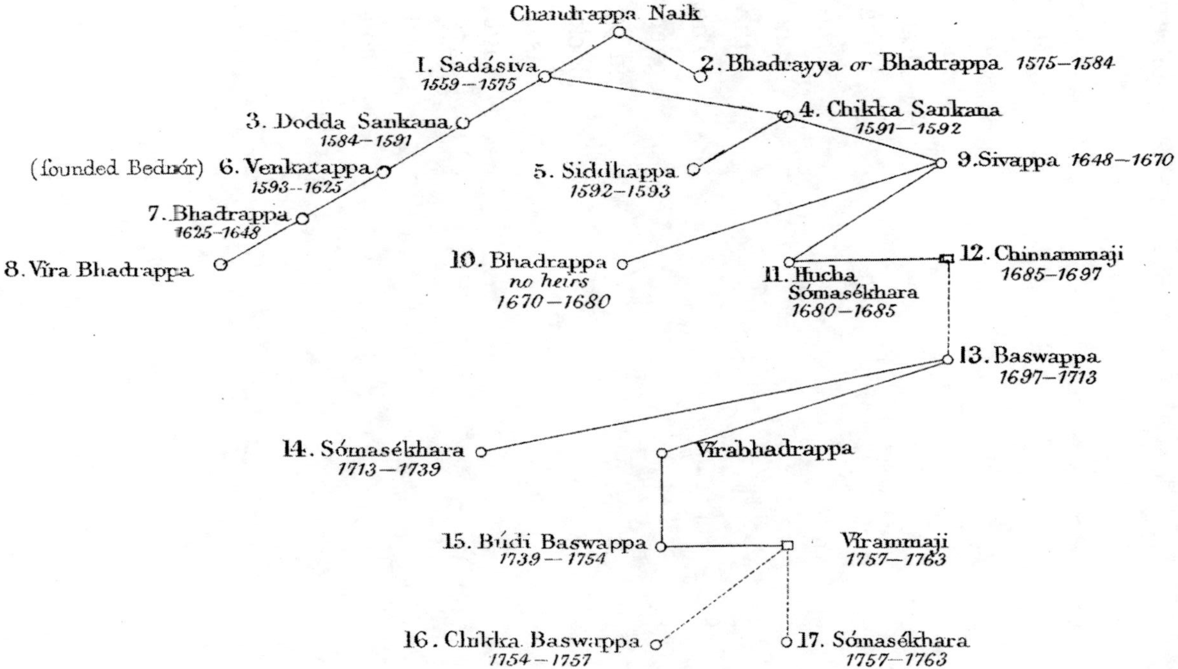

PEDIGREE OF THE **NAIKS** OF **KILADI** OR **IKKÉRI**, *the rulers of* **BEDNÓR**,
according to Buchanan "Journey through Mysore." Vol. III. p. 125.

But, in 1639–40, Sivappa Naik, who was conducting the administration as regent, deeming Bednór to be the most eligible seat of government, owing to the strength of the position, fixed upon that place as the ruler's abode, and the dynasty reigned there for more than a hundred years with considerable prestige. Sivappa Naik ascended the throne in 1648, and besides conquering the whole of the hill country, including the small fiefs held by the Jain chiefs, won for himself much renown as a ruler. The Vijayanagar dynasty had by this time become so weak, owing to the incursions of the Musalmáns and the revolt of the Mysore Wodiar, that Sivappa Naik had no difficulty in asserting his independence, and in overrunning the Malnád, but it is more to his credit that he was the first of his race to introduce a settled form of government, some of the traces of which exist to this day.

The rule of the successors of Sivappa Naik appears to have been wholly devoid of interest, although they retained their possessions in the hill country in despite of the rising power of the Hindu sovereigns of Mysore, with whom they frequently waged war. The chronology attached to the pedigree now given, is somewhat doubtful, as there are various versions of the descent of the successive chiefs, but the writer has in his possession the following grants issued by them, with the dates attached.

	A.D.
Venkatappa	1600
Sivappa	1651
Bhadrappa	1671
Baswappa	1697
Chennammaji	1699
Sómasékhara	1726
Búdi Baswappa	1740

Two of these grants, those by Sivappa and Bhadrappa, are written on palm leaf, and the rest on paper, while they all refer either to assignments of land and money to particular individuals, or to the nomination of the grantee to certain offices, for which a consideration had been paid to the sovereign.

In 1763, the dynasty was subverted by Haidar Ali, who stormed Bednór, and seized the vast treasures that had accumulated there, from the time of Sivappa Naik. The Rání Vírammaji, with her adopted son Sómasékhara Naik, fled to Belálraidrug, a strong fortress built by one of the old Belál kings at the head of the Kúdúdúkal pass, but, being surrounded by Haidar Ali's troops, she was taken prisoner and sent to Madagiri in the Toomkoor district, where she shortly afterwards expired. Her adopted son is supposed to have been killed, and the rule of the Naiks of Kiladi thus came to an end.

The family were by caste Sivabhaktaru, that is, devotees of Siva, whose worship still prevails throughout the hill country, and all the high offices in the country were held by people of this persuasion, although the Naiks made liberal offerings to Brahmans. Since the restoration of the Hindu Rajas of Mysore, when the Malnád came for the first time under their direct rule, the Sivabhaktaru or Lingáyats have lost all authority, their places having been usurped by Brahmans, who now hold most posts of importance.

The Kiladi family distinguished themselves by planting along the roads which led to their capital avenues of the Dhúpada tree (Vateria Indica, or black dammar). These superb trees, which will not grow in the plain country, excite the admiration of all visitors to the Gairsoppa falls, and will long remain to testify to the civilisation of the extinct dynasty. They yield a gum, and grow luxuriantly from young shoots in their native locality, but are not found on the Ghát ranges.

It is not known what mode of assessment prevailed in the Malnád prior to the time of Sivappa Naik, but, as there are few villages in the country, it is probable that, as at present, it was divided into farms, called wargs, a certain number of which comprised what was, for the sake of convenience, called a village. The farmer held, besides rice land and betel-net gardens, a certain proportion of forest and grazing, for which he paid a lump sum to the state, and, subject to the periodical payments, had the power of selling and transferring his holding, a right unknown in the plain country, where, as in most parts of India, the sovereign is considered the proprietor. It may be safely asserted that the existence of tenant right was never acknowledged by the old rulers of the soil in the plains, the occupants, excepting those holding land irrigated by tanks or wells and a few privileged proprietors, being regarded as tenants at will, who could at any time be ejected, their land being given to others. At the present day, if unirrigated land is required for railways, or other public purposes, there are few native rulers who would consider that anything more is necessary than to remit the assessment on the land, compensation to the occupant being deemed absurd. But, in the Malnád, or hill country, as also in Manjarábád, in Coorg, and on the Malabar coast, the proprietorship of the soil is vested in the farmer, and in the case of the latter, that is, Coorg and Malabar, it is known by the name of Jama or Janam tenure, signifying a birthright.

The farmers of the Malnád hold tenaciously to their ancient rights, and some of them pay from 100*l.* to 200*l.* yearly rental, but their position is not so good as it was in former days. The climate during the rainy season is very severe, and labor in the rice fields is extremely trying. All agricultural operations were consequently carried on by the Holiars, a low caste, of hardy and active habits, who were serfs on the farms, and whose ancestors had from generation to generation lived on the estates to which they were attached. They are identical with the agrestic kinds of Manjarábád and Coorg, and their present freedom is much resented by their masters, whose estates are often only partially cultivated, owing to the difficulty of procuring laborers, when high prices and tempting offers from coffee planters allure away those upon whose exertions in the fields the prosperity of their farms depends. Such Holiars used to receive barely 4*s.* a month from their feudal superiors, together with a blanket and some clothing, and presents on marriages and holidays, whereas planters pay them 8*s.* or 10*s.* monthly, so that the temptation to desert their masters is well nigh irresistible.

Sivappa Naik, in order to ascertain what assessment the land of the Malnád would bear, cultivated under his own eyes various descriptions of soil, noting the quantity of seed sown within a given area, the out-turn of each crop, and the value at the selling rates. He then fixed the Government share at one-third of the gross produce, which is nominally the proportion determined in most modern settlements in India, and prescribed the rental payable by the several qualities of land. The basis of the system was the quantity of seed required to sow a certain extent of land, this mode of calculation being known as the Bíjwari, from the Sanskrit word 'Bíja,' a seed. The actual assessment was called the 'Shisht,' and the total rental of a farm or village the 'Bérij.' The valuation appears to have been moderate, but the equitable assessment fixed by Sivappa Naik was soon disturbed by his successors, who enhanced the sum payable, by adding various extra charges called 'Pattí.' It was not difficult to find a pretext for these extortions on charitable grounds, or on the plea of defensive operations; but the result was that, in the time of Haidar Ali, the extra charge amounted to so large a sum that the pattí stood to the shisht in the proportion of $1\frac{1}{4}$, or thereabouts, to 4, or an addition of about one-third to the proper rental. This was no doubt far in excess of the real value of land, and, in consequence, the revenue commonly fell into arrears, while the balance, which yearly accrued on the uncultivated portions of the farms, was held like the sword of Damocles over the head of the unfortunate proprietor, who, moreover, was unable to resign portions of his holding without throwing up the whole farm. Of late years, permission has been accorded to resign what cannot be cultivated, and the introduction of the revenue settlement according to the Bombay system will speedily remedy existing defects and discrepancies; but for the moment, the Malnád farmers are certainly not so well off as their fellows in the plains. This is, in a great measure, owing to the paucity of agricultural labourers, but also because the majority of the farmers are in the hands of money-lenders.

The most remunerative produce of the hill country is betel-nut, from which the Mysore State yearly derives an income of about 45,000*l.* in the shape of excise. The original outlay on a betel-nut garden is however heavy, and it is said that sixteen years elapse before the trees yield any profitable return. The gardens are generally formed between hills in a position protected from the winds, where there is an abundant supply of water, of which there is no lack naturally for the most part in the Malnád. The trees are planted at regular intervals of from twelve to twenty feet, eighteen and a half feet being the ancient Ikkéri standard, and the ordinary nominal mode of assessment is to fix a certain valuation on each 1,000 trees; but a comparison of the ruling rates shows the existence of a confused and arbitrary taxation, varying in every portion of the district in the most perplexing manner. In fact, the difficulty of remedying the abuses which had grown up in a long course of years was so great, that it was wisely resolved not to attempt any tinkering on uncertain data, but to leave the revision to the regular survey, which would apply a remedy on a well-defined and recognised basis.

Other reasons have combined to affect unfavourably

betel-nut cultivation. The Mysore produce pays an excise duty,* whereas that of Bombay does not. There is no apparent reason why an article of pure luxury should not pay an excise, as tobacco does in England, and the sum raised (45,000*l.*) is too large to sacrifice heedlessly; but the Mysore farmer naturally grumbles at the immunity from taxation enjoyed by his Bombay neighbours.

Again, most of the cultivators are in the hands of money-lenders called Sútigidárs, who advance, or pay on behalf of the farmers, the Government demand, taking the crop. The prices of betel-nut for the season in the low country at Wálájápett, Arcot, and other places, is not fixed till May or June, when the whole extent of the year's crop is known, as well as its quality; but as the instalments of Government revenue fall due long before this time, the cultivator had either to dispose of his produce at a great disadvantage, or to borrow money in order to meet his obligations. This has been remedied by postponing the instalments to a time when the selling rates in the Madras Presidency have been ascertained.

The betel-nut of the Malnád, called 'adiké' in Kanarese, and 'supiári' in Hindusthání, is a very elegant endogenous tree, shooting up quite straight to a height of sixty feet, the fruit growing in bunches immediately underneath the spreading leaves at the top of the tree, like cocoa-nuts. The nuts are gathered by men, who

* Nagar betel-nut of the first quality pays a duty of 2*s.* 6*d.* on the maund of 24 pounds; the second quality 1*s.* 6*d.*; and the third 9*d.* In the plain districts, the duty is only 6*d.*, but the nut grown in them is very inferior.

swing themselves from one tree to another without descending, so that no time is lost in collecting the produce, which, after being boiled and split in two, is sent away in the winter months to the plains. In the intervals between the betel-nut trees, other products, such as jack-fruit, limes, plantains, &c., are grown, while the pretty pepper-vine is seen, twining round the lofty betel-nut, so that the appearance of the plantations is very picturesque, and brilliantly green. By far the best betel-nut is grown in the Malnád of the Kadoor district.

As there are few cart-roads in the hill country, the betel-nut is generally carried on pack-bullocks and donkeys, of which large droves are brought in the cold weather months by gangs of Lambádis and Korchars, two of the wandering tribes, who have the reputation of combining with their more honest calling a predilection for thieving and gang robbery. The principal depôts are Bii úr in the Kadoor district, and Tipatúr and Gubbi in the Toomkoor district, where reside the more wealthy merchants, who export the nut beyond the Mysore frontier.

In the jungles which line the western ranges of the Ságar sub-division certain tribes of Mahratta descent used to carry on a species of cultivation called kumari, which is now strictly prohibited. It was their practice to fell the trees on a hill side, and after burning the jungle, to sow millet and some other crops which require no irrigation. The return is large for a year or two, but the destruction of valuable timber is great, and the ground requires to be constantly changed.

The principal castes in Ságar are the Haiga or Havika

Brahmans, who hold a great many of the betel-nut gardens, and are a grumbling and discontented people; the Halépayaka, who, besides being agriculturists, have a good reputation as soldiers and sportsmen; the Holiar or hereditary serfs, above mentioned; and the Jains, of which interesting people a few members are found near the old passes of Govardhangiri and Hinni. They live in a very simple fashion, each on his own estate, but exercise considerable authority over their retainers. They export rice largely to the towns on the coast, and some of them are in easy circumstances. Their great desire seems to be to keep the Brahman officials at the furthest practicable distance, while few of these delicate gentry care to penetrate the wild and difficult country where the Jain farmers still preserve a faint trace of the former ascendancy of their race. The country, however, on their side, produces little but rice, and some pulse, the Jains never touching animal food of any description. They are not a powerful race; indeed, all the people of the hill country are very inferior to the dwellers in the plains, in point of physical appearance and strength. This may, to some extent, be accounted for by the prevalence of fever, which, at certain seasons, is very common, and generally attacks all new comers, so that, to the people of Bangalore or Mysore, service in the Malnád is equivalent to banishment, or to life in a penal settlement.

The simple races who live in this remote and inaccessible part of Mysore are ignorant and superstitious, and hold in reverential awe the spirits of the woods. In marching through the country one frequently sees in the heart of the forest singular sheds erected over deserted white-ant hills, inside which are deposited numerous little horses of wood and clay, many of which have riders on them. Such a shed is called a 'jetga-mané,' or spirit-house, and is dedicated to the local deity, Bír Dévaru, or Nágappa, in whose honor a festival is held yearly in the month of February, when the curious hobby-horses referred to are offered to propitiate the sylvan snake-god, to avert murrain among cattle, and to secure offspring. It is not improbable that serpents do often take up their abode in old ant-burrows, and are therefore feared with good reason. These strange temples of nature are reverenced by the Jains among others.

The sub-division of Nagar closely resembles Ságar, but is more hilly, and less easy of access. Nagar, the capital of the Kiladi or Ikkéri princes, originally bore the name of Bidurúru, or bamboo-town, from 'biduru,' a bamboo, and 'úru,' a town, and is still surrounded by thick forests of this useful tree. That which constituted its strength in olden time, namely, its secluded and strong position, has in these days proved its bane. When there were no roads anywhere, and, consequently, no carts, all the produce of the country was exported on pack-bullocks, which, with immense labor and many casualties, managed to scramble down the natural gorges in the hills, which here and there, in the most difficult places, were paved with flights of steps. At the present time the plain country is covered with a net work of roads, but the communications in the hills are worse than they used to be, as the old passes have never been kept in proper repair since the subversion of the Ikkéri dynasty, while the gradients on them are so severe, that it is impracticable to convert them into roads fitted for cart traffic. Three new Ghát routes have, indeed, been opened in the Shimoga district, namely, the Gairsoppa, Kolúr, and Águmbi roads, and these are of great service; but the internal communication is still defective, and cultivators who live in immediate proximity to the old passes, prefer to use these, steep and rugged though they be.

The principal of these passes is Haidargarh or Hosangadi, about twelve miles from the town of Nagar, the worst portion of which is so frightfully rough, steep, and slippery, that it is a marvel how laden bullocks can possibly climb up it. This particular point is called the 'Áne Jeri,' or Elephant's Drop, from a tradition that one of these animals here fell over the precipice. There are remains of fortified places at the summit, and at various convenient places on the pass, which made the approach to the capital well nigh impracticable to an enemy, while these outposts constituted also the toll-gates, where duties were levied on all exports and imports. It has recently been proposed to make a new road over the hills near the Haidargarh pass, a good line with an easy gradient having been traced for the purpose, and the points of departure and arrival being the same as those of the ancient route. This will be of great benefit to the country, but the engineering difficulties are not small, while labor is hard to get.

The town of Nagar presents a melancholy picture of decay. It is said once to have had 100,000 inhabitants, but, after its capture by Haidar Ali, it gradually dwindled away, till it has become an insignificant village, containing only 300 houses. Its prosperity depended so intimately on the presence of the Ikkéri prince and his court, that the extinction of the rule of that family and the subjection of the territory to the Seringapatam ruler, had necessarily a depressing effect upon the people and upon trade. The town in 1763, when it was stormed by Haidar Ali, was undoubtedly wealthy, and a rich booty was acquired by the conqueror, which laid the foundation of his future fortune; but there is no trace now of former grandeur, except a few ruins of the palace and deserted gardens. The place lies in the centre of a basin of thickly-wooded hills, at a few points in which there are openings communicating by steep and rough-paved steps with the country beyond, so that no wheeled vehicle can enter the town. Fortifications crest all the hills, and a second line of outworks at some miles' distance gave further security to the capital. In troublous times, such as formerly prevailed, it may well be imagined that traders resorted in large numbers to a capital which afforded them ample protection, so that it became the chief mart, not only for the rice, but also for the betel-nut cultivation of the hills. It is impossible to restore its lost prestige, but something has been done of late years to assist trade by opening new roads, and it has been proved that an excellent approach to the town can be easily made, at no great cost.

The town had several gateways, of which one was named the Delhi, and another the Kodiál or Mangalore gate. Of the latter an amusing story is told that, on the late Raja's visiting Nagar, on his return from a pilgrimage to Udipi on the coast, the Amildar, or local official, being apprehensive that his highness's elephant could not pass through the gate, broke down the upper portion. Unfortunately for this zealous individual, the Raja made his entry in a palankeen instead of on an elephant, and the Amildar was publicly flogged for having acted without orders. Worse punishments than this were, however, inflicted in the time of the Ikkéri chiefs, for one may still see, on the so-called Shúla battery hill, a hole in the ground, in which was inserted a pole for impaling criminals, who were hoisted up and exhibited *in terrorem* to the whole population. It does not appear, however, that the Ikkéri princes were more tyrannical or despotical than their neighbours; and the memory of some of them, and particularly of Sivappa Naik, is still preserved with respect in the country, while the people were probably in better circumstances under their rule than when subject to the Musalmán sovereigns of Mysore, or even to the late Raja's government.

About ten miles north-west of Nagar there is a remarkably fine peak called Kodachádri, 4,111 feet above the sea, and a conspicuous landmark. The mountain is more than 2,000 feet above the level of the villages below, and is clothed with splendid forests, but the ascent is very steep indeed in one place near the foot. When ascended by the writer the barometer stood at the bottom of the hill at 28·10 at 8 A.M., and on the summit at 10 A.M. at 25·92. Bangalore having a mean of 27°, representing a height of 3,031 feet, Kodachádri is consequently 4,111, as remarked. The view from the top of the hill, which has a bluff appearance from a distance, though it is as sharp as a knife in reality, is very fine, commanding a long stretch of the great Ghát range, a considerable portion of Canara, and a wide view over the Malnád. The ascent is about three miles, and the mountain is easily reached from Nágáwádi, the head of the Kolúr Ghát, where there is a rest-house for travellers, and whence it is only four miles distant. It is a peculiar feature of the highest peaks in the Mysore Gháts that the summit is a narrow ridge, with a precipice on either side,—so narrow indeed is the top of Kodachádri, that in some places the ridge is only 12 feet across. As in many other instances, the stones on the top have magnetic properties, and at once affect a compass, if held over it.

A small isolated strip of country in the Nagar subdivision, called Hanar, belongs to the British Government. It was given as an endowment to the Kolúr pagoda in the Canara district, but, being an integral part of Mysore, ought not to have been included in the schedule of territories assumed by the English after the fall of Seringapatam in 1799.

The people of Nagar resemble those of Ságar, but there are few Jain farmers of note, though there is an old colony of this sect at Húmcha, where their priest resides.

A very rough march of fourteen miles over broken and stony ground, and with numerous ascents and descents, takes one to Kaulidrug, which gives its name to the sub-division south of Nagar, though the present head-quarters are at Tirthhalli, a flourishing town on the river Tungá and on the Águmbi Ghát road. A great part of the march is paved, but, however convenient this may have been in former days to people on foot, carrying heavy loads in the rainy season over slippery ground, the mounted traveller finds to his disgust that the broken and uneven pavement soon causes his horse to cast his shoes, and as there are no farriers in the hill country, he must, if he has not learnt the trade, content himself with walking, leaving his steed to be led. In truth, so bad are the paths, except along the main lines, in the Malnád, that even pack-bullocks cannot traverse them, and the beasts of burden in use are the men of the country.

The old town of Kaulidrug is prettily situated on a lake, above which towers an ancient fort of considerable size and strength, built by Sadásiva Naik, though fable assigns its construction to the mythical Pándavas. There is a curious block of stone in the old palace, eight feet long and seven feet wide, called the 'Ráni's Cot.' It is well carved, and has on it an inscription showing that it was made in the year Bháva (1694 or 1754, probably the former). The isolated position of Kaulidrug in the centre of a difficult country has led to its abandonment, Tirthhalli having taken its place. Its ruins and those of Árgá testify to its former importance, while the beautiful avenues of the Dhupada tree give an attractive appearance to the country, which is naturally rich, producing excellent betel-nut and abundance of rice. To the eastward are fine forests of teak, which clothe all the sides of the hills down to the Tungá, which, at Tirthhalli, only forty miles from its source, is already, owing to its numerous affluents, a formidable river, and difficult to cross except in the dry season. At that time of the year one can step over the great boulders in the bed, the difficult places, where there is a rush of water, being temporarily bridged over by benevolent Brahmans, partly out of charity, and partly to enable pilgrims to perform their ablutions in the sacred stream, from which they themselves derive a profit. There are two maths, or monasteries, close to the town of Tirthhalli, so that every facility is afforded to devotees to comply with their religious obligations.

The natural productions of Kaulidrug resemble those of Nagar, but, in addition to sandalwood, which is found in the more open parts, though of inferior quality to the Mysore wood, the coffee-plant begins to make its appearance. There is a prejudice on the part of the natives against growing this plant in the country farther north, arising from a superstitious feeling that its cultivation will bring them bad luck, nor have the few farmers who have ignored their fears been very successful, as the soil and climate appear unsuitable.

Those who possess betel-nut gardens bestow great pains in fencing in private woods, which are strictly preserved for the sake of the leaves of the trees growing in them, these being extensively used in manuring the betel-nut. Such enclosures are known by the name of Hádia and are numerous, evidencing careful cultivation on the part of the proprietors. In singular contradistinction to this, one cannot but comment upon the reckless way in which the people in all parts of the country suffer their cattle to stray into the gardens of European coffee-planters, a loose practice which they carefully guard against when their own interests are concerned, as above brought to notice. Coffee has not been planted with much success in Kaulidrug however, as the jungles are too dense to the east, and the Gháts near Águmbi are fearfully exposed to the full force of the south-west monsoon, which brings a deluge of rain with it. In the forest ranges which here bound Mysore, cardamoms grow wild, as also cinnamon, but the latter is of a poor description and not worth cultivating.

In Kaulidrug, the majority of the landholders of influence are Brahmans of various sects, the worshippers of Siva or Lingáyats being few in number, while there are no Jains of importance.

The Anantpur sub-division is not specially interresting. Part of it is covered by thick woods, and there are magnificent avenues in it of the Dhúpada tree. Some of the finest villages are held by Brahmans on a rent-free tenure, the grants having been made many hundred years ago by the Vijayanagar sovereigns, and being mostly on copper plates. One, in the possession of the Brahmans of Gautama Agrahár professes to have been given at Harihar by Janméjaya, son of Parikshit of the Sómavansi tribe and of the royal race of Hastinapura or Delhi.

The town of Anantpur is on the high road from Shimoga to the Gairsoppa falls, and is encompassed by thick bamboo jungle which, beautifully green as it is, soon becomes monotonous, while it has the reputation of being extremely unhealthy.

KADOOR.—(*Kadúr.*)

The Kadoor district has an area of 7,023* square miles, a population of 262,000, and a revenue from all sources of 99,000*l.* It contains only seven sub-divisions, of which three, Koppa, Wastára, and Lakkuwalli, form the Malnád or hill country, while the other four, namely, Chikkamugalúr, Kadoor (Kadúr), Tarikere, and Bánáwár are comparatively open country, though even in these there are several ranges of low hills. In the mountain tracts, the scenery is exceedingly fine, and is probably in its savage grandeur as picturesque as any part of southern India. Three of the higher hills in it are more than 6,000 feet above the sea.

The Koppa sub-division is intersected by the Tungá river, which is here, near its source, a beautiful swift-flowing mountain stream, of considerable depth in the rainy season, and abounding in fine fish. It runs past the celebrated shrine of Sringiri or Sringagiri, where resides one of the most venerated Hindu priests. This Guru, whose name is Narsinghácházri, is the successor and representative of the famous sectarian Shankaráchári, whose doctrines are widely spread throughout southern India, and who is said to have exterminated the Jain religion. Owing to the extended influence which he possesses, the Swámi is called by his dis-

* Not reliable.

ciples the Jagat Guru, or the teacher of the world, his followers asserting for him a superiority to all other religious preceptors. He is the venerated high priest of all Hindus holding the Smárta faith, whose doctrines are handed down in writing from recollection (Smriti), as distinguished from mere tradition (Sruti). The principal tenet of the Smártas is that everything in the world is illusion or máyá, and that there is no reality in what we see, which led a sagacious Brahman, who was asked to contribute towards the expenses of the Sringiri Guru, to observe that, if all the world was illusion, the Guru himself must be an illusion, and therefore that it was absurd to expect him to pay anything to a non-entity.

Narsingháchári is an ascetic and a celibate, living very simply, his diet being, it is said, exclusively milk. His manner and address are good, and besides having a great reputation as a Sanskrit scholar, he speaks with fluency Kanarese, Tamil, and Telugu, and has a fair knowledge of the Mahratta and Hindusthàni languages, having, in his younger days, travelled much. He wears a tiara like the Pope's, covered with pearls and jewels, said to have been given to him by the Péshwa of Poona, and a handsome necklace of pearls. On his feet he has sandals covered with silver, with the usual peg between the great toe and the next toe. He is about seventy-five years old, and has adopted as his successor a boy to whom he has given what is called the 'upadésa,' that is, the religious instruction in the sacred rites which qualifies him to assume the functions of Guru. This youth accompanies him in all his periodical tours, receiving all the tokens of respect which are due to the successor of so famous a preceptor.

On these circuits, Narsingháchári travels in great state, riding in an adda palankeen, that is, one which is carried crossways, thus preventing any other conveyance from passing him in a narrow road. An elephant is always in attendance, for the sake of effect, and a numerous cortège of Brahmans and disciples accompanies the Guru wherever he goes, all the Hindu inhabitants of a town being obliged to turn out to welcome him on arrival, a mark of respect from which even the Raja himself is not exempt.

On the few occasions when he has visited European officials, it has been necessary to receive him either under a tree or in a pandál (a temporary erection of boughs and leaves supported by poles), as nothing would induce so holy a personage to enter a house or a tent which has been polluted by the presence of Mléchas, or outcasts, as all Europeans are in the eyes of Hindu priests. The building where he receives return visits from Europeans is a stifling little hole, which no doubt needs extensive purification afterwards, but he is very polite, and, though he never shakes hands, that being out of the question, he generally presents consecrated rice and cocoa-nuts colored with turmeric, which is considered a high honor. An amusing story was told of his visit to the writer in 1864, to the effect that various dishes of meat and other unorthodox food were presented to him, which, by a few magical words, he changed into fruit and flowers, a fiction for which, of course, there was no foundation.

As a mark of his rank, he is accompanied when he travels by an honorary guard of ten men of the Mysore Horse, a distinction which, however gratifying it may be to his pride, is of little use in these peaceful days for his defence, while it is rather provocative of a collision with intolerant Musalmáns.

The Sringiri Math is in the centre of a fertile tract, which is held rent-free, having been bestowed on a former Guru about 400 years ago by one of the Vijayanagar sovereigns. It has a rental from all sources of about 5,000*l.*, besides which the establishment holds several isolated villages, and the Guru receives 1,000*l.* a-year in cash from the Raja. Notwithstanding this large income, the Math is said to be in debt, in which respect it does not differ from other similar institutions. To replenish his empty exchequer, Narsinghácharí is in the habit of making frequent and protracted tours, in order to levy contributions from his disciples; but he complains greatly of their want of faith in these perverse times, and of the stinginess shown by them in their donations.

Leaving Sringiri, one passes through a neat village called Vidyáranyapur, inhabited by Brahmans, all the houses nearly being painted red, and, following the course of the Tungá, arrives at Nimár, where an adventurous officer formed a coffee plantation under the Súji Gudda, or Magnet Hill, in the heart of a very wild country. The scenery is lovely, but wild, and so difficult are the communications and so scanty the means of subsistence, that nearly all the trade is in the hands of two Brahmans residing near the Kig mountain.

A very rough and difficult march of nine miles, over rocks and stones and numerous small streams, takes one to Kerré, a village of twenty houses, and the last inhabited place towards the great Gháts. There is an old pass here, under the bluff side of the Wolkonji hill, but it is in a frightful state and is little used.

A final march of nine miles, with many steep ascents, leads to Gangá Múla, the source of the Tungá and Bhadra rivers. The exaggerated account given by natives of the difficulty of reaching this spot, has led to a general belief that it is inaccessible, and to a wild fable that the two rivers issue from the tusks of a boar, the hill where they rise being called the Varáha Parvat, or boar hill, from a tradition that it was visited by the boar incarnation of Vishnu. It is in truth a wild country, and has a desolate grandeur about it, seeming to be the end of the world. On every side tower up magnificent mountains, spreading for leagues in every direction, and covered with immense forests, while nowhere can one detect the faintest trace of human life, either in the shape of houses or of cultivation. Prominent among the higher hills are the Kudurémukha to the south, the beautiful Kalasa peak, and an immense mass of mountain called Angrikal. Ascending the Varáha Parvat, one reaches the spot where trickles out the tiny stream of the Bhadra, while, in another part of the hill, issues its sister the Tungá, their sources being held in great veneration by the few pilgrims who have had the courage to penetrate these wilds. The two streams meet about 100 miles from their joint source at Kúdli in the Shimoga sub-division. There is a third stream, the Nétrávati, which natives imagine to rise at the same place as the other two; but this is an error, for, as it flows westward towards Mangalore, it is obvious that it cannot run up hill, and that its source is on the other side of the Ghát range.

A pious pilgrim, many years ago, being desirous of leading an ascetical life in this wild region, commenced building a temple, and had already erected a dwelling for himself, when some marauding Moplas from Canara, climbing the mountains and discovering his retreat, pillaged his house, so the unfortunate man quitted the desolate spot, leaving behind him the ruins of his abode, and the unfinished temple, of which the foundations still remain, with an image which he brought from Kalasa.

The head-quarters of the Koppa sub-division are at Hariharapur, a flourishing town on the Tungá river, which, however, is unbridged, so that during the rainy season, the rapid stream, with its high banks, is a formidable obstacle to traffic. Hariharapur is on a second road to the Águmbi Ghát, running through the northern portion of the Kadur district, and meeting the other line which passes through Tirthhalli, at the town of Águmbi.

A trip of four marches through a wild but most beautiful country, takes one from Hariharapur to the southern limit of the Nagar Malnád, part of the line being in the Koppa and part in the Wastára subdivision. As one ascends the steep hills which lead to the great saddle that separates the Tungá and the Bhadra, one enjoys splendid views of the fine mountain scenery which gives such a charm to a tour in the west of Mysore, while virgin forests of grand timber trees are contrasted with the rich betel-nut gardens which on all sides meet the eye. The woods abound in birds, including hornbills, woodpeckers, parrots, doves, jungle fowl, and a beautiful little bird with two long white tail feathers, which utters a shrill cry of 'trêt, trêt.' Mouse-deer, and the large red squirrel are common. In the thick mists which hang about in the early morning in the vicinity of the bamboo forests which shut in the Bhadra, one sees myriads of spider webs glistening in the dew, some of them of immense size.

The climate is notably damp, so much so indeed that at Bugunji, one of the principal places where the excise on betel-nut is levied, the people, during the rains, keep all their grain and other perishable articles in immense long boxes, like exaggerated coffins. Fever is rife at certain seasons, and the country is dreaded by those not inured to it from early childhood. To a delicately nurtured native of Bangalore, the tremendous forests, full of wild beasts and devils, and the terribly steep hills, each apparently loftier than the other, which he is obliged to climb, are a source of unmitigated disgust and terror, while he is cut off entirely from his little luxuries, and, instead of travelling at ease in his favourite bullock coach, must trudge the whole way.

Several years ago, an excellent trace of a new road was made between the towns of Hariharapur and Wastára, but the project was not at the time carried out. Recently, it has been revived, and there is a fair prospect of its being successfully accomplished; but it is an engineering task of no small difficulty, for not only does the road run over spurs of hill 4,000 feet above the sea, but the river Bhadra, the Sítá Holé, and several other smaller streams are crossed, which, in the rainy season, are all mountain torrents with a furious current. Such, however, are the attractions of trade, that, even at the present time, notwithstanding the difficulty and terrors of the route, some 50,000 pack bullocks, laden with betel-nut and rice, annually traverse it; while, thanks to some recent improvements, one solitary cart is said, with extreme pains, to have reached Báléhonúr from the north, that is, half way to Wastára from Hariharápur.

The forests contain the fragrant champaka, (*Michelia champaka*), nandi (*Lagerstrœmia microcarpa*), honi (*Pterocarpus marsupium*), bíté (*Dalbergia latifolia*), and other fine timber. Besides these well-known trees there are many others which attract attention, and among them the picturesque Sanhalli Bhógi, which has a white flower, and the Chetumbé Bhógi, a fine tree, with wide-spreading top branches like a yew. In the denser woods, tigers are rarely met with, but they frequent the lower jungles in the neighbourhood of villages, and occasionally commit great ravages among cattle.

The Koppa sub-division, though naturally rich and

fertile, is in a depressed state, owing to the arbitrary manner in which the rental of the betel-nut gardens has been levied, during a long course of years, at the caprice of the local officials, and also to the impoverished state of the landowners. Unlike the cultivators in the plains, who can procure with facility at the adjoining markets all that is not produced on their land, including such articles of dress as they may need, the agriculturists in the hills of Koppa, having hardly any produce but the betel-nut grown in their gardens, which few of them are able personally to export, are obliged to borrow money for all their wants from the wealthy merchants who take the crop off their hands. Many of them complain that they have nothing beyond rice to eat, water to drink, and fuel to cook with, and that, having long been entirely in the hands of the money-lenders, whose terms used to be 24 per cent. interest yearly, they have not the means to procure the simplest luxuries. Their condition has been of late much ameliorated by the suspension of the Government demand till a period beyond the close of the official year, so as to enable them to dispose of their crop after the selling rates at Wálájí, Arcot, Vellore, and other places have been ascertained, but a long time must elapse before they can get rid of the incubus of the heavy debt which now presses on them. Nearly one-third of the Government revenue is still paid by money-lenders, but the monopoly which left all the cultivators in the power of two or three individuals has ceased, so that, with the increasing competition, the rate of interest on money lent is reduced to one-half of what it was formerly.

In the plain country, the agriculturists frequently carry their grain on their own carts to distant markets, thus realising a handsome profit, without the intervention of any agent. But, in the case of betel-nut, which is moreover a precarious and delicate crop, capital is needed for the costly enterprise of transporting it beyond the limits of Mysore, after paying the excise due to the Government. When, however, the system of roads now in hand is completed, there is little doubt that wealthy traders will bring their carts into the hill country, and purchase direct from the owners of gardens, who will then reap the fruit of their industry, and repay the loans which now are as shackles round them. The three great wants of the Malnád were good communications, an equitable assessment, and payment of the Government demand at times which are convenient to the cultivator. The last of these requirements has been already met, and it is to be hoped that the other grievances will shortly disappear, as a good system of communications has been devised, which only needs funds to carry it out, while the revenue settlement department, which is already at work in the Sórab sub-division, will apply an effectual and sure remedy to the existing inequalities of taxation.

The greater part of the betel-nut grown in South Koppa finds its way, by Wastára, to Chikkamugalúr and Belúr, whence it is exported eastward. All the rest is sent to Bírúr in the Tarikere sub-division, where reside many merchants of substance. It is calculated that about 60,000 maunds (the maund being 24 lbs.)

are sent to Bírúr, and 20,000 in the other direction, the total exports from the single sub-division of Koppa in an average year being thus 80,000 maunds; the excise on which is collected at five principal stations.

Proceeding due south from Bugunji, and crossing the Sítá river, one reaches Nítlé, the excise station. The scenery at this gorge is singularly picturesque, and quite alpine in character, a splendid mountain called the Áne Gudda, or Elephant Hill, towering up on the right hand. Beyond this, there is a considerable ascent, through a grand forest, to the Sítá Kaniwé or gorge, and, after passing the ruined town of Hosapatan, one reaches the Ghanté Venaikana Kaniwé, the top of the saddle that separates the Tungá and Bhadra rivers, and the boundary between Koppa and Wastára, which latter sub-division one here enters. A good deal of coffee has been planted along the line of road, but, with rare exceptions, that grown in Koppa is not of such good quality as that produced farther south.

At Báléhonúr, the second stage from Hariharapur, an extremely difficult mountain path leads W.S.W. to the secluded Kalasa Mágani (Mágani is a name given in the Malnád to a portion of a Táluq, or sub-division, which in the plain country is called a Hóblí). This curious region is quite unique, both the country and the people having many peculiarities. A concise description of it is given in the following Kanarese saying—

Múrú Sávira Varahá
Áru Sávira Gudda
Hanéradu Sávira Paisách
Kádella Champaka
Úrella Heggadé

which, being translated, signifies—

Three thousand pagodas (i.e. 10,000 rs. revenue)
Six thousand hills
Twelve thousand devils
In every thicket the Champaka (a tree famous for its fragant flowers)
In every village a Heggadé (a Jain Headman).

The inscription is not inappropriate, save perhaps the devils, though the people of the country are firmly persuaded that these are as thick as they can stand, and, as in the Ságar country, one frequently sees sheds in the jungles, dedicated to Daiva Kuppina, or Panju-walli, a sylvan spirit, who, in his malevolent qualities, seems to rival the Bír Dévaru of that region. A series of severe ascents and descents, through thick forests, takes one to the Bird's Pass, 4,200 feet above the sea, where are the remains of a barrier which, in olden time, must have made the road nearly impassable.

Descending with much fatigue to the Bálé stream, one reaches a small village, near which is a splendid view of the superb Kalasa peak, called, from its pre-eminence, the Mêrti Gudda, that is, the mountain above all. It is 6,500 feet above the sea, and after a toilsome climb up its steep sides by the 'Windy Gorge,' one revels in a view which surpasses all one's expectations. On every side tower up hills of various shapes and sizes, stretching far away to the horizon, and presenting a wonderful spectacle of wild sublimity. At the foot of the steep ridge which runs up to a sharp point forming the actual peak, the barometer at 10.30 A.M. stood at 24·22. This point is called the Tural Bágalu, or Tural Gate, and is in a gap between the Mêrti Parvat and another hill to the south, and a very tough pull of twenty-five minutes takes one hence to the summit, the higher of two peaks, between which there is a dip. The writer's barometer being only adjusted to 6,000 feet, became deranged after ascending beyond that height, and the altitude of the mountain is therefore only put down approximately at 6,500 feet, which is probably, however, below the mark.

In a clear day, one can see the great Kumár Parvat in Coorg, a distance of fifty miles in a straight line, the fine Kodachádri hill in the Nagar sub-division a like distance, while to the south-west is the magnificent Kuduré-mukha, which is really the highest mountain in Mysore. The top of Mêrti is quite bare, but its sides are clothed with fine forests, in which are splendid specimens of the champaka tree, so much esteemed by natives for its fragrant white flowers, while one sees beneath one in secluded nooks and sheltered vallies stretches of paddy land in successive layers, one below the other, and numerous gardens of betel-nut, which, in this remote corner, attains an excellence surpassing that of any other place where the fruit is grown. The superiority of the nut of Kalasa is attributed to its ripening in the hot weather, which hardens it. It is smaller than the ordinary nut, is of a deeper color, and is considered to have a far finer flavour, so that it fetches a higher price in the market. The sides of Mêrti, where the nature of the ground admits of it, are cultivated in a series of terraces, in which abundance of rice is grown, with a little coffee, which however does not succeed well, owing to the humidity of the climate.

About fifteen miles south-west of Mêrti, but twenty miles by any road practicable for ponies, is Kóté Kán, or the Kuduré Mukha hill, the latter name having been given to it by the people of the coast from its resemblance to a horse's head, when seen from the sea. The mountain path to it leads by the Jain estate of Samsé to the Bangar Baligé, or Somáwati hill, a bluff-faced mountain with a perpendicular drop, between which and the adjoining Brahma Parvat issues the Kádigal or Sóma-wati, one of the affluents of the Bhadra. From this point there is a good road or path from Nágúr in Canara to the top of the mountain, made by the officials of that district, who have built a house on the hill as a pleasant retreat in the hot months. It is however in Mysore territory, as there is no practicable ascent on the western face of the mountain. It is some 200 feet from the house to the summit, which is about 6,800 feet above the sea, and is not only the loftiest hill in Mysore, but probably the highest between the Himá-layas and the Nílgiris. It commands a remarkably fine view of the Kalasa Mágani, as also of Manjarábád, and a considerable portion of Canara; while, in the far distance, one sees the pleasantest sight of all to the exile, namely, the sea, shining brightly to the westward in the rays of the setting sun, recalling visions and thoughts of home.

In assuming the altitude of this fine mountain to be about 6,800 feet above sea level, it may be observed that three miles from the house the barometer stood at 24° 15′ at 7 A.M., and that, allowing 300 feet per mile for the ascent, the latter half of which is very steep, the house referred to would be at an elevation of 5,881 + 900 = 6,781.* Adding 200 feet to the summit, the elevation would be 6,981, or more than the height just assumed.

Extremely fine views are gained all along the crest of these gháts, between Gangá Múla, the source of the Tungá and Bhadra, and Balálraidrug, the boundary of the fastness of hills within which the Kalasa country is enclosed. Charming as the country is under a clear sky in the bright sun, it is a frightful region to dwell in when the periodical rains pour down the mountains in countless torrents, rapidly swelling and rising, till tiny brooks become impassable rivers, and the wretched inhabitants scarcely dare emerge from their houses. All the devils are let loose at this time, and from June till October have it pretty much their own way, tormenting the people with fever, and the cattle with murrain. The superstitious inhabitants, from the highest to the lowest, dread these sprites, and, it is currently asserted, offered human sacrifices to them in days gone by. Nor can one be astonished that a primitive race, far removed from civilisation and imbued from their earliest youth with fear of the gnomes and bogies that haunt the woods, should still place implicit faith in the efficacy of sacrifices.

The principal proprietors in Kalasa are Jains, and Námdár cultivators who reverence Vishnu. Who the old inhabitants were it is hard to say, as accounts re-

* The mean of the barometer at Bangalore, based on many observations, is 27°, its height above the sea being 3,031 feet at the commissioner's flag-staff. Taking this as the fixed point of departure, 1,000 feet had been allowed for each degree registered by the barometer.

garding them differ. Some assert that the country was held by Bédars and Kormars, and that the Jain Chief of Kárkal, Bhairasú Wodiar, invaded it from the north, dispossessing the old rulers; but it is more probable that the present Jain landholders are the descendants of chiefs who, after the subversion of the Halibede dynasty, were driven into these remote hills, where they could defy the malice of their enemies.

The leading Jains are called Heggadé, and their wives Heggaditi, and, though no longer wielding absolute authority, have such great local influence that no one, without their aid, can move through the country. The chief of the Jain landholders, the Samsé Heggadé, is a man of substance, paying 200*l.* yearly to Government, and resides in a large farm, which, with its extensive out-offices and barns, greatly resembles a respectable farm in Europe, though to a person accustomed to the ordinary Indian village with its small mud houses, the contrast is striking. Such houses present a solid wall to the force of the south-west monsoon, having no windows on that side, but there is usually a court-yard in the centre, into which the gutters from the thatched roof empty themselves. In the house and barns are stored up all food, forage, and other articles needed to carry the family safely through the season of heavy rains, and the farmer is rarely without a supply of fire-arms for the defence of his house against chance robbers, and of his cattle against wild beasts. Near the residence of the proprietor one sometimes sees a temple dedicated to Sántnáth, or some other Jain incarnation, the officiating priest being of the Viswamitra, or other brahmanical caste. The idols in the temples are of black stone, the figures standing erect, with their arms hanging down at their sides.

The Samsé Heggadé has a grant given to him by Vénkatádri Naik of Balam, to which Kalasa for some time belonged, but long before the Aigúr chiefs or even the Ikkéri princes were heard of, Kalasa was a famous place of pilgrimage, as being near the source of the sacred Bhadra. This fine stream, here also called the Samp Holé, passes near the Samsé estate, running under forests filled with magnificent trees, creepers with immense leaves, and a profusion of orchids, and makes its first appearance in civilised life at Kalasa.

The Kalaséshwar temple is one of the neatest buildings of the kind in the province, although not beautiful architecturally. It is ascended by a long flight of steps nicely painted, and is surrounded by a strong wall as if it were a fortification. In the court yard there are twenty-six stone shásanas in Kanarese (one with the date 1132 Sálivâhan on it), and one in Nágari, while the Brahmans possess also two grants on copper plates. The institution has no doubt a great antiquity, and has large resources, both in money and land, but the priests are exacting landlords. It is to the credit of the people of Kalasa that they have established a grant-in-aid school, which promises to be beneficial to this remote part of Mysore.

The tourist, retracing his steps to Báléhonúr, above mentioned, proceeds south to Baswanakotta, crossing the Bhadra on a rude raft made of súpiári or betel-nut trees. In the jungles beyond, he will perceive some comical wooden figures with grinning mouths, like rude toys, representing Mariamma, the small-pox deity, and her younger sister. They are supposed to exercise a potent influence in averting the scourge of small-pox. At various places on the road too, are to be seen stones called másti-kallu, which are commonly believed to be commemorative of sattis performed by faithful widows.

Beyond Baswanakotta is a fine hill called Kanchinkaldrug, so called from its bold face resembling bell-metal, 'Kanchu.' The fort on it was built by Vír Balál, one of the kings of the Halibede dynasty, who constructed Balálraidrug, and is a strong place, though it has been deserted for a hundred years. It commands the approach to the Kalasa Mágani from the east, as also the route to the north. After crossing the Hakki Makki pass, which is 5,000 feet above sea level, one descends into the less mountainous country near Wastára, to the west of the great Bábá Budan hill. Near the village of Ánúr is a remarkable hill called Madakal, or Murakal, one of the heights of which terminates in a singular knob, which some facetious planters nicknamed 'Cannon's nose,' from a fancied resemblance to the nasal organ of this gentleman, who was the first European to establish a coffee plantation in this part of Mysore. He formed another fine estate at Bálúr, a few miles distant, and since his time numerous other gardens have been opened near the sources of the Hémáwati river, the produce being sent out of Mysore to the western coast by the Kodekal or Umbrella Ghát, so called from a curious rock on the road resembling that useful article.

The coffee grown here is of fine quality, except in some estates near the Gháts, where the climate is very damp and the winds blow with great violence. All the eastern side of Wastára consists of steep hills and narrow valleys, rice being grown frequently on the sides of the hills, which are cut away in successive layers for cultivating purposes. The headmen are well off, proud of their ancient privileges, and fond of appearing in public with umbrellas and other insignia, granted to their ancestors by the old chiefs of the country. The town of Wastára is wholly unimportant.

The Lakkuwalli sub-division is traversed throughout its length by the Bhadra, which, near the town of Lakkuwalli, runs through a gorge, where it has been proposed to construct an immense reservoir, in connection with the works of the Madras Irrigation Company. Whether this stupendous project will ever be carried into execution, it is premature to say, but, considering the nature of the ground, the great force of the river at the narrow pass, and the dread unhealthiness of the jungles, it may safely be asserted that the project would cost an immense sum (not less than 300,000*l.* probably), and entail great sacrifice of life. As the river flows between deep banks, flanked by high hills, any irrigation channels taken from the head dam could not be utilised till they have passed over a considerable stretch of country, while the Mysore frontier is more than sixty miles off, so that, either the channels would run unprofitably to waste over this great distance, or an arrangement must be made with the Mysore State that the villages in its territory should have the first claim to the water, in which case, the certainty of the supply to Her Majesty's country below would be endangered. The imposition of a water cess by a private company in a foreign state would be a hazardous venture, yet, unless this be done, it is highly improbable that the project would be profitable, considering the large outlay required for constructing the head works. It may be observed moreover that, as a large tract would be submerged by the reservoir, including several villages, there would be a heavy bill for compensation.

Lakkuwalli is one of the teak-producing sub-divisions of Mysore, but most of the older and finer trees were felled many years ago, necessitating the formation of fresh plantations, which, however, promise well. A thick jungle stretches from the north to the south up to the slopes of the great Bábá Búdan mountain. This remarkable hill was called in former days Chandradróna, but derived its present appellation from a Musalmán saint, who lived and died on its summit, and who is reputed to have brought from Arabia the coffee tree, which he planted near his dwelling, whence it gradually spread to other parts of the country. His successor, Ghaus Sháh Kádiri, resides near the grave of the saint, which is in a dark cavern, that is occasionally lighted up at night for the benefit of visitors, who wish to show respect to the memory of Bábá Búdan. Ghaus Sháh has a good house at Búdannagar, where the climate is delightful, and streams of the purest water issue on every side. He has extensive plantations of coffee, held free of rent, in recognition of the service rendered by his predecessor, and is consequently in easy circumstances, and much respected, not only by those of his own creed, but by the whole surrounding population. When he leaves his mountain abode, he travels in a palankeen, a mode of conveyance little used now in Southern India, where the bullock coach has superseded it, but still adhered to by a few people of rank.

The Bábá Búdan mountain is in the form of a horseshoe, the ends fronting the west, and its highest peaks, called Mulaingiri and Kalhatti, attain an altitude of 6,300 feet. It has a very fine appearance from the south, the country on that side being open. In the centre of the space enclosed by this magnificent hill is a densely wooded tract, called Jágar, much feared for its unhealthiness, as it lies at the bottom of a cauldron, surrounded on all sides by lofty mountains, except where the swift-flowing Bhadra rushes by it to the west, thus completing its isolation. In this jungle tract there are numerous small hamlets, a great deal of coffee being grown by the leading Gaudas or headmen, who are wealthy and independent. The forests produce, besides fine timber, which is, however, not easily removable, the lac insect, and the Kapila powder of the *Rottleria tinctoria* tree. Elk are found in numbers on the mountain, affording good sport, while bison are occasionally met with, and tigers sometimes cross the hunter's path.

On the Kalhatti peak is a house built for the accommodation of the European officials, and beneath it, at Santaweré, are some fine coffee plantations at an elevation of 4,000 feet. In the vicinity a plantation of cinchona trees has been formed, which promises well.

Several thousand plants of the *Succirubra* species have been raised, of which 2,000 have been distributed among the planters and leading native proprietors of the country around. There is every prospect of this plantation proving a great success, as the elevation and climate seem both to be suitable; but in the absence of any local means of extracting the quinine and other essential properties of the bark, it is probable that the natives will content themselves with using the bark itself as a febrifuge. But, in any case, the dissemination of the cinchona tree will be a great blessing in a country where fever of a bad type commonly prevails, and where the price of quinine now places it beyond the reach of the native community.

Chikkamugalúr, though a small sub-division, is one of the richest in the province, being abundantly watered by streams from the Bábá Búdan mountain, to the south of which it lies. The town of the same name is one of the most thriving places in Mysore, carrying on an extensive trade with Bangalore and Madras, but it is an unpleasant residence in the rainy season, being much exposed to the force of the south-west monsoon. It is connected with Shimoga by a fair road through the lower hills; but the stupendous Bábá Búdan mountain, and the difficult ranges of hills already described, offer an almost insuperable obstacle to the communications with the north and east.

Though badly wooded, and apparently bare, the sub-division produces fine wheat, sugar-cane, rice, gram, tobacco, castor-oil plants, and other crops, the best being raised in the black soil about Sakaraipatan, an ancient town, said to have been built by Raja Rukmángada Rao, of whom nothing is known. It is connected with Chikkamugalúr by a difficult pass called the Írané Kaniwé, practicable, however, for carts. Four miles west of the town is the Madaka tank, one of the largest reservoirs in the province. This splendid sheet of water is of considerable depth, and the sluice is ingeniously constructed so as to carry off the mud accumulated in the bed of the tank. From the escape issues the Avati stream, which, being joined by the Véda that waters Sakaraipatan, forms the Védávati, and flows eastward through the barren Chitaldrug district.

Bánáwár, the next sub-division, is in the open country, and is not specially interesting, though good tobacco is grown in it, and there are very fine groves of the date palm, which are utilised in making toddy. There is a curious old gun in the fort, called Ráma Chandra, which is supposed by the people, if worship is paid to it, to be efficacious in curing stomach-aches.

The Kadoor (Kadúr) sub-division gives its name to the whole district, and the town is one of the healthiest places in the province, being in a fine open country 2,400 feet above the sea, and commanding a grand view of the Bábá Búdan mountain. The crops raised are the same generally as those grown in Bánáwár.

Tarikeré is also one of the sub-divisions in the plains, but portions of it are covered with wood, and the low hills contain much scrub jungle, in which tigers and other wild beasts are common. One of these beasts, which used to infest this part of the country, as well as the adjoining sub-divisions, is said to have killed 200 persons, carrying off the agriculturists in broad daylight as they ploughed their fields, and committing such ravages among gangs of labourers on the roads as to deter them from working. A reward of 50*l.* was offered for the destruction of this man-eater, but, though frequent expeditions were made to hunt him, and he had been more than once wounded, it was never shown that he had been killed, though this was inferred from the fact that he has not been heard of for some years.

At Tarikeré itself tigers often made their appearance, and an amusing story is told regarding their boldness. Two gentlemen, who were travelling, stopped at the rest-house, and ordered dinner. The first course was brought in and disposed of, but a long time elapsed before the second was brought. At length one of the gentlemen, tired of waiting, got up, and going into the veranda, called out to his servant, who was in the adjoining cook-house, enquiring the cause of the delay, upon which he received an answer that tigers were prowling about between the rest-house and the out-offices, prepared to carry off any servant who might incautiously show himself. It was said that a tigress and three cubs were thus lying in wait for their prey.

The people of Tarikeré are a stubborn and refractory race, and ill-disposed to submit to the authority, either of the Government or of their own headmen, who possess little inflence in their villages. The greater part of the sub-division was formerly held by Pálegárs of the Bédar caste, who, after the extinction of the

Vijayanagar dynasty, conquered a considerable tract of country, up to the borders of Chitaldroog, which was also in the possession of Bédar chiefs. They were turbulent and disaffected in the days of the late Maharaja, and took advantage of the misrule practised by His Highness's Brahman officials, to instigate the people to revolt. Both Bédars and Lingáyats, which latter class included most of the influential landholders, cordially hated the Brahmans, and resented their ascendancy. The unpopularity of the Government was, however, in great measure owing to the faulty system of renting out large tracts of country to the highest bidder, a practice which led to great oppression and discontent, the renters being generally outsiders, and as rapacious as they were venal. In 1830, dangerous symptoms of disaffection showed themselves, and in the ensuing year all the country side was in open revolt, holding large indignation meetings, called locally 'Koot.' The Raja's officials vainly attempted to suppress the rebellion, notwithstanding that severe measures were taken under his immediate orders, and at length it became necessary to call in the aid of British troops. The Tarikeré Pálegár, Sarja Hanumánappa Naik, offered a strenuous resistance, which he continued till 1834, when he was seized and hanged.

The Government of India attributed the rebellion entirely to the Raja's mismanagement, and consequently, in 1831, took the reins of power out of his hands. The action of Lord William Bentinck in this matter has often been questioned, for though the Raja was engrossed in pleasure, and in the hands of sycophants who played upon his wilful and stubborn nature, it does not appear that he intentionally oppressed his subjects, or that he ever did actually fail to pay the subsidy due to the British Government, while it is certain that the people of that part of Mysore where disturbances broke out were indifferently loyal and prone to disaffection.

It is further to be observed, that the manners and language of the Nagar population differ considerably from those of Mysoreans generally, and show a closer affinity to those of the ryots of Canara, where about the same time an insurrection broke out. In both cases oppressive taxation was the alleged ground for the discontent which prevailed, a feeling which was certainly fomented by the Tarikeré Pálegár, as also by a pretender to the Nagar throne, called Búdi Baswappa.

The character attributed to the Tarikeré people by natives of other parts of Mysore is confirmed by Mr. Stokes in a very able report on the old Nagar division, and is certainly true at the present time.

The professional stranglers, called Thugs, forty years ago were as formidable in Tarikeré as tigers are now, but were entirely suppressed, many being hanged, and others imprisoned for life, of whom a few old men are still to be seen in the Bangalore prison. The crime is now rarely heard of, but seems to have been known as early as 1800, for, in the old records at Bangalore, mention is made of the capture of a gang of thugs, who buried their victims in some deserted temples at Krishnarájpur, eight miles from Bangalore.

The present generation, however, at that place are wholly ignorant of the evil repute attaching to it, and have never heard the story, though a detailed account was given at the time of the disinterment of the murdered persons.

There is considerable variety in the crops raised in the Tarikeré sub-division, according to the respective prevalence of black and red soils, the existence or absence of woods, and the supply of irrigation, which is somewhat uncertain, as large tanks are scarce.

The Tarikeré iron is of good quality. The ore, having been reduced to powder and sifted, is smelted in furnaces filled with heated charcoal, underneath which a pair of bellows is worked. When the iron melts, it passes through the charcoal by a hole in the side of the furnace underground. The cost of manufacture is about 9*d.* a maund, which sells for about 1*s.* 6*d.* Such iron is extensively used for agricultural implements, a portion of it being sent to other subdivisions, and the total out-turn yearly exceeds 1,000 maunds.

CHITALDROOG. (*Chitaldrug.*)

The Chitaldroog district has an area of 4,205 square miles, a population of 378,000, and a revenue of 97,600*l.* It is, *par excellence*, the 'drug (droog) shíme,' or hill country, the surface being covered with hills, although few of them attain any great height. In the centre of the district there is a quadrilateral, twenty miles square, containing a most difficult hill tract, with only a few villages: a bare and rugged region, which has never been scientifically surveyed, and which is only interesting to the geologist. Indeed, more than half the district is a wretched country, with little cultivated ground, and deficient in water. The rainfall is surprisingly small, being in certain sub-divisions in some years only ten inches, and as the soil is in many places very light, and wholly dependent on a good monsoon season, the people are not unfrequently in great straits. Anyone standing on the top of the great Bábá Búdan mountain in the Kadoor district, and looking westward towards the ocean, sees beneath him a richly wooded and fertile country, with never-failing streams and heavy fogs, holding the moisture in suspension over the hills; but if he turns round and looks eastward, nothing meets his view but barren rocks, scanty cultivation, and a parched-up soil, with only a few stunted trees. It is difficult to account satisfactorily for the remarkable change thus exhibited within a distance of not more than fifty miles, especially as at Bangalore, which is considerably further east, the rainfall in the south-west monsoon is invariably much heavier, and during the year the total fall aggregates thirty-five inches on an average. There is therefore, probably, some peculiar property in a great mountain like the Bábá Búdan in diverting the rain-clouds.

The people have done what lay in their power to avert distress by excavating tanks where this was practicable, several of these works being of large size; but many have been breached, and in the course of years, many more have silted up, owing to the friable nature of the sandy soil. In such cases, there is nothing for it but to elevate and strengthen the embankment, and to raise also slightly the escape-weir, excavation of the bed being both costly and impracticable. In fact, this latter process is never expedient, except where the tank is in a town, in which case the raising of the embankment and the extension of the water-spread would be hazardous, or even impossible.

The Government has for many years had under consideration the formation of an immense reservoir, at a gorge called the Márí Kaniwé, at the point where the river Hagri or Védáwati issues from the eastern side of the quadrilateral above mentioned. This stream has its source in the Madaka reservoir underneath the Bábá Búdan mountain, and, though there is rarely much water in it, it is occasionally swollen during the periodical rains, and rushes through the gorge referred to in a large volume and with great velocity. Nearly seventy years ago, the people of the neighbourhood pointed out to Dr. Buchanan, when he was travelling through Mysore, the eligibility of the site for a grand reservoir, but the work was one of too great magnitude to be undertaken by the late Maharaja's Government. Years rolled on, and the matter seemed well nigh forgotten, when it was again revived by the superintendent of the division, now General Dobbs. Since that time, levels have been taken, contour lines have been laid down at 60, 80, and 90 feet above datum, estimates have been framed, and everything seemed to be in a fair way for prosecuting the work, when differences of opinion arose among professional officers regarding the embankment, the sluices, and the wasteweirs, and the question still hangs fire. It is calculated that in the basin of hills behind the gorge, sufficient water could be stored to irrigate 50,000 acres, the drainage area of the reservoir being about 400 square miles. The work would cost probably 150,000*l.* when completed, but, if eventually carried out, it will be a signal boon to a country which for many generations has been subject to visitations of famine that have greatly impoverished the people.

In former days, the Chitaldroog district was much exposed to the depredations of the Mahrattas, whose principal leader, Parsurám Bháu, ruthlessly plundered the northern part of the Mysore province. It was no uncommon thing for the whole population to desert their homesteads, leaving their houses, and carrying with them all their portable property, while, under the appellation of the 'Valasé,' they wandered about the country till the invaders retired, and circumstances enabled them to return to their native villages. The remarkable affection displayed by Indians towards their homes is perhaps unequalled in any country, the dreary barren hills of the Chitaldroog district being as much prized by the people as if they were a paradise upon earth.

It is not improbable that this portion of Mysore may have been less sterile formerly, as on many of the hills traces are to be seen of forests cut down long ago. In fact, old records mention the existence of fine timber where such has wholly disappeared, owing, no doubt to the reckless way in which the cultivators have cut down whatever they required for agricultural implements, regardless of the destruction caused to young trees and saplings. No one ever thought of planting new trees to replace those that had been felled, and so, as population increased and agriculture spread, the few remaining forests rapidly disappeared. The denudation of trees under which the district suffers has probably had much to do with the prevailing drought, there being scarcely any vegetation to arrest the passage of the monsoon clouds, which float onwards, without depositing their valuable contents.

In the year 1866, the crops failed generally throughout the province, most of the tanks running dry. In the Chitaldroog district especially, wide-spread distress prevailed, the cheapest grain selling at 8 or 10 pounds the shilling, or about ten times its price in fair seasons. As the labouring classes receive only about 7*s.* 6*d.* a month, and much less when working for their own people, the poor, with their families, suffered greatly; and, notwithstanding the stimulus given by Government to the importation of grain, and the number of relief works designed to give employment and wages to distressed localities, it is believed that many persons perished. It is to be observed, however, that the higher castes, even though in indigent circumstances, will not perform manual labor, while it often happened that able-bodied men would not work in making roads and repairing tanks, unless in the immediate vicinity of their own homes. Subscriptions were readily raised through the province, all officials who were able to do so contributing a portion of their salary, while wealthy merchants aided liberally in the good work, so that the distress was much mitigated. Although oriental notions regarding the duty of charity differ from ours, and although they rarely give money to the needy, they are not backward in distributing grain and other food, and during the famine-year their assistance was freely rendered. The late Maharaja maintained an open kitchen at his own expense, and behaved with marked liberality and bounty.

Little is known regarding the history of the Chitaldroog district prior to the time of the Vijayanagar dynasty, although it has been surmised that the Kadamba Rajas, who ruled at Banawási in North Canara, extended their sway over this portion of Mysore. No remains have, however, been found to warrant this belief. There is abundant evidence, though, of the power of the Vijayanagar or Anagundi kings, of whom numerous vestiges are found at Hampé in the Bellári district adjoining Mysore. They were celebrated for their rich benefactions to Brahmans, and their names will be deservedly handed down to many future generations in connection with some of the valuable irrigation channels in Mysore, which were undertaken during their rule.

At Harihara, where there is a large temple dedicated to the combined deities Vishnu and Siva, one may see, in the courtyard of the shrine, more than twenty Sásanas, recording grants of land made by the Vijayanagar sovereigns, most of which have been maintained till the present day. All through the Chitaldroog district, similar grants are found in temples, though nowhere are they so numerous as at Harihara, owing to its position on the sacred Tungábhadra, a fine river, which has recently been bridged at this place at a large outlay. Harihara is on the Bombay frontier, and only 1,800 feet above the sea.

During the ascendancy of the Vijayanagar family, an individual of the Bédar or Bhoi caste, left his home at Jádikaldrug near the shrine of Tirupati, and settled at Haleúr, near Chitaldroog. The Bédars are an active and hardy raçe, sportsmen by profession, and inured to war and athletic sports. They do not, however, bear a high reputation, and there is a common Kanarese proverb 'Bédana sanga bédá,' i.e. do not associate with a Bédar. Their advent in Mysore was about the year 1475, but they do not seem to have acquired much importance till 1634, when Kastúri Rangappa Naik, the head of the clan, formed the design of building a fortress at Chitaldroog, a hill well adapted to such a purpose, it being very strong by nature.

The Naik immediately set to work, and, under his directions, the many crags which form the drug were girt round by strong walls and projecting battlements. From this vantage-point, being secure against attacks from outside, he commenced to seize all the country round, and in a short time annexed a territory yielding a revenue of between 40,000*l.* and 50,000*l.* He defied the Mysore Raja, who was then beginning to conquer the rest of the country, and his successors remained in undisturbed possession till the time of Haidar Ali, who resolved to reduce the stronghold, and accordingly besieged it. The Bédars, under their chief, Madakere Naik, made a brave defence, and opposed the whole force of the Musalmán leader with such effect that he was obliged at first to raise the siege. In 1778, the ensuing year, the place was again invested, and, notwithstanding a firm resistance, was at last taken, owing to treachery on the part of some Musalmáns belonging to the garrison, who were won over by Haidar Ali. Since that time, the Pálegárs have sunk into insignificance, although the family is still respected by the Bédars of the country, who regard them as their natural leaders, and assist them when in need with money. Thirty years ago, when a few of the Pálegárs showed a rebellious tendency, the Bédar clan readily mustered to follow their standard. From the Red Battery, on the summit of the hill, there is a fine view of the picturesque cluster of rocks beneath, and of the wild country in the neighbourhood, but beyond numerous fortified crags and a sorry building, misnamed a palace, there is little to attest the influence formerly enjoyed by the Chitaldroog Naiks.

In the vicinity of Chitaldroog is the Múragi Math, where resides the high priest of the sect of Lingáyats, who, as their distinctive mark, invariably wear, suspended round the neck in a silver box, the lingam, or emblem of the god Siva. They are wealthy and influential, being keen traders, but rarely enter the service of the State, and despise government education, regarding as useless any education, beyond a mere knowledge of writing and accounts. They are found in great numbers at Dávangere, a large town north of Chitaldroog, which carries on a considerable trade in cloths and grain with the Bombay districts. They hold tenaciously to their own tenets, and invariably resist the pretensions of the Brahmans, with whom they have frequent collisions at the great processions of either sect, both parties attempting to force their way through the quarters of towns inhabited by their adversaries, by whom they are as stoutly resisted.

Of late years, the jealousy which actuated rival sects in Mysore has somewhat abated however, and serious affrays between members of the right hand and the left hand, as the contending members of the lower castes are called, are of rare occurrence. In former days, when Colonel Wellesley commanded at Seringapatam, the quarrels were so fierce as to call for the interposition of the military. In Southern India, faction fights between the Shias and Sunnis, the rival sects of Musalmáns, are little known, for so much Hinduism has been grafted on the orthodox belief, that the Moharram, which is properly a season of mourning, is observed in Mysore by Musalmáns as a time of rejoicing, when they give themselves up to dancing, acrobatic performances, and all manner of mummery. It is true that these amusements are sternly reprobated by the puritanical Wahábis, who inculcate a rigid adherence to the letter of the Korán, but Musalmáns generally fondly observe the Moharram saturnalia, which the Government rather encourages, as being free from any bigotry which might unsettle the minds of the people.

Musalmáns are essentially intolerant, though powerless now to inflict any serious injury upon Hindus. A few years ago when the high priest of Sringiri, the most venerated Guru of Southern India, visited Bangalore, the driver of his elephant, which formed a part of his following, beat his kettle-drums defiantly in front of one of the principal mosques in the town. This was sufficient to excite the ire of the true believers, who assembled in great numbers, and pelted with stones the Hindu procession. Fortunately for himself, the Guru was in a palankeen, and escaped the shower of missiles, but he was compelled to beat a hasty retreat, while it was found necessary to call out a party of sepoys to assist the police in preserving order, and in restraining the fanaticism of both sides. A very small spark is sufficient amidst such inflammable materials to kindle a fierce flame, but the principle of non-interference, except when a breach of the peace is imminent, has been productive of the best effect. Formerly, the Government used to prescribe the particular limits of contending sects, and to prohibit one from invading those quarters of a town where the other resided, but this custom only fanned the flame, and prolonged the quarrel.

One of the principal grounds of dispute was the assumption by particular priests, in contravention of alleged former practice, of the right to carry in procession certain insignia, such as a gilt umbrella, or a palankeen borne sideways. The latter privilege, which was tantamount, in a narrow street, to stopping the way, was only enjoyed, and this under special orders from the sovereign, by the Sringiri Swámi, who strenuously objected to the pretension of any other ecclesiastical dignitary to exercise it.

Disputes regarding the unauthorised use of religious

insignia, not unfrequently find their way into the civil courts, and are sharply contested, not only by the rival priests, but by the whole of their flocks. In fact, the influence of the leading Gurus is still very great, and the exactions which they levy from their followers on their tours of visitation are often heavy. It is their custom to wander about the country for months together, during which time they receive neophytes by stamping them on the breast and shoulders with the seal of initiation into the sect, while, in return, they expect handsome donations from their disciples, which, in the case of government officials, generally amount to a month's salary. Whenever the funds of the Guru fall low, this course is resorted to to replenish his exchequer, his visit being anticipated with more dread than pleasure, for, if he takes a fancy to any town, and resides in it for some months, his disciples find his constant presence rather onerous.

When the Sringiri Swámi visited the late Mysore Maharaja, he was lodged in handsome quarters, and received about 30*l.* a day for his expenses, besides various gifts of cloths and other articles. In addition to this, whenever His Highness paid his respects to this incarnation of the deity, as he was reputed to be, he was, by custom, obliged to make the Sáshtánga Pranám, or eight-fold prostration, consisting in throwing himself at full length before the Guru, and reverently touching the ground with his forehead, breast, shoulders, hands, and feet, a mode of salutation anything but palatable to a sovereign far advanced in years. It may be said, however, in favour of this Guru, and of many others, that on the occasion of pilgrims visiting them at their monasteries, they entertain all comers free of expense for a certain number of days, a practice which during great festivals entails heavy expenses. Indeed, most of the religious establishments in Mysore are in debt, notwithstanding their periodical quêtes.

In the Madras Presidency, a great blow has been dealt to Hindu temples by the Government altogether abstaining from interference with their management, and by its directing the nomination by the people themselves of churchwardens, to look after the interests of the establishments. This policy, though it is said to have resulted in peculation of the funds and in the decay of the temples, is undeniably sound, and no exception to it could legitimately be taken by Hindus; it being no part of the duty of government officers to manage their temples for them. In Mysore, owing to the country being administered in trust, on behalf of the Maharaja, such a course was not practicable. The difficulty was, however, met by nominating the Hindu assistants in each district to superintend the endowments, and to exercise a general control over the management of those religious establishments to which the State contributes funds.

Four miles south of Chitaldroog is a hill called Jógi Math, about 3,700 feet high, which is well adapted for a sanitarium, having a good climate and a fair supply of water, while it is well wooded. Most of the districts in Mysore have, within easy reach of the head-quarters station, high hills, to which the officials can betake themselves during the hottest season, a precaution which, in the case of a feverish place like Chitaldroog, is necessary. Chitaldroog was for some time a military cantonment, but was abandoned owing to a virulent fever breaking out, of which many officers died, and it still bears a bad reputation in this respect, all new comers being liable to be attacked. Rife as fever is in most parts of Mysore, there is no portion of the country which is so generally unhealthy as the barren Chitaldroog district, for which reason it is much dreaded by government officials accustomed to the south of the province.

The other principal hills in the district are Nidigal, which is 3,680 feet, Hosdrug 3,280, and Paugarh 2,970 above the sea. The former of these is a very fine peak, and although its altitude is not great as compared with some other hills in the province, it rises 1,400 feet above the town at its base, and is seen from all sides, being a prominent land-mark. The town is 700 feet lower than Bangalore, and the level of the country falls rapidly eastward and northward. The tract of Nidigal and Paugarh was formerly in the possession of the Harti Naiks, a powerful family, which succumbed to the Chitaldroog Pálegárs, who regarded with covetous eyes this fertile strip, which is abundantly watered by natural springs, called Talpargis. Nidigal is at the entrance of a difficult pass not practicable for wheeled carriages, and the hill is fortified. Paugarh is, however, a much more formidable place, and differs from most Mysore forts in being covered with rocks and crags, while, in lieu of the steep slippery precipices which form the sides of the Drugs, art has been brought into play to supplement nature, and the only practicable ascent is up steps with intervening gateways strongly fortified. One of the batteries is called the Sultáni, after Tippu Sultán, and the place was well provided with war material—more than 12 guns, 20,000 shot, and a great number of rockets having been found in it. The rockets were still serviceable, although they were of the time of Tippu—a proof of the dryness of the climate.

Hosdrug does not differ from other fortified hills of the same class. The fort was built by the Pálegár of Chitaldroog, in opposition to Bágúr, the ancient chief town of the country, which was subject to the Balál kings. Traces of an older site are found at a place called Nílawati, of which a romantic story is told, that the daughter of its lord was wedded to one of two brothers, who, though princes from afar, came in disguise as thieves, and tried to carry off the girl.

Although there is comparatively little arable land in the Chitaldroog district, there is excellent pasturage in some portions of it, where the grass is thick and abundant, large flocks of sheep being kept by the villagers, who sell them to dealers from Bangalore, at prices varying from 2*s.* 6*d.* to 6*s.* per head. The wool is of fair quality, and a superior kind of blanket is made from it at Dávangere and other places. Some of the best grazing grounds for cattle are found in the Hosdrug sub-division.

The most northerly point in the district is Molakálmuru, so called from a story that the Chitaldroog Pálegár broke his knee in ascending the rugged rocks which surround the town on every side. There is a fine echo in the centre of a basin of hills behind it; but the natives firmly believe that the rock only gives back the word 'Jógappa,' the soubriquet of a certain Jógi, or ascetic, who lived here. This is, however, a fable, the echo being remarkably clear and distinct, whatever words are called out. In the Molakálmuru sub-division there is a curious forest of the *Hardwickia binata* (called by the people *Asina mara*), extending over an area of ten or twelve square miles. The trees are of great age, and are not now propagated, either by seed or by cuttings. They look like pollards, and have a very stunted and weird look, the ground beneath them being hard gravel, on which nothing will grow. In many instances fig trees are seen grafted on these old trees, embracing and even hiding the trunk, from which their age may be inferred. In the Búdihál sub-division, the same tree flourishes well, and yields a fine dark wood, suited for building purposes.

Great exertions have been made to plant trees along all the high roads of the district, the people of the adjoining villages being responsible for watering and tending them, and having a right to the produce of all fruit grown on them, but the hardness of the soil, and the great depth at which water is found, have thrown obstacles in the way, and constant vigilance is needed to prevent the trees from dying out.

The agricultural products of the district are, in the south, the same as in the Tomkoor district, namely, millets of different species, beans, linseed, and the castor-oil plant. In those sub-divisions where black soil is found, the larger millet, wheat, sugar-cane, and Bengal gram are grown, while, near the Tungábhadra, cotton is tolerably abundant. The better kinds of exogenous cotton, including the New Orleans and Bourbon varieties, have been introduced, but have not found much favor with the people, who aver that, though these are longer in the staple, they are less hardy than the native kind. A few showers, at opportune periods, are sufficient to produce a plentiful crop in the black soil; but, as stated above, the rainfall is very precarious, and as the nature of the country in many places does not admit of the formation of tanks, wells are more used than in any other part of the province. The Persian wheel is unknown, and the process generally employed for raising the water is by lowering a large skin, which, when filled from the well, is hoisted by two or more bullocks being driven down an inclined plane, the ropes attached to them drawing up the skin by a pulley to the surface, when it is emptied, the water being conducted by small irrigating channels to the land where it is required. These wells are called Kapilé wells, and though more effective than the common Yátam or Pékotta, which is worked by men only, they are very inferior to the wells in Upper India, where the Persian wheel is in use. If water is close to the surface, a hand-bucket, called a Nirú Gudé, is lowered, and raised by two men standing opposite to one another, each holding two ropes attached to the skin.

Iron is found abundantly in some of the sub-divisions of the district, and, after being hammered into bars, is manufactured into a variety of agricultural implements, which are not only used by the people, but exported elsewhere. Steel of fair quality is made in some places, the dried branches of the *Cassia auriculata* (also used for tanning purposes), and some fresh leaves of the *Convolvulus laurifolia* being put into a crucible, with iron which has been cut into small pieces, eight inches long, two inches wide, and half an inch thick. The crucibles are closed with red mud or loam, and are put in a hole filled with charcoal, on which bellows are made to play for five or six hours, till the contents are completely liquified. The steel thus manufactured at one time promised to attract attention in Europe, but of late years it has not been in special repute.

A vast quantity of glass bangles are also manufactured in the Hiriúr and other sub-divisions, and are hawked about the province by itinerant pedlars. The glass is of various colors—red, green, and black, but possesses no particular beauty.

An attempt has been made to collect together in the museum at Bangalore specimens of all the natural productions of the province, as well as of all the articles manufactured in it. Among the former is an interesting series of all the various woods which have a commercial value, or are used for domestic purposes; the specimens having been prepared so as to show in sections the properties of each species. All the grains of the country, as well as the various oils, gums, drugs, seeds, and agricultural and forest productions are exhibited. A fair collection of the woollen, cotton, and silk manufactures has been made, and the processes followed in smelting iron, making steel and glass, and extracting gold are shown. Models have been collected of most of the agricultural implements of the country, as well as of those used in various trades and manufactures.

The geological and natural history departments are making fair progress, and attention has been directed towards the antiquities, literature, numismatology, and the arms of the country.

The museum is much frequented by natives, and promises to be a useful and interesting institution.

ADMINISTRATIVE.

The reader is referred to Wilks' 'History of Southern India' (recently republished at Madras in a convenient 8vo form) for an accurate and valuable account of the vicissitudes of the Mysore State from the commencement of the sixteenth century till the year 1799 A.D., when the power of the Musalmán usurpers was broken at Seringapatam.

The pedigree of the present Hindu dynasty, so far as it can be ascertained, is given opposite, but it may be remarked that, owing to its temporary extinction by Haidar Ali, there are few trustworthy records available that reach back to a remote period.

The period when the two brothers, Vijairáj and Krishnaráj, came to Mysore was an auspicious one for adventurous spirits, as the celebrated Vijayanagar or Anagundi kingdom was then near its end; but, although they obtained a footing by one of the brothers marrying the distressed daughter of a petty baron, who, on her father's demise, was persecuted by a neighbouring Wodiar, or ruler, it does not appear that the family attained any pre-eminence in the country till the time of Ráj Wodiar. This chief rebelled

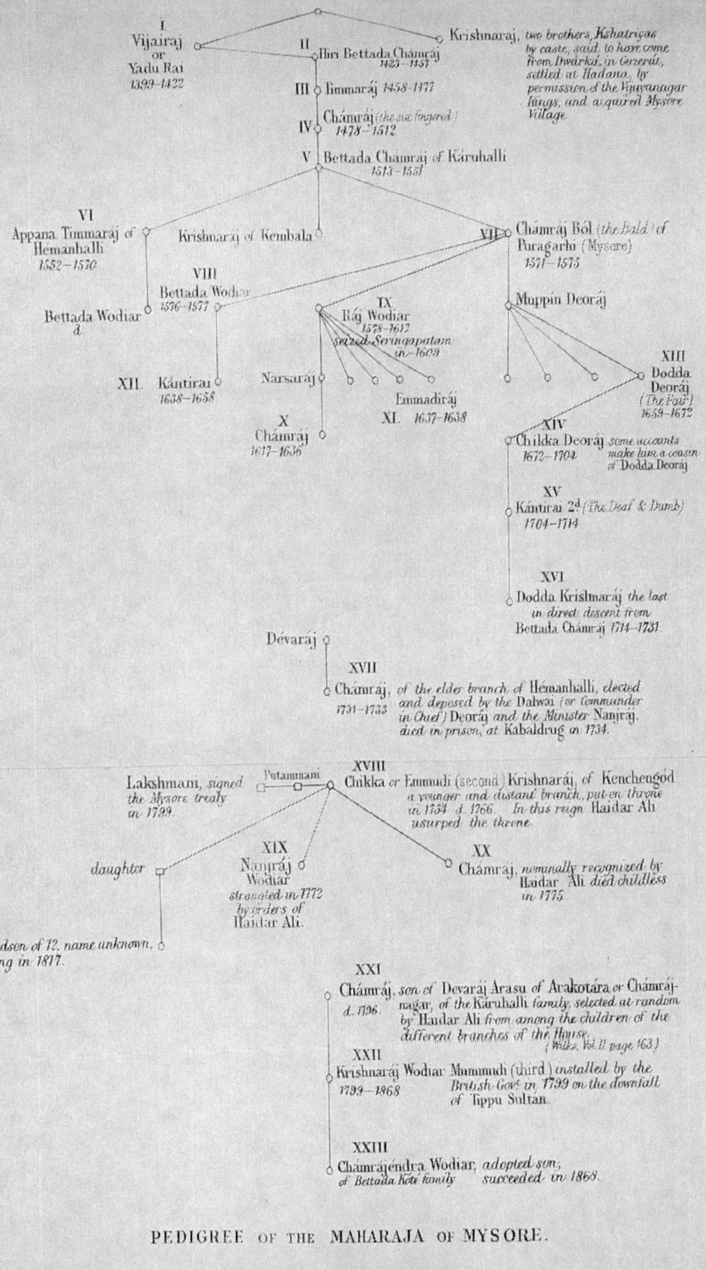

PEDIGREE OF THE MAHARAJA OF MYSORE.

against the Viceroy of Seringapatam, and, in 1609, wrested from him that celebrated stronghold. Before this, in 1588, the power of the Vijayanagar kings had been annihilated by the Musalmán chiefs of the Dekkan, and the discomfited rulers had abandoned their capital on the Tungábhadra, and retreated to Pennakonda, 100 miles to the south-east, where the dynasty shortly afterwards became extinct.

Ráj Wodiar, having secured the fortress of Seringapatam, speedily enlarged his possessions, and commenced a series of aggressions which lasted for more than a hundred years. He and his successors subdued the following tract of country.

Ráj Wodiar	conquered	20	Forts or	circles of country.
Chámráj	"	18	"	"
Kántirai	"	31	,	"
Dodda Deoráj	"	12	"	"
Chikka Deoráj	"	40	"	"
Kántirai II.	"	5	"	"
Total	.	126	"	"

The districts specified comprise the whole of the Ashtagrám division, and more than half of that of Nandidrug, besides parts of the Koimbatór and Salem districts in Madras. The total area may have amounted to 15,000 square miles, with a revenue of 500,000*l.*, or half that of the present Mysore state.

The further extension of the Mysore dominions was the work of Haidar Ali, who subdued all the hill districts of the Ikkéri kingdom, and the large fiefs held by the several Pálegárs, leaving no part of the present native state unconquered, while he carried his victorious arms down to the western coast, and to the north and south of the ancient limits of Mysore, till he became the most formidable Muhammadan chief in India.

It will be seen from the pedigree given above, that the direct descent failed on the death of Dodda Krishnaráj in 1731. To him succeeded Chámráj, of an elder branch of the family, but this ruler was set aside and imprisoned by those who had put him on the throne; and here ceases the genuine descent, 'for,' as Wilks says, 'whatever slender ground may be conjectured to exist for acceding to the regularity of the succession in the person of Chámráj (No. XVII. in pedigree), the murder of that prince, the rejection of his lineal heir, and the election of an infant of a younger branch, extinguishes all imaginable pretext to hereditary claim in the person now elected to the rank of pageant Raja from which he never emerged; and from this period forward, the mock successions to a faulty title,' &c.[1]

Of the sons of Chikka Krishnaráj, in whose reign Haidar Ali assumed supreme power, one was strangled by the usurper's orders, and the other died childless. It is not known what caprice induced Haidar Ali to select as a nominal sovereign the boy Chámráj (No. XXI. in pedigree), though it may be surmised that either some feeling of compunction, or an idea that the act would strengthen his own position, influenced him. This apparently trivial proceeding, however, probably led to the restoration of the old Hindu dynasty in the person of one of its scions, the son of Chámráj; for, had not a son of that chief been forthcoming in 1799, the Mysore

[1] Wilks, vol. i. p. 234.

territory would, there is reason to believe, have been divided between the British Government and the Nizám.

Tippu Sultán would most likely not have hesitated for a moment to put to death any member of the Mysore family, whose claims might endanger the position of his own sons, and it was therefore fortunate that, owing to his extreme youth and the obscure condition to which his father had been long condemned, the future Raja escaped the notice of the tyrant.

Tippu Sultán having been killed, and the British Government having, from motives of policy, determined to restore the Hindu dynasty, it signified little what individual was selected for the purpose, provided that his nomination was approved of by the members of the family, and it is certain that the selection of the late Raja Krishnaráj was acceptable to the widow of Chikka Krishnaráj who died in 1766, as also to the widows of Chámráj above referred to, who died in captivity not long before the fall of Seringapatam. These ladies acknowledged the boy as their son, and the other influential members of the house intimated their assent.

The commissioners appointed by Lord Mornington to carry out the intentions of Government, and to secure the execution of a treaty with the new state, notwithstanding the approval thus obtained, were careful to designate the youthful chief as a 'descendant' rather than as the 'heir and representative' of the ancient Rajas of Mysore, for, in truth, it would have been difficult to prove that no member of the family of a senior branch was in existence. It is, therefore, clear that Raja Krishnaráj, the young sovereign, was an entirely new creation, deriving his claim solely from the favor of the British Government, and not in right of inheritance.

Both the official and the native reports of the time describe the installation of the young chief as affording the utmost joy to the people of the country, who had long groaned under the tyranny of Tippu Sultán, a remorseless ruler, who had forcibly converted to his own faith thousands of Hindus, and driven his subjects to despair by his cruelty. The restoration of the old family was to the mass of the population a cause of unmitigated rejoicing, and probably no Indian chief ever ascended his throne under such favorable circumstances.

The minister Púrnaya, a Mahratta Brahman by descent, was a man of consummate ability, a skilled financier and a vigorous administrator, who left the impress of his authority for many years on the country, and managed to husband its resources so well that, on the Raja's attaining his majority, a large sum of money had accumulated. His rule was rather arbitrary, and he did not hesitate to punish severely those who disobeyed his orders, while exception might be taken to some of the methods employed by him to extract money; but when he assumed charge of the regency, the finances were in a deplorable state, and his own credit was at stake to retrieve them. As time wore on, and his authority became more firmly established, he could ill brook opposition and viewed with chagrin the prospect of the young Raja ruling in person. Púrnaya, being of the old school, who considered that Brahman ministers should govern kingdoms, while Rajas enjoy themselves and content themselves with receiving homage on state occasions, had taken little or no trouble about the education of his sovereign. Perhaps he was too old to devote much thought to the subject, nor did the British Government evince any special anxiety about it, being no doubt satisfied that a minister who was so much extolled by the Residents at the Raja's Court, would not neglect so important a point.

Púrnaya, calling to mind the supremacy of the Brahman Péshwas at Poona, and the thraldom in which they held the Satárá Rajas, their legitimate sovereigns, was probably anxious to preserve his own authority, and to make a puppet of the young Raja. The latter, however, in 1810, when he was in his sixteenth year, instigated by those who had already commenced to work upon his impressionable temper, expressed a desire to take the reins of power into his own hands. This led to a violent outburst of rage from Púrnaya, who forgot the respect due, even from a man of his age, to his sovereign, and the result was that the minister, shortly afterwards, resigned his authority to his master, and retired into seclusion at Seringapatam, where he died in 1812.

The young Raja Krishnaráj appears to have behaved well during the trying circumstances attendant on Púrnaya's resignation of office, and commenced his rule under the most favorable auspices, with a treasury well filled by the minister's careful management, and with plaudits from the whole province. But the fatal facility with which he listened to the insinuations of favorites, and the insincerity of his disposition, soon clouded over the bright prospect.

In 1814, the Resident was compelled to report to Government that the Raja had already dissipated the treasure accumulated by Púrnaya on worthless persons; that he had exceeded the bounds of prudence in giving large benefactions of land and money to temples, and that the Resident's remonstrances fell unheeded on his ear. While the Resident's advice was flouted, a lute-player, named Venkata Subayya, with other indifferent characters, obtained an extraordinary influence over the young chief, whose mobile disposition seems to have lent itself to the parasitical charmings of courtiers who praised his generosity and encouraged his evil tendencies.

The disinterested counsels of the few respectable native gentlemen at his court met with no more attention than those of the Resident, and although sharply rebuked by the British Government and warned of the inevitable result of his extravagance and sensuality, the Raja turned a deaf ear to all remonstrance. In 1817, he was foolish enough to enter into political intrigues which gave umbrage to the Government, but did not proceed from any want of loyalty on his part.

The extraordinary adulation paid by the people of Southern India to those in authority had a mischievous effect upon a man of the Raja's temperament, the obsequious conduct of those about him encouraging in his mind the idea that he was above all control. No natives, save one or two of his own relations, sat in his presence, and it was *de rigueur* that everyone should appear before him with the waistband fastened, a custom only observed by the people when presenting themselves before the sovereign or other personage of rank.

In letters to him the full address was to the following effect: 'To the presence of the divine feet of the great lord ——— Wodiar[1] Bahádur,' a blank space being left for the name Krishnaráj, which it was deemed disrespectful to use in writing.

The infatuated Raja still pursued his evil courses, always vowing amendment, but never acting up to his promises, till the country began to suffer sensibly from his imprudence and spendthrift habits. It does not appear that he at any time failed in paying the subsidy due by him to the British Government, but he was frequently at his wits' ends to find the means of discharging his obligations, and his constant want of money led him to resort to that most objectionable mode of raising revenue, namely, the leasing out of portions of territory to the highest bidder. So long as the stipulated payments were made, no questions were asked as to the manner in which the rents were levied by the lessees, and the unfortunate cultivators were, so to speak, stripped to the skin by the merciless agents of the government contractors.

Once, in 1826, the venerable Sir Thomas Munro, actuated by a sincere desire to avert the ruin which

[1] 'Wodiar' is a Kanarese word for ruler.

threatened the Raja, visited Mysore, and remonstrated personally with him; but the effect of his advice was at best transient, and between this time and 1831, the year of his dethronement, matters went from bad to worse, till a crash was inevitable.

The Resident, Mr. Casamaijor, strove ineffectually to arrest the Raja's downfall, but did not succeed in securing his confidence. His Highness seemed destined to place his trust always in unworthy advisers, and it is said that he delighted in showing those about him how little he cared for the counsels of one of the earlier Residents, by promising verbally anything and everything to that officer, and by putting his tongue in his cheek to the amusement of his courtiers, the moment the Resident left his presence. So suspicious was one of the Residents of the Raja's fickleness, that he made a practice of noting beforehand the subject of a proposed interview, lest His Highness should afterwards altogether deny that they had conversed about it.

In 1831, sparks of disaffection showed themselves in the Nagar division, and, being fanned by the rapacity of the government officers, the turbulent character of the people, and the insidious designs of some of their leaders, soon broke out into open revolt. For the reasons assigned in the account given by him of the Tarikeré sub-division, the writer does not consider that this insurrection was in itself a sufficient justification for depriving the Raja of his sovereign power; but there can be no question that eighteen years of misgovernment had greatly alienated the respect of the people, diminished the resources of the country, and endangered the stability of His Highness's rule. Though he had not failed in paying his subsidy regularly, he had done more than disappoint the expectations of his benefactors, to whom he owed his very existence as a Raja: he had abused the trust confided to him, had weakly allowed the people whom the British Government had placed under his protection to be plundered and oppressed by the scum of the province, and had disregarded and despised all remonstrances, even though these had been urged upon him by no less an authority than Sir Thomas Munro.

In extenuation of his short-comings, it may be observed that a more authoritative right to interfere should have been given to the Resident, and that the subordination of the latter to the Madras Government was productive of unfortunate results. To offer advice to a character like the Raja, in soft conciliatory words, unsupported by warnings of the consequence of non-compliance with the counsel tendered, was tantamount to preaching to the wind. The position of the Madras Government, in relation to the Resident and the Supreme Government of India, was also anomalous, and afforded the Raja's unscrupulous followers opportunities of intrigue which damaged his reputation.

Had he lived in these days, it is more than probable that a man of his great natural intelligence would, with the advantages of a sound education, have proved a successful ruler. Instead of sacrificing the welfare of his people to his personal pleasures, he would have been compelled to render a strict account of his proceedings, and, in lieu of passing his time in frivolous pursuits and empty shows in the company of designing and venal favorites, he might have taken a lively interest in the administration of his country.

The state receptions held by him at the great vernal and autumnal festivals were not devoid of picturesque effect. It was the custom to depute a regiment of the Mysore Horse,[1] accompanied by the body-guard, to escort the Resident to the palace, and their gaudy uniforms, together with the green apparel of the running spearmen, the gaily caparisoned elephants, and the tumultuous assemblage of retainers, Brahmans, and fakirs made up a pleasing, if distracting spectacle. On entering the fort a salute was fired from the ramparts, and when the narrow streets were traversed, and the cortège defiled into the large square in front of the palace, the household troops were seen drawn up on either side. Then commenced the din of musical instruments, the band playing 'God save the king,' the elephants trumpeting, and the mob shouting the Raja's praises, while the troops presented arms, and amidst all this characteristic pomp and hubbub, the Resident alighted, and was received at the foot of the staircase by the Raja's nearest relations and courtiers. On the rare occasions when the Governor of Madras visited Mysore, it was the custom for the Raja to descend himself to the bottom of the steps at the entrance of the

[1] The Mysore Horse are the native cavalry of the province, comprising at present six regiments, each composed of 300 troopers. They are well-mounted and equipped, and are commanded by native officers, under the general supervision of the Military Assistant. In former days they did good service under the Duke of Wellington and Sir John Malcolm, and if properly led, are efficient troops. Their uniform is red, with a white turban, which is fastened over the head by a white cloth passing under the chin.

palace, and there embrace him, stage fashion, over both shoulders. The same etiquette demanded that the Governor-General should be met by the Raja, at the gates of the fort, and thence escorted to the palace.

From the time when the administration was taken out of his hands, the Raja ceased to sit in open darbár, and the longing of his old age to lift the curtain, which, in 1831, hid him, metaphorically, from public view, was never realised, visitors receiving an audience in the inner apartments, which were not remarkable, except for a superabundance of highly-colored paintings, among which were likenesses of most of the Chief's European friends during his long life. Immediately before entering the reception-room, which was on the upper storey, visitors were astonished to see two fine pet cows comfortably chewing the cud in a small pen sunk in the centre of the floor of the anteroom.

Raja Krishnaráj was undoubtedly clever, and refined in demeanour, although persons accustomed to the etiquette followed at darbárs elsewhere in India, were surprised to see that he did not rise from his chair to receive visitors, while he wore shoes during an audience.

His conversation was generally seasoned by shrewd and sarcastic remarks, and he was fond of jokes, not unfrequently stopping short, in the midst of a discourse on grave subjects, to quiz one of his English or native friends. He spoke fluently, and not without a certain eloquence even, in Kanarese, his mother tongue, and preferred making use of this when dwelling on diplomatic topics, but he generally addressed English officials in Hindusthání, with which he was quite conversant. He had, or seemed to have, a vivid recollection of the Duke of Wellington and Lord Harris, and of the circumstances attending the ceremony of his being placed on the throne when he was a child five years old, constantly reiterating, when conversing on his claims, that he was the same individual who was then raised to power.

The long deprivation of his sovereign rights to which he had been subjected, had made him somewhat testy and querulous, and he was naturally of a quick temperament, but he rarely showed this in the presence of English officials, and in his demeanour was urbane and gentlemanlike. For some years after he ceased to rule, his official correspondence was of an acrimonious character, but this is not to be wondered at, when one considers the bitter humiliation which he had undergone.

Though short of stature, he had a pleasant and dignified expression of countenance, and must, as a young man, have been good-looking, while his dress was ordinarily in excellent taste, being less gorgeous than the attire of Sikh chiefs, but more striking than that of the Princes of Rájputána. His complexion was fair, and in the centre of the forehead he wore the royal spot, called the Tíká, the emblem of sovereignty, while round his neck was suspended a splendid triple necklace of pearls, and girt round his waist was a much-cherished sword, with a medallion of the Queen upon the belt.

During the course of the interviews, if not of a private character, the court retainers remained in the room, calling out from time to time 'adab sé,' 'with respect;' 'tafáwat sè,' 'from a distance,' meaning that the Raja must be addressed with reverence and from afar. When the audience was concluded, the Raja placed round the necks of his visitors garlands of sweet-smelling white flowers, while to each were distributed a few drops of atar of roses, and a sprinkling of rose-water, from elegantly-chased golden vessels, the never-failing betel-nut and a few cloves or cardamoms being placed in the hands of each person as a sign that the interview was over. During this ceremony the retainers shouted 'Mahaswámi parai,' 'the supreme great lord,' a common mode of applauding any action of the Raja.

Although he exacted the utmost respect on all public occasions, and was naturally tenacious of his personal dignity in the absence of sovereign power, the Raja gladly divested himself of all state in private, and was accustomed to sit up to a late hour at night, listening to the gossip of the 'village,' as he called the town, with its population of 70,000, in contradistinction to the royal abode in the fort, hearing tales and poetry, and sometimes discussing politics or religious themes. On these occasions, a few confidential friends and servants attended him, and when the night was far spent, a meal was brought in of such pungent dishes that they were said to make the bearers involuntarily sneeze. 'Early to bed and early to rise' was an axiom which, in his later years, the Raja did not study, but when young he is said to have been active, and to have performed wonderful feats in slaying tigers and capturing elephants single-handed, these gallant exploits being commemorated by the court painters in glowing frescoes in one of his residences. Latterly, he contented himself with fondling pigeons and with keeping a small menagerie.

After he was deprived of power, he ceased to observe with splendour the great festivals of the Vasant, and Dashara, but when an old man, he celebrated with rejoicings the annual return of his birthday, on which occasion he used to invite all his European acquaintance to the Mysore races and the attendant ceremonies in the palace, where he regaled his visitors with a dinner in English fashion, and amused them with fireworks and circus performances.

His expenditure on himself was not perhaps excessive, but the cost of his immense establishment of 10,000 persons, his open-handed charity, and the great drain on his purse which the prosecution of his claims in England entailed, involved him deeply in debt. Between 1846, when they were previously discharged, and 1868, the year of his decease, his debts amounted to 420,000*l.* although during this period he had received annually, out of the revenues of the territory, about 130,000*l.* for his personal expenditure, his palace establishments, and other incidental charges unconnected with the administration.

Of course, Brahmans shared largely in the Raja's benefactions, and foremost among these was the family chaplain, Parakála Swámi, a priest of some note, and an exponent of the tenets of Vishnu. It is the custom when the Guru, or priest bearing this title, is about to expire, to crack his head with a cocoa-nut, so that his last breath may issue through the skull, and his spirit ascend this way to the skies.

The Mysore family appear to have been originally followers of Vishnu, as is evidenced by the name of the brother of the first Wodiar, and the use of the words 'Sri Krishna' on the earlier state seals; but it would seem that at one time the head of the house leaned towards the teaching of the Saivas, while some branches even now adhere to this persuasion. It may be observed, too, that Chámundi, otherwise Káli, the wife of Siva, is the tutelary deity of the Rajas.

The rival sects of Vaishnava and Srí Vaishnava Brahmans on the one hand, and of Sivabhaktaru on the other, form the majority of the population of Mysore, or at least of the more influential portion of it. Of these, the Srí Vaishnava, or Ayengár sect, is of foreign origin, and speaks Tamil as the house language, according to the Hindu custom of preserving in all domestic relations the tongue spoken by the ancestors of those who have settled in other parts of India, far away from the birthplace of their race. The Ayengárs are able and astute men, holding high official positions, and are said to have exercised much influence over the Raja. The Sivabhaktaru, or worshippers of Siva, otherwise called Lingáyats, wear suspended round their necks, in a silver box, the emblem of their god; but notwithstanding the apparent impropriety of this strange custom, they bear as high a moral reputation as their neighbours. They are independent in character, despise government employment, and detest Brahmans of other sects, from whose hands they will not even take water.

The late Raja favoured alternately the professors of both faiths, according to the impulse of the moment, or the ascendancy which the ladies of the household, and influential relations belonging to one or the other of the rival parties, severally gained over him.

During his long reign of sixty-nine years, he had contracted several marriages, both orthodox and otherwise, and his blood relations and family connections were numerous. He left at his death, two Ránís and four other ladies, three illegitimate grandsons, and two illegitimate great grandchildren, besides a host of other persons, more or less nearly related to him. Those who claim a common descent with the Raja are called Arasus; illegitimate descendants are styled Kumárs; while the relatives of ladies holding the Siva doctrines, who had been introduced into the palace in somewhat irregular fashion, are known as Siváchárs.

Among the various branches of the family there are a certain number (thirteen) with which alone legitimate marriage connections can be formed, and from which alone adoptions can be made, in default of direct heirs. Of all these, the Dalwai, or Commander-in-Chief, whose functions are the same as those of the Sénápati of other parts of India, ranks first. Indeed, at one time, this officer exercised so much authority as to bid fair to supplant that of the Raja himself; but the family in which the post was hereditary fell into decay, and now possesses little influence.

The term usually employed to designate members of

the royal stock is Rájbindé, a word which is equivalent to the designation of Thákur in Rájputáná. Few of the families of this class now in existence have any weight in the country, most of them having been impoverished by their own extravagance. The various departments of the Raja's household were, however, superintended by a member of one or other of the Rájbindé families, although His Highness was rarely on good terms with the majority of this class, owing to the harshness with which they had been treated by him formerly.

As the acknowledged head of the clan, he was the arbiter and referee in all marriages and other family matters, a pre-eminence which he asserted with great tenacity, occasionally pushing his authority beyond its legitimate limits.

Some Indian princes, to whom nought but a barren title remains, still preserve a semblance of those administrative functions which their predecessors formerly wielded, maintaining heads of various imaginary departments, a kind of skeleton, as it were, which, should the revolutions of time perchance bring about the restoration of lost authority to the prince, would speedily start into life and full vigour. Thus, in his limited sphere, the late Mysore Raja organised his palace establishments into departments which were apparently modelled on the system pursued by former chiefs of his house, but which admitted of future expansion. The uncouth Kanarese titles sound strangely to the ear, but were substantially not different from those in use by other Hindu potentates.

The Raja, notwithstanding his natural shrewdness,

was apt to be swayed by the divinations of the court astrologers, who consulted horoscopes, and pretended to explain the course of political events by fancied combinations of the constellations. It is improbable that he placed implicit faith in their predictions, but, all through life, he was superstitious, and prone to lend a ready ear to the suggestions of wily advisers, although he was rarely fortunate in his selection of confidants. He was fully alive, however, to the importance of securing the support and co-operation of the most influential Brahmans in the country, on whom he frequently bestowed rich rewards.

The bountiful hand with which, in the days of his power, he gave away land and money, had much to do with the misfortunes which overtook him in 1831. The temples which he chiefly favoured received from him splendid gifts of jewellery, the precious ornaments presented by him to the shrines of most repute being valued at from 10,000*l.* to 20,000*l.* each. These benefactions won for him the blessings of the Brahmans, but his donations were not confined to men of learning and sanctity, worthless and corrupt parasites being too often the recipients of his generosity. To the poor, however, he was ever charitable, and maintained at considerable cost an establishment at Mysore, where a dole of rice was daily given gratis to the needy.

The Raja's pretensions as a literary man were not great, but in the Saraswati Bhandáram, or royal library, there is a collection of 600 manuscripts, written partly on palm leaf and partly on paper.

These relate to various subjects connected with Hindu religion, literature, and science, and are mostly written in Kanarese characters, though many are in Nágari, Telugu, or Grantham. In the same wing of the palace is a fair collection of native weapons of all kinds, such as muskets, fusils, swords, battle-axes, maces, daggers, the Mahratta wághnak or tiger's claws, and many curious and ancient arms formerly in use in Southern India. His display of jewels, though not so splendid as that of many other Hindu princes, was well worthy of his rank, and like other sovereigns of India he had amassed a large store of gold brocades, mirrors, and pictures, besides a great variety of costly European objects.

Raja Krishnaráj Wodiar expired in March 1868, having been conveyed from the upper apartments of his palace to the ground floor, in order that he might, like an orthodox Hindu, breathe his final breath on mother earth. His last thoughts were fixed upon the faint hope that he might still grasp once more the reins of power, a gratification wisely denied him. His obsequies were celebrated with much pomp, the funeral pyre being of sandal-wood, while rich gifts were presented to those who officiated at the ceremony, a dole being also distributed to all the poor of the town. Most of his charitable subscriptions were maintained, and ample provision was made for all his relations and retainers.

Raja Krishnar was the oldest sovereign in India, and was one of the very few persons whose recollection went back to the time when Lord Wellesley was

Governor-General, and Sir Thomas Munro and Sir John Malcolm were young field officers. To considerable natural capacity, he added a retentive memory, and had his common sense been equal to his shrewdness, he might have proved an excellent ruler; but the bane of his character, which was strikingly exhibited from first to last, was that he always distrusted the official representatives of the British Government, and placed his confidence in those who counselled him from interested motives. A few English officers, who had held appointments in the Mysore Commission, gave him disinterested advice in the later years of his life; but, in the heyday of his power, not even Sir Thomas Munro, one of his oldest friends, had any influence with him. As a necessary consequence, the people of the country placed no confidence in him, and his restoration to power would have been a grievous error, from which the province was happily preserved. Few, however, of those about him had the courage to tell him that this devoutly wished-for consummation was never to be, and, till the last moment of his life, he fondly hoped that the large sums spent by him in contesting his claims would not be barren of result.

Natives of influence in the province, who regarded with ill-concealed alarm the possibility of the absorption of Mysore into the Madras Presidency, strongly counselled the Raja to adopt an heir as the only means of preserving the integrity of native rule, and the motives which actuated them are certainly deserving of respect. Not only did the project placed before the Raja of adopting an heir elicit their warm sympathy as

Hindus, to whom adoptions, on failure of male heirs, are recommended by every feeling of religion and policy, but they regarded with anxiety the probability of an influx of a host of highly educated Madras officials, hankering for posts in Mysore, should the province become a British possession. It was not difficult to persuade the Raja that if an adoption made by him received the assent of the British Government, such a recognition of his sovereign rights would ultimately lead to his own restoration, the real point for which he had so long contended.

It had indeed been asserted that, in the event of his restoration, the Raja would drop the question of adoption, and consent to bequeath his territory, *proprio motu*, to the British Government, but such an arrangement was, on the face of it, impracticable, and based on false policy. There was abundant evidence to show that the Raja had for eighteen years grossly misgoverned the country, and that Lord William Bentinck was at least not without a show of justification in placing his sovereign powers in abeyance. It was also well known that no unbiassed person could regard with other feelings than those of alarm the contingency of the Raja wielding, as an old man, that authority which he had failed to exercise wisely when young.

The right to adopt an heir is however inherent in all Hindu rulers, and Lord Canning's action in abstaining from issuing a patent to the Mysore Raja was only justifiable on special grounds, which in any case were open to debate. It is true that adoption had not, so far as the annals show, been the custom in the Mysore family, but there was nothing in the peculiar circumstances of the Raja's case to debar him from the common Hindu privilege of adopting an heir, except the British Government avowedly put him on a different footing from that of other Hindu chiefs on the ground of his being a first creation, and of the right of nomination to the succession resting with itself. But it does not appear that any intimation to this effect was ever communicated to him, or that the Government even laid down such a course of action as proper to be followed. In fact, the sovereign rights of the Raja were on all occasions acknowledged, and the treaties with him at all times enforced, even at considerable inconvenience to both Mysore and British territory, as regards judicial procedure.

Taking into consideration all the facts of the case, that is, the justice, *primâ facie*, of the claim, the feelings of the leading natives of the province, the anxiety of other Hindu princes as to the result, and the possible pretensions of the Nizám of the Dekkan, it is probable that the English Government acted wisely in recognising the adoption made by the Raja.

To the Raja himself, however, the decision of the authorities in England brought little comfort, and he could not divest himself of the feeling that his own interests had been sacrificed to those of the boy whom he had selected as his heir. And so, with the craving still strong within him to raise, even for a few hours, the curtain which fell before him in 1831 and hid him from his people, the old man died, full of sorrow and unfulfilled desire, at the age of seventy-four. His strong constitution was undermined by violent attacks of coughing and swellings of the lower extremities, which in a few months caused his death.

Among the leading Rájbindé families was that of Bettada Kóté, to which belonged Lakshmani, the widow of Raja Chikka Krishnaráj, as also the first and third wives of the late Raja, and from this the future ruler of Mysore was taken. He was the third son of Chikka Krishna Arasu, who, like his father before him, had been a favourite of the old chief, and, on his adoption, in June 1865, received the name of Chámrájendra, after his adoptive grandfather.

He was installed, with all the pomp and ceremony demanded by Hindu etiquette, six months after the demise of Raja Krishnaráj, on an auspicious day during the Dashara festival.

In the centre of a large circular enclosure in the palace, where the old chief used to sit and witness the performances of his circus troupe, was placed a throne, said to have been presented by one of the Delhi Emperors to Raja Chikka Deo Ráj,[1] and to have been found in Tippu Sultán's palace at Seringapatam, whence it was taken to be used at the installation of Raja Krishnaráj in 1799. The young chief was conducted up the steps, and when he took his seat, was pelted from every corner of the court by a storm of flowers, which lay several inches deep at the foot of the throne, while

[1] Some accounts assert that this throne belonged to the Pándavas, and that it afterwards was the royal seat of the Vijayanagar kings, on whose downfall it came into the possession of the Mysore Wodiars. It appears to be of fig-wood, inlaid with ivory, and is now covered with gold plates.

a royal salute was fired, and the troops presented arms. The officiating Brahmans then pronounced some benedictory prayers, and offered to the young Raja water of the sacred streams, with consecrated cocoa-nuts and rice. After this, the genealogy of the Mysore family was read aloud, and on its conclusion, where the young chief's name and titles were recited, the building resounded with the shouts and applause of the people.

The next step was to present him with a khilat of twenty-one trays of shawls, cloths, and jewellery on the part of the Viceroy, while all the Rájbindés and high officials of the court came forward in turn, made their obeisance, and tendered their offerings, the ceremony being terminated by a distribution of pán, betel-nut, and garlands of flowers. During the whole time, the little Raja behaved with the utmost decorum, neither allowing himself to be moved by the storm of bouquets, nor by the vociferous adulations of his courtiers.

In the afternoon, he held a darbár in the great balcony fronting the court-yard of the palace, having first walked round the throne, scattering at its foot flowers, in token of taking possession. On his ascending his seat, he was again pelted with flowers by the bystanders, while a tumultuous shout of applause rose up from the dense crowd below. To the latter, great amusement was afforded by the combats of the jettis, or boxers, who wear on the right hand a cæstus of horn, with which they deal out most severe blows, and as wrestling is combined with the boxing, and their motto is 'spare not,' both of the combatants are speedily covered with wounds, blood flowing freely. It is in fact a savage sport, but used to be much in vogue, three or four couples of men being kept expressly for the purpose. They are extremely active, and their power of endurance is great.

The afternoon's ceremony was concluded by fireworks, and the next day, the young Raja had to undergo the fatigue of doing homage to the State Elephant, Cattle, and Horse, this being an indispensable ceremony on ascending the throne. These animals are supposed to have certain auspicious marks, and a specimen of each must always be present in the royal stables. Should any one of them die suddenly, the Raja can only take one meal a day, till a successor is found, having all the lucky marks required by the Shástras.

The British Government has shown its anxiety to give a becoming training to the young chief, and to preserve him from the ignoble fate of the late Raja, by nominating a guardian, whose duty it is to educate the boy in such a manner as will fit him to fill worthily the high position to which he is destined. The able and judicious officer (Colonel Malleson) who was selected for the purpose, has directed his attention both to the mind and the body, and while instilling a desire for learning into the young chief, has not neglected those manly and healthy exercises which are needed both mentally and physically.

The ancient Hindu literary routine takes the goddess Saraswati for its muse, and treating mythology as if it were genuine history, and ignoring geography altogether, contemns all modern science. Any deviation from the Brahmanical teaching imparted to his predecessors was viewed as an error by the older members of the family, and especially by the ladies of the household, and no little tact was needed to overcome their objections. There is every prospect, however, of the young Raja receiving a sound education, and of his excelling in athletic sports. It was wisely determined to associate with him in his studies, and in his hours of relaxation, the sons of the principal Rájbindés, so that, on his attaining his majority, his court will be composed of well-educated men, who will strengthen his government, and enter cordially into all his measures of improvement.

He has a difficult task before him, but one of great interest. He will come into possession of a fine country, free from debt, and already far advanced in civilisation; but the people, who have for forty years enjoyed the benefits of a strong yet sympathising government, will not be contented with a *roi faineant*, idling away his time in unworthy pleasures in evil company, and leaving the cares of state to others. The Raja will have to work, and work hard, as a ruler, and although he will not be able, like his celebrated ancestors, Kántírai and Chikka Deoráj, to conquer territory, he will be able to gain for himself an equally lasting reputation, and, by governing well, justify the liberal policy of the British Government, and win the esteem and gratitude of his people.

From the year 1834 till 1860, the administration of the province was in the hands of Sir Mark Cubbon, a distinguished officer who, having previously served in the country, was well acquainted with its resources, and the character of the people, and who, by his wise measures and thrifty supervision, rescued it from anarchy, and put its finances on a sound footing. A man of noble heart, and dignified presence, as generous in private life as he was economical in the management of public funds, he was popular in the best sense of the word, by his urbane manner, and the strict justice and impartiality which regulated all his proceedings. When compelled by the infirmities of old age to lay down the reins of office, he left behind him a reputation which had endeared him to all classes, and his name will always be remembered in Mysore with veneration and respect.

During his long administration, the presence of the Maharaja in the country was naturally embarrassing, for, although His Highness's lavish private expenditure conduced to the prosperity of the town of Mysore, the occasions were not unfrequent when questions arose affecting his personal dignity and position, and the Commissioner and the Resident (which office was retained as a separate post till 1842) were not always in accord regarding his pretensions. After the abolition of the office of Resident, he made strenuous efforts to recover the administration of his territory, urging his appeal in 1844, 1845, and 1848, and, lastly, just before Sir Mark Cubbon resigned his charge. All the correspondence on the subject of the Maharaja's claims is to be found in the papers printed by orders of Parliament in March 1866; and it need only be observed here, that His Highness had an accurate knowledge of everything that took place, all letters emanating from him being carefully scrutinised before they were despatched.

The future of the Mysore province is a problem which is hard to solve, mainly because the territory is far in advance of most native states, and because retrograde measures must at all hazards be avoided, if the people are to receive the same protection and the same equal laws that they have hitherto enjoyed.

They are undoubtedly desirous to see a native chief ruling over them, but not one vested with the arbitrary and irresponsible power formerly wielded by the late Raja. Indeed, the majority are probably content with the existing system, under which everything is done in the name of His Highness, although he has no voice in the matter. All this must, however, be changed when the young Raja attains his majority; and the question is, whether the administration should remain unaltered till that time, or whether steps should meanwhile be taken betimes to remodel the governing agency with a view to the future.

It appears to the writer that it would be unfair to the Raja to carry on the government of the country at high pressure, that is, with a great preponderance of English officers till the last moment, and then to withdraw suddenly, leaving His Highness to manage for himself, with a warning that the British Government will expect from him that everything shall be as well conducted as at present.

The radical defect of all Indian States managed according to the native system, is that too much is left to the caprice of individuals, whether Raja or minister, and that the will of one man often overrides the true interests of the many. That such power may be exercised wisely and well is true, and Raja Dinkar Rao, Sir Sálár Jang, and Sir Mádhawa Rao, are in the present day notable examples of able and excellent ministers.

The object in view, however, is rather to enable an intelligent chief, such as the Mysore Raja, to manage his territory himself, aided by experienced persons, without being wholly dependent upon them. In order to accomplish this, the Raja must first be highly educated, and the people have a right to demand that he should be. There is every reason to expect that the present chief will fulfil the expectations formed of him, in which case he is not likely to be a puppet in the hands of any minister.

But it appears essential that the Raja should be guided by the law, and by a fixed system—that is, that he should not be at liberty to abrogate existing laws without the assent of the British Government being first obtained. A contrary course would lead to chaos, and the interests that have grown up, and have been fostered during the last forty years, are too important to be surrendered to irresponsible power.

Those who sympathise most with native States, and who have seen how they are administered, are conscious of the great risk to which their stability is subjected by idle or headstrong rulers seeking to set aside all law, and to act on the impulse of the moment. No native territory governed in this manner can be well governed, and the numerous instances of mal-administration exhibited of late years among the chiefs of Rájputána and elsewhere, show the evil engendered by such a want of system.

In order to secure the happiness of the people and the good name of the ruler, the simplest plan seems to be to assimilate native rule as much as possible to that of the British Government. It is not meant by this, that every act and regulation in force in Her Majesty's territory is applicable to native States, or that the stringency of particular enactments should not be relaxed when required; but the essential feature is that there shall be a written law, which judges and other functionaries shall not be at liberty to set aside, and that even the Raja shall be bound by it.

There is a written law at present, and this should be adhered to, unless modifications are needed, in which case such amendments or alterations should receive the assent of the British Government.

There is much in the English system of administration that is distasteful to the native mind; but it is probable that exception is taken, not so much to the laws administered, as to the officers who administer them. It is true that the Indian Government has been accused of passing laws that are not needed, that little or no trouble has been taken to explain their purport before they were enacted, and that they are enforced with undue severity. But, even admitting the cogency of these arguments, and the rigid nature of the English system of government, the sum total of them does not give so much umbrage as the incompetency of those who administer the laws.

Imperfect knowledge of the vernacular dialects, and of the first principles of law, and want of an intuitive perception of native ideas and requirements, are disadvantages which beset many English officials, and which no ability or high moral qualities will wholly make amends for. It would seem that, thirty or forty years ago, Englishmen associated more freely with natives than is now the case, and knew more of their ways of thought; but there were few lawyers in those days. Now, more attention is paid to a legal training, but an intimate acquaintance with native prejudices is rarer than it used to be. A combined knowledge of the law, the languages, and the disposition of the people, appears to be beyond the ken of all but a very limited number of Englishmen.

It will be apparent at once that some of the defects specified do not exist in a territory administered by native officials who, being men of the country, are of course well acquainted with the people, their language, and their habits. There is also another recommendation in the nature of the service attainable, namely, that great latitude is left for rapid promotion, and that any man may rise to the highest posts.

In British India the most distinguished native officer of Government cannot at present hope to attain a high administrative appointment; and, although he is not excluded altogether from the High Court bench, and many inferior posts are open to him, he may as well hope to grasp the moon as to become a Commissioner of a Division, or even a Collector of a District. All the professions of the Indian Government of its desire to raise the position of its native servants, and all the proposals to admit leading natives to seats in Legislative Councils, however specious and commendable, will not compensate for the real grievance that influential and distinguished Indians feel at their virtual exclusion from the government of the country. Whatever Secretary of State may have the courage to open this double-locked door, and admit to the sacred precincts inside the people of the country, will win for himself everlasting renown in India, and attach to the British Crown the allegiance of all classes. A limited number of civil administrative posts of the grade of assistant should be thrown open every year to general competition in India, so as to spare natives of the country the risk and expense of proceeding to England.

In the case of Mysore it is most desirable, if not indeed essential, to commence the experiment of placing the leading native officials in posts of higher importance than they have hitherto occupied. In doing so, it will be incumbent to provide adequately for any European officers who may be displaced; and any charge which this may entail may fairly be debited to Mysore.

It must not be concealed that the success of the administration hitherto has been mainly due to the strenuous exertions of the European officers, who have worked hard, and offered to their native subordinates an excellent example of devotion to duty. The faults of many native employés are want of punctuality and occasional slackness in performing their work, and in keeping them up to the mark the supervision of European officers has been invaluable.

It will, in any case, be advisable to retain the superintendents of divisions till the last moment, that is, till the Raja's majority; but all the minor administrative posts, such as district charges, and the duties of assistant, should be gradually made over to native officials, and, as five years will elapse before the young chief becomes of age, the arrangement is quite practicable. A bonus should be given to every European officer displaced, calculated according to the length of his service in Mysore, the compensation being fixed on liberal terms and being payable at once out of the revenues of the province. To the native substitute a salary equal to two-thirds of that of his European predecessor would probably suffice. In this way, the services of several Europeans could be dispensed with without giving cause for dissatisfaction, and the vital measure of forming a strong native agency would receive fair play, of which there is little prospect at present.

A few offices, which it is needless here to give in detail, but not amounting to more than ten or twelve altogether, including medical charges, must at all times be filled by Europeans, even after the Raja attains his majority. In this category are the future Resident and his staff.

Some appointments of a temporary nature, such as the Survey enquiry and the Inám Commission, must be retained till the completion of the duties concerned, which are of the highest importance to the welfare of the province. The thirty years' leases given to the cultivators will effectually protect them against the rapacity of any of the Raja's officials hereafter, and the investigation into rent-free holdings, and the grant of title-deeds to the possessors will give a validity to this kind of property which it never enjoyed before.

The tendency of recent legislation in India is to strengthen the judicature at the expense of the administration. Now this is unexceptionable in territories where the latter can implicitly rely on the loyalty and obedience of the people, but in an oriental country, whenever a great convulsion agitates the land, and the administration is weakened, the courts of justice immediately collapse. In foreign territory particularly, the Government, to be efficient, must be strong, or the courts would become corrupt, while there is not much fear, under a settled system and with a vigilant Resident, that the Raja would unduly influence their decisions.

The present judicial system in Mysore is closely assimilated to that in force in British territory, and does not need much modification. The people are too intelligent to desire a return to the times when common sense and simple rules are said to have sufficed. Common sense in judicial proceedings is but too often non-sense, while the cry for simple rules may be affirmed to argue simplicity on the part of the crier. Unless all native officials are gifted with innate light and superior wisdom, it is better to teach them a methodical procedure, and to give them some legal training, than to leave them to their fallacious instinctive ideas of right and wrong.

The financial system now in force in Mysore is sound, the budgets being carefully prepared, and a watchful control being maintained over all miscellaneous and contingent expenditure. For the efficient superintendence, however, of this radically important department a European officer, or a native versed in the European mode of keeping accounts, will always be needed, as the treasury transactions relate, not only to Mysore, but to all the requirements of Her Majesty's forces stationed at Bangalore. In the accounts of the province, the substitution of Kanarese for English is an easy matter, the former being already in use in the accounts sent in from the sub-divisions. It will be seen from the schedule of revenue at the beginning of this paper that the income-tax is not in force in Mysore, the Moturfa, or tax on trades and professions, taking its place; so that only English officers pay income-tax. The Moturfa is an ancient impost, well suited to the country, and being subject to revision every year, is as free from objection as any direct tax can well be.

Only nine articles now pay custom duties, betel-nut producing more than half the whole sum raised.

There is only one department of the administration the future constitution of which will need anxious consideration, inasmuch as native prejudices on the subject are strong. It is that of the Public Works, the efficient supervision of which is of vital importance in a country, containing 20,000 tanks and numerous irrigation channels.

It is useless to bring against the department stale charges of bad work, rotten contracts, and knavery of subordinates. Allegations to this effect were not unfrequently substantiated, but a remedy for them has not yet been found. Subordinates may be punished, contracts may be annulled, and better work may, perhaps, be secured by higher payments, but by none of these contrivances will the department be made capable of being managed by a native agency.

It is often recommended that natives should be trained to serve in the department, a scientific education being imparted to them; but the reply to this advice is that eligible young men will not become engineers, and it is idle to suppose that they are to be had for the asking. The writer can assert, without fear of contradiction, that natives of good family dislike the active professional life of an engineer, that they shun the exposure and hard work, and that they infinitely prefer sedentary pursuits, such as are open to them in revenue employ.

To add to the present unfavorable state of matters, the few trained natives who, in former days, performed the functions of surveyors, and were competent to superintend extensive works, are no longer available, being old and worn out.

In the present dearth, therefore, of competent native engineers, and the improbability, to say the least, of such officers being forthcoming in this generation, there is no help for it but to maintain a certain portion of the Public Works Department as it now exists. Indeed, a superintending Engineer of Irrigation, to counsel on all important projects, and to supervise and control local officials will be indispensable.

Under native rule the obligations of the cultivators to attend to the up-keep of the tanks of the country, when once brought up to the required standard, can be more strictly enforced than at present. Some show of despotic authority appears to be absolutely necessary to secure the desired end, the agriculturists, like most other classes, requiring a certain amount of pressure to ensure prompt action, which is of the utmost importance when heavy floods threaten the stability of irrigation works.

If the attention of the Government of India is directed towards the points above enumerated, and if steps are taken to introduce the native element more freely into administrative offices, there is no apparent reason why the Raja, on attaining his majority, should not be able to form a strong governing agency, which will conduct the affairs of the province to the satisfaction of the Supreme Government, and to the contentment of the people. But, if matters are allowed to train on as at present, without an effort being made to forestal future difficulties, it is much to be feared that the young chief will be unfairly beset by perplexities, the solution of which devolves properly not upon him, but upon the British Government.

Are native States a tower of strength, or a standing menace to the British Government? It is useless to discuss the errors of the past, and to criticise the policy of twenty years ago. 'Tempora mutantur, et nos mutamur cum illis.' As regards the future, the minds of all native Princes in India have been tranquillised by the Queen's Proclamation of 1858, and by the wise steps taken by Lord Canning to recognise the right of adoption, so that annexation will be unknown, except in rare cases of bequest or rebellion. The utmost that the paramount Power would do would be to set aside an incompetent ruler, and to nominate his successor, or to superintend the affairs of a State for a few years, or during a minority.

Most of the native chiefs maintain larger bodies of armed men than are needed, either for show, or for the security of their territories, and, although the pay given is individually small, the total outlay is large, and the heavy expenditure not only entails on the people many a vexatious impost, but retards the improvements of the country. The other main defect, to which attention has already been drawn, is that too much is ordinarily left to the personal caprice of the ruler, owing to the absence of a well-regulated form of government; and this unsettled state of matters may, in the case of obstinacy and folly on the part of the chief, engender revolt among his subjects, necessitating the intervention of the British power, or hurry him blindly into hostilities against it. Ill-governed native States, with a large standing army, are undoubtedly a source of danger, and it should be the object of the paramount Power to reduce their armaments to the lowest possible limit, consistently with treaty obligations. Any political cohesion among native princes, of a nature adverse to our interests, is now scarcely practicable, and it may be hoped that an appeal to their religious prejudices would fail of effect, as, during the last twelve years, they have witnessed the inauguration and consolidation of a new order of things, in which their rights and privileges have been jealously guarded by the British Government. They have therefore every motive to be loyal, and could not look for greater consideration, either from a foreign invader, or from any indigenous power which might rise up supreme in India.

There is ample scope for improvement in all the native States of India, and some of them indeed are notoriously ill-governed, but they offer to their subjects a field for eminent talent and ability, which is sought for in vain in British territory. Everyone of good family has a chance of rising to the summit of power, and it is needless to point out the attraction of this to men of mark. Though much remains to be done, the force of circumstances has compelled the chiefs of India to improve in many respects the condition of their States, but, in all substantial points, such as the security of life and property, the regular administration of justice, and the mode of collecting the land-tax, the residents of British territory are better circumstanced than their neighbours. Gross oppression, such as is not unfrequently witnessed in native States, is, if not wholly unknown, extremely rare, and, when detected, is severely punished; but the oriental mind dislikes rigid rules which work with the regularity of a machine, leaving little latitude for the talents of individuals, and it is therefore not surprising that to men of ability, notwithstanding the precariousness of their position, service under a native ruler should be more attractive than employment under the British Government.

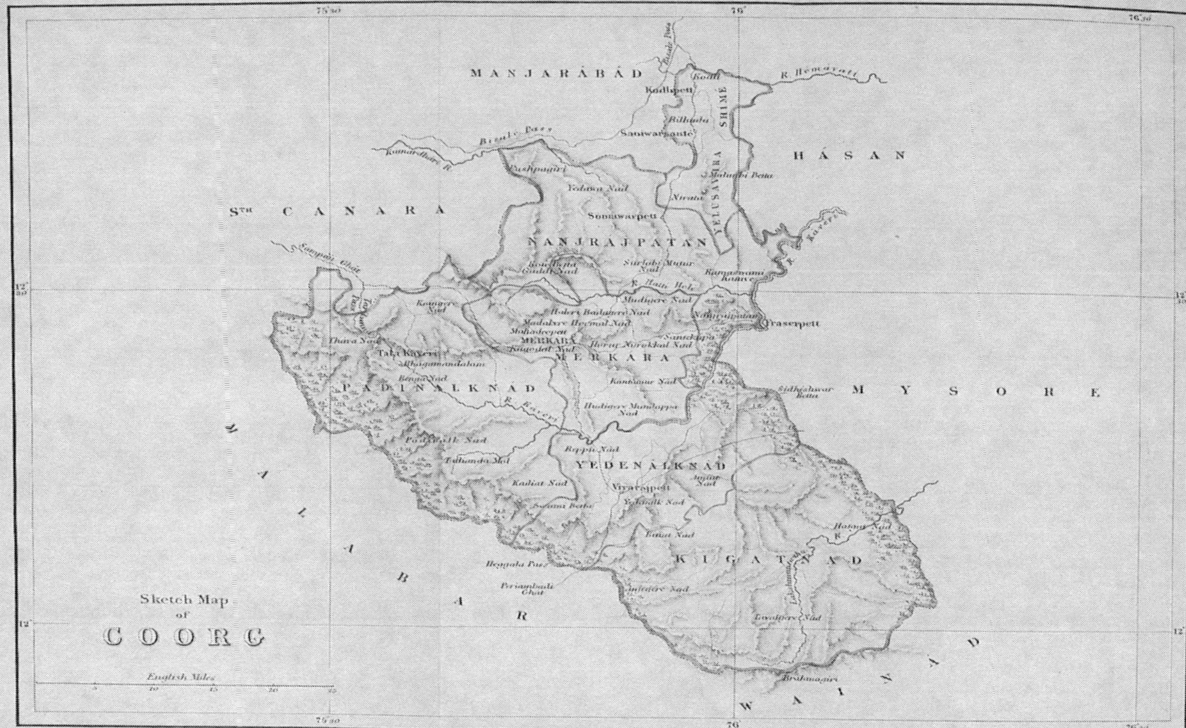
Sketch Map
of
COORG
English Miles
MANJARÁBÁD
HÁSAN
S^TH CANARA
MYSORE
MALABAR
WAINAD
NANJRAJPATAN
MERKARA
PADINALKNAD
YEDENALKNAD
KIGATNAD
YELUSAVIRA
SHIMÉ
Somwarpett
Fraserpett
Virarajpett
Kodlipett
Saniwarsante
MERKARA
Bisale Pass
R. Hemavati
R. Kaveri
Sampaji Ghat
Heggala Pass
Periambadi Ghat
Brahmagiri
Tala Kaveri
Bhagamandalam
Pushpagiri
Sidheshwar Betta
Malambi Betta
Ramaswami Kanave
R. Hatti Hole
Nanjarajpatan
Mohadeopett
London, Henry S. King & Co. 65 Cornhill.

COORG LAND.

FEW parts of India are more picturesque than the little hill province of Coorg, and nowhere can be found a more gallant and loyal race than its inhabitants.

Shut in on three sides by stupendous mountains, and on the fourth by an almost impenetrable bamboo jungle, this primitive country might long have remained unknown to the world, had not the insane folly of its last ruler precipitated a conflict with the British Government, which led to his dethronement, and the annexation of his territory, with the free consent of all his subjects, to the English Crown.

The history of Coorg barely reaches back 250 years, and there are in fact no native records of an older date than the commencement of the present century; from which unfavorable conclusions might be drawn as to the character of the population, were it not that personal contact with them fully absolves them from the charge of barbarism.

It could not well happen, indeed, that the denizens of a country where the aspect of nature is singularly beautiful, should be without some traits of character to interest and attract, and we find accordingly that the Coorgs are a hardy and athletic race, rejoicing in field sports and manly games, and with a justifiable pride in their fine fatherland.

Coorg, properly called Kodagu, or Kurg, is a small mountainous province on the eastern slope of the great Ghát range of Southern India. It lies between Manjarábád in Mysore, and the British territory of Wainád, and, like both of these districts, is now well known in connection with the coffee trade.

It contains 2,400 square miles of country, and a population of 113,000, or only forty-seven to the square mile, classified as follows:—

Coorgs	24,585
Hindus, not Coorgs	73,638
Muhammadans	5,774
Aboriginal tribes	7,050
Jains	224
Parsis	22
Native Christians	1,071
Eurasians	490
Europeans	98
Total	112,952

The total receipts of the Province in 1869–70 were 59,446*l.*, the taxation falling at the rate of five shillings per head.

The various sources of income are given in the accompanying table:—

	Rupees.
1. Land Revenue	2,86,560
2. Forest	1,06,658
3. Excise	66,375
4. Assessed Taxes	3,028
5. Stamps	33,742
6. Post-office	7,010
Carried forward, Rupees	5,03,373

	Brought forward	5,03,373
7.	Telegraph	1,864
8.	Judicial	5,075
9.	Registration Fees	1,847
10.	Public Works	70,480
11.	Miscellaneous	7,302
12.	Local Funds	4,519
	Total, Rupees	5,94,460 or £59,446

It is a notable fact that out of the total raised as land revenue, namely, 28,656*l.*, about one-third was produced by the assessment on land bearing coffee, which product therefore contributes greatly to the resources of the province.

During the same period the charges were—

		Rupees.
1.	Civil and Political Establishments	1,54,763
2.	Judicial Charges	19,308
3.	Stamps	2,533
4.	Police Charges	1,152
5.	Military	2,13,944
6.	Superannuation Payments	1,973
7.	Ecclesiastical	4,836
8.	Allowances under Treaties	21,470
9.	Public Works	1,24,651
10.	Education	14,088
11.	Miscellaneous	7,873
12.	Local Funds	2,322
13.	Post-office	5,386
14.	Telegraph	19,859
	Total, Rupees	5,04,158 or £59,415

The province therefore pays its way, including the charges for an entire regiment of native infantry, but the grant for Public Works is wholly insufficient.

Coorg comprises six divisions, which are sub-divided as follows :—

1. Mérkára	2. Yedenálk Nád [1]	3. Pádinálk Nád	4. Kigat Nád	5. Nanjrájpatan	6. Yélusávira Shímé
1. Madakere Hormal nád	1. Yedenálk nád	1. Pádinálk nád	1. Anjegere Mare } nád	1. Gaddi nád	1. Kodli Hóbli
2. Kagodal nád	2. Beppu nád	2. Kadiat nád	2. Távalgere Kurchitore } nád	2. Yedawa nád	2. Bilhada Hóbli
3. Horúr Núrokkal nád	3. Amiat nád	3. Tháva nád	3. Hatgat Aragere Tirunálk } nád	3. Surlabi Mutúr nád	3. Nirata Hóbli
4. Kántámúr nád		4. Benga nád	4. Bitiat Kirigúr Kutta Beruli } nád	4. Nanjrájpatan Hóbli [2]	
5. Hudigere Mundappa nád		5. Kuingere nád		5. Rámaswámi Kaniwé [3]	
6. Mudigere nád					
7. Haleri Badigere nád					

The whole of the Náds are hill country. The Yélusávira Shímé, and two sub-divisions of Nanjrájpatan are outside the hill barriers, and in the plains.

The only towns in the province are—

Name.	Locality.	Population.
1. Mahádeopete or Mérkára	Mérkára sub-division .	3,859
2. Virarájpett . . .	Yedenálknád sub-division	2,922
3. Fraserpett . . .	Nanjrájpatan sub-division	1,181
4. Sómawárpett . . .	Nanjrájpatan subdivision-	915
5. Kodlipett . . .	Yélusávira Shímé sub-div.	733
6. Saniwársanté . . .	Yélusávira Shímé sub-div.	500

With these exceptions, there are neither towns nor villages, the people living in farm-houses, each man on his own estate, a certain number of such farms comprising what, for administrative purposes, is called a village.

In order to obtain a tolerably accurate idea of the configuration of Coorg, it is desirable to ascend the principal mountains of the country, splendid hills that tower aloft above their compeers, and open to view the numerous secluded vallies and dense forests with which the province abounds.

On the northern frontier, in the Nanjrájpatan divi-

[1] A Kanarese word used in Coorg and Mysore to denote a division of hill country.

[2] A division of plain country.

[3] A gorge between hills.

sion, the Kumár Parvat, called by the Coorgs Pushpagiri or Pupgiri, that is, the Flower Hill, by its bold and almost inaccessible sides seems to oppose an insurmountable barrier to the invader. In fact, all access to it from the north is impracticable, except by a long and toilsome climb of twelve miles up the slopes of the hill from the Subhramani temple in Canara. On the Coorg side, the approach, though much shorter, is very steep and difficult, while the natives regard with some fear the dense jungles at the foot of the mountain, as they are frequently infested by herds of wild elephants. These animals, notwithstanding that the mountain is 5,500 feet above the sea, often contrive to climb up the steep wooded sides to the summit, feeding on favorite trees as they make their way upwards. The Coorgs have another reason for regarding the hill with superstitious dread, as on the extreme point one sees, within a small stone enclosure, apparent marks of two feet, which are regarded as of celestial origin. The few devotees who have the courage to visit the lofty mountain, put up, in commemoration of their pilgrimage, heaps of stones, of which one observes great numbers all around.

Looking over the rugged precipitous northern face, the whole of the coffee district of Manjarábád lies like a map beneath one, the stupendous Ghát range of the Nagar country towering up in the distance beyond. Turning round, one sees to the south the great chain of mountains which encircles Coorg on the west like a high wall, shutting it out from the low country on the coast, and terminating in the lofty Brahmagiri which divides Coorg from Wainád. To the east is the Mysore plateau, dotted over with drugs and peaks, while to the west, if the day be fine, a distant view of the ocean rewards the observer.

This grand hill has not often been visited by Europeans, but being a prominent landmark on all sides, it has of course not escaped the attention of the Trigonometrical Survey, whose officers have planted on its summit one of their triumphant marks.

In the centre of North Coorg, the Highlands of the district, with an average elevation of 3,500 feet, is the fine mountain called Kóté Betta, or the Fortress Hill, an immense mass, with a flat black summit, which, on a misty day, looms out like a great whale. Kóté Betta is also in the Nanjrájpatan division, and is a favorable point of view for studying the topography of the northern portion of the district, as it commands a great stretch of country, and because, as in the case of the Mysore Drugs, good water is found on the summit. The hill is about 5,000 feet above sea level, but is comparatively easy of access.

The Coorg Highlands are the wildest part of the province, a mass of hills, in fact, with but little forest, and sparsely inhabited. The people are mostly Lingáyats,[1] and not pure Coorgs, the latter being found chiefly in the central tracts, where cultivated land is more abundant. The climate, however, of the Highlands is eminently salubrious, and Sómawárpett, a small town on the outskirts, enjoys a good reputation in this respect.

[1] So called from their wearing the 'lingam,' or emblem of the god Siva.

The third mountain which calls for remark is Tadianda Mól, a beautiful peak in the Pádinálk Nád division, which rears its head to a height of 5,600 feet, and is the loftiest in the province. Being in a central part of the Ghát range, Tadianda Mól is perhaps the best elevated point from which to survey Coorg, while the ascent from the Naiknád palace at its foot only occupies two hours. It is an easy climb till one reaches the actual peak, where the ascent is naturally steep. As soon as the fleecy mist which generally covers the country in the morning clears off, a splendid view is obtained of the little Coorg paradise, as well as of the distant Mysore ranges of hills, and of the sea to the westward. All the mountain sides are clothed with primæval forests full of the finest trees, while in the vallies far beneath one descries the emerald bits of cultivation which denote the presence of the Coorg farmer, whose substantial dwelling is seen hard by, half hid, however, by bamboos, plantains, and umbrageous trees.

Fourth on the list of the higher hills is the Brahmagiri, called in Mysore Dévasi Betta, a long range which separates Coorg from Wainád, and which is nearly as substantial a barrier on the south as the Pushpagiri on the north. It is in the Kigatnád division. The ascent to the highest peak is not less than six miles, passing over alternate rises and falls for three miles, when a tough pull takes one to the higher range. Here one passes over undulating downs, with occasional patches of forest in the gullies, called in Southern India 'Shólas,' till one reaches the foot of a sharp ridge leading to the top of the peak. Perched on the summit, one has a strikingly fine view of Wainád at one's feet, with its numerous coffee plantations, and the Nílgiri mountains in the distance beyond. To the eastward is the dense jungle which divides Coorg from Mysore, the Mugudu, or triple boundary of these provinces and of Wainád, being eight miles off. The Kigatnád division of Coorg, which is, as compared with the central and northern parts, an open country, lies much lower than the rest of the province. Owing to this circumstance, though the ascent to the Brahmagiri is toilsome, the descent on the Wainád side is not very severe, the level of that province being higher than that of South Coorg. The Coorgs of Kigaṭnád are of somewhat darker complexion than those farther north.

The Brahmagiri has an elevation of about 4,500 feet, being, therefore, considerably lower than Pushpagiri or Tadianda Mól, but it is equally revered by the Coorgs, as from it issues the Lakshmantirtha river, one of the affluents of the sacred Kávéri, and itself a stream of no small repute. It is a picturesque little burn, springing from a fountain two miles from Kúrchi, where there is a small temple of indifferent construction in honor of the deity.

Besides the four hills mentioned, there are many others of local celebrity, of which that where the Kávéri rises deserves notice. The source of this sacred stream is called Tala Kávéri, or the Head of the Kávéri, the tiny rivulet trickling out between two hills called Brahmagiri and Agnigiri. It is received into a small reservoir, which is greatly venerated, and visited by hosts of pilgrims. Further on, at Bhágamandalam, it meets another stream called the Kanké. There is only a petty temple at Tala Kávéri, which is in an elevated wild tract three miles from civilisation, but at the October festival, crowds of devotees encamp on the spot, and perform their vows. At Bhágamandalam there is a large temple which enjoys an endowment of 600*l.* a year, and is reputed to be an ancient edifice. Inaccessible as is the country about Tala Kávéri, there is a pass in the vicinity, called Tarikanna, which was formerly much in use, but is said to be now impracticable.

Although the general direction of the Ghát range is north and south, the hills which intersect the interior of the province are so varied in shape, height, and direction, and, at the same time, so numerous, that, small as is the area of the country, it must be repeatedly traversed, and much fatigue must be undergone in climbing the principal mountains before an accurate idea can be formed of the peculiarities of the district. Besides the hills already mentioned, there are a few others of note, such as Swámi Betta, called by Europeans Mt. Remarkable, near the Periambádi Pass, and Málimbi Betta, a fine conical hill in the Yélusávira division. This division is, however, beyond the barriers of Coorg, and formed no part of the province originally, having been a recent conquest. It derives its name from its revenue 'yélu' seven, and 'sávira' thousand, that is the seven thousand (pagoda) territory, this amount being its assumed revenue. The division is in the low country, and in its characteristics resembles Mysore rather than

Coorg, while the people are essentially different from the true Coorgs.

The commencement of the Hindu year is generally signalised on the Coorg mountains by deafening claps of thunder, which reverberate and roll through the vallies with a roar which appals new comers. The thunder-storms are often accompanied by heavy showers, which suddenly chill the air, and portend the coming up from the sea of the regular monsoon. The barometer frequently changes, and its rapid alternations show that strife is waging among the elements, wind and calm, hot air and cool sea-borne breezes, following one another in rapid succession. At length, about the beginning of June, this fitful state of things ceases, and the south-west monsoon obtains the mastery, retaining it till the end of August, and pouring forth during this period those beneficent showers which bring with them plenty and happiness to the people. But the raw damp cold is very trying to those not inured to the climate, the country is enveloped in perpetual mist, communications are interrupted, and those who can get away, take refuge below the hill barriers.

As the north-east monsoon passes first over the Mysore plateau, its effect is not much felt in Coorg. At this season, a few heavy showers fall, after which the weather clears up, and uninterrupted sunshine characterises the glorious winter of the Coorg mountains.

Coorg, being visited by copious torrents of rain, is the treasure-house from which the districts of the plains draw much of their wealth, but the considerable rivers which rise in the province cut their way through such high banks that their fertilising properties are not utilised in Coorg itself, and it is only when one enters Mysore that the great value of their irrigating powers is practically tested. In Coorg, though there is an abundant rainfall, averaging in some parts yearly 120 inches, there are few works of irrigation, but the reason is apparent when one considers that in this mountain tract there are a thousand streams, coursing down the hillsides, and supplying water at every man's door nearly.

The Kávéri, with virgin modesty, steals its way silently under the cover of lofty overhanging banks and thick forest for the greater part of its course through Coorg. One may be encamped only a few yards from the stream, and yet be unaware of its proximity, owing to the dense growth of wood on its sides. When swollen by floods, however, it is very deep, and becomes impassable, cutting off all communication between the chief towns of Mérkára and Víraréjpett. It is bridged at Fraserpett where it leaves Coorg, but nowhere else.

As in the case of all the great Indian streams, mythology and poetry have combined to cast a sacred halo over this river, investing it with the rays of divinity and the charms of modesty; and, in truth, when one reflects upon the priceless boon which its waters bestow on the parched-up lands of the plains, it is no wonder that the grateful recipients of its bounty should weave a romantic tale about its celestial origin. This Indian Undine, in silence and seclusion, performs her penitential homage in order to obtain the beatitude of her foster father, the sage Kávéra Muni, while the stream into which she is transformed, after stealing almost unperceived away from its birthplace, when it enters Mysore, assumes the majestic mien of a goddess, and thundering over rocky channels, pursues an impetuous course till it dashes itself over the magnificent falls at Sivasamudram.

The Lakshmantirtha, which rises in the Brahmagiri hills of South Coorg, is an affluent of the Kávéri, and is also utilised as soon as it enters Mysore, several irrigation channels being taken from it in that province. In Coorg, it flows through forests, and has steep banks, so that no direct benefit is derived from its waters, but the supply is constant.

The other rivers of the province, namely the Hatti Holé, or Fish river, flowing into the Kávéri, and the Kal Holé, or Stone river (mentioned in the despatches of the Duke of Wellington), are of inferior note. The Hémáwati, which is a Mysore stream, traverses a portion of the Yélusávira division, and offers considerable impediments to the traffic between Coorg and Manjarábád.

Before the annexation of the country in 1834, and for many years afterwards, there was no cart road in it, the only available means of carriage being pack bullocks or coolees. In the days of the Coorg Rajas, trade was very restricted, and the hills so rarely traversed by British troops, that their little territory remained almost unknown. The only communication much used was a defile passing under the Sidhéshwar hill, where a strong okhad, or outpost, defied all approach on the frontier: a stone was erected with 'Vi,' for Víraráj, on one side, and 'Dé,' the Mysore device, on the other, marking the boundary between the two provinces. The pass at this point led over hills, covered with thick wood, into Coorg; but the country is so difficult, and the bamboo jungle so impervious to troops, that the Coorg chiefs were able to offer a formidable resistance to an attacking force.

After the dethronement of the last Raja, one of the first duties undertaken by the British Government was to secure a thorough communication, for military purposes, with the coast. This was accomplished by the formation of two roads, one entering Coorg at Fraserpett, and leading *viâ* Mérkára, to Mangalore, by the Sampáji Ghát, and the other entering the district a little to the south, and leading, *viâ* Víraréjpett, to Cannanore by the Periambádi Ghát. The first of these comprises a descent of twenty miles from Mérkára to Sampáji, the pass being well and skilfully laid out. The second is a descent of thirteen miles from Periambádi to the Stony river on the frontier; but, though the gradient is not severe, the line is not so well laid out as the first-named, and is more difficult to keep in order.

These two great arteries, though quite sufficient for military purposes, are altogether inadequate for the requirements of the district, now that every corner of it has been opened up by European enterprise, and it has consequently been found necessary to devise communications north and south, in deference to the repeated applications of the planters, to whom the country owes so much of its prosperity.

Coorg is an example of a small hill district, with a limited revenue of 57,000*l.*, where the communications are at all times maintained with great difficulty, and where large streams are so numerous that to bridge them all would swallow up for an indefinite period the whole revenue of the country. To bridge the Kávéri, for instance, between Mérkára and Víraràjpett, where such a work is much wanted, would, at present rates, probably cost not less than 20,000*l.*, its width during the rainy season being considerable, and its velocity great. Even during the dry months, its rocky bed contains nearly three feet of water, with deep pools at intervals, so that boats are generally needed to cross it.

It may also be remarked, that the maintenance of roads in a hill-country like Coorg, where the gradients are steep, and bridges are liable to be carried away by the impetuosity of sudden floods, is a fruitful source of expense. Even the industry of the planters, who have done so much for the district, has a prejudicial effect upon the communications, for which there is no adequate remedy. Formerly, when the monsoon burst on the crest of the Gháts, which were covered with dense wood, the contents of the rain clouds, which descended on the hills, were absorbed in the rich mould which lay at the feet of the stately trees, and the moisture made its way only gradually to the lower levels. But since the hillsides have been denuded of the giants of the forests, and slender coffee plants have taken their place, the heavy rains have washed away the surface soil, and the waters rush violently down the hillsides, meeting with no resistance where the deep mould formerly stayed their course; and, should they encounter a bridge in their descent, too frequently tear up its foundations, and destroy the roadway also.

The magnificent trees which clothe the Coorg mountains, not only embellish greatly the landscape, but have, it is said, a potent influence on the annual rainfall by attracting the clouds. The Coorgs assert that, since planting operations have been extensively carried on, their country is much drier than it used to be; but although, as above pointed out, the denudation of trees has the effect of precipitating the showers violently down the face of the hills, no proof has as yet been adduced that the actual yearly rainfall has diminished.

Upon a copious rainfall mainly depends the prosperity of the district; for although an adventitious stimulus has been given to it by growing coffee, rice is the staple food of the people, and abundant showers are necessary, in the absence of artificial irrigation, to produce the yearly crop. Even for coffee, tea, and cinchona, plentiful and timely rain is needed, the absence of the periodical fall bringing with it not only drought, but the destructive insects which follow a dry season.

Of all parts of Coorg, the Kigatnád division appears to be most fertile, owing probably to its lower level and the abundance of water consequently supplied to it. The soil is of a darker hue than in the other divisions, which is attributed to the thick deposit of vegetable substances brought down from the hills; but this seems to affect the climate prejudicially, South Coorg being so unhealthy that Europeans residing in it almost invariably suffer from a bad type of fever; and even the natives, by their dusky complexions, show the effect on the constitution of the moist black soil.

In Northern and Central Coorg, the soil is mostly dark red, and in the vallies is highly productive; but there is a large proportion of waste and unculturable land in the Highlands. Rice is the great crop of all the hill country, but in the plains, in Yélusávira Shímé, and Nanjrájpatan, the productions are similar to those of the adjoining parts of Mysore, dry grains being extensively grown.

Were it not for the heavy rains which deluge the country, its elevation and favorable temperature[1] would lead a person to think that the European fauna would thrive in Coorg. Certain fruits do succeed well, especially oranges, limes, shaddocks, and plantains; but these are natives of the soil. European vegetables have been tried with fair success by planters.

The appearance of the Coorg farm houses in the spring is very picturesque, as, besides the cultivated plants, the hedges teem with a profusion of roses and other wild flowers.

Of the products of the forests mention will be made in treating of the results of coffee planting as carried on in the district.

In former days, when, to a native mind, the merit of

[1] At Mérkára, 3,700 feet above the sea, the extreme range of the thermometer is about 80° indoors, and the average 60°. Sómawárpett also enjoys an equable temperature, but, south of Víraréjpett, the thermometer stands much higher.

a territory was its inaccessibility, few States enjoyed such an immunity from invasion as Coorg, the only approaches to it being through dense tangled woods, or up the face of steep mountains, clothed with forest trees, and cut up by stony water-courses. The Sidhéshwar route already mentioned, and the Heggala Pass to the west, were the only communications practicable to troops; and even these could be easily defended against superior forces.

Owing to this seclusion, and the poverty of the country, this little Alpine region remained almost unknown till the time of the sturdy Haidar Ali, who, having conquered all the hill tracts of Mysore, carried his arms also into Coorg, meeting with little resistance. Having established his ascendency, he built a fort at Mérkára, now the chief town of the province, inside which was afterwards erected the Raja's palace.

It is not to be supposed, however, that, prior to the advent of Haidar Ali, there was no settled government in the country, for, at an early date, it appears to have been parcelled out into Náds, or communes. The extent and configuration of these depended in a great measure upon the natural boundaries furnished by the various chains of hills which cross the province; but as, owing to the prevailing system of compulsory labour, slaves were available in large numbers, the limits of each nád were also defined by cutting deep ditches called 'kadangs.' These still constitute the boundaries of divisions and villages, and are scrupulously maintained, so that any attempt to alter such landmarks is immediately resented. In the case of individual holdings, stones are generally put up to identify the limits of each property. Disputes regarding such boundaries are not uncommon, it being easy to remove the stones clandestinely.

Tradition says that the thirty-five náds into which Coorg was anciently divided, were shared by twelve chiefs, who enjoyed the privilege of being preceded by Kombhukárs or hornmen, six of them being of note.

The primitive Kodagaru, or Coorgs, were divided into Amma Kodagaru (who anciently exercised priestly functions, but fell under the displeasure of the goddess Kávéri), and secular Coorgs. The latter were of three branches—San, Bud, and Malé, of which the San only are numerous at present.

About 250 years ago, a Lingáyat of the Ikkéri country emigrated to Coorg, and pursued there, it is said, the calling of a teacher. It is not stated whether he professed to be a religious preceptor, though this is probable; but in course of time he contrived to levy a share of the grain of many villages, and at length acquired so much influence, that he usurped the sovereignty of the whole province. He was the ancestor of the Coorg Rajas, who wielded an authority which was so implicitly obeyed, that one cannot but suppose that so brave a race as the Coorgs must have attributed to their rulers a divine origin, or rights derived direct from the deity, or they would scarcely have shown such unbounded respect to Rajas who seemed to have madness in their veins.

The first chief established himself at a place called Haleri, about eight miles north of Mérkára, and gave to

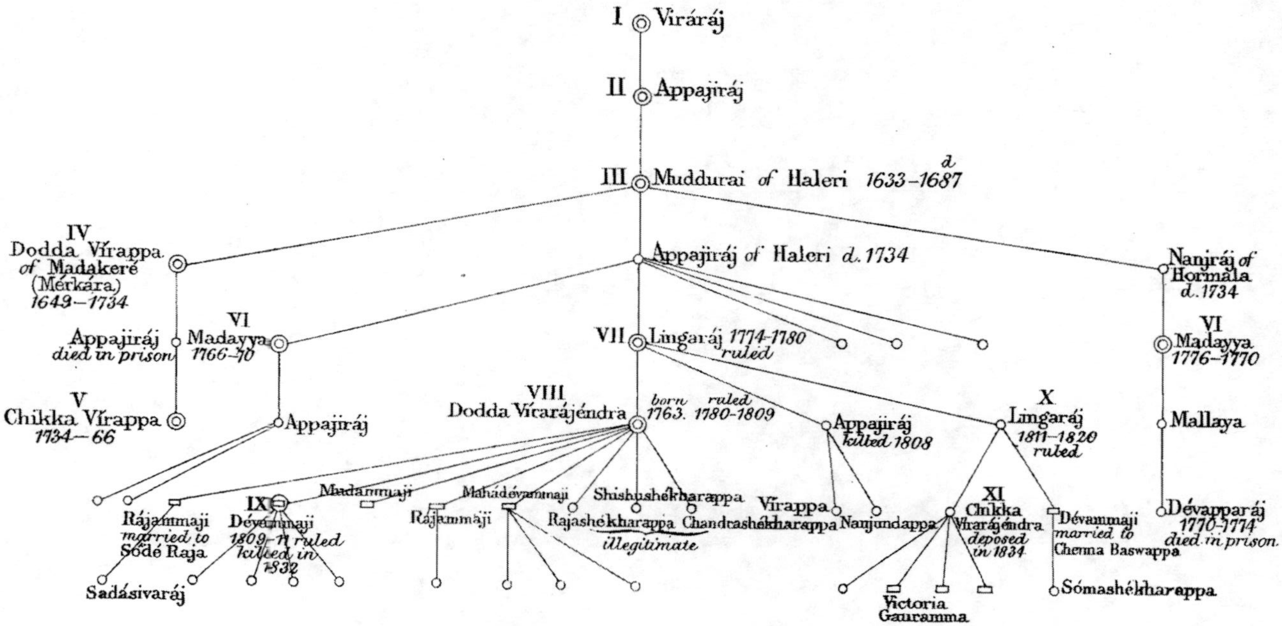

PEDIGREE OF THE COORG RAJAS.

his newly-acquired possessions the title of the Haleri Samasthán, or Haleri sovereignty, an appellation which it continued to bear, officially, down to the dethronement of the last Raja. The family pedigree, so far as it can be traced, is given opposite :—

The history of the family is almost a blank till the invasion of Haidar Ali, to whom little resistance seems to have been offered, as the Coorgs, however individually brave, were unable to resist the conqueror's entrance into their country, or to encounter him in the field. But, although his troops were far superior to the Coorg levies, the subjugation of the province was difficult and unprofitable, as the country was inaccessible, and the simple habits of the people promised little spoil. As commanding, however, the approach to Mysore from the west, the occupation of Coorg became a necessity, and both Haidar Ali and his son Tippu Sultán were fully aware of its importance. To the latter, the Coorg Wodiar, though a fugitive or a prisoner, was a dangerous enemy, as being the head of a hardy race of mountaineers, who could ill brook subjection, and might at any time be a thorn in his side. Accordingly, at the close of the first war with the British, when Sir John Kennaway was deputed to negotiate the treaty of Seringapatam in 1792, although the Mysore sovereign agreed to cede half his territories to the allies, he for some time stoutly resisted the surrender of Coorg, even although little or no revenue had been received from it for several years. His agents called it the gate of Seringapatam, and pleaded hard for its retention by their master, their persistence being so great that it was only cut short by a positive refusal of the Governor-General to abandon his faithful ally the Raja. During our long struggle with Tippu, the Coorg chief had uniformly aided us to the best of his power against the tyrant who had held his country in thraldom, and was rewarded for his steady allegiance. The province was, however, only valued at 8,000 Kántirai pagodas, out of a total of more than 13,000,000 ceded to the Company.

In fact, although no regular revenue had been collected from Coorg, it had constantly been harried by the Mysore troops and its Raja imprisoned, so that it seemed a worthless possession financially. Nor did matters improve much till the close of the second war with Tippu in 1799, when the gallant chief of the Coorgs, who had invariably defied his power and assisted his enemies, was at length able to breathe freely.

Dodda Víra Rájéndra or Víra Rájéndra the Great, was the Wodiar or Raja, who had struggled through the troublous time of the Mysore usurpers, having succeeded in 1780 his father Linga Ráj, who, however, left him nothing but a bare title. On his accession to the throne, after the fall of Seringapatam, he came into an impoverished inheritance, but as he conducted his affairs with prudence and economy for several years, he was soon enabled to display some of that pomp and circumstance which are so dear to Hindu rulers. The feudal tenure on which the Coorgs hold their lands, rendered it possible for their Raja to make a great display at the principal yearly festivals, when all his subjects attended in person and contributed to the *éclat* of his petty court. So, when the chief went to hunt elephants or bison, it was the custom for all the headmen of the Nád which he honoured with his presence to accompany him so long as he remained in their commune. The few Englishmen who held communication with the Raja, describe him as most solicitous to show them every attention, to amuse them by sporting excursions and fights between wild beasts, and to testify markedly his respect for the nation which had rescued him from the oppressor.

Unfortunately, a year or two before his death, Dodda Víra Rájéndra showed symptoms of insanity, and although he maintained his friendly relations with the British Government, he gave way to great excesses, and took away the lives of hundreds of his subjects during sudden bursts of rage and madness. During lucid intervals, his conduct was irreproachable, but the fits of insanity became more frequent and fearful, till they terminated in his death in 1809.

He had three illegitimate, but no legitimate sons, his legitimate offspring being confined to five daughters. Of these, one married the Raja of Sódé, or Sunda, in North Canara, a small territory which subsequently lapsed. The second, Dévammaji, was selected as successor to her father, and placed under the guardianship of her uncle Linga Ráj, younger brother of Dodda Víra Ráj, a crafty individual, who assumed a character for sanctity, and pretended to abjure all wish to ascend the throne. He soon, however, threw off his disguise, and in 1811, having placed his niece in confinement, usurped her authority.

Like his brother, Linga Rájéndra continued on good

terms with the British, but ruled his country in a tyrannical manner. He was not, however, devoid of ability, and directed his attention to the resources of the province, forming a valuable record of the revenue of each Nád in a kind of Domesday or Visitation Book, called a 'Shisht,' wherein is entered the holding of every farmer, with details of cultivated land, grazing land, and forest, the whole forming a valuable and tolerably accurate register of the landed tenures of Coorg.

Linga Ráj reigned from 1811 to 1820, when he was succeeded by his son Chikka Víra Rájéndra, or Víra Rájéndra the Less. This chief's reign of fourteen years was one long course of unmitigated tyranny, and it is a marvel that the Coorgs should have endured during that time the frightful cruelties which this bloodthirsty ruler perpetrated. He had, seemingly, not even the excuse of madness that condoned the wild bursts of passion which moved his uncle, but his jealous and suspicious disposition led him to murder in cold blood all who fell under his displeasure, or were fancied foes to him. Short shrift was given to those who incurred his wrath. In the dead of the night, the unhappy prisoners were taken out secretly through a postern of the palace, conducted to a thick jungle, and there decapitated, the corpses being thrown into a pit, previously dug for the purpose. His own relations were the chief victims, and it is confidently stated that the whole of these were murdered by his orders, except his own wives and children, and his sister Dévammaji, who fled to Mysore to avoid his persecution. All the descendants of his uncle Dodda Víra Rájéndra were ruthlessly killed, including women and children; and that the fidelity of this story may not be impugned, it may be stated that, only three years ago, a pit was discovered near the Naiknád palace, where were found the remains of some of the victims, those who executed them being present, to attest the truth of the horrid tale.

In a corner of the courtyard of the Raja's palace at Mérkára, is a rudely fashioned elephant of the size of life. It is said that the Raja used to take up a position in the balcony of the palace, armed with a rifle, and causing wretched prisoners to run across the yard from their place of confinement to the elephant, fire at them as they sped along, with the promise, however, of sparing their lives if they touched the elephant. As he was an excellent shot, the victims rarely succeeded in reaching the elephant unharmed.

In course of time, the Raja, forgetting all dictates of prudence, imprisoned and threatened the lives of British subjects, which necessitated the interference of the English Government. Being reminded of his obligations, and warned of the consequence of neglecting them, Chikka Víra Rájéndra cunningly denied all the charges against him, but secretly practised still greater cruelties. At last, in 1834, having insulted his own sister, she, with her husband, fled to Mysore, putting herself under the protection of the Resident at that Court. Her brother, warned too late of her flight, ordered an immediate pursuit, but this proving fruitless, he demanded her surrender from Mr. Casamaijor, an application which that officer properly refused compliance with.

The Raja then, despising all remonstrance, defied the British Government, and hostilities shortly after commenced. A feeble resistance was made to the English force, but it was clear that the Coorgs had little sympathy with their Raja, who, finding his position untenable, fled from Mérkára and took refuge at Naiknád, where he soon surrendered without a struggle. Before giving himself up, however, he wreaked his last bloody vengeance on those who had been his prisoners. Among those who then suffered was his minister, who was found hanging dead, though whether he was despatched by order of the Raja, or whether he had hung himself from fear of the consequences of having abetted his master in his cruelties, was never ascertained.

Chikka Víra Rájéndra was at once removed from Coorg, to the great delight of the people, and sent to Benares. After a residence there of some years, he proceeded to England, where he died. One of his daughters, who added the august name of Her Majesty to her heathenish indigenous appellation of Gauramma, married an English gentleman. Two other daughters married Sir Jang Bahádur of Nepal, but the younger was sent back in disgrace to the family residence at Benares. Although attempts have been from time to time made by members of the family, by sending emissaries, to keep up their connection with Coorg, their overtures have not met with any response.

As soon as the Raja was removed from the country, the Coorg people, without a dissentient voice, voted for the annexation of their territory to the British Crown, the province being one of the very few British possessions in India which has become such, not by conquest, but by the free consent of the population. Perhaps owing to this fact, the Government, to which they announced their adhesion in 1834, has, not without good reason, shown them constant indulgence, and an exceptional deference towards their feelings and prejudices. For instance, the slaughter of cattle in Coorg is, and is likely to remain, forbidden, so long as the people deprecate it, nor would it be prudent or just to ignore their feelings on the subject, in the face of a distinct promise given to them by Colonel Fraser at the time of annexation.

While they yielded implicit reverence and devotion to their chief, the Coorgs exacted complete submission to themselves within their own demesnes. The patriarchal system, under which they lived, vested the landed proprietors with great authority, and as slavery was rigidly enforced throughout Coorg, and each farmer had a considerable number of agrestic hinds on his land, undeviating submission to the head of the house was required.

The more substantial proprietors reside in strongly-built thatched houses, with an inner court-yard in the centre open to the sky, provision being made to carry off the heavy rainfall, which in Coorg often amounts to 120 inches in the year. Outer rooms are devoted to business and the reception of visitors, but the inner rooms are appropriated to the various members of the family, all of whom live under the same roof. The rooms are small, and have no outer windows, so that it is difficult to understand how sometimes sixty or eighty members of a family, comprising three or four generations, manage to reside together. Indeed, owing to the superfluous inmates, it has of late years been necessary to depart from the ancient usage, the juniors being sent to live elsewhere. But a short time ago, the custom of polyandry prevailed among the Coorgs, to which it was partly owing that the brothers of a family lived together. This practice is nearly extinct, however, and any reference to it is unpalatable. In most of the farms are to be seen guns, and bows and arrows, hung up on beams, and many proprietors can turn out twenty fighting men at least. Quantities of provisions are stored up between the rafters and the roof, while outside, grain and stock are kept, cattle, pigs, and fowls being tolerably abundant. Vegetables of various kinds, plantains, jack-fruit, oranges, &c., are grown close to the farm-house, and in the neighbourhood dwell the Holeyaru or labourers, who, from time immemorial, have lived on the estates of their Coorg masters.

The non-Coorg Hindus, as distinguished from the Coorgs, who are the lords of the soil, amount to 74,000 souls, comprising nearly three-quarters of the whole population. In this category are Holeyaru, Yerawas, Páleyas, Kurubaru, and various other low castes, the majority of whom are sons of the soil, and were serfs, till manumitted by the British Government. It is with difficulty that their former masters can retain their services now that planters pay them readily double wages, and many of the Yerawas, who are numerous in South Coorg, have emigrated to Wainád, leaving rice-fields uncultivated, or the crops standing unreaped, for want of hands. The Coorg landlord will not do the heavy work of planting and transplanting rice himself, exposure in the rainy season and toiling through thick moist mud being only endurable by one inured to hard labor.

In truth, in the time of the Coorg Rajas the number of serfs attached to each holding was specifically mentioned in the Sanads or grants issued by the State. These title-deeds were called Jamma Sanads, that is, birthright grants, from the Sanskrit 'Janam,' a birth; signifying a proprietary right inherent in the possessor, and inalienable from his family, so long as he complied with the conditions of his feudal tenure. The assessment is 10*s.* on 100 battis,[1] that is, about three acres, and is regarded as half the full assessment, the remission being made in consideration of feudal service, the conditions of which extend to military service in time of war, and police duties during peaceful times. A due proportion of grazing land, called Badiké, and of forest, called Báné, is attached to each Warg, or farm, and is specified in the grant, on receiving which a fee of 2*s.* is paid, the farmer getting a handful of the soil of the holding in confirmation of his right. He has further to make a payment to the State of 1*l.* per 100 battis on entering upon possession; the amount

[1] A batti of irrigated or wet land is dependent on the quantity of grain which will suffice to sow it, so that the extent comprised is not a standard superficial area, and varies greatly, according to the quality of the soil. On an average, 100 battis equal three acres.

being, however, payable in instalments, while the grant is unlimited in duration at the pleasure of the cultivator.

Only a few classes are permitted to hold land on the above easy terms, all the remaining farmers holding land on Ságu tenure (Kanarese, 'ságu,' to cultivate), at the full assessment of 1*l.* per 100 battis. Such farmers form no portion of the militia of the country. Indeed, the services of the Jamma ryots are now never required in a military capacity, while the obligation to carry arms, of course, does not extend beyond the limits of the Coorg province.

For many years after the annexation of the country to the British dominions, the Coorgs remained in their pristine state of simplicity, only known to the few European officials whom duty or curiosity led to visit this interesting alpine tract. Their knowledge of the outer world was absolutely *nihil*, as no Coorg ever left his native land. Their leisure hours were devoted to athletic sports, including hunting bison and beasts of prey, and to the great periodical festivals which hailed the advent of the rice crop, or implored a blessing from the goddess Kávéri, in whose honor a special feast is held in October.

Little is known of the faith anciently held by the Coorg mountaineers, but, as they bear a resemblance in many respects to the Nairs of Malabar, and as one of their greatest peculiarities is an aversion to leave their own country, it appears probable that they are aborigines of the soil. It is remarkable, however, that in many parts of the province we find traces of an earlier race, the remains being similar to those discovered on the Nílgiri mountains, and in various other parts of Southern India. Unfortunately, Coorg history, as already observed, does not extend further back than 250 years, so that it is impossible to assign any trustworthy period as the time of the construction of the monuments so frequently met with. Near Fraserpett, nearly 500 cairns were discovered within a limited space, and hundreds of others have been found elsewhere. Whether these erections were mortuary kistvaens, or dwelling-places, has not been decided satisfactorily, as neither bones nor ashes have been found, on the one hand, as an indication of their having been used as burial-places, nor, on the other, is there in them any trace of smoke on the roofs, pointing to their having been inhabited.

The cairns consist of a small chamber, enclosed between three or four stone slabs, with a large slab on the top, the rear stone being generally pierced by a round hole rather larger than a man's body. They vary much in size, being from six to ten feet long, and three to six feet wide, some of them being more than three feet deep. A few of the structures have double chambers, and many of them are surrounded by circles of stones, forming a kind of verandah, a few feet wide. In a few instances one sees large stones standing erect at the entrance of the edifice, but this is rare.

These monuments do not face in any particular direction, and are seen scattered about the side of a hill in close proximity to one another, which gives them the appearance of a burial-ground.

By the people they are called either 'Pándú póré,'

that is, 'Pándava stones,' after the mystic heroes of the Mahábhárat, or 'Pándara mané,' that is, 'pygmy houses,' both these phrases portending a dwelling-place. They are also sometimes called 'houses of the dead' in Kanarese, but it is evident that the Coorgs are wholly ignorant of their original use.

In some of the structures urns have been discovered, which are not without artistic merit, some of them being tripods, while a good many specimens of glazed pottery have occasionally been found. In one instance a human jaw was found, together with pieces of bones. Husks of grain, principally paddy, bits of iron, and fragments of necklaces, made up the list of treasure trove, but it can hardly be asserted that anything of special interest has been brought to light, while the kind of pottery found, though not resembling that now in use, appears to be too carefully modelled to be the handiwork of pre-historic times. One cannot, however, avoid the conclusion that the cairns are of a date prior to the present era, as the Coorgs do not employ such a mode of sepulture, nor have they any tradition on the subject.

There is very little of Hindu religious doctrine among the Coorgs, and they have a positive antipathy to Brahmans. Their ancient worship seems to have been given to the God 'Ayappa,' a sylvan deity, to whom some of the finest woods in the province were dedicated. These 'dévara kádu,' or divine woods, are often regarded by European planters with longing eyes, but are likely to remain for many a day untouched by the axe, as the Coorgs invariably demur to their occupation. It is said that the caste called Amma Kodagaru were originally the national priests, but more than 100 years ago they fell under the wrath of the deity, and lost their purity, and their priestly office in consequence, since which time Brahmans of the Siva faith have discharged all ceremonial functions for the Coorgs. Once in the year, the forests dedicated to Ayappa or Pan, are visited by the Coorgs (who, at other seasons, are afraid to enter them), when the Brahmans offer propitiatory sacrifice.

The few temples in the country are served by Brahman priests, that is, the buildings at the sources of the Kávéri and Lakshmantirtha rivers, and those at Mérkára, Víraréjpett, and Fraserpett. From the earliest times the sacred spring at Tala Kávéri was regarded with veneration by all Hindus, and Brahmans officiated at the yearly festivals in honour of the goddess. So also at the fountain head of the Lakshmantirtha. It is, therefore, difficult to reconcile the aversion of the Coorgs to the sacerdotal caste with the fact that Brahmans must always have exercised their priestly functions in the country, and particularly when it is remembered that the Coorgs themselves occasionally avail themselves of their services. In all official posts, however, the ascendency of Brahmans is resented by the Coorgs, partly perhaps from a consciousness of their superior intellect; and we accordingly rarely find one of the twice-born holding high employ in the province.

In many parts of Coorg reside priests who profess Saiva tenets. These persons are called Jangamas, and their habitations Maths. They wear a reddish-yellow dress, and are held in much respect by the people o

North Coorg, though few of them are learned men. Many of the maths however are prettily situated in parklike scenery, surrounded by clumps of stately trees, under the shade of which the hermits may be seen, seated with their disciples. There is apparently more superstition among the Lingáyats who dwell in the north of the province, adjoining Manjarábád, than among the real Coorgs. The former form marriage connections with their neighbours over the frontier, and have much in common with them, whereas the Coorg 'aristo' keeps to his own domain, and never sets foot on foreign land. All his joys and all his sorrows are to be found on his native hillside, and although in these days of excitement some curious Coorgs could not resist the temptation of making a journey to Bangalore, and thence on by rail to Madras, the mass of the people remain contentedly on their own farms, marry and die like their forefathers, and care not to seek their fortunes among strangers.

A miserable pittance in his own beloved country, coupled with the dignity of office, is a stronger inducement to a leading Coorg to serve the State than the most remunerative employment beyond the province. To the credit of the Coorg officials it may be said that, notwithstanding the meagre pay received by them from the Government, they discharge their duties worthily and without reproach. Their wretched stipends are, however, but a nominal addition to the income they derive from their lands, and the sweets of office consist, not in the emoluments, but solely in the status conferred on the holder.

The Coorgs are one of the few races in India who take a genuine pleasure in athletic sports. They are good at running and jumping, capital mountaineers, active sportsmen, and able to sustain severe and continued exertion. It is asserted that, since so many of the finest forests of the country have fallen before the axe of the planter, the scarcity of game which used to form a portion of their repast, has had an injurious effect upon the frame and constitution of the Coorgs, who now eat much less meat than they did formerly; but, if there be any truth in this statement, it does not appear that any immediate ill consequences have been produced, as they are at present an eminently hardy and sturdy race. Their stature is not ordinarily above the average, although some big men are found among them, but most of them have a gallant, erect bearing, and a demeanour which, though perfectly polite and respectful to superiors, is not without a proud consciousness of innate dignity. Many of them have handsome features, and, with the exception of the residents of South Coorg, they are much fairer than the people of Mysore or Canara. Their women are good housewives, and have considerable influence, but they are less remarkable for good looks than the men, as is often the case among mountaineers elsewhere.

The Coorg dress is simple and becoming. It consists of a blue surtout reaching down halfway between the knee and the ankle, and midway on the arms, and is folded to the left. A handsome thick red sash confines the waist, and in this is stuck a short dagger, of which the hilt and a portion of the sheath are covered with silver, a silver chain being also attached to it.

On the head is a thick white turban, generally with some gold lace in it, of a fashion quite different from the head-dress of the Mysore people, whose turban is less raised. When passing through the woods, the Coorg carries on his back a strong wood knife, double the size of his dagger, the handle being stuck in his girdle, while the broad blade lies naked on his back. Under the surtout is worn white clothing, and during the rains and cold season a rough blanket is in common use.

The principal amusement of the Coorgs consists in national dances, which are far more picturesque than those of the Gaddis of the Kángra hills. The first of them, called the 'Balakáta,' or Whisk-dance, is danced by a circle of fifty or a hundred persons, who, holding chauris or whisks in their hands, dance in slow measure round and round, waving the whisks, and singing a chant in honour of the goddess Kávéri, while a group of musicians sit in the centre, accompanying the performers with their voices and a drum, called a Duri, which resembles an hour-glass, being pinched in in the middle. In another dance, called the 'Kólháta' or Strike-stick dance, each Coorg holds in either hand a stick, something like those used in the game of 'la grace.' These he strikes alternately on those of his neighbour, as the ring revolves, all the dancers singing as they move. The effort is very pleasing, although the chanting is somewhat monotonous, and the songs not very interesting, even when intelligible. The action of the performers is, however, remarkably graceful and dignified.

Another curious amusement is called the 'Kól Peria,' or stick and shield play. In this game, two men enter the arena, each armed with a long swish in the right hand, and a shield, or a handful of whisks, in the left. After defying one another, and jumping about in a strange manner, they slash at their adversary's ankles and legs with the swish in their right hand. Hard blows arė dealt out, and if their fence is broken down, the performers' ankles tingle with the smarting pain produced, which is not unlike the effect of the Dominie's rod in an English school. If the men become excited, they slash at one another without mercy, and the bystanders are sometimes compelled to interfere; but the Coorgs are such good-natured fellows that this is rarely necessary, and the performers always embrace each other at the end of the play.

When this game is over, the lookers-on also take a share in the fun, dancing about vigorously with a kind of war-flourish, which culminates in the 'Tengina Pór,' or cocoa-nut fight, which consists in one strong individual taking a cocoa-nut, and trying to keep it against all comers, while there is a general scramble to snatch it from him, and carry it off. Whoever succeeds in keeping it, in defiance of the rest, breaks it on the ground, which brings the games to an end, but in the scuffle which takes place, some time elapses before this is accomplished.

On the recurrence of the great yearly feasts, several hundred Coorgs assemble together to perform these dances and feats of strength, and no doubt such exercises have had a beneficial effect on the people, both physically and morally. Every commune has its band, so to speak, that is, a collection of drums, horns, and pipes, the performers on which invariably turn out to meet high official authorities, preceding the little processions of the Coorg farmers, and accompanying great personages with music and chanting to the encampment ground prepared for them. When the traveller reaches the 'Kadang,' or ditch, which forms the boundary of the Nád, he finds, drawn up in a long row, all the headmen, who salute him, according to Coorg custom, by raising both hands to the forehead. They accompany him so long as he remains in their commune, and should he halt within it, they remain during the night in the farm-houses of the village in the precincts of which the halt is made, and proceed the next morning with the traveller to the boundary of the next nád.

The language spoken by the Coorgs appears to have an admixture of Tamil and Malayálim words, but the base of it is Kanarese. The latter tongue is used in all official documents, but in their domestic relations the Coorgs employ the Kodagu, or indigenous dialect.

The following sentences are taken from a small Coorg Grammar, published by Captain R. A. Cole, who, for some years, efficiently superintended the administration of Coorg.

English	Kodagu	Kanarese	Tamil	Telagu
What is the *name* of this village?	í úruda *peda* ennu?	í úrinå *hesaru* enu?	inda úrin *pér* enná?	i úri *péru* émi?
Is the *water* good?	*níru* nallada?	*níru* voḷḷédó?	*taṇṇir* nalladá?	*niḷḷu* manchivá?
What is your pay?	ningu sambala *echchaku*?	ninagé sambala *eshtu*?	unnoḍaya shambaḷam *enná*?	niyokka jitam *émi*?
I *must go* to bed.	nángu buḍḍavaku *póndu*	nánu malaguvadakke *hóga béku.*	nán paḍukka *póga véṇum.*	nénu pandu konédániki *póvalénu.*
Are *plantains* to be had here?	illi *báḷé paṇṇu* kittuwa?	illi *báḷé haṇṇugaḷu* shikyávó?	inge *váḷapaḷangaḷ* agappaḍumá?	ichhaṭa *araṭi pandlu* dorakuná?
Say if bearers and bullocks can be had at the next stage.	minyelaṭu mokámulu bóyealádu eṭṭádu kittuwa killeya ennu *eṇṇu.*	mundina majalugaḷalli bestarágali eṭṭugaḷágali shikkuvadillavó enu *héḷu.*	mun majalgaḷil bóyigalávadu mádugelávadu agappaḍumaṭṭádó énna *shollu.*	mundari majaluló bogilugáni eddulugáni chikkavó émi *cheppu.*

From the above few phrases the general resemblance of the construction of Kodagu to that of the other so-called Dravidian languages of Southern India will be apparent. Its pronunciation is peculiar, the letter u being pronounced somewhat like the same letter in French.

Missionary efforts have not been successful among the Coorgs, notwithstanding their simple and unsophisticated habits, but, till within the last few years, they have remained in a state of comparative ignorance. The whole of the native Christians in the district do not number much more than 1,000 souls, and these are almost exclusively Konkanis, or people from the coast, whose ancestors settled in Coorg during the troublous times of Haidar Ali and his son Tippu Sultán, who carried fire and sword into the low country. The latter, especially, by his brutal attempts to circumcise the Christian population of the territory overrun by him, was the cause of an extensive emigration of these unfortunate people into the high lands above the Ghâts.

Scarcely ten years have elapsed since the enlightenment of the Coorgs was really commenced by the establishment, under the auspices of the Basel Mission,[1] of a superior school at Mérkára, the capital of the district. It was subsequently taken under government management, and, thanks to the intelligent and praiseworthy superintendence of the Principal, has made fair progress; but the prejudices of the chief Coorgs are still strong, and it is, perhaps, too much to expect that

[1] One of these missionaries, the Rev. Mr. Mögling, published some years ago an interesting little book on Coorg.

they should abandon their old ways till the present generation of grey-beards has passed away, and a new one has sprung up, thoroughly permeated with the knowledge acquired by a superior education. A proposal to establish a boarding-school for Coorg boys and girls at first met with warm support from the people, and subscriptions flowed in freely, but the conservative headmen took alarm at the possible tendency of the education of their children away from home, and the project has hitherto proved less successful than it deserved to be. At the same time it may be observed that a fair measure of success has been attained in forming schools in the various communes into which the district is divided.

If the progress of enlightenment among the Coorgs has been slower than could be desired, their material progress has been remarkable. This is mainly owing to the extensive operations of the coffee-planters, who, some fifteen years ago, began to colonise the country, the splendid forests in which promised a rich reward to the enterprising settler. In truth, nothing can be finer than a Coorg hill side, covered with a luxuriant growth of stately trees, including the splendid spars of the kúvé mara or poon, the lofty nandi and wild jack, the sweet-scented champaka, blackwood, ebony, and many others.

Shorn as the province is of many of its woods, the forests now produce 10,000*l.* yearly, including realisations from the sale of sandal-wood, which flourishes in the eastern divisions. All along the western slopes of the Ghát range, where the climate is too humid to admit of planting operations, and in the Dévara Kádu, or sacred forests, trees are to be seen which, for height, size, luxuriant foliage, and brilliant tints, can scarcely be surpassed.

On the crest of the Gháts flourish cardamoms, called in Kanarese 'Yálakki,' of a superior kind. They grow in the thickest jungles, where there is ample shade and moisture, the forests being leased out for a term of years. The ordinary mode of obtaining the spice is to fell one of the giant trees which grow on the hill sides, when, after a time, the cardamom plant makes its appearance, but it may be cultivated apparently, with a fair measure of success, without resorting to this wasteful mode of securing its spontaneous growth. The picking of the spice entails much exposure to inclement weather, and is not unattended with risk, as snakes are extremely fond of cardamoms. A useful little manual on the subject of cultivating them has been published by Mr. E. Ludlow, of the Forest department.

As in Mysore, sandal-wood was in Coorg a royal monopoly, and still remains so, the quality of the wood being scarcely inferior to that of the adjoining province. The tree is taken up with the roots, and costs, including carriage and labor, about fourteen shillings the kandi of 560 lbs., the average selling price being 8*l.* 12*s.*, that is, 1*l.* for 65 lbs. of wood, the Mysore rate being 1*l.* for 62 lbs. The price, however, varies every year according to the briskness of the demand at Bombay, where the wood is not only required for local purposes, such as funeral pyres and other religious ceremonies, but whence it is also shipped in large quantities to

China. The material for most of the beautiful carvings in sandal-wood, sent from Bombay and China to England, comes from Coorg or Mysore, the latter province deriving a large revenue from this valuable article. In Coorg the amount received is between 4,000*l.* and 5,000*l.* on 528 kandis of wood. In Mysore the quantity sold in 1869-70 was 2,354 kandis, and the amount received 19,300*l.*, or 8*l.* 4*s.* a kandi, the cost of collection averaging, however, nearly 1*l.* a kandi.

Sandal-wood is found growing in the vicinity of, but not actually in, a forest country, and appears to be a very sensitive tree, requiring a particular climate to bring it to perfection. It is found sparsely in the eastern parts of Mysore, but flourishes best near the western hills, growing in hedgerows and singly, apart from other trees. Attempts have often been made to rear it from both plants and seed, but without success, owing, probably, to a want of knowledge of its apparently capricious nature.

It is collected either by the forest officers themselves, or by contract, and is stored in depôts, after being prepared, and sorted according to the fineness of the wood, which is narrowly scrutinised by the dealers who frequent the half-yearly sales. It is ranged in several classes, and every portion of the wood is disposed of, including logs, roots, chips, and powder. From the chips a strong oil is extracted, which, to the uninitiated, resembles atar of roses, while the powder is used for domestic and religious purposes. Most of the logs and roots find their way to Bombay.

From the time when Europeans began to settle in

the district to plant coffee, the forests, with which the country was covered, began to acquire a new value. But, at first, any applicant received permission to commence operations in woods not claimed by private individuals, or regarded as sacred forests. Very little trouble was taken about securing proper grants, permission to cultivate coffee on payment of the government excise being deemed sufficient. As years went on, the number of planters increased greatly, large sums were laid out in clearing, planting, and establishments, and the estates began to acquire a value in the market. As soon as the question arose of transferring properties from one person to another, the simple permission to cultivate appeared insufficient. In the next place, those who had expended large sums on their estates, and anticipated bumper crops, complained, with some reason, that the excise duty, though only sixpence on a maund of 28 lbs., pressed unduly on capital and industry. It is true that the excise was only 5 per cent. on the value of the crop, and that it was self-adjusting in regard to the yearly out-turn, but the best estates paid most and the worst least. The latter belonged chiefly to natives, who took little or no trouble about the cultivation of coffee, but retained many of the finest woods. A sliding-scale duty, like the excise, was in consonance with their ideas, and they desired no change.

In compliance with the request of all the influential European planters of the province, an acreage was substituted for the excise, title-deeds being at the same time given to them, instead of the permission to cultivate, which previously constituted their only grant. The terms prescribed seemed fair enough, the forests being given free of assessment for four years, so as to admit of all the preliminary operations of clearing and planting being carried out before any demand was made on the part of Government. From the fifth to the ninth year, the rate fixed was two shillings an acre, and after the ninth year, four shillings an acre, a certain deduction being made for unculturable grass land.

As the above change necessitated a measurement of each estate, in order to ascertain its area, a survey was commenced, and is still in progress, but the difficult nature of the country has interposed serious obstacles to its rapid advancement, and, in the case of unsurveyed estates, it has been necessary to adopt the rough estimate of area given in the cultivation permit, as the basis of intermediate assessment.

Then a difficulty arose about the rights of the Coorgs holding on Jamma tenure to cultivate coffee in the woods attached to their farms, free of assessment. This was compromised by allowing them a certain number of acres free, and assessing the rest, on the ground that they previously paid the excise.

Further intricate questions started up about the acreage on cardamom forests leased for a term of years, in which coffee had been grown instead of, or in addition to, cardamoms.

When the knotty points which presented themselves had been disposed of more or less satisfactorily, the Hindu cycle began to draw to a close, and, verifying the predictions of the Brahman soothsayers, one year after another of drought came to mar the prospects of the planters. Large sums had been spent, heavy loans raised, and no expense spared to open the way to fortune, some planters having even undertaken the felling of bamboo jungle in order to realise a more speedy return for their outlay.

The dry seasons brought with them that most destructive of insects, the borer beetle, together with the grubs of moths, which committed great havoc among the coffee trees. It was supposed by many persons, and particularly by the Coorgs, that the planters had erred in felling all the jungle on their estates, and that this was the cause of the drought, the rainclouds floating away eastward without discharging their contents, owing to the absence of the trees which formerly arrested them. Others said that the Brahmans were quite right, and that the periodical drought at the close of a cycle was a well-ascertained fact, based on the experience of ages.

Whatever the truth may be, it is certain that the continued dry seasons proved a heavy blow and a great discouragement to the planters, who had toiled for many years and expended all their resources, to be foiled just when the shower of gold appeared likely to descend upon them. The European colonist is, however, a resolute and persevering individual, and if, as is most probable, a series of propitious seasons prevails, and coffee cultivation elsewhere does not prove too formidable a rival, there is no reason why the long expected fortunes should not be made. It would be a great misfortune should Coorg lose one of the main elements of its prosperity,[1] for not only is a considerable portion of its revenue now derived from coffee, but its colonization by Europeans has imparted a new stimulus to the people of the country.

Although causes of collision between the planters and the Coorgs do from time to time arise, it may be affirmed that, in the main, good feeling subsists between them. In one respect, it is to be feared that contact with Europeans has had a prejudicial effect upon these mountaineers, and that is that the love for strong liquors appears to have increased among them. It has been checked as far as possible by imposing the highest still-head duty that spirits will bear before they leave the distilleries, and a limit has been put upon the number of retail shops, but, notwithstanding, drinking has spread. Some excuse may, however, be made in favor of the Coorgs, founded on the humidity of the climate.

The towns of the province offer little worthy of notice. The tombs of the Coorg Rajas at Mérkára are handsome buildings, but are rather of a Musalmán than a Hindu type. The palace in the first is a huge structure, surrounded by a flagged basement, and is an exaggerated copy of a Coorg house, built to resist the monsoon storms, and, therefore, very substantial, but having no pretension to architectural beauty. The panorama presented to view from a place of public resort near the fort, called the Raja's seat, is singularly fine, as it comprises a great portion of the splendid mountain range which encompasses Coorg.

[1] The coffee area is 80,000 acres, and the exports aggregate between 3,000 and 4,000 tons yearly, which may be valued at £150,000.

The palaces at Haleri and Naiknád are not deserving of the name, being in no way remarkable.

Perhaps the greatest panegyric which can be pronounced upon the Coorgs is that, owing to their staunch and approved loyalty, they were exempted from the provisions of the Disarming Act, a recognition of their good service during the insurrection in Canara, which they always refer to with pride and pleasure. Their loyalty was, in a great measure, owing to the confidence which they felt in the European officer who, at the time, superintended the affairs of the province. Few parts of India, indeed, have been more fortunate in this respect than Coorg, which has had many superintendents who have gained the esteem and affection of the people.

THE PANJAB

BEFORE ANNEXATION.

THE soil of India has ever been fruitful of adventurers, who have raised themselves to prominence, founding dynasties, which the folly or weakness of their successors annihilated in the course of a few generations.

Foremost among those who, in modern times, achieved such a success were Sivají, the daring but unscrupulous head of the Mahratta race; Haidar Ali, the ablest and most skilful native general whom British troops ever encountered in India; and Ranjít Singh, the one-eyed warrior of the Panjáb, who, while overrunning and conquering many provinces north of the river Satlaj, sedulously maintained friendly relations with the English.

All these chiefs were illiterate. It is doubtful whether Sivají could sign his name. Haidar Ali used as his mark the letter 'H' in Persian reversed. Ranjít Singh, again, scrawled 'Sahí' or 'signed,' in Gurumukhi characters, on grants of land, but, in his correspondence, contented himself with attaching a small seal, with his name on it, as his attestation to letters.

The sovereignty founded by Sivají was expanded by

the Pandits Pradhán, commonly known as the Péshwas,[1] who were at first merely ministers of the Satára Rajas, till the Mahratta hordes threatened to usurp the paramount power in India. The attempts made by the Emperor Aurangzéb to check the progress of Sivají were but partially successful, and, after his death, the Mahrattas rapidly extended their conquests, founding the States of Nágpur and Tanjore, now lapsed, the still flourishing houses of Baróda, Gwalior, Indore, Kolhápur, and Sáwantwári, as well as a principality in Bundélkhand, where the Banda, Jhánsi, and Jalaun families held large possessions, now incorporated with British territory.

The Mahratta confederacy owed its ascendancy alike to the daring and prowess of its military chiefs, and to the astute policy of the Péshwas, who were seconded by able men like Bálàji Janárdan, commonly called Náná Farnavís, an uncompromising opponent of the English. To Sivají, however, is due the honor of raising from comparative obscurity the Mahratta race, and of founding an empire, of which the branches still extant contain a population of nearly six millions, with a revenue of more than two millions sterling.

Sivají died in 1680, and when, after a troubled interval, his grandson Sáhújí mounted the throne as Raja of Satára, the Péshwa Bálájí Biswanáth laid the foundations of that supremacy of the ministers which made the Rajas who succeeded puppets and captives

[1] The word 'Péshwa' corresponds closely with the English word Premier, signifying foremost or first. Pandit Pradhán means the chief Pandit or learned man.

in their hands. On the dethronement, in 1817, of the treacherous Péshwa Bají Rao, the rightful sovereign was restored, but, after a few uneventful successions, the dynasty became extinct in 1848. The last Raja, Sháhjí, adopted an heir, but this act was disallowed by the British Government, and the State lapsed, not without much protest and discussion.

Haidar Ali's ancestors came from the Panjáb, while his mother was of Arab descent, to which circumtrances may perhaps be attributed the energy and bravery which eminently distinguished him. His long rule of twenty years was signalised by the subjugation of the whole of the present Kingdom of Mysore, and of considerable portions of provinces to the east, west, and south of that country, now comprised in the Madras Presidency. He was a resolute and skilful commander, a good soldier, and a wary tactician, who, though he fought bravely against the British Government and its troops, showed a frank wish for friendship, which the ruling policy at Madras of that period was incapable of appreciating at its proper value.

The fatuity and obstinacy of his son, Tippu Sultán, shattered the fabric constructed by him, and the short-lived dynasty expired with the fall of Seringapatam, only thirty-eight years from the time when Haidar Ali first seized the reins of power. Short as was the rule of himself and his son, it was a brilliant one, and had it not been for the masterly operations of Lord Cornwallis in 1791–92, and the subsequent war entered on by the directions of the 'glorious little man,' Lord Wellesley, the Mysore sovereigns would probably have made themselves masters of all Southern India. The capture of Seringapatam, however, in 1799, and the death of Tippu Sultán, extinguished finally all the hopes of the followers of Islám that their faith would recover its former supremacy in Hindusthán.

Ranjít Singh was possessed of most of the qualities which fit men to rule, and although he was never, like Sivají, regarded by the Hindus as an incarnation of the deity, he succeeded during his lifetime in establishing for himself an almost unbounded influence over the Sikh nation. The race of Játs to which he belonged, and which is found in many parts of Northern India, is brave and industrious, sturdy in fight, and skilled in agriculture. To this caste belong the majority of Sikhs, and while part of a family serve as soldiers, the rest remain at home, tilling the ancestral lands. Indeed, some of the bravest of the Hindu races are careful cultivators, while those who leave their fields to be ploughed by the lower castes have rarely a reputation for bravery. Ranjít Singh rose to power at a time when the Móghal star was beginning to fade away, and when the Panjáb, the highway of invaders of India, had, since the irruption of Ahmad Sháh, become a prey to anarchy.

In its origin, the faith taught by Guru Nának, the first of the Sikh saints, was an ascetical deism, shorn of many of the superstitions of Brahminical belief; but as his teaching and that of his successors attracted many followers, the sect caused alarm to the Musalmán authorities, who attempted, with the usual result in such cases, to suppress it by persecution. The vitality which it thus gained, received a further stimulus by the murder of Tégh Bahádur, the ninth king, as the Sikhs style their teachers, and by the cruel massacre at Sirhind of two of the sons of Guru Góvind Singh, the tenth and last teacher, who, before he died in the Dekkan of a broken heart, inflamed the minds of his followers to a determined and prolonged resistance to the despotic Moghal rule.

The thirst for vengeance thus evoked was gratified by the sack of Sirhind; but the Sikh nation, though all its military qualities had been called into action, was split up into numerous bands, which rallied under the standards of certain celebrated leaders who had little in common. These confederacies, or Misals, as they were called, generally took their names from the homestead or the profession of their chiefs, as, for instance, the Bhangí, the Singhpuria, the Alhuwália, &c., and among the least important was that called the Sukarchakia, to which belonged Charat Singh, grandfather of Ranjít Singh.

In Cunningham's excellent history of the Sikhs will be found a full and accurate account of the rise and progress of Ranjít Singh, and of the history of his dynasty till the Satlaj campaign. During the course of the construction and consolidation of his rule, the strategy of Ranjít Singh and the bravery of his troops were often severely taxed. No less than three attacks were made, at different times, on Multán, whose nawab, Muzaffar Khán, offered a desperate resistance, being finally slain in the breach with five of his sons. On the first invasion of Kashmír, the Sikh army was betrayed by the Chief of Rájáuri, and decoyed into the snow, from which, as narrated by an old greybeard, Sirdar Gurmukh Singh Lambá, nicknamed 'Piyálchí,' or 'the Toper,' it had to fight its way back, sword in one hand and staff in the other. The second invasion was, however, more successful, and Ranjít Singh wreaked his vengeance on the Rájáuri Rájá by carrying him off to Lahore in a cage. The Afgháns for many years waged a constant warfare against the aggressions of the Sikhs, who, owing to the difficult nature of the country, and the martial qualities of the Trans-Indus races, were unable, except, perhaps, at Pesháwar, to establish on the further side of the river a settled government, generally confining their efforts to a yearly extortion of tribute, or, at best, forming standing camps in the enemy's country.

Although much resistance was encountered by Ranjít Singh in various parts of the Panjáb from the hostile Musalman races, his rule was gladly welcomed by the Hindu population, and the want of union, and the mutual distrust among his opponents, gave him strength and confidence. Indeed, the name of Afghán or Pathán, and of Kashmírí, is considered in the north of India as synonymous with treachery and double-dealing, as is shown in the Persian distich:

> Agar khalal mardán uftad, az ínán na bagírí : yakam Pathán, duyam Kambóh, seyam badzát Kashmírí.
>
> If mankind should be coming to an end, do not select (for its restoration) first the Pathán, secondly the Kambóh, thirdly the rascally Kashmírí.

implying that the races named are bad stocks for reproducing the human family. Even now, the various clans of the Afgháns appear to be ever at variance with one another, tribe against tribe, family against family, and house against house, the demon of discord showing himself in bloody feuds and murders, while the strange spectacle is seen of stalwart borderers fighting desperately under the English colors against their own countrymen. All the Afghán race are brave individually, and a few tribes may be loyal, but loyalty to a foreign government is liable to be tarnished by accidents caused by avarice or religious impulses, and no man can foretell the future of the wild country of Afghánistán.

When the Panjáb was annexed, there can be little doubt that we succeeded to an awkward inheritance in the possession of the Trans-Indus frontier, and that its retention is both costly and hazardous; but, on the other hand, its abandonment might be equally fraught with danger. Those who advocate its retention observe that we must keep what was virtually an integral part of Ranjít Singh's territories, and that the value of the Pesháwar and Kóhát districts, which may be assumed at 80,000*l.* yearly, fully justifies this course on mere financial grounds; while the adjacent tract of the Déraját, which also lies beyond the Indus, and which yields a revenue of 130,000*l.*, must also be given up if the northern districts are surrendered. Further, it is alleged that the possession of the frontier up to the Khaibar, and the passes of the Suláimán mountains, gives us a vantage ground which we should lose if we retired beyond the Indus; and that we are now able to meet successfully the inroads of aggressors, to pursue them into their hills, and to punish them not only on their own soil, but by cutting off their trading connection with the people of our territory. It is said, again, that the disunion among the several Afghán tribes, and the facility with which we can subsidise those who seek our friendship, would enable us to cope successfully with any force of invaders who might rally against us. Moreover, the constant hill warfare in which our frontier force has been engaged, has been invaluable in keeping the troops up to the highest point of discipline and daring. A mountain range is, it is asserted, a far better boundary than a river, as, in the one case, there is frequently antagonism between the tribes on either side of the hills; while, in the case of a river, the people on both its banks are knit together by an identity of language and manners, and by family alliances which constitute the closest of social relations. Finally, great stress is laid on the damage to our prestige which a withdrawal behind the Indus would cause throughout Hindusthán.

The opponents of these conclusions, on the other hand, call attention to the fact that the British Government must look beyond Afghánistán for its invaders, and that Russia is the real power to be feared, as she might either pour in her own troops, through the Afghán country, to the borders of India, or indirectly incite the Afgháns, by lavish rewards or the promise of territory, to combine against us. If the passes were once occupied, we should, it is said, have great difficulty in maintaining our position; and if we fell back beyond the Indus, the most disastrous results might ensue, the river being, at certain seasons—which the enemy would certainly select for its operations—extremely difficult to cross, owing to its rapidity; while this very difficulty would constitute the security of a Cis-Indus frontier. Again, the climate of the Pesháwar valley is notoriously unhealthy, and greatly feared by our European troops; while the native regiments raised in Hindusthán detest the country, notwithstanding the cheapness of grain in it. To the sad expenditure of valuable English lives, must be added the outlay on the many hill forts which line the frontier. There is little connection, moreover, it is said, between the people of the Panjáb proper and the Pathán tribes—the Musalmáns of the former being either Awáns, or of other races, who are at feud with the residents of the Trans-Indus country. In respect to the effect on our prestige, it is asserted that a voluntary withdrawal in a time of peace, on the grounds partially stated above, would be a far less risk to run than a forced abandonment of our position in the face of a foe—a step which would inevitably create widespread alarm, and sow the seeds of serious disaffection throughout the whole continent of India.

Such were a few of the arguments adduced on either side when the question was mooted in the time of the late Lord Canning, and they appeared to be so equally balanced that the subject was dropped after the mutiny, and the *status quo* accepted as a practicable, though not very satisfactory solution.

Kashmír was the only portion of Ranjít Singh's dominions which remained eventually under native rule.

It was sold to Raja Guláb Singh on the termination of the Satlaj campaign of 1845-46 for 750,000*l.*, or four years' assumed revenue, and the expediency of this transaction has since frequently been called in question by Indian journalists, the bargain being denounced as a needless sacrifice of a paradise which would have been a suitable tract for European colonization. Irrespectively, however, of the circumstance that at the close of the war the subjugation of this outlying province would have been an arduous task in the hot season, and with our army in a weakened state from its recent encounters with the Sikh soldiery, it may be doubted whether its possession would not have entailed great and unforeseen expenditure.

The revenue of Jammu is about 275,000*l.*, and of Kashmír about 250,000*l.*, the former province being a separate possession, though both are under the rule of Maharaja Ranbír Singh, son of Guláb Singh, whose family were Dógra Rájputs of the Jammu territory. The land revenue of the thirty-six pergannahs, or subdivisions which comprise Kashmír, is at present probably not more than 150,000*l.*, and of the remaining 100,000*l.*, about 40,000*l.* are yielded by the duty on shawls, other taxes, such as customs, duty on timber, taxes on shops, and a variety of small imposts, making up the balance. The land tax is heavy, half the gross produce being commonly taken from the cultivator; and much of the valley is said to lie waste, notwithstanding its intrinsic fertility, the people having deserted their lands, and fled over the border. But the valley of Kashmír is a very small strip of land, surrounded on every side by hills, which, to the north, are comparatively barren, yielding little revenue.

As one approaches the northern confines of the province, the people are turbulent, and a constant source of anxiety. When the writer was in Kashmír, the people of Chilás had invaded Hasóra, and carried off the inhabitants into captivity. Guláb Singh, on learning intelligence of this inroad into his territory, organised with great energy an expedition, which, after extraordinary fatigue, and a loss, it is asserted, of several thousand coolies, attacked the stronghold of the lawless mountaineers. After several months' unsuccessful siege, the tank which afforded a supply of water to the garrison was accidentally exploded, and the besieged were compelled to capitulate. No sooner were the Maharaja's outposts admitted than they seized the gateway, and let in the whole army, when an indiscriminate slaughter of the Chilásis took place. The chiefs were made prisoners, and the fort was razed to the ground. Guláb Singh was very proud of this achievement, as it is said that Chilás had defied the Emperor Akbar. In extending his sway over Tibet, Gilgit, and the north, the old chief encountered much opposition, but the outlay entailed was comparatively small, as the soldiers only received four shillings a month wages, being authorised to levy a 'quête' on the people in whose district they were quartered when they wanted fuel, fodder, and other necessaries.

To the British Government such an unruly and troublesome frontier would be an endless cause of expenditure, which would greatly counterbalance the possession of Kashmír. In any case, so long as the sovereign remains faithful to our Government, and there is no valid ground for questioning the loyalty either of Guláb Singh or of the present Maharaja, we are bound by our own acts, and have no right to cast a longing eye on the famous valley. During the Panjáb campaign of 1848–49, Guláb Singh's conduct was challenged, mainly, probably, because he had formerly been on intimate terms with some of the leading rebels; but beyond a desire to keep well with both sides, no imputation against his proceedings could be substantiated.

That Englishmen should be popular with the Maharaja cannot be expected. The yearly visitants pry into the details of the administration, and proclaim in all the papers of India the griefs and misery of the people, which is naturally very unpalatable to their ruler. Moreover, before the appointment of a Resident at Srínagar, during the season when the valley is frequented by Europeans, the Maharaja had just cause for complaining of the conduct of some of his visitors. In one instance all the prisoners were let out of jail by an angry officer, whose servant had been confined on some trivial charge, while in another case one of the soldiers died, it was said, from the effects of a blow on the head administered to him by a second officer. It is well known that no Oriental sovereign likes his territory to be overrun by strangers, his rule to be criticised, and his proceedings animadverted on; and we must bear in mind the reply given by one potentate to an Englishman who asked him why he did not make a good road through his country up to his capital, 'What! for your

Government to march its troops along with ease to take it?' answered he.

Guláb Singh was rapacious and penurious, but, though illiterate, he had great natural capacity, and a wonderfully retentive memory. He amassed large sums of money, the popular belief being that all his vast treasures were stored in the fort of Riyási, in the Jammu territory, and that the people who conveyed them thither disappeared, and were never heard of afterwards. The crime of shedding the blood of cattle was severely punished by him, as an orthodox Hindu ruler, and he is said, when Governor of Hazára, to have flayed Musálmáns alive for this offence.

The Kashmíris are a cowardly, lying race, but of a happy temperament, and always civil and obliging; while the women are certainly beautiful, and, when decked out for show at their festivals, present a striking appearance. Lahore, Amritsar, and other great cities of Northern India abound in Kashmírí women, not of the best repute, while the ranks of native officials number hundreds of Brahmans, whose forefathers emigrated from the valley, and who, for ability and astuteness, are worthy rivals of the Mahrattas of Bombay, or the three-marked Brahmans of Southern India. The majority of the population are, however, Musalmáns, and although their ancestors were forcibly converted in the time of the Delhi emperors, the present generation appears perfectly content with its faith. It appears strange to those who have seen this charming country in its spring-tide of flowers, or in its glorious summer, when the snow on its hill tops is kissed away by the hot beams of the sun, to return again on the cold approach of night, or again in its rich autumnal profusion of various fruits, that the people should have tamely succumbed to successive invaders, but such seems to have been the fate of most of the hill races between Hazára and Nepál. The fiery Gurkhas of the latter territory overran like a swarm of ants the Kamáon and Simlá districts, plundering and ejecting the Rájput chiefs, till their progress was arrested by the strong hand of the British Government. In fact the hill tribes were no match for the dwellers in the plains, and the Sikhs, in the time of Mahárájá Shér Singh, resisted with success the combined efforts of the Afghán races on the frontier, though these were urged on by the strongest incentives of religious zeal and patriotic opposition to a hated foe. The success of the Khálsá army was no doubt in great measure due to that discipline which they had acquired under the skilful French generals whom Ranjít Singh had entertained in his services.

The following schedule of the income of Kashmir from various sources, irrespectively of that derived from land, is curious:

	Chilki Rupees.
Tax on shawls	7,17,200
" Pashmína	50,800
" worked borders	9,100
" shopkeepers	1,53,200
Customs	1,60,700
Mint	50,700
Duty on wool and Pashmína	10,200
Tax on sugar manufacturers	9,400
" Timber	93,400
Duty on saffron	22,000
" silk	12,800
Carried forward	12,89,500

	Chilki Rupees.
Brought forward .	12,89,500
Duty on charas[1]	10,000
„ tobacco	17,700
Tax on sheep	45,600
„ buffaloes	11,000
„ floating gardens	18,400
„ Singhára nuts	40,000
„ produce of islands.	11,700
Income of Kótwalí	7,600
„ courts of justice and stamps . .	16,400
„ other courts	4,500
Tax on houses let on hire	8,500
Income of Government gardens.	2,200
Duty on lime	2,500
Tax on sellers of wild fowl	500
Tribute from petty Rajas	74,000
Income of newly-acquired territory	17,000
„ temples and Vazírs' dues	27,000
Basant, Dashara, Naoroz festivals	48,000
Miscellaneous	15,000
Total Chilki rupees . . .	16,67,100
Equal to Company rupees . .	10,41,938
Equal to	£104,193

The above return was made out several years ago, but is probably fairly accurate at the present time, and, excepting a few items, the taxation does not appear to be particularly oppressive. A fee was formerly, and is perhaps still, levied on marriages, from which, however, the privileged classes were exempted. This is a legitimate source of revenue, which might with advantage be raised in our own territory, as it is readily paid by the people, who are always lavish in their outlay on such occasions. We have indeed so far adopted this form of taxation, that in some provinces of British India a registration fee is demanded for entering domestic occurrences.

[1] An intoxicating drug.

If a more equitable system of collecting the land revenue is introduced, there is no apparent reason why Kashmír should not regain its pristine prosperity, and the increase of cultivation which would follow on low assessments with long leases would not only bring in a larger income, but admit of the abolition of some minor items of taxation which are objectionable. It is to be hoped that the present Maharaja and his successors will, in regard to fiscal administration and judicial proceedings, endeavour to imitate the excellent example set by Hyderabad, Mysore, and Travancore among the native states of India.

During the winter season, the Bárámulla Pass is the only outlet from Kashmír which is open for traffic, and the moment one passes the gorge, which, tradition says, was cleft out of the mountain by the Muni Kasiapa to afford a passage to the long pent-up waters of the lake which filled the valley, the character of the scenery suddenly changes. The Jhilam is no longer a quiet sluggish stream, flowing lazily along through a level verdant country, but a fierce hill-torrent, pouring impetuously down over a rocky bed, and bounding along a rugged mountain side, round which winds a narrow path for travellers.

A march of a few days takes one to the borders of Hazára, where, thanks to the influence which his benevolent administration obtained for him, Major James Abbot was enabled to hold his own throughout the rising in the Panjab in 1848-49, when all the European officers located elsewhere were compelled to abandon their stations. This gallant and distinguished officer protected the mountaineers from the oppression of the Sikh functionaries, and was so much beloved that the people used to point out the very place where he had sat down when he visited their several villages.

The day seems to have passed away when the personal influence of a single Englishman was a tower of strength to his government, and it may be that the progress of enlightenment and civilisation since the great mutiny of 1857 makes it no longer essential; but if those great administrators Sir Thomas Munro and Sir John Malcolm could rise from their graves, and see how codes and regulations, with their attendant routine, have cramped and weakened the power for good of those placed in authority, they would probably smile with compassionate contempt. As it was said of the Muscovites, 'grattez le Russe, et vous trouverez le Tatare,' so it is asserted by many that the superficial gloss which modern education has given to the Indian mind would at any moment be rubbed off under the pressure of religious fanaticism or political bias, and that the British Government would then find an enemy acquainted with its weak points, and just sufficiently educated to feel the bitterness of being subject to the sway of foreigners. Doubtless it is becoming every day more difficult for local officers to maintain their influence, as the people progress in knowledge, while their comparative ignorance of the language and habits of those among whom they dwell places them at a disadvantage with educated natives, equally conversant with the modes of thought and action of their own countrymen and of Europeans. Under such circumstances they must rely solely on their own integrity and honesty of purpose, and on those high principles which are inculcated by the Christian faith.

The Hazára district borders on classic ground, for on the opposite side of the river Indus towers up the Mahában mountain, believed to be the 'Aornos' of Arrian, which the troops of Alexander the Great surmounted with such labor and difficulty, and which in our own day was the haunt of fanatical Musalmáns whom the Pesháwar force pursued to their fastnesses at Sitána and severely punished. Thirteen centuries passed away from the epoch of the Macedonian conqueror till the invasion of Mahmúd of Ghazni, and more than two thousand have elapsed up to the present time, but the fidelity of the account of the Greek historian can still be established, notwithstanding the ages that have since run their course.

Indeed, the exact locality of the combat with Porus may fairly be insisted on, owing to two natural features of the country which remain unchanged. The first is the existence of a promontory, 'akra,' round three sides of which, Arrian says, the river (Jhilam) winds. This is the case at Mangala, on which there is at present a fort, belonging to the Kashmír ruler, while there is no other place on the river, from the point where it emerges from the hills, which corresponds with Arrian's description.[1] Again, the historian mentions the fact that a short dis-

[1] Some antiquarians suppose that Dárápur, lower down the river, was the scene of the contest, but, although subsequent invaders of India frequently took the route through the so-called Ghórigalla Pass which leads to Dárápur, the promontory at that place does not answer to Arrian's description.

tance above the scene of battle there were islands in the river, on which grew trees. Such islands with trees on them are still to be seen at Sukhchainpur, a few miles above the town of Jhilam, and between it and Mangala. Of the towns said to have been founded by Alexander the Great on the Hydaspes or Jhilam, one, Boukephala, was presumably built on a high mound close to the present town of Jhilam, and the other, Nikaia, on the opposite bank, the former having been designed to perpetuate the memory of the famous charger Bucephalus, and the other as a record of the victory gained over Porus. In the mound referred to many coins and ancient remains have been found, and it is possible that, were it completely excavated, some trace might be found of the burial-place of the conqueror's steed.

Owing to our ignorance of the history of the Panjáb between the expedition of the Greeks and the first invasions of the Musalmáns, it is impossible to fill up the intervening gap with any precision, but it is not impossible that Porus was a Rájput of the Powár or Pramára tribe, which belonged to the Raghuvansi stock of the Solar race, and came originally from Ayódhia or Oudh, whence its members spread themselves over many parts of Hindusthán. Rájputs, both of the Solar and the Lunar dynasty, are found in great numbers to this day in the Simlá and Kángra Hills, the small dynasties which they founded centuries ago being for the most part still extant. Foremost among these was, however, the extinct house[1] of the Katóch Rajas of Kángra,

[1] The present Raja holds a small estate yielding about £3,500.

whose ancestor Bhúm Chand is said to have issued from the ground, of full stature, and completely armed, like Minerva from the brain of Jove. His race, for purity of descent, was considered the highest among the Rájputs of the Panjáb, but the territory fell a prey to the Sikh invader, who looked with a covetous eye on the lovely Kángra valley, which, with its famous fort, was surrendered to the British Government after the campaign on the Satlaj in 1845-46.[1] With the sole exception that it is wanting in lakes, the scenery of the Kángra valley is equal to that of Kashmír, the hills being covered with splendid forests of oak and ilex, while in the far distance towers up the stupendous Chambá range to a height of 15,000, a snowy wall which looks like an impassable barrier at the end of the world. Beyond it is, however, the picturesque Chambá territory, and, on the extreme border, the wild tracts of Láhaul and Spiti, at an elevation of from 7,000 to 10,000 feet, where the climate is intensely cold and the population but scanty. There are several other Rajas in the beautiful Kángra district, with long pedigrees and short purses, but the chiefs of Nadaun, Sukhét, and Mandí enjoy a fair income and receive salutes from the British Government.

North of the river Chanáb, the population of the plains of the Panjáb is mostly Muhammadan, though of Hindu origin, a great share of the *credit* of its conversion being due to Aurangzéb, who is said to have forcibly circumcised the people of several hundred

[1] The fort of Kángre capitulated in the year 1008–9 to the celebrated Mahmúd of Ghazni, when an immense treasure was found in it.

villages in a single day. Two of the principal of these tribes are the Awáns, a stalwart race living between the rivers Jhilam and Indus, who, in former days, had constant border feuds with the adjoining Pathán villages; and the Tawánas, an influential and brave people, inhabiting the desert south of the Salt range, whose chief, Fatah Khán, gallantly held out in a fort at Bannu against the Sikhs during the rising of 1848-49, till he met his death from thirst. There is also a singular tribe called Gakkars, who dwell in parts of the Ráwalpindi and Jhilam districts, and who are said to be descended from the fire-worshippers of Persia.[1]

The Sikhs, though so long the dominant race in the Panjáb, form but a small proportion of the population, deriving, however, their strength, partly from their inherent martial instincts, and partly from their religious cohesion, which rests upon the fact that all castes, including Musalmáns, are alike eligible as professors of the Khálsá faith. In the Panjáb proper, that is, the country north of the river Satlaj, the principal homestead of the Sikhs is in the Mánjhá, or the 'middle land,' between the Beás and the Rávi. Here they are found forming the entire population of villages, whereas elsewhere they are only to be met with partially. Generally they are Játs by caste, although many of the most influential Sikh leaders were Kshatriyas, such as the brave Sirdar Hari Singh Nalua, who was killed near Pesháwar, fighting against the Afgháns. The Sikh

[1] Muhammad Ghórí was assassinated by the Gakkars in 1206, on his return from India to his capital. They are described as being at this period a barbarous race of mountaineers.

Gurus were also Kshatriyas, and the race of the Sódhis, who derive their descent from Guru Haragóvind, is both numerous, and revered by all the Khálsá.

The Játs are undeniably a sturdy race, and good agriculturists, both in the Panjáb, and in the North-West Provinces, where some powerful chiefs belong to this stock. The Bharatpur (Bhurtpoor) Raja is a Sinsanwál Ját; the Dhólpur Raja is also a Ját; the one having a revenue of 210,000*l.* and the other of 60,000*l.* During the mutiny, a strong regiment of Ját Horse was raised by Major Murray, and performed excellent service.

The Játs have been supposed by some persons to be identical with the Getæ, and to have entered India at a later period than other Hindu races, but their social observances bear a close analogy to those of orthodox Hindus. They are divided into numerous gótras or families, of which the principal are the Sánsi, Gil, Virk, Sindhu, and Sidhu, &c. To the first belonged the royal family of Lahore, as also the Sindhánwálás, an influential house; to the second the Majítias, of whom Lehna Singh was an accomplished scholar, and Ranjór Singh, the hero of Badiwál, a bad general. The Atáriwálás, who headed the insurrection of 1848-49, were Sindhus, but as it is forbidden to Hindus to intermarry within a certain number of degrees of relationship, the principal Panjáb families were closely connected with one another, to which cause may be in a great measure attributed the resistance which they made in common to the British Government.

The state of the Panjáb, when the lamented Sir

Henry Lawrence assumed the post of Resident at the court of Lahore, was such as to tax all his energies. The army, like the Janissaries, or the Prætorian Guard of Rome, had virtually usurped all authority, and had constituted themselves the arbiters of peace or war; and, though they had received a rough lesson in the Satlaj campaign, their numbers and discipline made them still formidable. The Darbár was corrupt, and while money was lavishly wasted for private ends, the State was insolvent, the payment of the troops being much in arrears; while most necessaries of life were inordinately taxed. The land revenue was high, and collected arbitrarily, it being no uncommon thing to see the people of 300 or more villages resort to Lahore from a long distance to complain of the oppression of the local officials, waylaying the Resident on his visits to the Darbár, and lighting torches at mid-day to show, by an apt illustration, the darkness of the land in which no justice was to be found.

As the Darbár was not strong enough to contend alone with the prevailing disorder, the Resident was, unwillingly, compelled to assume a greater share in the conduct of affairs than would otherwise have been justifiable, and this interference was afterwards put forward by Raja Shór Singh Atáriwálá as one of the grievances which had led the Sikhs into revolt. The Resident took steps for reducing all exorbitant expenditure, disbanded superfluous troops, settled on an equitable basis the land revenue, giving the cultivators leases, abolished vexatious taxes on necessaries of life, put an end to slavery, gave permission to the Musalmáns to cry the Azán, or call to prayers, which under Sikh rule was prohibited, and introduced a variety of other administrative improvements. In all these measures, most valuable assistance was given to Sir Henry Lawrence by his brother, Mr. John Lawrence, afterwards so eminently distinguished as Lieutenant-Governor of the Panjáb, and Viceroy of India.

It must be admitted that, however consonant with our ideas of justice and good policy all these measures may have been, a native State could not but regard some of them with jealousy, and others with positive disapprobation; but it is very difficult for a Resident to watch abuses and not to attempt to reform them, while the minority of the young Maharaja Dalíp Singh, and the weakness of the Darbár, appear to have justified the course taken. Absolute non-interference would have precipitated matters in all probability, and have led to utter anarchy.

A brilliant surface covered over and partly concealed what was unsatisfactory beneath. The Lahore Darbár was the finest in India in regard to its appanage and the gay and gallant appearance of the chiefs, who, on great festival days, when it was the custom for the pillars of the State to make their obeisance to their young sovereign, came arrayed in gorgeous red and yellow dresses, glittering with gold and jewels, richly embroidered cloaks, and the handsomest of swords at their sides. Some of the Sirdárs of the highest rank were striking-looking men, while many of them had fought bravely against the English, and their frank and independent manner contrasted favorably with the exaggerated politeness of Hindusthánis. Grey-bearded and martial-looking old Ghórcharhas (troopers) of Ranjít Singh's era; fanatical Akális, clad in blue, with turbans encircled by their favourite war weapon, the quoit or disc; solemn priests, chanting out verses of the Granth, or Sikh Bible; pundits and astrologers, and a motley assemblage of richly-clad officials and retainers made up a picturesque *tout-ensemble*, which gave a special prestige to the Panjáb Court, when the Resident, with his assistants, was present at the deliberations of the Council of Regency.

The scene was, however, soon clouded over. Raja Lál Singh, formerly prime minister, had been banished to Agra, in consequence of his intriguing to prevent the surrender of the Kángra fort to the British Government, and Rání Jhandá, the mother of the young Maharaja, with whom he was a great favourite, was enraged at his deportation. She was a woman of great spirit, vindictive and resolute, and ill-disposed to submit to the dictation of the Darbár, who prohibited her interference in state matters. Having once virtually ruled, through her brother Jawáhir Singh, and, later, through Rajá Lál Singh, her forced seclusion became unbearable to her, and her crafty mind led her to sanction a plot for the assassination of the Resident and Rajá Téj Singh, the head of the Council, a feeble chief, but well affected and a friend to the English. The conspiracy was organised by Prém Chand, a Brahman of Jammu, the Ráni's native country, but was detected, Prém Chand being banished to Hindusthán, and the Ráni removed to Shékhupura, a fort in the jungles beyond the river Rávi. Her rage and indignation at this step exceeded all bounds, but her power for mischief was not yet at an end.

Shortly afterwards, Sir H. Lawrence was compelled by ill-health to proceed to England, and, during his absence, circumstances occurred which led to a general rising of all the discontented spirits of the Panjáb. The Governor of Multán, Díwán Múlráj, who had succeeded his father, Sáwan Mall, in the administration of that province, expressed a wish to be relieved of his charge. At the subsequent trial of this individual at Lahore, it was not conclusively shown what was his real motive in wishing to resign his post, that is, whether he hoped to get his lease renewed on more favourable terms, or whether he was playing into the hands of the Rání, who, it was said, had previously sent to Multán one of her attendants, on pretence of making a pilgrimage, bearing a branch of the ák, or white-willow tree, as an inducement to Múlráj to revolt. His conduct, on the murder of Messrs. Vans, Agnew, and Anderson, showed vacillation and cowardice, and his subsequent proceedings were marked simply by the courage of despair; but it does not appear that the assassination was really premeditated by him, nor is it easy to see what object he could have gained by defying both the Lahore Darbár and the British Government. At the same time, it is probable that the minds of the soldiery had been worked upon, and that they were adverse to the change of governors contemplated by the Darbár, who had nominated Sirdár Kánh Singh to relieve

Mulráj, the English officials being deputed to aid him in his charge. These gentlemen committed the error of proceeding by river to Multán, while the troops marched by land, so that there was no cordial understanding between them, and no attempt was made by the latter to rescue the English officers when first wounded by Múlráj's people.

It is not the writer's design to dwell upon the siege of Multán, of which full details are given in the official records of the time, but it was thought by some persons that the Government erred in forcing upon the Lahore Council their responsibility for suppressing the first outbreak, and in not taking matters into its own hands. It was said that, had Sir H. Lawrence been at his post, he would have proceeded at once, accompanied by a flying corps and a few guns, to Multán, and have forced Múlráj to succumb. It is true that the assassination took place in April, when the sun is fiercely hot, and marching is often fatal to European troops, but the effect on an Oriental mind of prompt and resolute measures is beyond price, and during the celebrated mutiny of 1857 our troops were constantly in the field during the hottest months of the year.

As time wore on, the rebellion gained head, and notwithstanding the actions fought against Múlráj by the gallant Major Edwardes, and the subsequent siege of Multán, the infection spread throughout the Sikh army, whose patriotism and religion were appealed to by disaffected persons on every plea which could excite their courage and their bigotry. In a very short time the whole country was in a blaze, but six months elapsed before a British force, under the Commander-in-Chief, crossed the Rávi to contend with the Sikh rebels. In the early history of our career in India, and especially in the Madras territory, the Government was not so punctilious about fighting in fair weather, while during the mutiny, when its officers and troops were contending for their very existence, the order was to strike, and to strike hard and quick, without thought of time and season. The arguments adduced for postponing operations till the winter were plausible enough in a military point of view, but opposed to a sound policy, for during the long period of inaction, the disaffection became daily more formidable, and its suppression entailed the extinction of the Sikh dynasty, which might perhaps have been averted had our Government at once bestirred itself to prompt action. Many natives supposed that the Government, being determined to obtain possession of the Panjáb, knowingly let the rebellion spread till the chiefs should be irretrievably committed to revolt, while a few, who sided with us, expressed unfeigned surprise when the Government, at the end of hostilities, instead of seating the young Maharaja more firmly than ever on his throne, annexed his territories and obliterated his dynasty.

Those who were lookers-on when the English army crossed the Rávi, on leaving Lahore, to encounter the Sikh malcontents, predicted for it an easy victory, but, in the first engagement, a severe check was met with. A brilliant, but wholly useless, charge of the cavalry at

Rámnagar, on the Chanáb, brought them within the range of the Sikh guns on the further bank, and not only was there considerable loss, but the effect on the spirit of the troops was most disheartening. The next move to Sádullahpur ought to have been a great success, as the Sikh troops were ill-prepared for resistance, and Raja Shér Singh afterwards averred that, had a vigorous attack been then made, his army must have been completely discomfited; but the opportunity was lost, and the Khálsá army retreated to the heights of Múng Rasúl on the Jhilam, having the river on its rear. The next episode was the disastrous battle of Chilianwálá, called by the Sikhs Chélián Móza, from two villages of those names. Had it not been for the gallantry of the English regiments, and especially of H.M. 61st, in the division commanded by Sir Colin Campbell (afterwards Lord Clyde), there is little doubt that we should have been worsted. The fight was commenced in complete ignorance of the position of the enemy, and the troops as they advanced in columns suddenly found themselves in front of the Sikh batteries, which had been concealed by the jungle. The result was deplorable, certain English infantry regiments losing heavily, while many native infantry corps became disorganised, and a panic seized a portion of the English and native cavalry.

It may be remarked here that, in both the Satlaj and Panjáb campaigns, the loss among the Europeans was in the proportion of three to one relatively to that of the native troops, taking into consideration their respective numbers. The Hindusthání Sepoy felt himself no match for the redoubtable Sikh, even when led himself by English officers, and it is greatly to the national credit of the martial Panjábis that, with limited resources, and unaided by European commanders, they should have competed on such equal terms with the flower of the British army in India. There is no other race in Hindusthán which could have accomplished this; but the Sikhs were not only animated by religious fervor, but had profited by the superior discipline imparted to them by their French commanders in the time of the old Maharaja.

The engagement of Chilianwálá may perhaps be correctly described as a drawn battle, as neither side could claim an undoubted victory. The English army, however, was conscious that it had sustained a reverse, its losses being heavy, and a feeling of want of confidence in their commander spread itself through men's minds. The effect upon the Sikh army, on the other hand, was great, and it was currently asserted afterwards that hundreds of their soldiery were drowned in attempting to escape across the Jhilam. A long interval of inaction ensued, till the Sikhs marched upon Gujarát, on the Chanáb, a move which, if Shér Singh had made it earlier, with the object of raising Amritsar and the Mánjhá, would have greatly embarrassed the English Commander-in-Chief, who certainly could not have marched with the same celerity as the active and hardy Sikhs. Fortunately, however, the latter did not cross the river, which error, on their part, enabled the Multán force, which had, after many months of siege, succeeded in reducing Múlráj's stronghold, to join the main army under Sir Hugh Gough.

After the junction of the two forces, the battle of Gujarát was fought, and a brilliant victory obliterated all traces of the checks, the blunders, and the disasters which had before characterised the operations of our army. Gujarát was emphatically an artillery fight, for the Sikhs, with fewer guns, and those of inferior calibre, were wholly unable to contend with the powerful and numerous artillery brought against them, and after remaining some time in hell, as Raja Shér Singh aptly described their situation, they retreated in the utmost confusion. The Afghán cavalry, which had joined the Sikh army, made one ineffectual charge, but, being gallantly met and repulsed, fled precipitately, and, it is said, never drew rein till they had put the Jhilam between themselves and the enemy. The main army of the Sikhs also beat a hasty retreat, but were so hotly pursued by a detachment under Sir Walter Gilbert, that, seeing all resistance to be useless, they laid down their arms at Ráwalpindí, and their chiefs surrendered themselves as prisoners. With the termination of the campaign, ended also the dynasty of Ranjít Singh, ten years only after his death.

The annexation of his territories ensued, and was in accordance with the policy of Lord Dalhousie, who was no advocate for the retention of powerful native States, and whatever may be thought of the absorption of Satára, Oudh, and other provinces, the grounds for incorporating the Panjáb with British India were strong. The annexation might have been avoided indeed by taking the administration of the country into our own hands during the minority of Maharaja Dalíp Singh, but it must be admitted that the ample trial given to a native Regency, acting under the inspiration of an English Resident, had proved a failure, notwithstanding the eminent qualities which distinguished Sir Henry Lawrence, and the support given to him by a staff of assistants who, in point of ability, could not have been surpassed in India.

In fact, a dual government is an entire anomaly in an Oriental State. To secure obedience and preserve order under native rule, a benevolent despotism, so to speak, appears to be the most efficient of administrations, absolute power being blended with a due perception of native requirements, and the supreme justice from which there is no appeal being tempered by mercy and that occasional relaxation of forms which native rulers prize, and which their subjects expect from them.

Among the Sikh chiefs of the first rank there was not one who could safely have been intrusted with the responsibilities of a Regent, while most of the leading men had been arrayed in arms against us, so that the affairs of the Panjáb, failing its annexation, could only have been conducted under the control of an English commissioner, a step which did not commend itself to the Governor-General. Raja Téj Singh, the President of the Council, was feeble and timid; Raja Dínanáth, the Finance Minister, was crafty and unscrupulous; Raja Shér Singh Atáriwálá, who was tolerably straightforward and independent, though at first well-disposed, had been driven into rebellion by the perverse proceedings of his father, Chatar Singh; Shamshér Singh

Sindhánwálá, though a gallant and popular chief, was devoted to pleasure and fond of his ease; and the other members of the Council were quite unfitted to rule. The more hardy and resolute Sirdárs, such as Sirdár Surat Singh Majítia, who behaved so remarkably well afterwards at Benares during the mutiny of 1857; Kánh Singh Rósa; and other tried soldiers and brave spirits, had been carried away by the flood of disaffection. In short, there was no material left for instituting a strong native government; nor can it be said that the previous conduct of the Sikh Darbár, which, in its treachery and impotence, had suffered the Khálsá troops to invade British territory in 1845, had given the State any claim to generous consideration, such as would have been evinced by administering its affairs by British officers on behalf of the youthful sovereign during his minority.

It may be observed, however, that the land revenue of the province, as it existed in 1848–49, was less than one million sterling; that the extreme frontier was hard to hold and guard, and had in parts even to be conquered; and that the military and civil charges, on the introduction of British rule, far exceeded those of the native administration which it superseded. The Panjáb has never been a profitable possession, owing to the comparative poverty of the country and the great outlay required for the maintenance of the large army concentrated it it. The following is an abstract, made ten years ago, showing how limited were at that time the population and land revenue, as compared with the area, when contrasted with those of the North-West Provinces and Lower Bengal :—

	No. of districts	Average		
		Area	Population	Land Revenue
Panjáb[1] . . .	33	3,043	448,321	5,65,200 = £ 56,520
N. W. Provinces[2] .	26	2,328	974,436	13,08,481 = £130,848
Lower Bengal[3]. .	34	3,639	891,068	9,85,817 = £ 98,581

It will be seen from the foot-note[1] that the territory annexed after the Satlaj campaign was far more valuable than the Panjáb proper ; and here it may be remarked that, with the exception of Oudh, our more recent acquisitions in India generally have not tended much to fill the coffers of the State.

A highly developed system of administration, with costly courts of judicature, and an expensive army, presses heavily on the finances of Eastern countries, which are mostly poor, and often ill-prepared for the introduction of a government on European principles. There is not cloth enough, to use a homely simile, to cut the coat from, and thus, territories which, under native rule, yielded a sufficient income to enable the

[1] Includes the Jalandar and Ambála divisions (except Simla), annexed after Satlaj campaign, and the Delhi and Hissár divisions which, previous to the mutiny of 1857, were attached to the North-West Provinces. The following is an analysis of the statistics of these four divisions.

Division	No. of Districts	Average Area	Average Population	Average Land Revenue
Jalandar . . .	3	2,247	750,313	9,32,292 = £93,229
Ambála . . .	3	1,748	587,123	8,82,154 = £88,215
Delhi . . .	3	1,352	442,883	7,71,243 = £77,124
Hissár . . .	3	2,848	286,007	4,13,129 = £41,312

[2] Includes Meerut, Rohilkhand, Agra, Allahabad, and Benares divisions.

[3] Includes Patna, Bhágalpur, Rájsháih Bardwán, Nadia, Dacca, and Chittagong divisions.

sovereign to live in great state and splendor, do not, under our mode of government, pay their expenses. The time has not yet come when the British Government can with safety trust implicitly to the loyalty of the masses of India, and the necessity, therefore, of maintaining vast military establishments is apparent. The cost of these, added to the daily increasing requirements of the civil administration, is more than the country can bear; but the soundness of the policy of holding India by the strong hand is at present undeniable.

Great and sensible improvements have been effected, no doubt, in most of the local administrations, but many of these are costly, and it becomes a question whether the civil expenditure of a province should not, to some extent, be regulated by its income, and not by that of other provinces. It appears unreasonable to expect from a comparatively poor and thinly-populated country the same administrative measures and the same costly courts which are desirable, and indeed imperative, in wealthy and advanced territories. It is like a poor man keeping a carriage because his wealthy neighbour does so. Moreover, it is not much to our credit that a province should not be able to pay its own expenses, which, under native rule, accumulated stores of treasure, and was able to resist invasion from outside, without being a burden on other provinces. Most of the native States of India pay a subsidy for the protection afforded by the paramount power, but their contributions, being fixed by treaty, and having reference solely to the defence of their own territories, cannot be enhanced, except in special cases.

As regards the position of the people of the Panjáb, there can be little doubt that the mass of the population, whether agricultural or commercial, is better off than it was previous to the annexation of the country; but, on the other hand, many of the old families have lost their influence, partly from their own indebtedness and folly, and partly because all local power has been taken from them, while priestly influence is latently hostile, and the combative instincts of the Sikhs cannot be overlooked. During another generation of peace and tranquillity, it is to be hoped that most of these adverse elements will disappear, but it is unsafe to calculate with certainty upon what may be the disposition of the people and the times twenty years hence.

Of the English actors on the scene twenty years ago, most are still in the land of the living, but not so the great and good Sir Henry Lawrence, the chivalrous Edwardes, the fiery Nicholson, and the gallant Hodson. These have fought their fight, and rest in peace. Of the others, some are in retirement, well earned by long and faithful service, while many still uphold the honor of their country in distinguished posts in India.

THE SIKH INVASION

OF

THE CIS-SATLAJ COUNTRY.

In the ancient region of Brahmavartta are found the first landmarks of Indian history, and, although actual facts have been clouded over by the lapse of ages, by myths, and by the license of the poet, enough still remains to make the country classic ground in the eyes of Hindus, and not wholly uninteresting to others. Brahmavartta may be broadly described as the tract between the Yamuná (Jumna) and the Ghagar rivers, having the town of Ambála on the north and Pánipat on the south; but, in its more limited sense, it comprises merely the country between the Ghagar, or Gargarákha,[1] and the Saraswati, which latter sacred stream, after mingling its waters with the Ghagar, flows into thc sandy wastes of Hariána and Bhatiána, and disappears, to rise again, according to Hindu fable, at Prayág or Allahábád, at the triple junction (called the Trivéni) of itself, the Yamuná, and the Gangá.

In all times, and among many nations, the principal rivers of a country have been endowed with a sacred

[1] Anciently called the Drishadwati.

character; and, in the case of the Nile, the Kávéri, and the Ganges, it is not surprising that the immense value of their fertilising influences should have invested them with the attributes of divinity. It is not a little remarkable, however, that a small and insignificant stream like the Saraswati should be regarded with reverence, yet this may be accounted for by the fact that, in its vicinity, were fought the famous battles immortalised in the Mahábhárata.

If, as has been surmised, the Hindu race came originally from some farther land, the 'Paradésa,' or country beyond the borders of India, which, when quitted for ever, became holy in their eyes, like Asgaard to the Scandinavians, they would appear to have lost all traces of their exodus, for their history, prior to the tale of the Mahábhárata, is a blank. Many ages must have passed from the period when the Hindus were a nomad pastoral tribe, as described in their sacred books, to that second stage when they became an agricultural community, and from that time again to the epoch when they are shown to have been skilled craftsmen and thriving traders; but it seems probable that, at the time of their great epic poems, they were already far advanced in civilisation, having a settled form of government, a strong religious element, and an abstruse system of philosophy. Hindus themselves, not unnaturally, deny that their forefathers were foreign intruders, and, indeed, it is not easy to show from what particular centre they really did emigrate; but the fact that, excepting the priestly caste, the higher races comprised in the system of caste are found in greater numbers in the north of India than in the centre or the south, leads one to infer that their ancestors did immigrate into the country from some region beyond it, although this by no means presupposes that India was at the time devoid of inhabitants.

Kshatriyas, or Chatris, of many different stocks, and of the purest blood, are common in the Panjáb proper,[1] so that even the Hindus of Delhi eagerly seek the honor of alliances with them, while, as we proceed farther south, the sangre azul becomes thinner and more corrupted, till the inferior Rájputs, and the minor potentates of the south, have but little of the genuine Kshatriya blood in their veins. As a fighting class, however, the Kshatriya has almost ceased to exist, the people of this caste in the Panjáb being now mostly either traders or religious teachers.

The prevalence of Brahmans in every part of India, and even where the other three castes are rarely found, is an anomaly deserving of more minute research than it has hitherto received; but, in the majority of cases, it will probably be found that tradition points to their

[1] The Panjáb Khatris are divided into the following classes :—

1. Adhaighar, or Two-and-a-half Families.	2. Chàrghar, or Four Families.	3. Chhahzáti, or Six Castes.
Kakar	Bárá	Chópra
Malótra	Dhóné	Talwad
Kapúr	Malótra	Méndru
Khana	Kapúr	Kakar
4. Athzáti, or Eight Castes. Contains Eight Families.	5. Báràghar, or Twelve Families. Contains Twelve Families.	Dhóné
		Bárá
		6. Báwanghar, or Fifty-two Families.

In this classification a few of the branches have apparently an unsettled status, some of them claiming a higher position than is accorded to them by rival families.

Among Brahmans the Moyáls rank highest, and contain the following branches :—Datt, Bálí, Vaid, Chibar, Móhan, Law, Bambál.

having been invited by ancient rulers, who had been attracted by their reputation for learning and sanctity, to exercise their priestly functions, on the promise of their receiving handsome benefactions of land or money. At the present time, the farther we travel south in India, the greater is the influence of the Brahmans, till it culminates in Travancore, where their status is such as to make them all powerful in the country, their aid being, it is asserted, solicited, not only in the discharge of their sacerdotal duties, but for the very continuation of the royal line. If they were among the aboriginal inhabitants, one might expect to find the other three castes which make up the Hindu system having the same relative population which those of the Panjáb bear to the Brahmans of that province, but such is not the case.

Another argument in favor of the foreign origin of the Hindu race is that, on the one hand, there is a close analogy between Sanskrit and the ancient Zend of Persia, a tongue of which there is no evidence that its speakers came from India ; while, on the other, on removing the thick crust of the Sanskrit element which adheres to the common vernaculars of Northern India, the substratum bears an affinity to the languages of the South,—an affinity not very close indeed, and greatly warped by the action of centuries, but still pointing to an early connection between them. Such languages differ widely in construction from those of Aryan origin.

Again, the primæval worship of the Sun, which prevailed alike among the Védic Hindus and the ancient

Persians, appears to have nearly died out in India before the historic period, and, although traces of it are found, as in the famous temple of Mártand in Kashmír, in the titles of Rájput races, and occasionally in the names of individuals, it may be inferred that the gradual extinction of this form of worship arose from the circumstance that its professors had moved far away from the place of its origin. It does not appear to have been at any time the general popular belief in the South of India, so far as can be judged from the existing tenets of those who are least under the influence of Brahmanism, inasmuch as their worship is mainly rendered to snakes, to the sylvan god, or to material and inanimate earthly objects. On the whole, therefore, there appears to be good ground for believing that the Hindus, or, to speak more correctly, the four castes mentioned in their sacred books, did enter India from the North, carrying their religion and language with them, and imposing both gradually on the aborigines.

It may be added that there are no architectural remains in Southern India which can be compared with those of the North in respect to their antiquity, all the beautiful temples and works of art in the former having been built within the last thousand years. In the North, also, we find the majority of the places which are sacred in the eyes of Hindus.

The battle-ground of the heroes of the Mahábhárata, the Pándavas and Kauravas, can still be traced with sufficient accuracy to give an air of reality to the story, and it would seem from this, that tradition, among a people who are mostly illiterate, is not without its value. It is indeed not easy sometimes to draw the line between tradition and history, distorted and colored as the latter frequently is by the prejudices and imperfect information of the writers of it, while there is much worthy of note in the traditions handed down orally from generation to generation by professional genealogists, such as the Hindu Bháts and Chárans, who keep a careful record of domestic occurrences in the families to which they are attached.

The modern town of Thánésar is the northern limit of the tract called the forty kós (sixty miles), to die within which insures salvation to orthodox Hindus, and renders unnecessary the removal of their ashes to the sacred Ganges.[1] The holy pool bears to this day the name of Kuru Kshétra, in commemoration of the family whose dynastic struggles took place in its neighbourhood, and the cicerones of Thánésar profess to point out the exact spots mentioned in the Mahábhárata as occupied by the rival armies—that of Jayadratha, the Kaurava chieftain, having been drawn up to the east, and that of his opponents, the Pándavas, to the west. Oriental campaigns are not a summer's-day fight, but are carried on leisurely with varying success, sometimes for years, while the length of the epic appears to indicate a protracted struggle for supremacy between the contending forces, so that the events recorded in the

[1] Thánesar was anciently called Sthánéshwara, and also Bayusar, and is on the northern limit of the Forty Kós tract, the boundaries of which are, on the north, Ratnuyaksha; on the south, Arantuyaksha or Tarkhu, where is the village of Síkha; on the east, Bhachakru, where is the village of Amín; and on the west, Rámradha. This region is called Samant Panjak in the Gadá Parva of the Mahábhárata.

Mahábhárata must have been indelibly impressed on the popular mind. The legend, if such it be, of the Pándavas and their misfortunes, is well known throughout India, there being scarcely a district in which there is not some hill or other place of safety where the persecuted princes are reputed to have taken refuge from the malice of their revengeful foes.

A long blank follows this first glimpse of early Hindu history, the veil of obscurity being only partially raised in the Buddhistic period, when the king Asóka set up the columns of his law throughout his dominions, one of these having been erected close to the Jamuná where it issues from the hills. Of Alexander the Great and his victories, there is no trace, Brahmavartta lying south of the uttermost limit attained by any of his legions.

It is to the invading hordes of the Musalmáns that we are indebted for the next insight into the political and domestic relations of the Hindus in Brahmavartta, for, although inscriptions of some antiquity, that is, presumably, about fourteen centuries old, have been discovered at Pinjór, Pehówa on the Saraswati, and other places, these are too fragmentary to afford any connected view of the progress of events. But when once the path to conquest was discovered by the first followers of Islám who crossed the mysterious river Indus, the tide of invasion surged in, wave over wave, till it seemed as if all the hosts of Central Asia, incited by religious ardour and hopes of plunder, had poured into the devoted land, which fell an easy prey to the spoiler.

When Mahmúd of Ghazni[1] carried his victorious arms into India, the whole of the north of the continent was apparently ruled over by Rájput princes, of whom the chief exercised his sway from Hastinápura or Delhi, but a great part of the Cis-Satlaj country was held by the tribe of Kólís or Atras, a branch of the Raghuvansi Rájputs, who are said to have come from Oudh. To these succeeded the Chohāns, whose head was Rao Prithóra, the King of Delhi. The other leading tribes were the Powárs or Pramáras, also Raghuvansis; the Táonis who were Jádámvansis; and the Chandéls who belonged to the Lunar dynasty. The advent of these Rájput races dates from various periods, but tradition asserts that the earliest comers were the Kólís, who were a powerful tribe. It may be inferred that the Rájputs were at one time warlike, and the first among the combatant races of India, but it is well known that they afterwards succumbed successively to the Musalmán invader, the hardy Mahratta, the lithe and active Gurkha, and the stalwart Sikh. In fact their reputation for prowess has either been greatly exaggerated, or their martial qualities became gradually obscured by the indolence to which they are only too prone.

The system of adoption which universally prevails among Rájputs has no doubt tended much to the preservation of their dynastic repute, and one sees among them pedigrees reaching back to remote ages, which, though there may be much fable in them, there is reason to suppose are substantially correct. Thus, the

[1] Mahmúd plundered Thánésar in 1011 A.D. and destroyed the idols there.

Chóhán Raja of Mainpúri carries back his descent eighty-four generations, and the Raja of Dumráon in Behár ninety-three generations, while the more famous houses of Udaipur, Jódhpur and Réwah claim a still more voluminous pedigree. As adoptions must be made from among the descendants of a common ancestor, the purity of the blood is preserved, while in order to secure an accurate record of births, deaths, and marriages, the family genealogists make periodical tours, during the course of which they carefully note all such domestic occurrences. It is not, therefore, beyond the bounds of probability that Rájput pedigrees should be fairly reliable, or at least as trustworthy as those of most European families.

The cause of the decadence of minor Rájput houses may perhaps be traced to the extreme jealousy of one another which ordinarily prevails among them, added to their absurd pride of birth, and their lazy habits. The large dowries demanded from the fathers of marriageable girls, on their forming connections with families of higher rank than themselves, have been a powerful incentive to the commission of the frightful crime of infanticide, which still prevails extensively in many Rájput races, and which diminishes their numbers. Again, the strict seclusion in which the women of the poorest Rájputs are kept, prevents their working in the field, like the wives of most Hindu cultivators, while the men are generally too proud to handle the plough themselves, and their means of subsistence are therefore very limited.

Owing to the want of cohesion among the Rájput

races, Muhammad Ghóri obtained in 1192–93 an easy victory over them in a pitched battle in which they were signally defeated. Local tradition states that the Musalmán conqueror pursued Rao Prithóra from Bhatinda to a place called Chhat on the river Ghagar, where the Hindu prince was taken prisoner. The victor having been told that Rao Prithóra was a noted archer, his bow and arrows were sent for, in order that he might display his skill. His bhât, or family bard, stood hard by, and as the prince was about to discharge the arrow, recited a couplet having a hidden meaning, by which he instigated Rao Prithóra to shoot Muhammad Ghóri, and when the latter gave the signal, Rao Prithóra directed the arrow at his head, shooting him dead on the spot. The Hindu prince was of course immediately slain by his conqueror's followers, and both were interred on the spot of the tragedy. It may be observed that this tradition is at variance with the commonly received story that Muhammad Ghóri was assassinated in his tent by a band of Gakkars in another place, but the people of Chhat confidently point out his tomb, as well as that of Rao Prithóra.[1]

As in most parts of India, legends and traditions are rife in the Cis-Satlaj territory, though they are not specially interesting. Here is one:—The town of

[1] There is some confusion in Ferishta's history regarding Muhammad Ghóri, some of the achievements of Moyiz-ud-dín Muhammad Ghóri being also attributed to Shaháb-ud-dín Muhammad Ghóri (*confer* Brigg's Ferishta, vol. i. pp. 157–159 and p. 171). The incident narrated refers to the latter, who was apparently an uncle of Moyiz-ud-dín, and may have accompanied him to India, though there is no allusion to this in Ferishta.

Kharar, in the Ambála district, which in ancient times was called Ajainagar, was ruled over by Rájá Bainchak, a descendant of Rájá Aj, who was in the habit of playing at dice, on the condition that the loser should forfeit his head. As the king was always victorious, he formed a vast accumulation of heads, which he used to amuse himself by trailing along the ground, hence his capital acquired the name of Mundé-Kharar, from 'Mundé,' a head, and 'Kharar,' the sound which a heavy object makes on being dragged over the ground. From this evil propensity he acquired the name of 'Sirkap,' or decapitator. His queen was endowed with the wonderful power of drawing water from a well in a pot suspended by a single unwoven thread, but as she possessed no jewels, and was meanly attired, her husband, not perceiving that her magic virtue was owing to her simplicity and purity, sent to the Rájá of Lanká (Ceylon), to ask for some gold dresses for her attire. This prince, surprised at so unusual a demand, sent an ambassador to enquire who was the insolent chief who had made such a request. The ambassador, on reaching Kharar, found Raja Bainchak poorly dressed, and looking like a mendicant rather than a king; but when the ambassador was about to turn away with contempt, the Raja asked him to draw a picture of Lanká, and when he had done so, pointed out a particular bastion in the fortress, which he transfixed with an arrow, saying to the ambassador, 'Return to Lanká, and you will find that this tower has fallen to the ground.' The ambassador, on reaching home safely, narrated the words of Bainchak, and found that the event predicted had actually taken place, whereupon the Lanká prince, being greatly astonished at the miraculous power of the Kharar chief, sent him all that he had asked for; but when the queen went again to the well, decked in gaudy robes, and covered with gold ornaments, her magic virtue left her, the unwoven string broke, and her pot fell into the well, never to be recovered again.

With such tales, and narratives of the gallant exploits of former rulers, the people are wont to amuse themselves in the evening, as they sit under the village banyan trees, or on the raised platform which forms a rendezvous for all the gossips of the place. Without the aid of fiction, however, they have ample food for discussion, in recalling the visitations of the savage Tamerlane, and the fierce Nádir Shah, whose victorious hosts ravaged the Cis-Satlaj country on their way to Delhi.[1] The first brought in his train many individuals who settled in the country, and became peaceful landholders, their descendants being still numerous. The result of the invasion of Nádir Shah was to shatter the power of the great Móghals, of whom Tímúr the Tatar (Tamerlane) was the progenitor; and the Delhi emperors never rallied from the shock which, in the person of Muhammad Shah, they received from the famous Afshár conqueror.[2]

[1] Tamerlane, in 1398, after directing the massacre of the population of Bhatnér, assembled his army at Khaithal, west of Thánesar, before marching on Delhi.

[2] Nádir Shah, in 1738, encountered the forces of the Great Móghal at Karnál, 30 miles north of Pániput, where, in 1526, the celebrated Bábar overthrew the army of Ibráhím Lódí, the Afghán King of Delhi. At Pánipat also was fought, in 1761, the memorable battle between Ahmad Sháh Abdáli and the Mahratta hosts.

So long as they exercised their sway with moderation and clemency, the successors of the great Akbar ruled Hindusthán with fair success, and left many monuments of their magnificence; but when Aurangzéb, the most intolerant of monarchs, imitated the example of the first Musalmán conquerors, and ordained death as the punishment for non-conversion to his faith, a host of enemies rose up, and internal dissension paved the way for the destruction of the Móghal's dynasty and the invasion of Nádir Shah. It was to Aurangzéb's cruelty that the Mahrattas owed their subsequent ascendancy, and to the same cause that the Sikhs, from an obscure sect, became a powerful nation.

Up to the time of Guru Arjuna, the fifth of the Sikh high-priests, the Khálsá sect was an ascetical and insignificant body of devotees; but the unwise opposition to the extension of their tenets which the Muhammadan deputies offered, and the atrocious murder of their ninth Guru, Tégh Bahádur, led to their becoming a nation of warriors, full of fanaticism, and bent upon wreaking a bloody revenge on their oppressors.

On a lofty hill called Naina Dévi, on the bank of the Satlaj, there is a famous temple, sacred to the goddess Dévi, who was much venerated by Guru Góvind Singh, the tenth and last of the Sikh teachers: he who mainly imparted to his followers their martial training, and changed them from devotees into soldiers. It is related that one day, when he was offering sacrifice to the goddess, she manifested herself to him, and demanded one of his sons as an offering. The Guru, at first frightened, soon plucked up courage, and refused to sacrifice his son, whereupon the angry goddess told him that he should lose all four of his sons, a prediction which was soon after verified by the death of two of them in battle at Chamkór, and the assassination of the other two by the Subadár of Sirhind. It appears that Góvind Singh was engaged in constant struggles with the Ráj-put chiefs of the Náhan and Biláspur hills, and that these applied to Delhi for assistance. The royal troops attacked Góvind Singh, who long held out at Nandpur Makhowál, but, finding himself hemmed in by superior forces, sent away his mother and his two younger sons, Fateh Singh and Zóráwar Singh, who were, however, betrayed by a man named Duni Chand, and brought to Sirhind, the head-quarters of the Musalmán governor Vazír Khán. There was a Hindu at Sirhind named Sachánand, who had contemplated an alliance between his daughter and one of the sons of the Guru, who had, however, declined the connection. This individual had, in consequence, imbibed a deadly hatred against Góvind Singh, and when the boys were brought before the Subadár, said that they were of a brood of serpents, and counselled their death. The Nawáb of Malér Kótla, Shér Muḥammad Khán, vainly interceded for them, alleging that it was a sin to murder children only five and seven years old, but the counsel of the Hindu prevailed, and, after a fruitless attempt to convert them to Islám, they were taken to a tower by one Básu Bég, and stabbed with a dagger. Their grandmother was either killed, also, or died of grief.

Góvind Singh succeeded in escaping from Nandpur to Chamkór, where he was again attacked by the

Muhammadan troops, and in the engagement which ensued, his elder sons, Ajít Singh and Jujár Singh, were slain. A handsome temple was built in commemoration of their death by one of the Singhpúrian chiefs. At Nandpur Makhowál, where Góvind Singh principally resided, visitors are shown his sanctum, where is preserved a massive double-handed sword, which he wrested in single combat from an Afghán, whose name is engraved on the weapon. In the same building there is also a copy of the Ádi Granth, or collection of the sacred writings of the first priests, composed by Guru Arjuna, which was presented to the temple by the widow of Banda Bairági, the faithful follower of Góvind Singh, who, after his teacher's death, carried on a prolonged resistance to the Musalmán rulers of the country. Hard by is the tomb of Tégh Bahádur, who was killed at Delhi by the merciless Aurangzéb, his head having been brought to Nandpur by his disciples. His murder was, in truth, the cause of the rise of the Sikh nation, for had not his son Góvind Singh been inspired with a fixed determination to avenge his death, it is probable that the Khálsá would have been exterminated as a sect; but the gallant resistance made by his son, whose talents and energy invested him in the eyes of his adherents with the attributes of a saint and a hero, gave that consistence and discipline to the natural courage of these enthusiasts, which enabled them eventually to overthrow the oppressive rule of their persecutors.

Góvind Singh, after his disastrous defeat at Chamkór, proceeded to Máchiwárá and then to Mukatsar, where he had another engagement with the royal troops, but, being again worsted, fled to Bikánér, and, passing through the sandy desert, finally made his way to the Dekkan, whence he never returned. With him terminated the succession of the Sikh priests, but the warlike qualities which he implanted in the breasts of his followers continued to flourish, and after the invasion of Nádir Shah had rudely shaken the throne of the Móghal, the Khálsá collected their forces, and, crossing the Satlaj in large bodies under daring leaders, ravaged the whole country between that river and the Jamuná. The attempts previously made by Banda Bairági to raise the standard of revolt were only partially successful, the Musalmán power being still strong, and the issue was that he was captured, sent to Delhi, and there slain.

Among those Sikhs of the Cis-Satlaj territory who listened to Góvind Singh's teaching, and were among his firmest adherents, were Phúl and his sons, Játs of the Sidhu Barár caste. The family is now known as the Phúlkián Misal, and is the most famous house between the Satlaj and the Jamuna, owing its influence and its position partly to its large possessions, and partly to the respect in which it is held by all Sikhs as being descended from the faithful followers of the great Guru. The misal comprises the Patiálá, Nábhá, and Jhínd houses, besides minor branches, as shown in the family tree opposite :—

The Patiálá chief, though of the junior branch, was the first to assume the title of Raja, and owing to the energy and prowess of Raja Álá Singh, the princes of this family extended their sway over a large portion of

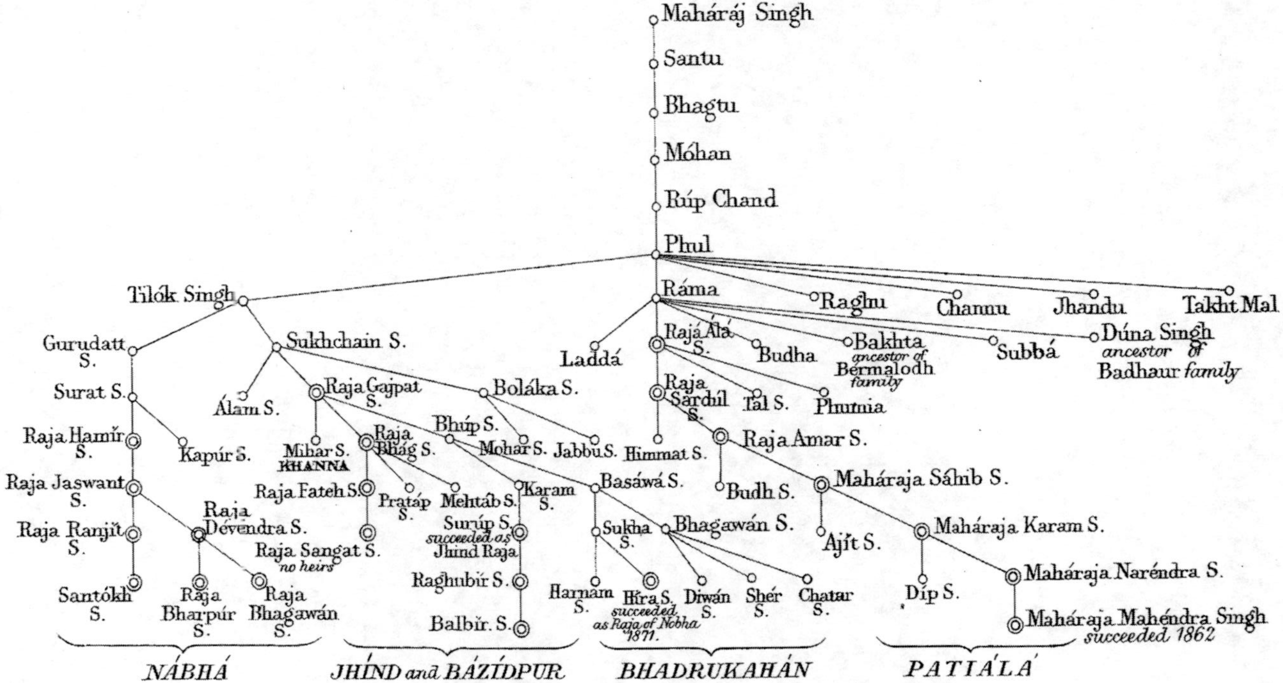

PEDIGREE OF THE PHULKIÁN MISAL.

the Cis-Satlaj country, the Mahárájá being recognised as the head of the misal.

The revenues of this State are probably not less than 300,000*l.* yearly; and those of Nábhá and Jhínd 40,000*l.* and 50,000*l.* respectively.

The Rájas of the Phulkián Misal have generally been well affected towards the British Government, both Patiálá and Jhínd having been uniformly staunch, alike during the critical period of the Cis-Satlaj campaign, and the momentous time when Delhi was besieged in 1857.

The Patiálá chief, Sáhib Singh, during the war with Nepál, rendered active aid in the Simla hills, where part of his possessions lay. His son Karam Singh, when the English supremacy trembled in the balance, did not hesitate to throw the weight of his influence into the scale, against his co-religionists. The late Maharaja Naréndra Singh, a man of noble presence, surpassed even his father by his gallant and unswerving co-operation during the mutiny. All his resources were placed at the disposal of the British Government, and it was mainly owing to his aid that the communication between the Panjab and Delhi was kept open.

The loyalty of these chieftains is of the highest importance, not only as representing the attitude of the Sikhs towards the British Government, but also because their territories are peopled by a warlike race, who would readily follow their direction and guidance. It is not too much to say that 50,000 fighting men could, without difficulty, be raised in the Cis-Satlaj country, where the Khálsá are commonly known as Malwéi

Sikhs, and their adhesion would have a great effect on whatever side of the scale their influence might be thrown. It is unlikely that any circumstances should arise which would alienate the fidelity of the great Sikh Rájás, especially since the extension to their families of the privilege of adoption; but, as the mass of the Khálsá are easily swayed by an appeal to their religious fanaticism, it is obviously desirable that these chiefs should feel that their own interests are closely connected with those of the paramount power.

When the Muhammadan power was beginning to wax faint, and the throne of the great Móghal was tottering to its base, the Sikhs saw that their hour for revenge was come, and, assembling their hosts under the banners of their most daring leaders, crossed the Satlaj *en masse*, and marched upon Sirhind. This town was anciently included in the province of Samána, which, in common with Thánesar, Pehówa, Bhatinda, Kharar, and a few other places, has a reputation for antiquity, but, owing to its central position, and to its being on the high road between Delhi and Lahore, Sirhind acquired great importance during the time of the Móghals, and was the head-quarters of a governor.

The Sikh invasion took place in 1820 Sambat (1764 A.D.), and was headed by three chiefs of note, namely, Jassá Singh Alhúwáliá, ancestor of the Kapúrthalla

[1] The following are considered to be among the most ancient towns in the country:—Thánesar; Pehówa, formerly called Prithudak; Kharrar, or Ajainagar, under which the Satlaj is said once to have flowed; Pinjór, called Adwitanagar, in the Vana Parva of the Mahábhárata; Samána, or Rinchin Khéra; Bhaváné, Bhatinda, Bhatnér, Bannúr, Indré, Kórí and Rúpar. Many other names might be added.

Raja, Kapúr Singh Singhpúria, and Jassá Singh Rámgarhia, who were all of different castes, but took their surnames from their respective villages. The other Sirdars, or chiefs, were of inferior rank, but ranged themselves under the following standards :—

Daléwália Misal	comprising the chiefs who seized Thánesar, Rúpar Siálba, Ládwá, &c.
Krórián Misal	comprising the Bassi, Biláspur, Léda, and Sadhaurá families.
Bhangi Misal	comprising the Búria, Jagádhri, and Diálgarh Sirdárs.
Nishánewalia Misal	including the Ambála, Sháhábád, and Ladhrán Sirdárs.

Besides these, there were the Shámsingián, Kátgarhia and Ghania misals, and many other chiefs fought for their own right hand, all being alike incited by fanaticism and hopes of pillage. Eventually, Baghél Singh, of the Daléwália Misal, appears to have become the most famous of the Sikh leaders, as he led the conquering forces of the Khálsá to Delhi, where he erected a tomb in memory of Guru Tégh Bahádur.

But little resistance seems to have been offered by Zain Khán, the Musalmán governor of Sirhind, who was at once slain by the enraged Sikhs, the town being sacked and destroyed. It is at the present day a dreary scene. For miles round one sees dilapidated mosques, grimed with smoke, with shattered domes, and their courtyards in ruins. Multitudes of bricks, and débris of buildings, lie strewn about in all directions, the whole area having a scathed and desolate look, showing how great must have been in former days the prestige of the place, and how fell the vengeance taken by the Sikhs on their oppressors. Musalmáns were ruthlessly put to the sword, those nobles who did not escape to the territories of the hill Rájputs being slain and their estates seized, the only exception being the Nawáb of Malérkótla, who, as it has been stated, interceded for the sons of Guru Góvind Singh, which compassionate act induced the Sikhs to leave his possessions intact.

After the capture and destruction of Sirhind, the Sikhs spread themselves over the country between the Satlaj and the Jamuná, the several bands seizing what territory they could, and dividing it among themselves, the chiefs of the Phulkián misal being however left in undisturbed occupation. Indeed, in the general confusion which ensued, they helped themselves largely, and still retain what they then won. The Panjáb chiefs do not appear to have observed any particular order in appropriating and dividing their spoil, and thus it happens that the descendants of members of the same Misal are found in different portions of the country. The land revenue of the country now comprised in the four districts of Ambála, Thánesar, Lúdiána, and Fírózpur may be estimated at 430,000*l.*, and is exclusive of the income of the Rajas of the Phulkián Misal and one or two other great chiefs, estimated at 370,000*l.* yearly; so that, when we first came in contact with the Cis-Satlaj Sikhs, they held a territory yielding 800,000*l.* yearly, with an area of more than 18,000 square miles, and a population possibly of 4,000,000.

It was a happy hour for this country when Sir C. Metcalfe, in 1806, succeeded in arresting the victorious progress of Ranjít Singh, Maharaja of the Panjáb, who meditated annexing it to his dominions. The crafty chief had no compunction in seizing any province that promised to be a valuable possession, and as the majority of the Cis-Satlaj chiefs still held their patrimonial estates in the Panjáb, he was not slow to assert his pretensions as their suzerain.

An amusing story is told of the avidity with which he grasped any opportunity of enriching himself at the expense of his feudatories. Among the leading Sirdars of the Cis-Satlaj country was Sóbha Singh Kalsia, whose grandfather, Gurbaksh Singh, accompanied the Krórian Misalin A.D. 1764. It is said that this chief, when a young man, was trimming his hair one day, when he perceived in his beard some grey hairs, which he endeavoured to restore to their pristine color by rubbing ashes over them. Ranjít Singh, hearing this, abused the Sirdár, saying that he had acted in a manner unbecoming a Sikh, it being unlawful for the Khálsá to dye their beards. The Sirdár took fright, and crossed the Satlaj the same night, whereupon Ranjít Singh immediately confiscated his territory in the Panjáb. Sóbha Singh never afterwards recrossed the river, and till the day of his death carefully hid his dishonored beard in a white cloth.

It may be observed here that on the death of any wealthy subject, Ranjít Singh is said, not unfrequently, to have declared himself to be the eldest son, confiscating the possessions of the deceased without any scruple, and reserving for the heirs only a small allowance.

Disputes between the several lords of the Cis-Satlaj

territory were common enough, and on various occasions Ranjít Singh's aid was invoked by one side or the other, so that, coupling this with the circumstance that most of the chiefs owned villages in his dominions, a tempting opportunity was offered to him of settling finally all dissensions by seizing the spoil himself.

When the British Government took the Cis-Satlaj Sirdárs under its protection in 1809, it wisely allowed to Ranjít Singh full scope for the extension of his rule throughout the country north of the river Satlaj, and he was not slow to avail himself of this tacit permission, though, no doubt, he reluctantly abandoned his cherished designs on the rich territory between the Panjáb and the Jamuná. The provinces of Multán, Kashmír, Pesháwar, and the trans-Indus Déráját all fell a prey to his victorious arms, while the discipline imparted to his troops by the French officers in his service, Court, Allard, Ventura, Avitabile, and others, enabled him to maintain and consolidate his authority. The first three of these officers bore a high reputation as soldiers, and were worthy representatives of their nation. Avitabile was uneducated, and not an experienced soldier. He was merciless in character, and used to pay largesse or grant estates in reward for the heads of the hill men; but it must be admitted that he successfully kept at bay the power of the Afgháns, and made himself the terror of the country side at Péshá-war. The large fortune amassed by him became the subject of law suits between his heirs, in Naples, of which kingdom he was a native.

It was owing to the circumstance that the small

escort of Sepoys attached to the service of Sir C. Metcalfe in 1806, successfully resisted the attacks on his camp made by a desperate band of fanatical Akális, that Ranjít Singh, to whom the matter was reported, formed so high an opinion of the value of European discipline, that he was induced to intrust the drilling of his troops to the French officers named above, and others of less note. The like had been done before by the Mahrattas with marked results, the success which their arms attained having been mainly owing to the excellent discipline taught to their soldiers by De Boigne, Perron, Baptiste, and others.

While, thanks to the exertions of Sir C. Wade and Sir G. Clerk, friendly relations were maintained between our Government and Ranjít Singh up to his death, the Cis-Satlaj country remained in a state of tranquillity, till the Sikh soldiery violated British territory in 1845. During the campaign which ensued, the greater part of the chiefs adhered to their allegiance, but the Raja of Ládwá, who was connected by marriage with the royal house of Lahore, the Bhai of Khaithal, the Rúpar Sirdár, and some others, forfeited their estates, owing to their having joined the cause of the Sikhs, while the Kapúrthalla Raja lost that part of his possessions which lay south of the Satlaj.

The great family, comprising the Phulkián Misál, with the exception of the Nábhá Raja, preserved an unshaken fidelity, which was highly creditable, as, after the battle of Fírózsháh, matters wore a gloomy aspect for the British power, which had rarely before received so severe a shock. It is not too much to say that, in the exhausted state of our army after this fierce struggle, the tumbrils of the guns being almost empty of shot, Raja Téj Singh might have obtained an easy victory, had he advanced with the fresh troops which he brought into the field. Fortunately, either acting from motives of cowardice, or from a suspicion that the English force before him was only a portion of our army, he, without apparent cause, withdrew his men, and the brilliant battle of Aliwál, with the subsequent entire discomfiture of the Sikh soldiery at Sabráon, placed the Panjáb at our mercy, and happily terminated a campaign, the issue of which was at one time extremely doubtful. In this, as in the Panjáb war, the Hindusthání sepoys proved no match for the hardy and resolute Sikhs, even though the latter were no longer under the command of French officers, and the brunt of all the engagements fell on the English troops.

Many lapses, owing to default of heirs, had occurred in the Cis-Satlaj country since 1806, and the position of the Government as the paramount Power gradually became far different from what it was at the commencement. Originally, the whole of the protected chiefs exercised sovereign powers within their own estates, an arrangement productive of great disadvantages and constant disputes. Many of the conquered tracts had been, in course of time, subdivided among cosharers, all of whom claimed equal jurisdiction, while there was no system for checking the caprice of individuals, the general control of the Political Agent being only partially efficacious in staving off gross oppression. Again, quarrels were rife as to the possession of particular villages, two or more chiefs striving each to assert his own jurisdiction in them, in order to secure payment to himself of their rental. The Government, therefore, after the Satlaj campaign, determined to maintain the sovereign powers of only the following nine houses, namely, Patiálá, Jhínd, Nábhá, Kalsia, Farídkót, Raikót, Diálgarh, Malérkótla, and Mamdót, the remaining thirty-four houses being disfranchised. The possessions of two of the greater families, namely, Raikót and Diálgarh, have since lapsed to Government.

The deprivation of their former powers to which the minor Sirdárs had been subjected, although unavoidable, was productive to them of serious consequences. The greater number of these chiefs had been in the habit of collecting their rents, either in kind, by a division of the crops, or by an arbitrary valuation, at the highest selling rates, of their proprietary share, the cultivators being virtually at their mercy. But, shortly after they lost their sovereign authority, disputes arose between them and their tenants, which necessitated the interference of the government officials. Collections in kind were obviously profitable to the landowners, as not only did they secure half the grain thrashed, but they also exacted a share of the fodder of their villages, besides various compulsory payments of stock, such as sheep, fowls, and the like, without recompense.

The cultivators, being freed from their old bondage, demurred to paying the exorbitant demands of the chiefs, and eventually it became necessary to make a revenue settlement of their holdings, which being based on the average collections of several years, with an abatement for bad seasons, fluctuations in the prices of grain, and the abolition of all unreasonable extra levies of the nature of heriot, naturally had the effect of considerably reducing the income of the Sirdárs, who remonstrated stoutly, but unavailingly.

Ten years afterwards, when the siege of Delhi was in progress, these petty chiefs aided actively in protecting the convoys on their way to join the army, while the mass of the cultivators stood aloof and inert, which gave the Sirdárs an opportunity of comparing the value of the assistance rendered by them in times of trouble with that of the Zemindars, to whose interests they supposed themselves to have been sacrificed. Bentham's maxim, *plurimorum maxima felicitas*, or 'the greatest happiness of the greatest number,' was, however, honorably carried out by the Government, and while few of the chiefs were capable of exercising worthily the powers wielded by them, much oppression and numerous serious disputes had been caused by the previous state of matters. Of late years, a few of the leading Sirdárs have been intrusted with revenue and judicial authority, and it is to be hoped that, as they advance in enlightenment and education, a farther and more extended trial may be made of the only system which can restore to them their self-respect, and win for them a ready allegiance from their tenants.

When the territory was partitioned on the invasion in 1764, to each chief was allotted, by mutual arrangement among the leaders of the Misal, a tract sufficient for the maintenance of himself and of a certain number of horsemen, rated at about 2*l.* a month per head.

According to the conditions of the subsequent tenure under the British Government, each Sirdár was bound to produce, whenever required, his quota of troopers for service in the field, the number being fixed on the above calculation according to the rental of his estate. In course of time, this obligation became inoperative, as, on the one hand, the Government never demanded the service, and, on the other, the Sirdárs perceiving this, ceased to maintain the required number of fighting men. It was therefore determined to commute the service to a money payment, which was fair in principle, though, perhaps, more advantageous to the State than to the chiefs. The descent of the shares of petty holders was also limited to male heirs in the direct line, all others being excluded. Some of the more stringent conditions have been relaxed in the case of those Sirdárs who rendered notable service during the siege of Delhi, but it is questionable whether the Government should bar from succession any descendant of the common ancestor, or refuse any adoption lawfully made to obviate lapses.

Although the Sikhs are, on the whole, a prolific race as compared with more effeminate Oriental nations, the effect of a strict rule regarding direct succession, when applied to sub-divisions of holdings, tends to diminish the income and lower the position of the proprietors. It is true that the perpetuation of minute holdings is disadvantageous; but if lapsed shares went to the head of the family, instead of reverting to the paramount Power, the measure would be popular, and the number of petty tenures would be diminished.

Under the existing system, as each share that lapses is swept in by Government, almost all the minor Cis-Satlaj Sirdárs are falling into insignificance, and descending to the position of ordinary cultivators.

The deprivation of their sovereign powers was also made the subject of complaint by the chiefs of the Lahore Council of Regency, who, on the annexation of the Panjáb, received a guarantee that they should continue to exercise in their estates the privileges enjoyed by them at the time. The apparent injustice of the treatment to which they were subjected was afterwards, however, remedied by granting to them the full powers of a magistrate and collector within the limits of their holdings.

The succession to landed property is not always of the same nature in the Cis-Satlaj country; for, although the shares are generally divided equally among male heirs, the head of the family, in the case of the great fiefs, succeeds to the title and the estate, provision being made for the younger sons, while, in a few instances, division is made, per stirpes, according to the system called 'chúdé bánt,' by which the collective issue of each wife of a deceased chief share alike. For instance, if there is one son by the first wife, two sons by the second, and three by the third wife, the one son receives a third, the two sons a sixth each, and the three sons a ninth each of the whole estate. This arrangement is not, however, common, and probably arises from partiality towards particular wives, either from their predominant influence or their higher rank, while, in some cases, the superiority of the sons may be the predisposing cause.

The effect of an equal division of landed property in a country where primogeniture is rare, and where caste prejudices offer a potent impediment to the cadets of a family finding a new sphere of employment, is inevitably to impoverish those small proprietors who do not actually cultivate their own lands. The numerous modes of life and the variety of occupations which hold out an inducement to such persons in Europe to better their condition, are unknown, or nearly so, in India; and the consequence is, that the service of Government is rarely sought by the landed gentry; nor can this be remedied till the diffusion of a sounder education extinguishes existing prejudices. Moreover, landed proprietors in the East are, as a rule, descendants of men who won their estates by the sword, and care little about intellectual superiority, so that almost all Government posts are held by those of the educated classes, who, from generation to generation, have made such employment their profession.

It must be admitted that the higher castes are naturally more gifted, and that the attempts frequently made to create a new class of public servants out of the sons of landowners, or from the members of the lower castes, have generally ended in failure. Hence we have before us a difficult problem in respect to the spread of education among the masses of the people; and until the natives of India can emancipate themselves from the trammels of caste and social prejudices which now prevent them from quitting the pursuits of their forefathers, it appears idle to give them an education which only makes them conscious of their thraldom.

For every Government post which falls vacant there are numerous competitors, of whom the vast majority must needs fail, and, failing, are unable to devise any other mode of subsistence for themselves. Such persons are discontented, and, having just enough superficial knowledge to enable them to lead others astray, may become, as their numbers increase, active agents of disaffection. To some extent, the general diffusion of knowledge is undoubtedly beneficial, as tending to give the people an acquaintance with their rights, and to curb the self-will and caprice of idle or oppressive officials; but it must be confessed that it becomes daily more difficult for English employés to preserve their ascendancy, while the time has not arrived when the Government can rely implicitly on the good-will and unfaltering allegiance of its native subjects.

Science and the fine arts are almost unknown among the people, except in translations from English books, such translations having rarely any originality in them; while there is in Indian literature a great want of that vigorous thought which characterises English works, though it seems to have flourished in times gone by among the ancient Hindus. Of the writings of any other nation than the English, the best educated Indians are almost wholly ignorant, while they are generally indifferent to geography, history, ethnology, natural history, and the various other branches of knowledge which comprise a liberal education. This is the more surprising, as their natural powers are great, while their readiness of apprehension is remarkable; but all education among them seems at present to cease when its foundations have been barely laid; and the moment that Government employment can be obtained by a candidate, he bids farewell to his books, and cares little about anything but his official duties and his hopes of advancement, even though he may have attached to his name the magic letters B.A.

It is impossible to say whether the Cis-Satlaj Sikhs are likely to retain their distinctive usages now that their prestige has been so sensibly diminished; or whether they will relapse into the Hinduism whence they sprang. But, whatever their religious tenets may be in future, they will always be a sturdy and fine race of men, whose allegiance is a matter of no little importance when war breaks out, either in India or beyond its confines.

A VISIT TO THE TAIPINGS IN 1854.

THE writer, being in China in 1854, had an opportunity of visiting Nanking, then in possession of the rebel Taipings. On May 25 the mail arrived from England, bringing news that war had been declared against Russia, whereupon the Admiral immediately sailed from Hong Kong in the 'Winchester,' in pursuit of the Russian Admiral, Pútiatín, who, with his fleet, was supposed to be in the neighbourhood of Japan. The writer was offered a passage as far as the mouth of the Yang-tsze-Kiang, where he left the flag-ship, and proceeded in the 'Styx' to Shanghai, which he reached on June 8.

The rebellion in China had for some time been spreading, and, in addition to the powerful party of Tai-ping-wáng, many bands of marauders, chiefly from the Canton and Fokien provinces, were actively engaged in plundering the country. One of these gangs had, in September 1853, suddenly seized on the town of Shanghai, and, at the time of the writer's arrival, was still in possession, though besieged by the imperialists, each party firing at the other, without doing much damage. In consequence of this state of siege, all the houses in the suburbs had been destroyed by the imperialists in order to enable them to breach the city wall. Only one gate of the town was open, and even that was kept barred, with a strong guard over it. The rebels were on good terms with the Europeans of the Settlement, who were admitted into the city without scruple; but no egress was allowed to the citizens, all the marketing to supply the necessaries of life being effected by letting down baskets over the walls. The city was a scene of great misery and desolation, almost all the houses being closed, while the few people whom one saw standing about the streets spoke with bated breath, and in evident terror of their masters. The rebels had compelled the citizens not to shave their heads, according to ordinary Chinese custom, and their unshorn polls had a most comical appearance. The walls were manned by the insurgents, each embrasure having a sentry, with a good stock of small guns, jingals, and ammunition close by. The rebels, who seemed to be terrible ragamuffins, to distinguish themselves from the inhabitants, mostly wore a red rag on their heads, or had some other article of dress of that color. All the temples in the town were closed. Great atrocities were said to be committed by the rebels, the chief of whom had been a horse-boy in the service of some English gentleman, and it was currently reported that many unoffending people had been beheaded, while others had been tortured, by being forced to sit upon heated stones, in order to extort money from them. Strangely enough, some of the missionaries had conceived an idea that the rebels were a promising field for Christian labor, while, in a few instances, low adventurers among the Europeans had sold them guns and powder without scruple.

The perpetual popping which went on between rebel and imperialist did not greatly interfere with the tranquillity of the European settlement, although in passing up the river between the city and the imperial encampment, some risk was run from the guns of either side.

The position of the insurgents under Tai-ping-wáng having at this time attracted great attention, both in China and in England, the Governor determined to send an expedition to Nanking, in order to obtain a more intimate knowledge of their condition and resources, and to form a conclusion as to their chances of ultimate success. Accordingly H.M.'s steamers 'Rattler' and 'Styx' were despatched to Nanking, and the writer joined the expedition. We left Shanghai on June 15, and after sundry mishaps during two days at the mouth of the mighty Yang-tsze-Kiang, in which the 'Rattler' got aground twice, and the 'Styx' lost an anchor and cable, we managed to clear the bar of the river, and anchored off Keashán. On the 18th we passed by the district town of Kiangyin, a place prettily situated in a bight of the river, with a fine pagoda in the distance, and a yellow temple on the bank of the stream, and proceeding onwards by the Keuen Shán pagoda, made our way up to Silver Island, a richly-wooded hill, adorned at its base with white temples, from which probably the island took its name. Two miles beyond this is the celebrated fortress of Chinkiangfú, which our troops took in the first China war, and which gave a title subsequently to Lord Gough, who commanded our army. On arriving opposite this stronghold, which commands the entrance of the Grand Canal, and was occupied by the insurgents, a shot was fired from the battery at its foot, which passed just under the bows of the 'Rattler.' Being thus brought to, we anchored for the night, and the next morning pulled ashore in a boat to demand an apology for the insult.

On our landing at the place whence the gun was fired, we received a note requesting us, if we wished to go on shore, to proceed up the stream to the regular landing-place at a jetty some way off. This we accordingly did, and on landing went to the house of the General, or Deputy-Governor, Kang, a young man, who at first seemed disposed to be uncivil, but yielding to persuasion or remonstrance, was at length very polite. As we sat and talked, the room became crowded by a mob of ragamuffins, who came to stare at us, and examined us and our dress very closely. They wore their hair, not in pig-tail fashion, like orthodox Chinamen, but twisted round their heads, and their polls being unshorn, the hair stood out in coarse bristles all over their heads in the most ludicrous way. Most of them wore moustaches and scanty beards. A few, who were apparently in office, wore yellow rags on their heads, drooping behind, like a lazzaroni's cap, while the General himself donned a peculiar head-dress of red cloth, inlaid with embroidery, with a sharp peak in front, a lion on the top, and a pendent tassel behind.

Having expressed a wish to see the Commandant of the fort, Wú-Jú-Kiaou, the General went to consult him, and returned, saying that his superior had consented to see us, whereupon we mounted our ponies, and, passing through a double gateway, entered the inner city where the Commandant resided. The town appeared to have been thoroughly pillaged, the houses having been gutted, and abandoned on all sides. Having arrived at the Commandant's abode, we were kept waiting for a short time, after which a crash of gongs was heard, and, an inner door being thrown open, we were admitted to the presence. The Commandant was seated behind a long table, and, without rising, motioned to us to be seated. He was dressed in a rich satin coat of a purple color, covered with gold, and wore the same kind of strange hat as our friend the General, though more richly decorated. He was a young man of about thirty, and, though at first extremely supercilious, soon became courteous. On our representing the insult that had been offered to the Britannic flag, the Commandant observed that he had no means of recognising foreign vessels, and had found it necessary to prevent ships from proceeding up the river, as the impish imperialists did not scruple to hoist the ensign of the English or any other nation. He promised, however, to write an apology, offered us assistance in procuring coal, and agreed to send some one with us to Nanking. Before we left, he politely gave us something to eat in the shape of several small, but not bad, dishes of duck, fowl, vegetables, and rice, which we had to discuss, however, with chopsticks, those curious inventions which remind the novice of the entertainment given by the fox to the stork in the fable. The Commandant also favoured us with copies of several of the insurgents' publications, among which were a translation of Leviticus; an account of the Establishment of the Celestial Dynasty at Nanking; a treatise on Land Tenures; an exhortation to exterminate the Tartars, &c.: all these books bearing a broad red official stamp in token of their genuine character. As we rode back, we saw some heaps of coal, and were told that plenty more was procurable. The town seemed large, but was very desolate, trade having ceased, and the population having been reduced to one-tenth of its original numbers, a sign that the rebels had not enlisted the sympathies of the people. We were told that there were 3,000 women in the city, but we did not see any, for it had been ordered that they should be kept separate from the men, on the ground that, while the place was in a state of siege, and the country generally unsettled, it was unadvisable to allow them to interfere with military operations. Proclamations to this effect were posted up all about the walls, together with others prohibiting the drinking of all intoxicating liquors, exhortations to citizens to return to their homes, advertisements for doctors, &c.

At a distance of about two miles, the imperialists were encamped with the object of recovering the city from the hands of the rebels, but they were too far off to breach the walls, and were afraid to come to close quarters. The fortifications appeared to be very strong, and were well guarded by large bodies of men, amply furnished with guns and ammunition, while the walls were surmounted by *cheveux-de-frise*. A canal also runs underneath the rock outside. The natural strength of the place is great, and as it commands both the river and the Grand Canal, its possession by an enterprising enemy would materially affect the trade of that part of the country.

After our return to the 'Rattler' we were favoured with a visit from the General, who was accompanied by one of his brigadiers and a colonel, if one may so dignify the respectable fraternity, and the three stayed to dinner, which they enjoyed greatly, forgetting the celestial denunciations regarding strong drinks. As we were far away from the batteries, and in the proximity of a besieging imperialist fleet, their visit to us betokened much confidence in our brotherly feeling, and some contempt for their foes. The General departed, highly delighted at having extorted a telescope and an umbrella from the Captain, and promising to present him in return a specimen of their peculiar head-dress, which however he forgot to do. The next day, the Colonel, who had been deputed to accompany us to Nanking, came off, and we steamed up the river, passing by Golden Island, a prettily wooded retreat, with a small pagoda and other buildings on it. Beyond this is Kwáchau, formerly a thriving town, which we found in a miserable state of ruin, and the desolate appearance of this and other places gave us an unfavourable idea of the conciliatory policy of the Taiping rebels.

On nearing Nanking, we had a good view of the place, which was surrounded by a strong wall, the Porcelain Pagoda standing out conspicuously in the distance. The inner city, being no less than four miles from the river bank, could not be clearly discerned, while the frontage of the suburbs was very mean, giving no idea of the proximity of a large capital. The approaches to the suburbs were all stockaded, large stakes having been driven into the ground crosswise, and, between them, innumerable pieces of bamboo with sharp projecting points, so that no troops could possibly advance over them in line. Several batteries commanded the river, and high look-out towers had been erected to survey the surrounding country and watch the arrival of enemies.

We sent a boat on shore with our friend the Colonel, who, on landing, was immediately mobbed by numbers of the rebels anxious to know our errand. The next day, June 21, we moved across the stream, and anchored close to the suburb, and after waiting some time fruitlessly for the Colonel's return, took a ship's boat and went on shore. After vainly attempting to pass through the wickets of the stockade, we pulled a little way up the creek, and landed where there was a ferry. Close by, a triangular flag of yellow denoted the quarters of the Taiping General in command of the outpost, which was outside the north-east wall of the city towards the Ifung Gate. We entered his house, and found him seated with two other officials, all three wearing the peculiar head-dress which we had seen at Chinkiangfú. Our reception was by no means civil, as they did not even rise to welcome us, a courtesy which Chinese politeness always dictates. On our seating ourselves, they enquired our object in coming to Nanking, and being informed that the British Government wished to cultivate friendly relations with them, and to receive information as to their power and resources, they told us to *petition* the Eastern King, whose name and titles were furnished in the following curious address:—'The Comforter—the Holy Ghost—the Honai Teacher—the Eastern King—Yang, Commander-in-Chief of the Celestial Forces.'

We promised to write to the Taiping Chief, to announce to this mighty potentate our arrival, and, having sipped some tea, took our leave. The Colonel never returned, and we shortly ascertained that the people had been forbidden to communicate with us, either on board the steamer or on shore, from which we concluded that something had gone wrong.

On examining one of the revelations which were presented to us at Chinkiangfú, we found out the origin of the blasphemous epithet applied to the Eastern King. The treatise stated that Yang, having given some excellent advice to Tai-ping-wáng, the leader of the insurgents, the latter, being well pleased with his devotion, said,—'Our elder brother, Jesus, in leaving this world, promised to send after him a Comforter. You are this Comforter, and I give you henceforward the title of the Holy Ghost.' In the same revelation, it was alleged that the Heavenly Father came down from heaven, and ordered that Tai-ping-wáng should receive forty strokes with a bamboo as a punishment for his misconduct in ill-treating various people, and his wives in particular, but Yang interceded for him, and he was let off with a severe reprimand.

On the 22nd, we passed through a part of the suburb, but were stopped at a wicket gate on our way to the city wall, and no persuasions would induce the rebels to admit us inside, so we entered the residence of a chief outside, who was very civil, but pleaded his positive instructions not to allow us to proceed beyond the gate. This man informed us that the 'second coming' had taken place the previous year at Nanking, and, in confirmation of the popular belief, we saw many people, when about to sit down to dinner, repeating, at their grace, a prayer 'in the name of God the Father, Jesus Christ the Son, and the Eastern King the Holy Ghost.' Some said this kneeling, others standing.

A great many junks were lying in the creek, full of fighting men, who, to the number of 10,000, were starting off on an expedition, in consequence of some news which they had received from the north, though of what nature they would not say. All the boats had flags, chiefly triangular, and the soldiers wore a uniform of red and yellow, with the common fighting cap, each man having the number of his regiment stamped on his coat, or a piece of wood suspended in front. Their arms were rude and inferior, consisting mainly of long spears, short swords, and halberds, but musquets or fusils were rare. The rest of the population were poorly dressed, and their heads looked exceedingly grotesque, owing to their unkempt bristly hair, but they were tolerably civil and used no abusive language. The taboo was rigidly maintained, on the alleged ground that, on a previous visit from the American steamer

'Susquehanna,' annoyance had been given by the rebels to the crew, but it is probable that they suspected our intentions. It was stated, however, that when the American minister was at Nanking, a middy who had wandered about the place in search of the Porcelain Pagoda, had climbed over the walls, and thereby created considerable sensation among the Taipings, who resolved from that time to keep all intruding foreigners aloof.

On the 23rd, while we were taking a walk in another direction, we were again stopped by a wicket. In reply to the request which we made for an interview, and for admission into the city, the General commanding the outpost wrote to say that he had received the 'golden commands' of the Eastern King, to the effect that he was too busy in sending off troops to see us, but he forwarded, for our initiation into Heavenly Precepts, sundry pamphlets similar to those we had received at Chinkiangfú. The following is a list of these productions :—

1. Leviticus.
2. Deuteronomy.
3. Joshua.
4. Important discourses on Heavenly Principles.
5. Discourse upon branding the impish den 'Chihli' (Pekin) with the name 'Tsuy le' (an opprobrious word).
6. Book of Declaration of the Divine Will, 2nd series.
7. On affixing the Golden Seal to Royal Proclamations.
8. Treatise on Land Tenures.
9. Calendar for 1854.

These pamphlets were all fairly printed, but were the oddest jumble of truth and falsehood, of sense and nonsense.

We then despatched a long letter to the Eastern King, putting a variety of questions as to the number of the Taipings, the extent of country they had conquered, the number of their troops, their laws and usages, and so forth, while a request was made to be supplied with coal, of which in our walks we had seen great quantities.

On the 25th, crowds of a force just returned from some warlike expedition came on board the 'Rattler,' and examined everything most curiously. Most of them were dressed as soldiers in yellow coats with a red border, having short swords swung on their backs. One of them, who said that he had been impressed into the service, stated that at Nanking provisions were scarce, and that the rebels had, latterly, been unsuccessful in the north. He further remarked that it was generally believed that we had come to extort money, which had led to the refusal to see us. All our visitors had unkempt heads and a savage appearance, and, though sharp enough, they were a disreputable set. One small boy, ten or twelve years old only, bragged of having cut off the heads of five or six men, and inspected the ship guns in a most inquisitive way.

Having received verbal permission to take in coal from Kiahwán, in a creek close by, where there was an extensive coal-yard, we dropped down by what is called in the maps 'Theodolite Point,' and anchored opposite the coal sheds. Soon after, a Colonel came on board to ask us to wait till the next day, to which the Captain of the 'Rattler' consented. In the afternoon a boat came off with a letter, written in the form of an order, telling us to go away, and demanding to know whether we wished to get into collision with the rebels. This letter, being offensively worded, was returned to the bearer. Two hours afterwards, a large gun was brought down by the rebels within a quarter of a mile of the 'Rattler,' while several others which were in a masked battery on the river bank, were disclosed, bearing directly on the ship. The officers on board were indignant, one young middy stamping on the deck, furious with rage at the impudence of the Taipings; but the Captain, who had received orders to avoid, if possible, any conflict with them, thought it prudent to send a boat on shore to demand the meaning of this apparent act of hostility. The rascals who had dragged down the big gun swore it was only intended for the imperialists, but as it bore straight on the 'Rattler,' and as, in the narrow creek in which we lay, we should have been exposed to the possible treachery of the 'Brethren,' the Captain judged it advisable to shift his quarters, so we weighed anchor, and passing up the creek again, anchored in the main stream, near some mosquito-haunted marshes. These insects are most annoying at Nanking. They devoured us in swarms, and as we had no curtains, and the heat was great, we were obliged to submit to be stifled under a sheet, or to be bitten frightfully all over. The men rushed about the deck at night, angry and sleepless, pursued by their pertinacious tiny foes.

The Yang-tsze-Kiang river at Nanking, though 250

miles from the mouth, is a mile wide, and runs like a mill sluice, at the rate of five miles an hour.

On June 27, we received a letter from some minor official informing us that the Eastern King would answer our communication. This letter containing an offensive appellation, a remonstrance was sent in. The messenger was also told to acquaint his superior that a salute would be fired by the 'Rattler' the ensuing day in honor of the Queen's birthday, it being deemed prudent to mention this, lest the Taipings should suspect hostile intentions.

On the morrow, we received another letter to the effect that the word 'barbarian' had been used to distinguish between the Brethren and us, thus assuming all the offensive superiority to which we had objected. The letter also stated, with reference to our intimation, that a salute would be fired in honor of our Queen, that the Eastern King had been graciously pleased to accord his permission to us to do so, but desired at the same time that we should learn that the use of the word 'imperial,' as applied to our Queen, was highly improper, it being employed solely to signify the Deity. No allusion was made to our application for coal, nor to the wish we had expressed to visit the far-famed pagoda. The letter was most offensively worded, and was accordingly returned by the bearer, while an answer was again requested to our previous communication.

In the evening, a boat came off, bearing a letter, or, so-called, 'order' from the Eastern King, enclosed in an immense yellow envelope, eighteen inches long and a foot wide. It was of great length, and contained answers to the questions put by us, while, at the same time, His Majesty, being greatly puzzled about the meaning of certain scriptural texts in his copy of the Pentateuch and the New Testament, put a great many questions to us in return, nearly all of them bearing on religious topics.

The letter commenced with a prologue to the following effect:—'I am the Holy Ghost, appointed by special orders of the Heavenly Father, who personally took the trouble to come down on earth to instruct me,' and a good deal more to the same effect. After this, our questions were answered, though, in most cases, very imperfectly and evasively.

The document asserted that the Heavenly Father, when about to enjoin His commands on mankind, came down personally on earth, taking the form of the Eastern King, and through his golden lips proclaimed his ordinances. Jesus Christ, it was said, similarly assumed the person of the 'Western King,' the next dignitary, and the name of 'Tien-Kwoh' was given to the dynasty founded by the rebels. We were informed that they had not, up to that time, struck coin, nor issued Government Gazettes, while their army was vaguely stated to be innumerable, and their range of empire to include the whole earth. Their laws did not appear to be well defined, but drinking was denounced under severe penalties, and many other crimes were apparently as severely punished as under ordinary Chinese law.

The theological questions put by Yang savored both

of shrewdness and absurdity. For instance, he asked, 'What length and breadth has God?' 'What is the color of His beard?' 'What clothes does He wear?' The same queries were made regarding our Saviour, with additional questions as to the number of his daughters and granddaughters. Then, some pertinent enquiries were made as to the right interpretation of difficult texts, such as, 'Repent ye, for the Kingdom of Heaven is at hand.' Yang asked why Jesus was nailed to the Cross, and why he rose again on the third day?

It appeared from this strange communication that, though the rebels had procured copies of portions of the Bible, they had no one competent to interpret to them the meaning of Scripture. The last remark made by the Eastern King was amusing enough. He enquired why we barbarians, who ought to bring tribute to the Celestial Kingdom, had the presumption to come to him and ask him for coal, thus showing our ignorance of heavenly precepts. In commenting upon our unenlightenment as to celestial doctrines, Yang compassionately observed that he was not much surprised at our ignorance, seeing whence we came.

The next day we formed a synod for the purpose of answering the questions put to us, by no means an easy matter, considering the absurdity of some of them. The rebels insisted that the Tatars must be the Satan mentioned in the Bible, and Yang ingeniously tried to establish this by several quotations which he thought apposite.

On June 30 we left Nanking, and just before we

got under weigh received a letter from one of the rebel Generals, requesting us to take to Chinkiangfú a brother of the Colonel whom we had brought up with us, and whom we had never set eyes on since we landed him. On the boat, which brought this missive, returning, we sent on shore our answers to the Eastern King's questions.

About three hours' steaming, aided by the rapid current, brought us to I'ching, on the left bank of the river, thirty miles below Nanking. Here we anchored, and, in the afternoon, pulled up a creek leading to the town, which is a large place, with a considerable population, but was pillaged and burnt the year before by the rebels. Though many houses in it were abandoned, there was an abundance of provisions, of which we were in need, and the inhabitants seemed much more respectable than the ragamuffin gang at Nanking. They gave us tea and pipes in one of the Joss houses, which had apparently been visited by the rebels, as the images in it had been destroyed, and we set out afterwards to visit the magistrate, who had the politeness to come out in his chair to meet us. He and all the other officials were very civil, supplying us with everything we required, and, in all respects, presenting a most favorable contrast to our Nanking friends. Most of them had, however, lost their buttons, for their unsuccessful resistance to the insurgents, who, only a few days before our arrival, had again attacked the town, and killed a great many people.

On July 2, we reached Golden Island close to Chinkiangfú, but, on landing, were refused admittance by the rebels. We found that this pretty little retreat of Boodhist priests had been quite ruined, all the temples having been unmercifully pillaged and burnt. We saw two handsomely carved marble pillars, one of which was broken, and some fine porcelain gable ends and tiles, but everything was mutilated, many of the houses having been knocked down to build a small fortification, behind which the insurgents had entrenched themselves. Failing to procure admittance to this famous sanctuary, we sent off to Chinkiangfú the rebel whom we had brought down from Nanking, and invited our old acquaintance, the General, to come on board, which he declined doing, saying that he had received orders not to visit us again.

The next day, we got into a boat and pulled down to Silver Island, visiting on our way the imperialist fleet, which was besieging Chinkiangfú. We went on board a square-rigged ship called the 'Glenlyon,' hired by the imperialists, on which were four Europeans, but no Mandarins, the latter being higher up the river. One of these men stated that the royal army encamped near Chinkiangfú amounted to 90,000 men, but this number must have been greatly exaggerated. We were told that, on the capture of the fortress by the rebels, 2,600 of the inhabitants were pressed as soldiers, and sent to Nanking, while their wives were locked up. and guards put over them. After having been subjected to every kind of indignity, these women were driven out in a body at night in the direction of the imperialist encampment, each with a lantern attached to her breast, which the imperial troops seeing, mistook them for a rebel force making a sortie, and, firing on them, killed a vast number.

The Glenlyon people said that the imperialists often charged up to the walls of Chinkiangfú, but were always driven back by the heavy guns mounted on the bastions, while the royal fleet, owing to the pusillanimity of the Mandarins, appeared to be useless. It was said that the rebels had fourteen or fifteen Europeans in their service, but that these were irregularly paid, owing to the uncertain position of the insurgent cause.

Silver Island, or more correctly Rocky Island (Tsiaou Shán), was formerly the site of a celebrated monastery, which, till destroyed by the rebels, was in a flourishing state. There was a very handsome temple, the images in which had been smashed, while the cloisters were destroyed and the sacred books burnt, every vestige of them having been made away with by the fanatical insurgents. We failed in obtaining any manuscripts whatever, though the library was formerly celebrated and extensive. From the monastery, a stone pathway leads to the top of the hill, whence there is a fine view of the surrounding country, including the course of the Yang-tsze-Kiang river, the Chinkiangfú heights, and the fertile low land on the left bank.

Passing by Kiang-yin, we proceeded down to Láng Shán, or Wolf's Hill, and, with considerable trouble, made our way across the river to Fúshán, a station of some importance, with a fort. At this crossing, we found only three and three-and-a-half fathoms of water, and even this depth with difficulty. Heavy rain detained us at Fúshán till July 6, when we steamed off again, but ran aground near Mason Island, where we had to wait till the next tide carried us off. On July 7, we got back to Shanghai without mishap.

The result of the expedition above narrated was to shake a belief which had prevailed among many persons that a pure type of Christianity had sprung up in China, inasmuch as an examination of the various publications brought back by us demonstrated that the rebels professed many absurd, not to say blasphemous, tenets on religion. It was further apparent that, although they had overrun a great part of the Chinese empire, and had, owing to the imbecility of the imperial rule, obtained considerable temporary success, they only occupied permanently a few towns of importance, while they had no hold on the revenue or trade of the country, and subsisted by plunder and pillage. They had certainly not enlisted the sympathies of the people about Nanking, who have little in common with the natives of the Fokien and Canton provinces, whence the insurgents came, and being, with but few exceptions, illiterate, they failed to command respect from the higher classes, even though many of the latter may have been opposed from patriotic feelings to Tatar ascendancy. It is to be feared that both they and the Mandarins oppressed the unfortunate inhabitants of the districts where the intestine feud was raging, and loud were the complaints of the cruelties practised by both sides. That the rebels were, at the time of our visit, only in possession of forts and other strong places, was proved by their inability to stop the flow of trade on the Yang-tsze-Kiang and the Grand Canal. They had no commerce of their own, nor did they seem to care about intercourse with foreigners, distinctly asserting that, if the latter did not come to pay tribute, they did not wish to see them.

It is probable that many persons sincerely believed in the reality of the conversion of these strange zealots, but some of the reports spread about them were evidently untrustworthy. For instance, in a book published by Vizetelly and Co., giving an account of their proceedings and of the interesting communications with them held by Sir G. Bonham, there is a print representing the rejoicings at Nanking on its capture by the rebels. This print is taken from a French book containing pictures of oriental scenery, in which the identical print is to be seen as representing the Chinese feast of lanterns!

The Colonel whom we took with us to Nanking stated that, at the capture of that place by the rebels, thousands of people were ruthlessly murdered, and it is notorious that the native Christians were among the victims. Had any missionary of any persuasion gone among the rebels and told them that they held erroneous doctrines, and that Yang's assumption of the title of 'Holy Ghost' was a blasphemy, there can be little doubt that he would have paid for his rashness by his life. In short, there never was a more egregious mistake than to suppose that these fanatical and blood-thirsty robbers were sincere and pious Christians.

The question arises whether it is justifiable or wise to disseminate broadcast among oriental races translations of the Scriptures without commentary or explanation, as has been done in China and elsewhere. In the first place, the translations themselves are not always free from error, as must needs be the case when a European renders into a foreign tongue, of which his acquaintance is partial and imperfect, phrases and words the exact meaning of which it is difficult to convey, when they are abstruse in signification, or when they represent a novel idea to an oriental mind. But, even supposing that the translations are perfect, and represent accurately the sense of the original, is it proper to let every man put his own interpretation on every passage, and communicate to others what may be an essentially faulty doctrine? It is not reasonable to say that the Word of God is sufficient, and will explain itself, or we should not witness such an absurd travestie as was exhibited by the Taipings in their religious tenets.

These deluded fanatics having procured from a Canton source copies of the Pentateuch and of parts of the New Testament, had blindly accepted the construction put upon the difficult passages by their leaders, and were consequently entangled in a maze of errors, from which, had they been actuated by the purest intentions, they would have had difficulty in extricating themselves. As matters stood, their chiefs misused the Scriptures to subserve their own political ends, and propagated a false and delusive belief, which did much harm to the advancement of real Christianity.

In the early days of missionary enterprise in China, *vivâ-voce* teaching was the weapon used by the Catholic missionaries, who, dressed like the natives of the country, penetrated into the interior in every direction. For more than two hundred years they labored in China, with the tacit, or even open assent and support of its sovereigns, making thousands of converts, and winning for themselves, by their literary and scientific attainments, the respect of the people. They neither received nor cared for the protection of European Powers, but, after the China wars, fought in the interests of commerce, had entirely changed the relations of the China Government towards European States, it is not surprising that the Catholic missionaries should endeavour to get themselves placed on the same footing as their Protestant brethren, and consider themselves equally entitled to protection.

The accusations preferred against them at the time of the Tientsin massacre, by certain writers in the daily papers, were based upon imperfect information as to the circumstances, and ignorance of oriental prejudices. It is notorious, and the fact has been observed in all ages, that converts to Christianity are regarded with dislike by many of their pagan countrymen, who have not been slow to prefer false charges against them before the local authorities. Formerly, the labors of missionaries, if not encouraged, were, at any rate, not proscribed by Chinese officials; but, after the humiliation to which their country had been subjected in its wars with European States, their repugnance and antipathy to foreigners were greatly intensified. Being unable, however, to resist, by force of arms, the objects of their dislike, they wreaked their vengeance in the only way which was practicable, namely, by courting false charges against helpless native Christians, and those who were devoted to the cause of religion and mercy.

The massacre at Tientsin appears to have arisen from a blind hatred on the part of the mob against all foreigners, rather than from purely religious bigotry, but both causes combined, no doubt, led to the outrage. It is to be lamented that certain daily prints took so little trouble to ascertain the real facts, but when allegations of petty larceny against an Emperor found admittance into the columns of a famous paper, it is perhaps not strange that Sisters of Charity should be deemed capable of imprudent conduct.

As regards the alleged arbitrary proceedings of French officials, it may be observed that, whatever may be their desire to push French prestige beyond due limits, their past history in the East does not lead to the conclusion that this is done in the interests of religion, to which, as is well known by those who have watched their actions, they are mostly very indifferent. Indeed, it may be mentioned in confirmation of this view, that the Bishop of Canton in vain applied to the French Consul at that port to procure the release of a native Christian woman who had been unjustly condemned to death by torture by the Chinese authorities, and that his object was only effected by the timely and humane intervention of the British Consul.

Without discussing further whether the indiscriminate dissemination of the Bible in China, where the copies are often applied to base uses, is judicious, or whether the publication of numerous tracts directly attacking the superstitions of the Chinese may not have aroused religious fanaticism on their part, it is evident that the diffusion of the Scriptures by ignorant zealots like the Taipings, with the wild and distorted commentary put upon the sacred writings by their chiefs, was productive of great mischief.

CHIT-CHAT WITH FRIENDS AT HOME.

Off Socotra, October 26, 1867.

DEAREST ——.—Such a delicious breeze! I am feeling as cool as a cucumber, and as fresh as a lark; and how we do all enjoy it, after the suffocating damp of the Red Sea! Notwithstanding all its miseries, the voyage is very amusing.

We left Aden, where there is not a vestige of vegetation (I was told afterwards that there is one garden), and which looks, what it is, the crater of a volcano, with strange fantastic mountains of lava, and small hills of coal, and numbers of seedy-looking camels trotting about, a regiment, and a few ships and shops. The chief amusement was buying ostrich feathers and watching native divers. About twenty of these fellows, quite black, and some with curly red hair, swam out to the ship, and dived for money flung out to them by the passengers, remaining, as it seemed, many minutes under water. They swam about the ship all day.

As we steamed away, we met the 'Malabar,' a transport, with troops for Abyssinia, and we gave them a cheer. Now we are fairly off for eight or nine days, with 400 passengers, the most crowded mail of the year! I wonder the purser can survive the journey, as all complaints go to him, and how John Bull does growl and grumble when he can't get all his home comforts, and is hot! Certainly, the passengers are great fun. There is Colonel R., a good-natured man, but now in a perpetual ferment, boiling over and exploding all day long. Mrs. R., having no maid, has cut off her hair in despair. Mr. N. and Mr. V., the former looking like a surly bear, the latter like a perspiring frog, playing whist from daybreak to sunset. There is Mrs. O., a gushing young woman of forty, going out to her husband. She laughs heartily all day, and flirts with all the gentlemen, who make great fun of her. She sings, too, with a stentorian voice, devoid of sweetness.

Mrs. G. is *very* interesting! She is also going out to her husband, the event being so near that it might take place on board. She thinks everyone dreadfully selfish, and is full of woes, which she is ready to pour into our ears, while two crying children do not contribute to her peace of mind, nor that of her neighbours.

Captain F. has the fever, and life is a burden to him. Mrs. F. is doubtless in his eyes a fine woman, but is a perfect feather-bed, and has a little girl, who is frightfully spoiled and screams all day long. Colonel and Mrs. S. sit apart from the common herd, and only associate with 'dear Lords,' and Sir W. S. If she sits aft, she cannot enjoy her baccy (cigarette)! She wears a wondrous chignon. She likes everything, and never grumbles, but is rather disconsolate at the prospect of losing 'her set' (the great people) at Ceylon.

Two Miss Downfalls are in charge of Mrs. F., who has given them up, because they will dance with the ship's officers, and go on the forecastle after dark. Dr. M. is a good Samaritan, and supplies Mrs. B. with Liebig's mixture and China tea. She looks very well, but is dreadfully spoiled, and is a very bad sailor, feeding the fishes so frequently as to be a source of discomfort to her gudeman.

To-morrow we hope to be at Ceylon, and to rest there forty-eight hours. What a luxury to sleep in a real bed, and not to be awoke by a donkey engine, screaming children, cocks and sheep, or a pig giving its expiring squeak!

Madras, November 8.

I wrote last on the Indian Ocean. It was a weary run to Galle of nine days, the sea calm, but with a heavy swell on it, and we just escaped a gale of wind. The 'Candia' rolled in grand style, like the pendulum of a clock. The single incident was meeting a native boat in distress, it having lost its way. They delayed us some hours, and the '*on dit*' on board was that the captain of the said boat wanted to be shaved, and that his wife was anxious to possess a chignon.

You can imagine what a relief it was to the eye, after the dreary grandeur of the desert and the ocean, to feast our eyes on the exquisite loveliness of the luxuriant vegetation of Ceylon. Even the rocks out at sea were covered with waving verdure, and the air really was scented with the spices and flowers.

We got safely into the rickety native boats managed by men in birthday suits, who shout and wail, and pull as hard as they can. When we landed, the feeling was like being in one of those tropical conservatories, but still it did not seem in the least oppressive. We put up at a fine new hotel, 'The Oriental,' our room being like a great barn, whitewashed, with an arch and wooden shutters for a window, the floor tiled, marble tables, and two iron beds, well protected with net curtains. How we did enjoy our champagne lunch! As it was Sunday, we drove to the Catholic church, our coachman and footboy being, with the exception of one small garment, both 'au naturel.' We found in the church an Italian Benedictine, who spoke English perfectly, and advised us to drive on through the cinnamon groves, which we did. What wonderful vegetation! date trees, cocoa-nuts, betel-nuts, and plantains, the natives running after the carriage with oranges, pine-apples, and flowers. When we stopped we were surrounded by pretty native children, bringing precious stones, pearls, feathers, and beautiful tortoise-shell ornaments for sale. I felt like a fairy princess. Some of the natives climbed up into a cocoa-nut tree, and having pulled off one, opened it, and offered it to me to drink. I thought it too sweet and sickly. Others brought sticks of cinnamon and lemon leaves for me to smell. They were very gentle, and seemed much amused.

What a luxury a real bed was, and did I not sleep

like a top! Next evening I walked with L. on the ramparts, and we saw such a sunset—gold, purple, blue, and green, with white spray, and a pink glow over all. At four o'clock next morning we were all on board; but, after leaving Gallé, we experienced strong head winds and currents against us, which sadly delayed our arrival at Madras.

Shall I ever forget that last night on board? I saw the sun set, without a sight of land; and, to add to our discomfort, it began to blow fresh, and an order was given to close the ports. Then the croakers, of whom there are always plenty on board, went about, saying the captain expected a gale, and that we should not be able to put into Madras for some days. L. made my bed up on one of the benches, as the heat below was stifling, and lay down himself on the deck beside me. It seemed but an instant afterwards when I was startled by the report of a gun, and, opening my eyes, found it was daylight. I had really slept soundly all night, and we had just dropped anchor off Madras. The 'Candia' was rolling about in a wonderful way, and everyone was saying what a dreadful night we had had; but I knew nothing of it. Of course, the voice of a croaker sounded in my ear. 'Do you see that flag, Mrs. B.? that's the danger flag! Sorry for you! Don't you wish you were were going on with us to Calcutta?'

I made a hasty toilette, no crinoline, only petticoat and waterproof, and prepared for a grand ducking. When I came on deck, a number of officers had, I found, come on board, and one of them handed me a letter from Lord N., asking us to go straight to

Government House. We accepted, and I was afterwards very glad we did so, for I enjoyed the visit exceedingly.

Until all was ready, I amused myself by looking at the strange scene. Besides the large boats that came off for passengers, numbers of naked men, seated astride on logs of wood with a long paddle in their hands, came to have a stare at the ship and her company, their long hair streaming in the wind, and one and all shouting like madmen. After all our boxes had been let down into one of the crazy looking boats, which were full of water, I bid good-bye to our friends on board, and descended the ladder. What with the yelling of the people, and the dashing of the boat, I felt very much like the Yorkshireman, 'clean mazed and stagnated.' Just as I was preparing to jump in, a large wave came and dashed the boat like a nut-shell under the ladder, and lifted us up with it. Then down we went again, and I jumped safely into the arms of the ship's officer. Then we were several minutes in getting clear of the 'Candia,' each great wave carrying us back to her; and when she rolled over on her side, as if to crush us, it really was terrific.

The twenty natives who rowed the boat were invoking 'Santa Maria' and 'Xavier' all the way to the pier. I don't know why we were not all swamped, as I never saw such frightful waves; and no ordinary boat could have lived in them. I suppose the lightness of the native boats, which are made of bark, sewn together with thick twine, renders them safe. Arrived at the pier a tub was let down, and we were hoisted up in it.

A deputation from Mysore awaited our arrival, and great wreaths of pink and white flowers were put round our necks, and bouquets presented to us.

Now, let me see if I can give you a description of Government House. It stands in a very pretty park, but the foliage of the trees is much richer than in England, and there are tall feathery trees like gigantic ferns. The earth is quite red, and there are great birds which scream, and little blue birds; and instead of deer, there are antelopes jumping and bounding about in an odd way. The house is painted to look like white marble. There are no doors, but you drive under a portico, and ascend a flight of steps thirty feet wide, through a grand open hall, up a very handsome branching staircase, and everywhere there are great vases full of exquisite flowers. You finally arrive at a drawing-room like a Grecian church—all white, with pretty chintz sofas and easy chairs, with punkahs waving slowly in a sleepy way over you. From this you enter smaller drawing-rooms, without doors, and with arches instead of windows, leading into a wide verandah with Indian matting to keep out the sun.

Native servants, all dressed in white, with white and red turbans, stand about here and there, watching to see if anyone wants anything. There are no bells, and if you call out, 'Peon,' instanter he stands before you. An Ayah with bare feet, rings on her toes, two large gold nails in her ears, besides earrings, a large ruby (?) inserted in one nostril, and a scarf gracefully wound about her person, was called up and told to take care of me.

We remained at Madras three days. The order of the day was—ten o'clock, breakfast; two, tiffin; and five, tea; and directly the sun set, we all turned out, Mrs. F. and I driving, while the gentlemen rode. All the grooms run, and are marvellously fleet. They wear short white dresses, scarlet and gold belts and turbans, and flourish long whisks of white and scarlet hair. Those who run with the carriage shout to the natives to clear the road. We drove up and down a fine road by the sea, the band playing, and all the world taking the air by moonlight. At eight we dined. Each evening we had a dinner party of thirty persons, and dined in the verandah, which was airy and cool, a band playing the whole time.

Bangalore, November 20.

As it is fourteen hours' journey to Bangalore, L. secured a through carriage, which is so comfortable that you can go to bed and sleep in it. As I stepped in, two neat square baskets were handed in, which turned out to contain a dainty dinner which Mrs. F. had kindly ordered to be sent—everything from ice to salt. We eat our dinner, and then I undressed partially, and went to bed with great comfort.

I was in the middle of a dream, when I became aware of a noise and something bright. It was quite dark, but a deputation had come down the line to greet us, and forty or more natives in white sheets, and with torches and tomtoms, were looking at me, much to my embarrassment. L. got out to speak to them, and they offered him fruit and flowers, one of them standing forward to make a speech. At four o'clock we stopped again, and there was another deputation, with more fruit and flowers, and atar of roses. There was a comfortable waiting-room, so I made my toilette, and enjoyed a cup of hot tea. Then we started again.

It was a glorious morning. L. said a litany and morning prayers, and, shortly afterwards, Bangalore came in sight, looking in the distance like an English village, with the spires of the churches peering up amidst the trees.

Inside the station were all the officers of the commission, with their wives, and outside the scene was most extraordinary. The whole native population had turned out. A rocky eminence in front of the station was one mass of human beings in white dresses, with every variety of colored turbans, producing a most picturesque effect. L. stood for a few moments on the steps, salaaming,—that is to say, bowing and touching the forehead with the right hand—and then we drove off, a detachment of cavalry galloping in front. As we neared our gates, we came to a triumphal arch—a mass of flowers, with 'Welcome' written above in white roses. Here the crowd was so dense that the carriage came to a standstill, and an address was handed in by one of the principal natives, accompanied by specimens of fruits. Then they insisted on putting a wreath of white roses and silver cord round my neck, and another round L.'s. When we entered our compound, guns fired, the flag was hoisted, and we were at home. The steps of the house were one mass of flowers, and a servant was waiting inside with a bouquet from the

Raja's own garden. As for myself, I was fairly bewildered, what with the dust, noise, and novelty of the whole proceeding.

Bangalore, December 4.

I enclose a list of our household; as each servant only does one thing, we are obliged to have a great many. Their costumes are light and airy. The three women, who are about our rooms, wear a scarf twisted round their persons, a jewel in one nostril, and all sorts of things in their ears, gold nails, &c., and on their toes they have silver rings. When I gave them their new scarfs they put them on, and then came and lay flat on the floor at my feet by way of saying, 'Thank you.' The butler and boys (we call them 'boys,' but they are all men, and some rather ancient), wear white muslin trousers, white calico upper garments reaching to the knees, and white turbans. The coachman and horse-boys wear blue cloth blouses, bound with scarlet, and fastened in at the waist with a scarlet and blue belt, white knickerbockers and scarlet turbans. In the hot weather, they wear all white, and they have bare legs and feet always.

I have a capital cook, but how he ever turns out such good dinners from the place called a kitchen is quite beyond me. They light little charcoal fires on the hearth, and there is no such thing as an oven or a grate, or a boiler or a jack! and yet we have joints and entrées, just as if we had one of Benham's stoves.

One thing is universal. They never express the least surprise. My butler, for instance, if you praise him, says nothing. If you scold him, and tell him he is a thief and a liar, he receives your information with the same passive indifference. Last week, he told me his brother had killed his wife with just the same nonchalance. A few days after, he asked to be allowed to go and be shaved, because his brother had been hung, and it was their custom to shave at such times. All the servants are alike in this respect. They are all most attentive, and run like hares if I want anything, and are really very clever. The first dinner-party I gave, I troubled myself to arrange the flowers, but the next party 'master's boy' did it all quite as well as I did it myself, so I never troubled myself about it again.

L. went to Mysore, to pay his respects to the Raja, who sent me a garland of flowers, and a betel-nut to chew. He told L. if he came again without me, he would not receive him, and said he had heard I was good tempered and *long-handed.* Some translate this to mean extravagant, others charitable.

December 6.

We are very early people in this part of the world. Last Sunday they kept the feast of St. Francis Xavier at the native church, and we sent word that we should attend at mass. Such a wonderful sight! It is a fine large church, built in the form of a cross. It was beautifully decorated with flowers by the Indians, and round the altar great exotic leaves had been most gracefully arranged. The church was quite full, and we had to pick our way over the people to gain the two prie-dieu's, which Père C. had placed for us before the altar. When the mass began, the people all sang in Canarese in a very touching and devotional manner. I should be afraid to say how many hundreds of the poor Indians went to Holy Communion, and their devotion was most edifying. Some of the men were grand looking fellows, with a single tuft of hair on their heads, and a white scarf twisted about their persons. The women, though of course very nude, were very clean, and wore all sorts of ornaments. Altogether it was a very strange sight! The priests dress all in white, and wear long beards. They look very worn and ascetic.

Now, C. will, I know, like to hear about the horses. Well! the stables are beautiful, and every morning before breakfast, I put on one of L.'s wide-awake hats, and hoist an umbrella, while L. lights his pipe, and away we go, down the front steps, through the flower garden. Of course I look very wise as I pass the gardener, and make believe I know all about his plants and flowers, while he, funny old fellow! wearing wondrously little clothing, bends down to the ground, and scratches the gravel and then his forehead, by way of saying, 'Your faithful servant.'

Arrived at the stables, there is a general neighing of welcome, for we feed the horses every morning with bunches of lucerne, of which they are very fond. A grand man in a blue coat and a scarlet turban, who looks so diabolical that Marie says she is sure he is the old gentleman himself, carries the bunches of grass. First comes Ajax, a wicked pony, but most handsome, who has a bushy mane and a mischievous eye. He affects to be shy and won't beg for his grass. Close to him are Black Prince and Erebus, two black horses L. bought for my special use. When we have passed them, Gay, the old brown carriage-horse, has thrust out his head and neighed, and begins to beg beautifully, holding up his leg in an exemplary manner. Melbourne, his companion, is white and uninteresting. Then come the pets Ruby and Topaz, a pair of chestnut Arabs, pretty creatures, but not yet thoroughly trained.

My other pets consist of two peacocks, the poultry, supplying the table with fowls, ducks, and turkies, some lovely white rabbits with red eyes like rubies, and some white doves.

I shall finish my letter with a verbatim copy of the bill of fare for my first dinner-party, as sent up by the cook, and I hope it may amuse you as much as it did me :—

Hotche-potche soup.
Poulay.
Cotholathe Mouthong, with Allusonby sauce.
Mouthong thongconsom.
Judthum Voulvang.

JOINTS.

Mouthong—Cocks Turky—Snips.
Blumanger—Sooka Poodang.
Maccaroning.

December 8.

Last week we had a most curious sight here in our compound. The great Gooroo, or Pope of Southern India, announced his intention of paying L. a visit. He is supposed to be an incarnation of the Deity. Of course he could not condescend to enter a Christian house, so L. had to receive him on the lawn. First came a number of natives dancing, shouting, and beating tomtoms, then an elephant bearing two huge drums, with a baby elephant. Then the Gooroo, carried in a magnificent cross palankeen, which is borne so as to stop the way, he being the only person permitted to be carried in this manner. He is an old man of seventy-eight. He wore a gold tiara, an emerald necklace, and silver shoes, and behind him was carried his successor, a child of seven, who is supposed to have the marks of the Deity about him. Gooroo senior lives on vegetables, and actually drinks (*horribile dictu*) cow's water. He sat on a wooden chair, and L. opposite him. I was peeping through the venetians all the while. Just under the window stood six dancing girls covered with ornaments. They were very handsome, and had chignons of flowers—a regular bouquet at the back of their heads. . . .

Christmas.

The time draws near the birth of Christ;
  The moon is hid, the night is still;
  A single church below the hill
Is pealing, folded in the mist.

A single peal of bells below
  That wakens at this hour of rest,
  A single murmur in the breast,
That these are not the bells I know.

Like strangers' voices here they sound,
  In lands where not a memory strays,
  Nor landmark breathes of other days,
But all is new unhallowed ground.

It was just so. The sound of church bells below the hill woke me up about eleven o'clock, just in time to get up and dress for midnight mass, and L. read me out those lines from Tennyson, as we sat awaiting the carriage. The church was all lighted up and looked very nice. The band of the 10th Regiment played Mozart's 12th Mass; Père C. gave Holy Communion, and we thought and prayed for all our dear ones at home.

After breakfast all the servants came with flowers and gilt limes, which they presented to us, wishing us a happy Christmas, and then the government peons assembled outside, with the bands, followed by messages and visits from the principal natives at the station. I have had to give all the servants Christmas boxes,—quite an undertaking,—and they took me in, and got double what they ought to have had, looking excessively pleased with themselves in consequence.

The Lancers the other day got up some theatricals, some of the men taking ladies' parts, but, as they had forgotten to engage a maid to superintend their toilettes, you can image how convulsed we all were to see a young lady appear on the stage with a crinoline and a tulle dress, of course quite transparent, which had never occurred to them, the heroine being quite unconscious of the cause of the excessive laughter which greeted her début, and attended her performance to the end.

January 6, 1868.

Once upon a time in Bungalum—somewhere down there in India, you know, or you don't know the exact whereabouts—it was early in the morning, so early that the sun was not up, though somebody else must have been, for, as the clock struck six, a cannon was fired off—bang! and Mrs. Commissioner, who had been fast asleep a minute before, dreaming all sorts of pleasant things, woke up with a start. She had only been in Bungalum a few weeks, and had not as yet become accustomed to the six o'clock and nine o'clock guns,—one to blow her out of bed, and the other to shoot her in again,—so she awoke, turned round on her pillow, and lay listening to the sound as it boomed away over the parade ground. Mr. Commissioner was awake also, or has been for some time, per force of habit, being a very early bird. Up he jumps. Of course he knocks his head or his back with the weights on the mosquito curtains, and, having given one or other, or both, a conciliatory rub, disappears into his dressing room, from which he is not long in reappearing in stout yellow leathern gaiters, booted and spurred. Of course he takes a peep through the curtains at Mrs. Commissioner. 'Well, did I ever! what a kitten it is for sleep!' he mutters, for she has relapsed into her former state of blissful unconsciousness.

Let her sleep, while we follow Mr. Commissioner, who, having gulped down a cup of tea and munched a piece of toast with relish, walks out into the verandah, on which exeunt peons for 'Ajax' with all possible speed. There is a cold feeling in the air, and a white fog envelopes the landscape. The redoubtable Ajax comes sidling along, winking first at the horseboy and then at his master out of his mischievous eyes. He does not want to be petted, not he! and he pretends to object to being mounted, but it is all in vain, and Mr. Commissioner has jumped on his back. Now for a spree, thinks the wicked pony, laying back his ears, and plunging out of the gate full tilt. Away they go, out of the civilised world of Bungalum, into the wild country, with its great boulders of rock, speaking of ancient earthquakes and upheavings, miles and miles. Not a soul, not even a policeman on his beat, sees the Commissioner ride forth, chuckling inwardly, as he reflects how he will take in the Amildar of Chitteldroog, and surprise all the native officials. He has heard of certain irregularities at the travellers' bungalow, and thinks there is nothing like going to the spot himself. It is a matter of eight miles, but, halt! here we are! Woh Ajax! A call from without the bungalow, a feeble response from within, and out comes a native servant, his swarthy limbs wrapped in a white sheet, wondering who on earth comes that way so early in the morning. 'What does the Sahib want?' 'Show me your price-list,' says Mr. Commissioner, taking no notice of the man's manner, which is not what it would be if he knew who his visitor was. 'You have not got one? then call the Amildar.' Native stares. 'So early in the morning, call the Amildar? and who shall I say wants him?' 'A Sahib,' replies the Commissioner, sitting back at ease in his saddle, while Ajax winks, as much as to say, 'Here's a pretty go!' The man in the sheet scuttles down into the village, reappearing after some time with the Amildar, not in the most respectful or pleasant mood at being so disturbed. 'Where is your price-list?' 'Haven't got one,' retorts the man, drawing near. 'Very well,' says Mr. Commissioner, rising in his stirrups with becoming dignity. 'If you don't send one in before four-and-twenty hours you lose your place.' The Amildar stares. 'And who are you, Sahib?' 'The Commissioner.' The Amildar is electrified; he has jumped out of his shoes (a sign of disrespect to appear in them), and is now salaaming to the earth. The Commissioner flourishes his whip, and Ajax is already a mile on his return home before the astonished Amildar has collected his scared senses. While the news goes the round of the village, Mr. Commissioner sits on the edge of the bed, chafing his cold hands, putting in his shirt studs, and amusing Mrs. C., who is by this time wide awake, with the account of the morning's adventure. How cold it was! how Ajax did pull, and how he tried to run away after a sixteen miles gallop, as he turned in at the lodge!

In the meanwhile, a very picturesque group has come up to the bath-room door. A white bullock, laden with a large black skin full of water, the contents of which are being emptied into a big tub. Yes! we all wash in tubs at Bungalum, reminding one of the days of our childhood, of nurses, and Saturday night. Mrs. Commissioner watches the shaving process, and then her lord and master sallies forth again, and having asked her in a pointed manner if she knows what time it is, retires to his study.

Scene 2.—Enter Mrs. L., all smiles, with a cup of tea. Enters also from the garden Poochao, the black maid, hiding her face in her hands, as a mark of deep respect. Poochao always hides her face in the presence of Mrs. Commissioner. No doubt she imagines the light of her countenance would be too great for her. Poochao's accomplishments consist in being able to wave a duster in the mildest manner possible, by way of dusting, and, with help, she can make a bed, and empty the basins and fill them, but Poochao is very honest and a good soul on the whole. Mrs. C. is dressed, and having called Mr. C., they say their orisons together before the ivory crucifix which stands, with their Prayer-book, at the foot of their bed. Then they sally forth, disturbing a small swarm of peons squatted on a mat in the verandah. The sentinels salute the Sahib. They wear a scarlet costume that looks well amongst the green trees, and would look well on nearer inspection, but for a white bandage which they wear under their chins, as if they suffered ever and aye from toothache.

Just as Her Most Gracious Majesty walks on the slopes, so daily do Mr. and Mrs. C. walk on the levels to the stables and poultry-yard. The sun is hot, the wind is cold, and when the solemn voice of the butler says, 'Breakfast on the table, Sir-r-r-r,' with such an 'r,' Mr. and Mrs. C. are quite ready for it and enjoy it.

Scene 3.—It is eleven o'clock. 'Garee mungow,' shouts the Commissioner to the peons—interpreted, 'carriage to the door.' Take it to Jericho, thinks Mrs. C., who always puts on a long face at this stage of the day's proceedings. At last Mr. C. gets to the door, but turns back and says, 'Let me see, did I give you a kiss or not?' Of course Mrs. C. says she thinks not, and so gets or takes another. Then Mr. C. sallies forth, putting on his office face, for the peons in the verandah would lose all respect for the great man if they thought he cared for Mrs. C. Orientals look upon women as inferior animals. Mr. C. frowns. Peon seizes the great gold-headed stick, that magic wand, the sight of which strikes awe and veneration into the hearts of the natives of Bungalum. Of what passes in the fort from that hour until half-past five let no man enquire. Mrs. C. says it would not interest her. No doubt the grapes are sour. She will go there at half-past five o'clock, but she will not be admitted within its sacred precincts.

Scene 4.—Missus can see! and soon gets out a smart bonnet, and in bustles with a rustle Mrs. Chatterbox, who is so anxious to see Mrs. Commissioner, and to have something to talk about. 'Ah, yes, she knew the house in dear old Sir ——'s time. He was her father's brother's mother's first cousin, once removed. She came to Bungalum herself as a bride, she won't say how many years ago,' &c. Having had her chat out, she departs. Enter Mrs. Alleyes, all curiosity to see the alterations. Mrs. C. feels that no great exertion is needed on her part in the conversational line. Mrs. Alleyes takes it all in. 'New carpets? handsome! Sofas re-covered! water-colors, embroidered table-cloth.' Alleyes shall write for some to-day. 'And so that is the fashion? tassels! nothing new in the hair line? Good-bye.' Exit Alleyes, and enter Mr. and Mrs. Pump, who let down the buckets at once. 'So sorry to hear Mr. B. is going away! to H——?' Mrs. Commissioner replies that she knows nothing about it. 'When is the Raja to be invested with the Star of India?' Mrs. C. wonders when, also. 'General —— will be down here soon, no doubt.' Mrs. C. thinks it is very possible. Buckets drawn up empty; and Pumps desist and depart.

Enter Mrs. Smalltalk. 'Have you heard of Mrs. Brown? What *do* you think people say of poor Mrs. White, because she took Colonel Blackbird home from the bandstand? And as to Miss Fickle, well, really! I don't know what to say!' She then departs. Enter young Jackanapes of the 11th with his bosom friend De Courcy Plunger. 'Haw! dull place, Bungalum! horrid slow place! nothing for a fellow to do! no balls this year! wish they were in a jungle, rather than in a half-civilised place like Bungalum.' One cackles while the other brays. D. G., exeunt both. Follows Mrs. Affirmative, and then Mrs. Negative. Shut up—two o'clock.

Solemn voice, 'Tiffin on the table, marm.' Mrs. Commissioner walks into her dining-room, and sits down at a large table in a big armchair to a nice basin of mutton broth. Four black faces, that is, eight eyes, are upon her. How loud that clock does tick! Mind wanders away thousands of miles to lunch going on at ——. 'My own dear daddy! mother darling! C—— love! how I wish you were all here! and there's Prince and Minette, and dirty old Tibby, and Tiny whining outside on the window-sill. Let him in.'

'Missus please.' 'Dear me, where am I? Oh, yes, all right!' and off Mrs. C. walks, to inspect a tailor recovering a sofa.

Scene 5.—Five o'clock. Chocolate and toast, and then away to the fort goes Mrs. C. in her easy barouche, with black horses, and the two running horse-boys, through the pettah, with its palms, temples, and shops, through crowds of natives staring and salaaming, through eastern sights and smells up to the old fort, under the gateway, up the hill through the inner gates, and then pull up. Mrs. C. pretends not to see the old madman, wrapped up in a ragged old shawl, who daily tries to intercept and get something out of Mrs. C., and the old crazy woman who has been every day for ten years with 'her case.' Mr. C. is long in coming, and a crowd has collected all staring. Some are handsome looking men, others dreadful objects with deformities. A stir! Mr. C.'s mysterious box, and the practical bottle of sherry and the empty biscuit-tin appear, followed by Mr. C. himself. Soldiers present arms, and then Mr. and Mrs. C. go for their evening drive, have a snug little dinner at eight, a little music, a little reading—petting? of course not—and then at ten retire to rest. So ends our day.

January 30.

Last week the Mahometans had their grand feast and holiday, after their fast. L. knew they would all go to the gardens (Lal Bagh) in the evening, so we made a point of going, no other Europeans being there except ourselves. The gardens were crowded with men and their children, all in their best, but no wives, who are never seen. The costumes were marvellous. Yellow satin trousers, crimson embroidered waistcoats, with a showy Cashmere shawl flung over the shoulder, that was the fashion. There was, however, an endless variety, pink trousers and blue vests, and I must say I coveted some of the latter. We walked about, and L. spoke to the men he knew. I had a chat with a man and his two little children, wonderfully got up. I asked him where he had purchased the lovely embroideries the baby had on. He replied, 'Our ladies make the things.' The little girl, five years old, wore on her head a gold metal cap set with pearls, pearl earrings and nosering, six gold bracelets on one arm, a sort of loose green silk chemise, and a shawl pinned on her shoulders. Such a little oddity! She was really pretty, with the most beautiful hands and feet. The natives seem fully to appreciate the gardens, and every evening numbers are there sitting under the trees, or looking at the flowers and animals. . . .

February 8.

The twelve o'clock gun has just fired. I am sitting at my writing table. The window is open; a pair of ring-doves are billing and cooing in the verandah; the fish are disporting themselves in the aquarium; there is a pleasant smell of mignionette and roses, a warbling of birds, and a chattering of squirrels. The sentry is walking backwards and forwards in the sun. What is he made of? It is Saturday, so L. is at home; but he is shut up in his study, seeing this person and that on important affairs! Official, of course! He has opened his door (to have a peep at me? it must have been for that). I have stepped in, and given him—never mind what—and have been packed out again in double quick time.

Last Sunday evening we had a row. The Gooroo went in state through the cantonment; and passing with his elephants and tomtoms in front of the mosque, where the Mahometans were at prayers, they sent out to prevent him passing—upon which the Gooroo's escort came back, elephants and all, and tomtomed louder than ever in defiance of the mosque and its inmates. This enraged the latter to such a pitch that they rushed out, and the Gooroo had to take refuge in a shop, from which he was afterwards conveyed away by the back door! In punishment for causing this row, L. has reduced his Holiness's escort from thirty to ten men, and forbidden him to come in future into the cantonment. Four hundred natives have signed a petition to L. against the insult offered to their high priest.

The Raja has just sent us a baby elephant, three months old. It was enticed from Mysore with sugar-cane, and now cries piteously for its mammy. We packed it off to the Gardens. It looks like a very old man who has lost his teeth. . . .

March 28.

A telegram has arrived announcing the Raja's death. He expired at eleven o'clock at night, and at twelve next day his body was burnt according to the Hindoo rites. At five o'clock, all the troops at Bangalore, mustering 2,000, were had out on the parade ground, about half-a-mile in front of our house. I did not go myself, but witnessed the scene from the verandah. It was a cool afternoon, the sun being hidden by a bank of clouds threatening rain, or rather rejoicing our hearts and eyes with the promise of it. In the distance, a cloud of dust and a beating of drums announced the arrival of the troops on the parade ground. On every side, crowds of natives in their white dresses were seen trooping towards that point. Major R. arrived in our compound in full uniform, and a few Silladars in their picturesque dresses came curvetting on to the ground. Then appeared the Commissioner on his beautiful Arab, in cocked hat and the Windsor uniform. The flag was flying half-mast high, and there was a great commotion among the crows, who doubtless were aware, not of the event, but of the coming rain. Then the bugle sounded to announce the Commissioner's arrival on the parade ground, followed by a salute of thirteen guns, fired in his honor. The wind dropped, and the flag hung motionless against the flag-staff. Somebody, given to feeling fidgety, strained her eyes through an opera glass, but saw nothing but a cloud of dust and an occasional flash of fire, when up sprang the breeze, and out floated again the flag, followed by a salute of twenty-one guns for the young Raja. *Le Roi est mort! vive le Roi!* and down came drops of delicious rain—which is, of course, looked upon by the people as a happy omen. L. returned, it got dark, and down fell the shower. We had our chairs placed in the verandah, and there sat, enjoying the smell from the thirsty earth, and the pattering of the rain on the leaves, till it was dinner-time. The frogs croaked, the lizards ran about, and the squirrels came hopping into the verandah, while we threw open all the windows and doors, and said, 'Oh! how refreshing!'

September 30.

On Saturday, September 19, a telegram was received from Mysore that the installation of the young Raja must take place on the 23rd, as the wise men and astrologers, having consulted the stars, found that that was the auspicious day, the hour to be between eleven and twelve o'clock. It was useless to remonstrate at this short notice, so L. said 'Fiat,' and I grumbled, and set Marie and two tailors to work and stitch their fingers off to get ready.

The Raja's stables having been reduced from unlimited supplies of horses and carriages to ten pair, it was no longer possible to post royally along the road of eighty-four miles in his Highness's carriage, as of old; so bullocks were laid, and, out of consideration for my bones, the bullock coach was discarded, and a pole adjusted to the office carriage, which makes up into a bed. I was only allowed the smallest portmanteau, which was tyranny and oppression to the highest degree, when three toilettes and a best bonnet, to say nothing of a crinoline, had to be stowed away. However, I could not remonstrate, when a Windsor uniform and a cocked hat had to travel ignominiously in a bundle!

A pair of bullocks having been pressed into the service with many blows and shouts, we set off at a famous trot, a Silladar curvetting in front, and several more kicking up a dust behind, while a peon ran in front, shouting to everybody to keep out of the way. Away we went, down through the native town, the people staring and salaaming, out into the wild rocky country beyond. As we passed through the different talooks or villages, the Amildar or Magistrate came out to meet us, followed by the inhabitants, and, whilst we changed bullocks, presented garlands of flowers and limes, and chatted with my husband in Canarese of the coming event.

After a time the road became more rough—very bad indeed—and the bullocks had hard work to get along. The difficulty was overcome by a native, with only his loins girt, sitting on the shaft, shouting and twisting the tails of the poor beasts, while the driver lashed, and the peons, running on either side, poked them with their sticks! Two wild-looking natives ran on ahead, as it grew dark, with torches, the smoke and smell of which were anything but agreeable. As we approached the villages, a native with a curious horn announced our arrival by a cheerful blast. During the night, in passing through the villages, we saw the people asleep outside their huts, rolled up in their blankets, white or coloured, looking like so many mummies. The great banyan trees looked so ghastly in the moonlight, with their gnarled branches and beard-like appendages.

Once during the night we were awoke by loud cries, and, stopping, found that the Silladar had given a whack to a pair of bullocks at the head of a train of carts, which had resulted in the animals upsetting the cart into a ditch. The cries were so piteous that we concluded that the driver was under his cart, and L. got out to render assistance, but found the man unhurt, sitting by the wayside weeping—I ought to say howling—and wringing his hands, Indian fashion, instead of setting to work to do anything.

At the Muddoor station, which was nice and clean, I made myself tidy; we had a comfortable breakfast, and, being joined by Major C., started again at six o'clock, in a comfortable carriage of the Raja's, with good horses.

We soon crossed the Cavery—the first Indian river I had seen. The country was very green with rice crops and mulberry trees, and is irrigated by water channels from the Cavery at this season of the year. We now got along at a great pace, and soon came in sight of Seringapatam peeping out amongst the luxuriant vegetation. There was the mosque, the fort, the tomb of Tippoo Sultan, the house and garden occupied by the Duke of Wellington, and the lofty monument erected to the memory of the officers who perished at the storming of the fort. In crossing an arm of the Cavery, we had a beautiful view at the Raja's bathing-place, beneath a very picturesque bridge. Great flights of steps lead down to the water, and women in bright clothes were filling their brass vessels with the water, and walking away with them on their heads. The river looked so deliciously cool that it is not very strange that these poor Indians should worship it when it is the source of such blessings to their country.

The next stage seemed very short, and we were

joined by a regiment of Silladars, who look very well in a body with their gold and scarlet dress and turbans. The native saddles also are very handsome, whilst the horses, adorned with colored ropes and tassels round their necks, add greatly to the general good effect. They certainly consider themselves fine fellows, and show off and kick up no end of dust. I was nearly choked.

Next we came upon a man with his horn; then a temple, with all the dancing girls outside in their best, with their priests and their everlasting tomtoms. A little farther on was a deputation of all the merchants of the city, with a congratulatory speech by a stout burly gentleman with much gesticulation, which, had we not been obliged to listen to it all most uncomfortably in the glare of the sun, would have amused me greatly. Then garlands and bouquets were thrown into the carriage. I was indeed rejoiced to reach the Residency, and get into the cool house.

On Wednesday, at eleven o'clock, we were all dressed and assembled at the Residency, which was formerly a palace of the Raja, and has in it one of the finest rooms in India. All the company at last arrived, and we went off in carriages, preceded by the Silladars, while natives ran on each side, bearing very long lances with scarlet streamers and gold cords and tassels. These lances they shake and clang in a peculiar manner, and to my mind most musically. In the procession were carried some curious batons and mitres, insignia of royalty.

All the people were thronging about, and when we turned under the gates of the fort, within which is the palace, and arrived at the great square in front of it, the noise was such that it was impossible to make any one hear. It was all dumb show. God save the Queen! Native music! Tomtoms! A great mass of human beings in the square, and every individual shouting! Had I not been told what to expect, I should have been frightened.

Upon driving up in front of the palace, one of the princes, by name the 'Prince of the Chamber of Cupid,' a grandson of the late Raja, came forward. I salaamed, he salaamed, and extended his two hands, upon which I placed one of mine, and he led me up the steps, surging with people, into the inner court of the palace to the chair on which sat the young Raja, to whom I salaamed, and with whom I then shook hands.

My husband and Major E. following, did the same, and then they took the little man by the hand, and, leading him up the silver steps, lifted him on to his throne. Then you should have heard the row! The lances were clanged, the English hurrahed, the natives shouted, and the bands and tomtoms played. I never was in such a din, and the crowd surged up, and there came a perfect shower of flowers. We were pelted on all sides, and L. had to protect the little Raja with his cocked hat, while Major C. did his best for me; but it was hopeless, and there was nothing for it but to endure. My dress was ruined at once, all the flowers being soaked in attar of roses! I looked up, expecting to see the little Raja terrified and in tears, but, like a high-born Oriental, he sat as cool as a cucumber.

I must describe the little fellow to you, and his throne. Chamraj Wodiar, Maharaja of Mysore, is going on for seven years of age. He is not dark, but of a rich olive complexion, with most splendid eyes. He has bare feet, coat and trousers of gold, and a beautiful turban, hung round with great drops of emeralds and diamonds. Major E. had the state rings and bangles made to fit his small feet and fingers. The throne is like what one reads of in a fairy tale, of solid gold, very ancient, and exquisitely chased and carved. From the arms hang ropes of real pearls. The umbrella above it is surmounted by a peacock in emeralds and diamonds. Two attendants stood behind, waving feathers tipped with diamonds, and two others waved in the air, in a peculiar way, Cashmere shawls, or what looked to me like them.

After a time, order was established, and we all sat down, the English on the left, the royal princes on the right. The little king looked about him with astonishing coolness, and began chewing a betel-nut! Had he cried, the people would have thought it a bad omen. As it was, he was a born king, and they were all delighted.

Then followed the ceremonies. First came the Brahmins, with incantations and prayers, sprinkling the child with the waters of the sacred rivers of India. Secondly, his pedigree, from the gods down to the present day, was read out. We gave him three cheers, and there was a great row. Thirdly, presentation of the fruits of the earth, carried in on trays, the Raja laying his tiny hand on everything with great dignity.

Fourthly, presentation of twenty-one trays of presents, and a very handsome necklace, from our Government, and my husband fastened the ornament round the little fellow's neck. Fifthly, descending from his throne, the Raja presented twenty-one trays to L., and fastened a splendid necklace of pearls, diamonds, and rubies round his neck, a shawl, embroidered in green and gold, being thrown over his shoulders. Then the Raja placed wreaths of flowers over L.'s neck and mine, but he could not get them over my bonnet, which seemed to amuse him greatly. Then he presented each with a rose, and a gold tray being handed in, he scented the roses with attar, and gave each of us a betel-nut, after which he was again placed on his throne.

Then followed the homage of all his relatives, who advanced one by one, and bowing down, placed their heads on the throne, each offering a present, which the Raja just touched. Then all the English officers salaamed and shook hands, and were handed out to the carriages as before, amidst renewed shoutings, the bands playing 'God save the Queen.'

I must tell you that the floor of the raised platform was carpeted with cloth of gold, which was soon inches deep in flowers.

In the afternoon of the same day we went a second time to the palace for a durbar. Inside the palace is a great room, looking on and opening into the square, but upstairs, and the throne had been placed in the balcony, so that all the public might see it.

First came the Brahmins, and the child had actually

to worship his throne, walking round it three times, and throwing lotus flowers at the foot of it, prayers being meanwhile recited. Then L. put him on his throne, while the mob below closed in, and there was another storm of flowers, L. protecting the Raja's face with my fan!

Then there were wrestlers below fighting, then sword-dancing, and, behold, the State elephant, painted, and done up for the occasion in his best. He was led up to the front of the balcony, and saluted with his trunk in the air. He was followed by the State horse, magnificently caparisoned, and lastly came the sacred cow, worshipped as an impersonation of the Deity, covered with pearls and cloth of gold. Finally, all ended with fireworks and 'Good night!'

On returning to the Residency, we had just time to dress for the grand dinner given to all the European officers. After dinner, we drank the health of the Queen, L. made a short speech, and then we drank the Raja's health. After dinner, we had music, and we got up some Christy Minstrels' songs. In fact, everything went off well.

On the following day L. and I drove round the town of Mysore, and had a very picturesque view of the old walls of the fort, an avenue of trees, and a large tank or lake-like sheet of water, with Chamoondee rising beyond, on the summit of which is a house, and a temple dedicated to the tutelary deity of the Mysore dynasty. On returning, we all went to the stables to see the horses, and feed the pigeons, great beauties, and formerly special pets of the late Raja.

After breakfast, we went to the palace, and saw all over it. It is a most curious and interesting place. We went first into the inner courtyard, where the installation took place the day before, and then took a squint down a long dirty-looking passage to the kitchen, which Major E. advised us not to visit. Passing up an open staircase into a low wide gallery, we saw to the left the ladies' apartments, and turned to the right into a small ante-room lighted from above, in the centre of which was a square place railed off, and slightly sunk, in which are kept the sacred cow and her calf. The former was evidently viciously disposed towards us, and made a thrust at the railing to get at us, ringing a silver bell. Her daughter, however, was more amiable, and allowed us to pat her. They were both as sleek as horses, and had each an attendant, watching to administer to their wants.

We then went into the inner durbar-room. In the centre the ceiling was hung with long chains of colored glass beads, and, as the sun shone upon them, the effect was very pretty. The doors were of massive silver, carved all over with hideous gods and goddesses. I wonder why the natives imagine their deities to be so very unpleasing in their appearance. The silver doors were certainly very handsome, but Baptiste, with his plate powder, would have greatly improved them. The room was low, except in the centre, and full of portraits, some of which were dreadful daubs. The Raja frequently slept in the passage, and was taken from it when dying, and carried down-stairs and laid upon mother earth, as is their custom. The staircase led up to some nice snug sitting-rooms. In the Raja's proper bedroom we were shown a pearl necklace, composed of 2,400 pearls.

We then went to another part of the palace to pay our visit to the queens. The gentlemen had to speak to them through a curtain, but I was allowed to pass behind it, with an interpreter, a Mrs. ——. On going in I found all the six ladies seated on chairs. I salaamed to each, and shook hands. A chair was then placed for me before the first queen, and I was asked to sit down.

As to their costume, as they were in mourning, no jewels were worn, and all had plain clothes, excepting the first queen, who had on a very magnificent green and gold shawl. She was a nice-looking old lady, with refined features, and after shaking hands with me, rarely spoke during my visit. Next to her sat No. 2, a jolly, good-natured, portly old lady, who talked all the time as fast as her tongue would go. She began by drawing my chair close to her, and seizing and squeezing both my hands in hers, said she was delighted to see me, and we had the following conversation.

Mrs. B.—'I hope you were not all much fatigued by yesterday's ceremonies?'

2nd Queen (tears rolling down her fat cheeks).—'My two eyes were not big enough to look at it all! but you must intercede that it may not be all show, but real!'

Mrs. B.—'There is no further need of intercession. The boy is crowned, and the British Government will protect his rights.'

3rd Queen.—'We are overcome with gratitude to Mr. B. We know that all the joy we feel is owing to him.'

Mrs. B.—'I should like to see the mother of the young Raja.'

1st Queen.—'We will send for her.'

Then the second began talking to my husband in Canarese through the curtain, and in a few minutes in came the young Raja and his mother, a very nice looking young woman, with splendid eyes like her son's. She salaamed down to the ground, and then, with all her heart in her eyes, she took up the little fellow and put him on my lap, saying, 'I give my child to you. He is not mine any longer, and you must protect him, and intercede for him.' Then women servants came in with a silver dish, with a garland of flowers, which the child took and put round my neck, and then placed a rose in my hand, scented by him from a gold scent-bottle with attar. Finally, he handed me a betel-nut, all of which I of course accepted with a salaam.

The little boy was superbly dressed, and had on such a necklace!

1st Queen.—'Do you admire the necklace?'

Mrs. B.—'It is most beautiful, but the child is far handsomer than the jewels.'

At which pretty speech, great satisfaction was evinced by all the ladies.

3rd Queen.—'I see by your face that you love children. Have you any of your own?'

Upon which an explanation followed of the loss of my baby.

2nd Queen.—'You have travelled a long way. Do you like India?'

1st Queen.—'We will show you our jewels. Lady D. could not speak for looking at them!'

2nd Queen.—'You speak more kindly to us than any English lady we have seen. We like you better than any one we have seen.'

But here a message came that I had remained long enough, and that I must come away, so I shook hands with them all, the second queen begging me to ask L. to send them to Benares, that they might finish their religious duties for their husband's soul. The little Raja gave me his two hands, and conducted me out with astonishing self-possession and gravity.

When I got out the gentlemen began laughing at me for staying so long, but I found they were, nevertheless, all curiosity to know what the queens were like, and what they had said.

We next visited the library. The books are all written on palm leaves, strung together, and compressed between wood, ivory, or silver plates. Poems and fairy tales comprise the literature of the country, and some of the books were illuminated.

We then visited the armory, a most curious collection, but some of the weapons were terribly cruel, and made me shudder! We then passed into a great durbar-room, full now of boxes of treasures. We had one box opened, and looked till we were tired at ladies' clothes made of cloth of gold, worth 1,000 rupees each. We saw shawls by the dozen, and our eyes ached with looking. Some of the boxes were marked outside with the name of the queen whose particular treasure they contained.

I was attacked by a violent cold, and could not go to the evening durbar, but was told that the little Raja complained of the great weight of his turban, and begged he might have a lighter one, which, I think, shows him to be a very sensible child.

On returning home, we travelled at different hours, and I was glad to see something of the country we had before passed in the dark, parts of which are strikingly picturesque. We entered Bangalore in the evening, and as we drove through the pettah, or native town, we came in for the procession at the close of the Dussera. All the gods and goddesses were being carried on cars with shoutings and tomtoms, the people being painted and got up in most extraordinary costumes, so that it really was a very singular sight, but I was so sleepy and tired that I could hardly take it all in. Thus ended our visit to Mysore, which I thoroughly enjoyed, notwithstanding the fatigue and my cold.

November 16.

I sit down to write to you in a distracted state of mind. I don't know how many times this morning I have said, 'I *shall* lose my temper!' but L. only laughs and says, 'When you do, let me see it!' and then I sit down and laugh. Sometimes I think if I had known the worry, fuss, and expense, no scenery in the world would have induced me to go into camp; but the pleasure of being with L. all day is so delightful that, after all, I think I shall perhaps not regret it. You can have no idea of the preparations for a three months march. The first detachment has just gone off, and the butler has been in, all smiles, salaaming down to the ground, to inform me he was able to start. He was evidently much pleased, no doubt having taken in the Mem-Sahib (me) nicely, and made a good thing of it for himself.

Just at the last I really had a great deal to think about. What with making arrangements for the camp and for servants left behind, beset by those going, who wanted an advance of wages, coats, and blankets, wives that wanted to go with their husbands, anxious mothers who preferred to stay behind with their children, but wanted their pay all the same, and 'boys' that had fever and could not find substitutes, I was 'sat upon,' and that too on a Monday morning, in my best frock, receiving visitors and friends who came to say 'Good bye!' No wonder I was distracted, and had disturbed slumbers, and that my temper was ruffled,—only ruffled, mind.

Chennapatam, November 18.

The clock struck four, and then it struck five, and a voice said, 'Time to get up.' Then somebody lighted a candle, it being quite dark, and coaxed somebody else out of bed. It was so cold, but Marie soon appeared with a cup of hot tea and toast, and at six o'clock we started. Poor old Poochao, the house-sweeper, came and knelt down at my feet and sobbed. She was not going; she was too old; and, as she does not speak

English, I was powerless to console her. The salute was fired as we passed out of the gates. A Silladar rode on before, and two others followed the carriage behind. As we passed through the native town, which was not yet astir, we saw the people lying asleep, rolled up in blankets in the verandahs in front of their shops. As we went by a temple, an old priest rushed out, and screamed out something that sounded like a curse, but was, I believe, intended for a blessing.

We were travelling in an open carriage, and so cold was it that I wore my wadded velvet jacket, a Scotch plaid over my knees, and a velvet wideawake to keep my head warm, and yet I shivered, yes! shivered in Southern India. As we drove along, there were beautiful lights from the rising sun on the wild rocks, and patches of highly-cultivated land, and vultures were sweeping and careering over the landscape in search of their breakfasts. The sugar-cane and rice crops looked most flourishing in the low wet land under the great tanks, which have all the appearance of natural lakes. Many of these have been most skilfully constructed, giving proof that the natives knew something of engineering, long before English rule and public works were thought of.

When we came in sight of a talook (village), a man with a long brass horn blew a not unmusical blast to announce our approach, and then out came a troop of Silladars on prancing steeds, in their picturesque dresses, and, joining our cavalcade, entered the village, where the Amildar or Magistrate at the head of the population awaited our arrival, with the usual complimentary wreath of flowers, lemons, &c. Then L. spoke to them, enquired about the crops, heard a few grievances, and on we went.

As we turned into the compound at the bungalow, the flag was hoisted, for it always travels about with us, when L. goes on an official tour, and I saw our camp pitched close by. Our tent was a large one, divided down the centre by a passage which went all round, and having two bath-rooms, the exterior of white canvas, and inside yellow and black stuff.

After breakfast, L. went out riding, to visit two curious tombs outside the town, the priests of which turned out in fine dresses, with tomtoms and two dancing girls, doubtful characters, all bedizened with finery, as is the custom when anyone of note arrives at a place.

I went to bed early that night, my first in a tent. It did seem so strange! Such an examination of the bed for fear of a snake! At last I slept, but was awoke often by the horses and other noises. At four o'clock we heard a row, and presently a horse galloping. It charged right at our tent, and stove in my bath-room. I fully expected it to come on to my bed! L. was up instanter, and it turned out to be 'Rex,' who had broken loose, and was amusing himself in an undignified and dangerous manner for his royal person. However, no legs were broken, and the horse-boy was reprimanded with a great many 'woppus lao,' whatever that may mean in Hindostanee.

Muddoor, November 19.

Out of bed at five o'clock, dressing by candlelight in a tent. It was so cold, but I had provided myself with a flannel dressing gown, and was soon comfortable in my warm English cloth habit. It seemed ridiculous to put on the large pith hat, with its thick white turban of muslin. 'Fritz' seemed astonished at being mounted by torchlight, arched his noble neck, and looked round in expectation, and was not disappointed, for I had saved him half my toast. Exit from the compound.

Picture the scene, a wild road, with large banyan trees on either side, with their fantastic roots, and great branches stretching far and low. A native going on ahead with the eternal horn, now and again stopping to turn round and blow the cheerful blast. He was followed by two peons, one carrying L.'s gun, and then came our three selves, Capt. C. on a large ugly Australian bay horse, L. on Tsar, the grey Arab, and I riding Fritz, the horse-boy running by my side, with his bare black legs, white knickerbockers, blue cloth jacket bound with scarlet, and scarlet turban. A little way behind, two mounted Silladars, whose costume I have already described as picturesque, more peons, and then the bullock-coach with Marie and Rosalie.

I enjoyed the ride so much, but was glad, after seven miles of it, to get into the palankin, of which this was my first experience. It was a very nice one, painted green outside, and has sliding doors and four little windows, and a sort of shelf with little drawers on the top, and a tin imperial which carries a change of clothes, books, &c. It has nice green leather cushions, and you can lie down or sit up. It is carried by twelve men, who take it in turn, six at a time, changing every hundred yards. The disagreeables are the motion and peculiar singing of the bearers, rather a dismal ditty, but I soon got to like the one and forget the other.

On reaching the bungalow at Muddoor, the priest turned out of the temple, and a man with the tomtom ran on in front, followed by a horn-man. Such a din! but it means respect, and you salaam and are grateful. Some natives were waiting on the steps with a dish of plantains and flowers, which they did to please us, poor creatures, and I was sorry that I could not speak to them. Crowds of people came with petitions, some of whom lay flat on the ground when they presented them, whining over their misfortunes or peccadillos. This man has not repaired his tank, and that one has been fined for insubordination, and when L. declines to interfere, they come round to where they can see me, and gesticulate until the peons come and send them off.

In the evening I walked out with L. to a large tank and got on to the 'bund' of it. The ground about Muddoor is white with incrustations of salt! We picked some pretty little flowers, but it got dark quite suddenly, and I was in a fright lest we should step on snakes. I had serious thoughts of asking L. to carry me, but, reflecting that he must know better than I the habits of these bêtes noires, I became reasonable, and we got home safely, dined, and turned into bed early, sleeping soundly.

Mullawallï, November 20.

Started by torchlight, a native running ahead of our horses, carrying a blazing stick, over which, from time to time, he poured oil out of a really elegantly formed brass bottle, which was so pretty that I shall try to get one. It was light by the time we came to the ford, and there was not much water in the river, in which the natives have large melon-beds that answer very well.

The country through which we then passed was stony and barren, but the lights in the mountains were lovely. L. pointed out to me Cubbal Droog, where a great many Englishmen were imprisoned by Tippoo Sultan at the end of the last century. The country became less barren at last, and we passed a pretty little temple on a rock in the middle of a wood by the side of a small stream which we forded. I looked back to see what would have made a charming sketch, blue mountains, green foliage, reddish rocks, white temple, river in foreground, riding party winding down the descent to the bank, and Silladars in scarlet uniforms on grey steeds, altogether just such a sketch as Simpson would have taken.

Soon after, we met Captain C.'s pony carriage, which I got into, for the sun was getting hot. 'Brandy and Soda' stepped out famously, but the road was so bad that we must have been upset, but for the running horse-boys to help us out of difficulties. Just as we reached Mullawalli, Soda performed a very eccentric trick, charging down a steep bank into the middle of a troop of Silladars, sending their horses flying in every direction, and very nearly turning us over. At Mullawalli we found the tents pitched around a nice small bungalow, which had been most tastefully decorated with large plantain leaves and flowers, on which evidently great pains had been bestowed by the Amildar to surprise and please us.

I passed a quiet day, and when it got cool we strolled along the high road, out of compassion for my fear of snakes. The country was well cultivated, and a very striking hill rose out of the valley, reminding me of Schloss Eltz on the Moselle. It is inhabited, I was told, by bears, and is very difficult to ascend on account of the jungle.

Sivasamoodrum and Billukwadi, November 21.

Started at half-past five towards the bear-hill, passing round its base. The country was wild and beautiful, with mountains in front of us, but the road so bad that I had continually to get out of the pony carriage and walk.

At last, we reached Sivasamoodrum, a most strikingly picturesque place, on an island in the centre of the river Cavery, closed in on every side by high hills. We crossed the bridge built by the father of the present Jageerdar, an educated man, who built and furnished a bungalow, where he entertained all comers at his own expense. His son met us on the bridge, mounted on a white pony. He looked unhappy, having just lost his second wife, who died of the fever of the Cavery, which is malignant.

As the place is unhealthy, L. had arranged to leave before sunset for Billukwadi, and as the great thing to be done was to see the Falls before the sun was high, we hurried on somewhat disheartened, for our breakfast basket had not turned up, nor the palankin, so I could not divest myself of my thick cloth riding habit, which was oppressively hot.

However, having taken a dry biscuit and a cup of milk, we hoisted our white umbrellas and 'topees,' and started at once for the Falls. Shall I ever forget it? First, shaken to pieces along the rough road in the pony carriage, scrambling down a rocky path, with the grass above one's head, in fear of my life for snakes and tigers, embarrassed by my long, hot, and heavy habit, and at last the glorious view of the Falls to repay me! Seated in the shade, almost on a level with the river, looking up at the foaming waters rushing over the rocks above, and falling thence a height of 250 feet! a rainbow adding to the general effect.

Scrambling up again in the full glare of the sun, but shaded by white umbrellas, we rested on the top of some big stones under trees near a temple which overlooks the Falls, or, rather, I should call it, the tomb of a Fukeer. Through the doorway we could see the tomb covered over with a scarlet and green cloth, embroidered with gold.

We then drove on, and descended again on foot to the Bhur Chookee, or lower Fall, which, to my mind, is by far the most striking, and here, at last, we got our breakfast under a big tree, with the spray in our faces. The spot is grand and picturesque, but there is a sad story connected with it, a young lady having fallen, or, some say, jumped over the fall, her body being never recovered, owing to the rapidity of the river rendering it impossible.

After breakfast, we were obliged to leave our shady retreat, and were well grilled before we reached the main road again, where I found my palankin waiting. I was glad to be carried off, the bearers all the while chanting in their quaint way. As far as I can make out, what they say is—

Grandmamma—diddle 'um.
Chorus.—Just so! Just so!
And she is all by herself.
Chorus.—Aye! Aye!
And a rare 'un!
Chorus.—Ah, do! Ah, do!
Charlie is a baboo—oo—oo.
Chorus.—Just so! Just so!

All of which L. declares means 'She is as heavy as an elephant.'

On reaching the deserted-looking bungalow, we found that great preparations had been made during our absence. The Jageerdar seemed to have been puzzled as to what English people would like to eat and drink, and had therefore done his best to satisfy every taste. On the floor were arranged bottles of pickles, champagne, claret, liqueurs, beer, soda-water, a Bologna sausage, cheese, and preserves, while a bat and a rat disputed possession of the apartment. The bullock-coaches having come up, we were able to bathe, dress, and take a nap, and afterwards to partake of the hospitable cheer, of which what we saw on the floor was only a small instalment, soup, a gigantic turkey, a ham, half a sheep, and a chicken curry appearing in due course on the table. We supposed that the Jageerdar wished to keep up his grandfather's reputation for hospitality.

In the afternoon, he came to visit us, accompanied by two Brahmins, who did all the talking. These men have three painted marks on their foreheads, the centre being yellow and the two others white, and they shave their heads in front, leaving a long tail behind. They wear long white clothes about their persons, and have great influence over the natives.

At five o'clock we started for Billukwadi, and found on our arrival the tents pitched and the dinner ready. A dense population thronged the entrance to the town, and of course we had from the Amildar the usual presents of flowers and fruit.

Bunnoor, November 24, 25.

A swingeing long march of sixteen miles, but, the road being good, we were able to get on well. Fritz was very troublesome, being as fresh as a lark and up to a spree. Bunnoor is a large place, and the people came out to meet us with a perfect din of native music, and a dancing girl who had rings on her fingers and bells on her toes (or ankles). The tents were pitched on a sort of green, surrounded on all sides by ruins of ancient temples, with hills in the distance. The people sent their offerings of fruits and flowers on the most delightful old metal plates, which I really longed to keep, as they were so quaint. In the evening crowds of women came inquisitively round my tent, and I went out with Rosalie and spoke to them. They said they had never seen an English lady before, were half shy, and kept hiding their faces in their clothes. They had all coughs, I observed, and no wonder, when, in the coldest weather, they only wear a strip of muslin round their persons. The crowd rapidly increased, and I was obliged to retreat. Afterwards we walked out and had a look at the curious remains of the old temples, the carvings of which had been beautiful. There were portions of gilding and painting on the outside, but the gates were locked, and we could not get inside.

Next day L. rode out twenty miles to Nursipoor, getting back to breakfast. He came back much pleased with his expedition, having visited at Somnath-poor a very fine temple built in the time of the Balal Rajas, who conquered this part of the country. He told me the carvings were most beautiful. The square courtyard contained fifteen cells, supported by finely-carved pillars, the roofs and entrances of the cells being exquisitely chiselled. It was only four miles from our camp, and I regretted having missed seeing these curiosities.

All the country round Bunnoor is agricultural, but, as the crops are now under water, the place is unhealthy.

Seringapatam, November 26.

Such an interesting day! As usual, we started by torchlight across country, a narrow path between cactus and aloe hedges, ten feet high at least, on either side, so that it was difficult steering to keep oneself and one's horse from being pricked. Before it was light we forded some streams, and skirted the margin of the

Bunnoor tank, when a gleam of daydawn appeared in the horizon. After riding some miles along the top of the tank embankments, we reached at last a little temple on a hill, where my palankin was to await me, but there was no sign of it, and the natives declared it had never been through, while, to add to the *embarras*, there were two roads, and we did not know which the bearers might have taken. L., with a few followers, took one, and Captain C. and I the other. The road was so stony that we could hardly get along, and meanwhile the sun was up, so that I was right glad that I had put aside all thoughts of vanity, and donned my pith hat, a headpiece which, owing to its air chambers, gives the wearer the appearance of having water on the brain. After scrambling along with many interjections, such as 'Steady there!' 'hold up, Fritz!' 'is it safe?' 'had I not better get off?' at last we met a native, who said the palankin had gone on through his village, so we pushed on whenever the stones would permit us to do so, until, joyful sight! I saw the white roof of the palankin, and, a little farther on, we were joined by L.

I don't think I shall ever forget crossing the Cavery river a little later, hoisted on the heads of a crowd of natives, all shouting, screaming, and gesticulating, the river, the costumes, the old trunk of a tree made into a boat, holding the peons, and dragged over by figures wading, while the riding party forded the stream on horseback. A great crowd awaited us on the other side with native music, but the heat was great, and we went on at once to our tents, which were pitched in the old fort. None of the carts had however arrived, and there was therefore no breakfast for us, but I was treated to, and refreshed by, a draught of milk. It afterwards turned out that the camp had marched thirty miles instead of twenty, and Marie, in her bullock-coach, did not arrive till four o'clock, but still in good humour, notwithstanding. In the evening, I sat in my easy chair on the ramparts, to witness such a grand sunset! quite pink, and reflected in the river, a sort of Turner gone quite mad!

Seringapatam, November 27.

We were lazy to-day, and did not sally forth from our tents before six. It had been arranged that we were to see Seringapatam on an elephant, and one of the Raja's had been sent out from Mysore, but we found it had only a native howdah. I scrambled up by means of a ladder into it, but we found it very uncomfortable, as we were obliged to sit cross-legged in it, so we got out and drove in the Raja's carriage, which had been sent to bring us into Mysore.

The fort is still a very strong place, although very ruinous in parts. A native population lives within the walls, and the mosque in the enclosure is really strikingly beautiful, but we had not time to go inside and ascend the minarets, from which L. said there was a grand view, as the sun, our formidable enemy, would not allow of our seeing everything, and we therefore gave up the proposed visit to the mosque and temple.

The tombs are about a mile and a half from the

fort. As soon as we reached the gate, we were greeted by a burst of native music from a room above the gateway, a horrid din. What can I liken it to? a band tuning up? a drummer gone mad? and a clashing and clanging of pots and pans, always fortissimo, with no piano? The priests (Mahomedans) and their attendants were waiting for us at the gate with a State umbrella, and two curious symbols. A long avenue of cypresses, with trim flower-beds neatly kept, led up to the tomb, and I had no idea that I was going to see anything so striking.

On a raised terrace at the end of the avenue stands the tomb, with an arcade all round it, and a mosque on the right-hand side. The base of the building is supported by polished black marble columns, which are very handsome, all the rest being pure white, and adorned with fine carvings. The doors are of ebony, inlaid with ivory, and at the principal entrance hangs a scarlet curtain embroidered with gold. Inside, in the ground, are the three tombs of Hyder Ali, his wife, and Tippoo Sultan, the greatest enemy we ever had in India. Each tomb was covered by a splendid Cashmere shawl, embroidered with gold, all of different patterns. Peacocks' feathers, and other insignia of royalty, lay about on the floor, and incense burnt in a niche, the people still venerating the memory of Tippoo, and calling him 'The martyr,' although he was one of the greatest tyrants that ever lived. We did not go into the mosque, as it is not popular to do so.

In the vicinity of the building are other tombs, all nicely kept, and one kind of grave struck me as a pretty idea. It was a flat stone, raised, the centre being hollow, and filled in with earth and flowers.

The graves of the English officers close by are a sad contrast to all the pagan magnificence, the ground being overgrown, not a sign of Christianity, and the names on the ugly flat monuments in nearly every case obliterated.

L. carried away a rose from the garden, and sent it to Prince Gholam Mahomed at Calcutta, who is personally known to him.

Near Seringapatam, on the road to the tombs, is the village of Ganjam, in which are twenty Catholic families, all people of high caste, who have built themselves a neat little church, which we visited on our way to the Duria Doulut. We found the little congregation all assembled, and the church very tastefully decorated with ropes of flowers. The statues, made by natives, were somewhat remarkable, and would no doubt be pronounced by some as uncommonly like idols, but I dare say the people appreciate their own ideas of the beautiful, more than anything we could produce in accordance with our notions.

After saying a little prayer in the church, which is only visited from time to time by a casual priest, we drove on to the Duria Doulut, or garden palace of Tippoo Sultan, which was occupied by the Duke of Wellington for some time after the siege. Government lately gave an order for its restoration, and 5,000*l.* were spent in renewing the decorations, and it is, in its way, quite beautiful. The exterior walls are covered with the most curious frescoes, representing the triumphs of

Tippoo over the English. Everywhere he is represented as complacently smelling a rose, either on horseback, in a palankin, or mounted on an elephant, in the midst of the most dreadful carnage, in which of course the English are shown as getting the worst of it. The perspective is amusing, and legs, arms, and heads are flying off in every direction, but, on careful inspection, the corresponding bodies will be found somewhere. The building is two storeys high, and, inside, the walls are covered with richly-painted arabesques, something in the style of the Alhambra at the Crystal Palace, only far more beautiful, and on a larger scale.

We breakfasted in the centre chamber of the second storey, although it seemed almost out of keeping with the spot to do anything so commonplace, the atmosphere and surroundings of the whole thing making me feel like an Eastern princess in a fairy tale. After breakfast we decided on remaining till the afternoon, so the Brahmins and merchants of Seringapatam came here to see L., who went into the verandah, and, seated in an armchair, listened to all they had to say, whilst they sat cross-legged, without their turbans, in front of him. Such a curious scene! I was a spectator from a balcony above. Afterwards, as it became hotter, I grew sleepy and dozed off on a sofa, my eyes dazzled by gilded walls, and my ears refreshed by the splashing of a fountain in the garden, the singing of many birds, with a pen-scratching accompaniment, for there were L. and Captain C. hard at work, while a delicious breeze laden with the perfume of roses, wafted through the chamber. What a strange incident in my life! I thought, and then—sleep overcame me, and I hope I did not snore.

At four we started for Mysore. I hardly recognised the Residency, as all had been brushed up and made so pretty by the good taste of Major and Mrs. C. In the evening there was a dinner-party, and imagine Marie's distress of mind, when she unpacked my box, and found she had left behind my chignon, wig-puffs, and all my white gloves. However, she contrived to do up my head, and, *entre nous*, I carried a pair of colored gloves turned inside out in my hand.

Mysore, November 28.

To-day we received an invitation from the Ranees to visit them at twelve o'clock, so I asked Mrs. C. and the other ladies to go with me. We went in state, the gentlemen in uniform, and we drove at a foot's pace, with the men bearing silver lances, and a troop of Silladars. As we drove into the courtyard, the band struck up 'God save the Queen.' Deva Parthiva, the old Raja's favourite grandson, came down to receive us, and handed me upstairs to the Ranees' apartments, where, on one side of the curtain, we found the little Raja sitting cross-legged on a chair. We salaamed, and shook hands. I thought he looked much thinner, and he seemed nervous.

The queens then requested us to go behind the curtain, which we accordingly did. I was not, however, received with the same cordiality as on my former visit, none of the queens rising, though they gave their hands. Fatima was sulky, saying that many of the servants had been dismissed, and begged Mr. B. would allow them all to be taken on again. Then she said to me, 'Ladies understand these things better than gentlemen.' She constantly cast her eyes up to the ceiling. I told her the crops in Mysore were very fine, whilst in other parts of India famine was expected, but nothing seemed to interest her.

The old Ranee sent for the little boy, and put him on my knee. We had a little chat, he saying, 'Good morning,' in very good English, adding that he remembered seeing me before, and then he presented me with flowers and betel-nut. I saw his sister for the first time, such a pretty child! two years older than himself. I told the Ranees that they ought to have their photographs taken; but Fatima shook her head, and said that, as no men ought to look at their faces, it was impossible. We then salaamed and retired, and the little Raja handed me out, a servant walking backwards before him, and singing his praises, salaaming as he did so.

As we returned to the Residency, there was a great crowd in the streets, and one man rushed after the carriage with a petition, looking very excited; but, on the whole, the people seemed quiet and contented, and are so, notwithstanding all the reductions that have been made in the late Raja's enormous establishments, so judiciously has all been managed.

Mysore, November 29.

We went to mass in the little Catholic chapel, the congregation being almost entirely native, and those whom I could see were very devout. The priest preached in Tamil very fluently. The natives recite litanies in a peculiar sing-song tone during the mass, which is rather distracting, and when they do sing, they shout in a most deafening manner.

Mysore, November 30.

Drove with Mrs. C. to the summer palace, which contains such a funny collection of valuable things, mixed up with rubbish, pictures, clocks, toys, plaster carts, beautiful Chinese lanterns, and Dresden glass.

Three elephants were in attendance, and Mrs. C. and myself, with Captain C., climbed up into the State howdah on the back of the largest elephant, which is over 9 feet high. We found it a very uncomfortable seat, the great creature swaying about as he walked, and nearly shaking us all out. However, we held on for dear life, and after many perils from branches, horses, and bullocks, not to mention a certain feeling of land-sickness from which we suffered, reached home safely. The trappings were magnificent, the seat of silver, the cloth scarlet, embroidered with gold, and he salaamed with his trunk in the air like a real gentleman. But he swore dreadfully at having to kneel down, and rose up once because the attendants had forgotten to place cushions under his legs, and he found the gravel walk hard for his royal knees.

We received visitors and played croquet in the evening, and went to bed as soon as we could, as we had to start early the next morning. Our camp had gone on straight from Seringapatam to Hoonsoor, our next halt, as it was a short cut by nine miles, a consideration for a number of people who have to march with baggage. Our camp consists of about 200 persons, which is considered moderate. L. always dispenses with everything that is not necessary, it being unpopular to march an army of people through the country, as they eat up all the supplies. Lord Canning's camp, with that of the Commander-in-Chief, used to muster 15,000 souls, so, in comparison, we travel in a very small way.

Hoonsoor, December 1.

We left Mysore in one of the Raja's comfortable carriages, a salute being fired on our departure. At the end of three miles, we passed the racecourse, with its two grand stands, the scene of much merry-making in the old Raja's lifetime on the occasion of his birthday, when the races annually took place. We stopped for a few minutes at Yelwall, nine miles from Mysore, one of the Government houses, standing on high ground in a well-wooded park, in which are deer and wilder animals, at least such is the on dit.

We posted on through a very barren district, with here and there a small village, and, where water was to be had, a patch of cultivation. At ten o'clock we reached Hoonsoor, the tents being pitched round a comfortable bungalow. Tents are so hot in the middle of the day, that I always rejoice in a bungalow, but L. and Captain C. prefer grilling.

At four, all the villagers came, and, as many as could find room, went into the tents, and sat down on the ground before L., telling him all their grievances, presenting petitions, &c.

Hoonsoor was formerly a place of some note, being a depôt of the Madras Government, and having large manufactories of military accoutrements, which employed many persons, but were given up as being expensive. It seems almost a pity, as they induced the people to learn, and they were taught many useful trades. Hoonsoor is also a great place for sandal-wood, and we went to see the depôt. On turning the corner of the street, we at once smelt the perfume of the wood, which was positively overpowering in the stores. The wood is not carved or made up here, but is almost all exported to China. . . .

Fraserpett, December 3.

As it became light, I perceived a great difference in the aspect of the country, and we had evidently got into a moister atmosphere. We passed through a real jungle, which I thought very picturesque; but having got, as usual, half-way, into my palankin, I had, to my disgrace, a sound nap. A summons to admire the view of Fraserpett awoke me, and it was really beautiful. On the bridge over the Cavery, we were met by the inhabitants, and, after taking in a supply of oranges, lemons, and flowers, were allowed to proceed to Captain ——'s house, which he had placed at our disposal. I now noticed a change in the dwelling houses, which were more substantial, and had thickly thatched roofs. Captain ——'s was quite a cottage *orné*—perhaps *orné* is not the right term, for it looked greatly neglected, and all he nice furniture spoiled.

I had a long sleep in the afternoon, and awoke to find my 'Darby' gone out, so poor little Joan set out to find him, and walked about a mile along a very dusty high road, meeting a herd of 200 buffaloes who, like their drivers, stared with amazement at me. When the cloud they had raised cleared away, a vision of delight appeared in the person of Darby, followed by as numerous a human herd, and, oh! the ingratitude and blindness of men! Darby actually enquired why Joan was so silly (that was the phrase) as to choose a dusty high road for her evening walk, when there were lanes equalling in beauty those of far-famed Devonshire to roam in. Joan could not reply at once, her utterance being choked—with dust!

Santecoopa, December 4.

As soon as it was light, we found ourselves in a dense jungle, with no view out of it. The variety of foliage, however, and the wondrous growth of the trees were a novelty. Every moment I longed to stop the bearers to pick a new fern, or an inviting cluster of roses, or a spray of some lovely creeper. One, a white convulvulus, with crimson centre, had found its way to the topmost branches of large trees, and hung down in graceful masses, a perfect shower of flowers. The air was quite perfumed with the scent of the various blossoms. Up we went, through the wood, higher and higher, and were joined by the Soobadar of the Mercara Talook, and a number of Coorgs in their picturesque costume, with drums and horns. They marched on in front of us, singing a quaint strain, and, now and then, blowing loud blasts of welcome on their horns till we reached Santecoopa.

We found the bungalow prettily placed on some rising ground, and the tents pitched under some large trees, and then, towards Mercara, such a view! the Abial peak, the coffee plantations, and the dense jungle beneath! I was enchanted, felt quite inspired, and tried to perpetrate a water-color sketch! It was rather like the crow's attempt to sing, and about as successful, but the motive was more praiseworthy.

Mercara, December 5, 6, 7.

Started in the palankin, L. mounted on Rex, up! up! through the wood, till we began to see over the tops of the trees, down into the vallies beneath, with peeps of distant hills. Half-way up the ghat, we were met by Captain and Mrs. C., who had very kindly driven down to meet us, he thinking that I should see the country better in an open carriage. We were joined by more Coorgs, and an orchestra of horns, drums, and fifes, in the midst of which we left L., and drove on ahead, the road being dangerous, lest the horses should take fright at the noise.

The road and scenery are very like a Swiss pass. Before reaching Mercara, we got out to see a cinchona plantation, which did not seem flourishing.

As I am not clever enough to depict Mercara in water-colors, I must try to describe it by my pen. It was a cold fresh morning, with a sharp feeling in the air, the clouds just rolling off the highest peaks of the distant mountains, which looked very blue, while the near hills were intensely green with coffee plantations. The coffee tree is a bunchy green shrub, with scarlet berries, and a blossom so white, that Captain C. says that, at the flowering season, the country looks as if covered with snow. There were deep jungly vallies between us and the mountains far away, and, on the height on which we stood, a fort, a palace, eastern tombs, a thatched town snug in a hollow, and sundry villas dotted here and there in cosy places. There was a foreground of Coorgs in white or blue coats, scarlet scarfs round the waist, silver daggers and chains, and a large knife fastened in a belt on their backs, and used to force their way through the jungles. They were fine tall fellows, with olive complexions. Captain C. introduced me to the leading officials, who presented fruits and flowers, and then we drove on to Captain T.'s house, which is romantically situated, looking down into a deep valley with the Mangalore and Cannanore ghat-roads winding beneath, the grand Brahmagiri range to the south, and Swami Betta and Tadiandamol to the west. We dined with Captain and Mrs. C., and I had my first drive in a bullock-coach, escorted by not less than twenty torches, enough to set all Mercara on fire, the sparks flying about in the wind in every direction; indeed, we heard next day that there had been a fire in the soldiers' lines, originated, some people said, by our torches.

Next day, all the Coorgs came up in a body, headed by the head Serishtadar, a fine-looking old fellow, and they sat down on the floor of a long glazed verandah in front of the house, and had a discussion with L. about their affairs.

In the afternoon Captain and Mrs. C. took us in their carriage to the tombs of the Rajas of Coorg, handsome buildings with gilt minarets. It is noteworthy that, inside, the stones above the graves of Dodda Virrajendra and Lingarajendra and their two wives are in the shape of a cross. The tombs were covered with flowers, a light was burning, and an attendant came out to present us with fruit. We did not go inside, but looked through the door. Some of the carvings about the buildings are very rich. The two tombs are exactly alike, a third building being a sort of sanctuary, in which the god Shiva is supposed to reside.

The Coorgs themselves do not believe in Shiva, and have no temples, but have a great respect for the god Pan, and the goddess of the Cavery river. They are very superstitious, and believe in wood demons, spirits, &c., and, except at certain seasons of the year, will not enter parts of the forest. Amongst the upper classes there are no conversions to Christianity, and although the children attend the Government schools, the slightest interference in religious matters would be resented at once, so in all the schools it is forbidden.

The Catholic missionaries have a school, not under Government, and after school-hours they give religious instruction to those who like to remain, but only the low castes ever venture to do so. It seems a sad state of things. We can educate them as much as we like, and many of the higher officials are clever and refined in manners, but we cannot convert them.

On the 7th I saw all over the fort, and went into

the rooms formerly occupied by Mr. K. when he was Superintendent. All the Coorgs ask after him with respect and affection, for they say they never had such a Superintendent. Troops now occupy the palace. Horrible stories are told of the cruelty of the last of the Coorg Rajas, a man who ended his days in England. It is said that he used to sit in a bow-window in the palace, and make people run across from the entrance to a stone elephant in the courtyard while he shot at them! In this way he killed all his relations but one sister, who escaped, and is still living. Certainly the Coorgs are much happier under our rule, and they are very loyal.

I expressed a wish to see some Coorg ladies, so one of the head men brought his wife and cousin to see me. They came thickly veiled, but uncovered their faces when in the drawing-room. They were fine young women, with large eyes, and were not very dark. Their hair was worn *en chignon*, only they had splendid gold ornaments on it, and bunches of white flowers. They wore white jackets with short sleeves, embroidered with red cotton, white muslin skirts, embroidered with a narrow gold lace, and very short. Their legs and feet were bare, and round their ankles they had massive silver bands, from which hung a number of little bells, with a silver chain from the band to each toe, held on a number of rings. Their arms were covered with bracelets, and round their necks hung a number of gold chains with jewel ornaments. L. was allowed to be present, but they were very shy. They showed me some work, a sort of fine embroidery, which they were doing, and with which they ornament their husbands' clothes. They also brought with them all their ornaments, and I showed them my Roman necklace, which is not very unlike what they wear, and it amused them.

In the afternoon, in honor of our visit, all the Coorgs assembled, to the number of 400 and upwards, and had a national dance in front of the old palace in the fort. We drove at a foot's pace, for the crowd round the carriage was so great that it was impossible to go quicker. They went, dancing and singing, in front of us all the way up to the fort, with drums and horns and war shouts. Such a row! I thought every moment the horses would take fright, and be off. All the English had assembled at the front windows of the palace, but we remained below in the courtyard, where we had a better view, and of course it pleased the people to see us among them.

About 200 Coorgs formed into a circle. The first figure of the dance was called Balakata, and was a slow movement, the men all dancing round, singing, and waving about gracefully chowrees (long whisks of hair like horses' tails), with an accompaniment of drums. This was followed by the second figure, called Kolhata, or stick dance, in which each man was provided with a couple of sticks, just like those used at 'La Grace.' They all moved round as before, beginning slowly, with a sort of prancing step, which got quicker and quicker. They kept tapping their neighbours' sticks in time, getting more and more excited, and hitting harder, as if they were going to have a fight, but at a given signal they all instantly stopped. The third figure consisted of a single combat. One man leaped into the circle with a war-whoop, armed with a long switch and a metal shield, challenging the ring. Then out sprang another, and away both danced. At last they rushed together, hitting as hard as they could. The laws of the game do not allow hitting above the knees, although some, in their excitement, certainly transgressed. The ankles, however, suffered most, and must have smarted terribly after an encounter. When one of the combatants gave in, the other embraced him, to show there was no ill-will. At the end of the third figure, the assembly had a grand flourish, dancing about, and leaping vigorously into the air. The entertainment was brought to a close by wrestling for cocoanuts, the victors coming forward and breaking them open before us.

They then formed into a long line, through which we passed to the carriage. Nothing could have been more orderly than the whole proceeding, nor more respectful than the manner of the people as they followed the carriage out of the fort and up the road. L. stopped and made them a little speech, after which they dispersed. Hundreds of people had assembled to witness the dance, and I shall never forget the scene. The old fort, the picturesque crowd, the fine men in their striking costume, and the graceful manner in which they danced. L. says it is quite unique, and that there is nothing like it in any other part of India.

Good night, and good-bye to Mercara! We were not sorry to leave for one reason. The cold was making itself felt. Many of the camp were down with fever, and most of our servants had been drinking to keep out the cold, fighting being the result.

Jumboor Báné, December 8.

What a cold morning it was! How the wind howled as I dressed by candlelight, and put on every wrap I could find! Captain C. drove me half-way, over such a road, twisting about, with frightful precipices and glorious views. I shall not soon forget the sensations of that drive. We passed great coffee plantations, and at last reached a valley and a river where we said good-bye to Captain C. I was carried across the river in my palankin, and then through a dense jungle wood, till I reached Jumboor Báné. The encamping ground was very picturesque, just like a park, with a fine view of lofty hills. A tiger had been in possession, I was told, when the tents came up in the early morning, but had disappeared in the jungle.

Somawarpett, December 9.

Left Jumboor by a very steep descent, the road lying through a dense jungle, where it was impossible to get any view, but the wild luxuriance of the vegetation, and the number and variety of the birds, made the ride very interesting. We encamped on some high ground, commanding a splendid view. The town is very clean, and the houses look more substantial and larger than most native habitations. We walked through the place in the evening, to the amusement of the population.

Saniwarsanté, December 10.

About three miles from Somawarpett we came to a bridge, in the centre of which the natives had erected a very tasteful little arch of flowers, and, on the other side, we found quite a crowd awaiting us with State umbrellas, horns, tomtoms, lances, &c., a regular turn-out. They wanted to adorn Fritz with a wreath of flowers, but he decidedly objected to the delicate attention. Tsar, however, quite approved, and stood quietly while he was beautified. In England people send their carriages to walk in procession, but in this part of India it is the custom to send your umbrellas, though only certain persons are privileged to use them. These are called Potails; of whom there are seventeen in this district, one of them having a right to have two lighted torches carried before him as a mark of precedence. No less than nine umbrellas, and the torches, were in attendance to do us honour. The umbrellas are of crimson silk, with gold fringes, or are red and white, of a large size. English horses would be terrified at them and the tomtoms, but Arabs do not seem to object to the display which accompanied us to the end of the march. As it is meant as a compliment, one cannot dismiss the people, but it is very tiresome, as one must go at a foot's pace, and the noise, after a time, becomes wearisome.

During the march we got off our horses, and climbed to the top of the Moree Betta, to see some curious structures, very like our European cromlechs. There are no less than fifty of these odd buildings at the top of the hill. The natives say that anchorites dwelt in them, but L. doubts this, as there are no signs of smoke on the roofs; but, if they were burial-places, it is strange that no skeletons, or jars containing ashes, have been found in them. Only a few pots, of a form not now in use, were found, with some rusty implements. Some of the pots we have in our house at Bangalore, the rest being in the Museum.

Sukrawarsante, December 11.

I decided on using the bullock-coach, and started most comfortably, but the bullocks were quite wild, and, after the most erratic movements, finally bolted into a ditch, where we stuck fast! I begged by signs to be left where I was, and when Marie came up in our own bullock-coach I got in with her, and jolted on safely to Kodlipett. Here I found the people had turned out, so I put my head out of the window, salaamed, and received a donation of fruit and sticky sugar-candy. Making an interpreter of one of my servants, I thanked the people, telling them how much I admired their country, and hoping they would have fine crops, to which they replied that they were very glad to see me. I noticed that the women and children were very pretty, the young ones being quite fair, but their clothing was scanty up to the age of seven or so, a few silver ornaments round the neck and waist being considered sufficient.

Soon after leaving Kodlipett, I got into the palankin for the rest of the march, and went fast asleep, slumbering till we reached Sookrawarsanté, where the tents were pitched on the side of a hill, with a very pretty view. Captain C. had an adventure with a tiger the last time he was here, but it made its escape from the party of gentlemen who had turned out to kill it.

Saklaspoor, December 12, 13.

A very pretty march, chiefly over downs, along a woody winding lane, like those of Devonshire. I rode Fritz, wrapped in my Chuddur shawl till we reached Oogahalli, where a Mr. L. has a house and a large coffee plantation, from which there is a superb view over Manjerebad. We remained a few minutes in admiration, and a mile farther on passed the fort of Manjerebad, built by Tippoo, who called the country 'The Misty,' from its being shrouded in mist during his visit. The fort is perched on the top of a precipitous rocky hill, and, as a matter of course, L. went scrambling up to the top. I completed my journey, and found a very comfortable bungalow, and signs of civilisation.

We halted here for Sunday, General —— and his son, who have taken to coffee planting, came in from some distance to lunch. He is called 'The Harmonious Blacksmith,' because he can play a sonata, and shoe a horse. He was very chatty. In the afternoon, a man brought me a wild leopard cat, which he called a young tiger. I made a present of it to Marie, who tied it up to the door of the tent.

Belgode, December 14.

Awoke this morning with the dripping of the dew from our tent, the fog being white and dense. However, off we started, I well wrapped up, with my shawl over my head, and just my eyes peeping out. The bridge over the Hemawati not being completed, we had to ford it, but the mist was so thick that we could not see the other side, and the stream was so deep in the middle that it was up to the horses' girths. Fritz and Tsar went very steadily through, but Rex did not like his cold bath, I suppose, for he began to dance about and plunge in a disorderly manner, so Captain C., who was riding him, went ahead and soon disappeared in the mist. On our reaching Belgode, he had not arrived, which made us anxious, but we found he had paid a visit to a planter friend, and he joined us at breakfast.

The ride was charming, through lovely woods, and our tent was pitched under a giant tree. In the evening we walked out to the jungle, but, coming upon a human skull in the wood, I felt quite disconcerted, and we turned back to the tents. The owls and bats made a great noise in the tree all night, and kept sweeping down upon the tent.

Beloor, December 15.

At Lukhoonda the road, after passing through woods, opened out. The rice fields are here cultivated in terraces on the sides of the hills under tanks, and at certain seasons are kept under water. My bearers had made a short cut, which proved a longer way, and L. having sent back a man on horseback to know why I was so long in coming, my bearers began running, and I was nearly shaken into a mummy.

I shall never forget the view on entering Beloor. It

was most lovely. Green rice-crops, sloping down to the edge of the tank, a fine sheet of blue water, surrounded by large trees, above which appeared the grey walls of the fortress, and the white dome and towers of the famous temple—beyond, the Bababoodun mountains looking purple and blue ; in the foreground, the procession come out to greet us, the people in white dresses, scarlet turbans, and scarlet uniforms ; a camel, with blue trappings and a big drum on his back ; and a crowd, one mass of gay color, moving along the road, while women, in their bright clothes, were descending the stone steps of the tank, with large brass vessels on their heads. It was, altogether, as beautiful a sight as anything I have seen.

Arrived at the bungalow, we found Captain H., the district officer, and his wife, encamped close by. After breakfast she spent the day with me. I found her very agreeable, and she had two lovely children with her.

In the cool of the evening, we walked to the temple. All the natives turned out to stare, and the road was lined with spectators as soon as we entered the fort. The temple is really very striking, and the carving as wonderful in its way as anything in Europe, only, instead of saints and angels, you have elephants, war-chariots, monkey-faced gods, and hideous monsters. Certainly, there is something very degrading in Pagan art. One of the idols, a huge lion, was visible in a large shed on one side of the building. We were not allowed to go inside, and, in fact, the doors were locked. The temple is said to be 700 years old.

Halibede, December 16.

We passed through a long range of hills covered with jungle, and said to be infested by tigers, but without seeing the whisk of the tail of one even. I suppose we were too large a party, as we heard that a man was killed a little while ago by one on the road, while trying to defend his bullocks.

We found our tents pitched under some fine trees close to the temple, which we went to see after breakfast. We carefully examined the carvings, which are considered finer than those at Beloor, though in the same style. The side chapels contain two gigantic bulls, which are held sacred. There is a fine lake close under the walls of the temple, and the view across it to the hills beyond is very picturesque. There was a fierce sun and a cold wind, and we were not sorry to regain our tents.

Halibede was formerly, no doubt, a very extensive place, but now it has a neglected poverty-stricken appearance. It is probable that much of the destruction was caused hundreds of years ago by the Musalmans, who sacked the place, and were it not for the grand old temple, nothing would indicate its having been the abode of the powerful Rajas who ruled over the west and south of Mysore. In the evening, we walked to the ancient Jain temples, some way from the town, supposed to be 700 years old. The exterior carvings are not so fine as those of the Hindoo temples, but they are more striking, and we were allowed to peep in. Lamps were burning before a great statue carved in black stone. There was much dignity in the figure, which was as high as the temple itself. Having visited two of these curious buildings, we walked to the third, but the people said that a leopard had taken up his abode in it, so we only walked round it, and got our legs well pricked by the spear grass, a really painful infliction.

Benkipoor, December 22.

A very pretty ride to-day, over an excellent road, so we went fast. Our route lay through jungle, but we did not see even a wild antelope, L. thinking that the scarlet uniforms of the Silladars who accompanied us frightened everything out of sight.

The bungalow is close to the Bhudra, which is a fine river, as wide as the Thames at Richmond, and spanned by a handsome stone bridge. As it was still cool, and the rushing of the clear waters over the rocks gave a refreshing sound, I strolled down to the bed of the river, and seeing how lovely was the view of the Baba Boodun hills, looked about for a snug corner to sketch from, when the voice of the butler above informed me there were plenty of alligators in the river. I did make a sketch, but from the safer ground near the bungalow, not desiring an encounter with a crocodile. In the evening, we walked to the bridge, from which we had a most enchanting view of the sunset, and I felt quite savage with myself for my inability to do justice to its glories on paper.

Shimoga, December 23–27.

Away early, by torchlight, in such a thick mist that we could see nothing of the country. We passed a temple on the road, and the people rushed out with fruits, and threw flowers into the carriage. On reaching Shimoga, we found that great preparations had been made, two arches of evergreens having been erected on the long bridge over the Toonga river, and the regiment of Silladars was drawn up a mile from the town, so that it was quite a gay sight.

L. rode on with Major H. and Mr. C. at a foot's pace, so I passed them in the carriage, and went on to the former's house, a fine large one, about a mile and a half from the town, having a glorious view of the Baba Boodun hills and the Kulus Peak. As the mist cleared away, it was like the rising of a curtain at a play, and as I had no idea there was any view from the house, it was a most agreeable surprise.

We had a very pleasant visit. Major H. is a very clever man, and his wife is charming. She married at eighteen, and has four children, of whom two are in England. She has one lovely little girl called Chickie. C. is a great sportsman. On Saturday he heard of a bear, and went after it, promising to bring it in to show the children, who were all assembled for a Christmas party, and before evening he returned with two baby bears, having killed their mother, which was brought in next morning. He has killed thirty-five tigers, and fifty bears, not to mention other game, so I think he is a public benefactor. Mrs. C. used to be in a perpetual state of alarm, but now, she says, she is hardened to it. He is going this evening to a wood near here, where a tiger has been killing cattle, and a bullock has been tied up to a tree, as a bait, poor beast!

I drove with Mrs. H. to *the* shop of the place, and we bought up everything in the shape of a toy to be had; but there were nothing but penny toys, which they sold for two shillings. However, we got enough to fill a bran pie for Chickie's party.

On Christmas Day, we went to seven o'clock mass, the congregation, numbering 500, being purely native. The chapel is small, in the form of a cross, but the scene was very edifying. The men of high caste knelt on the right, the women on the left. The dress of the latter, which, I am told, was introduced by St. Francis Xavier, was very neat, a fine white cloth, sometimes edged with lace over the head, and tied in at the waist, descending to the feet, rather like a shroud. They spread a colored handkerchief on the ground to kneel on, and kept the face concealed, all but the eyes. This costume is only worn in church. One or two of the children were remarkably pretty, and covered with ornaments. The low castes knelt behind us in the centre of the church. The men took off their turbans, and have their heads shaved, except a long tuft of hair on the back of the head. Some of them were very fine looking men, and not very dark. They chant out the prayers all during mass, except at the Elevation, when a little band struck up the only tune it *thought* it could play, and which nearly upset my gravity. It was 'God save the Queen.' The 'Adeste Fideles' was also sung, but it was not much like the beautiful melody we used to hear in Farm Street. We received Holy Communion, and I thought of all in England, as, I have no doubt, you all thought of us a little later.

Of course all the station dined in their best attire at Major H.'s that evening. Mrs. H. looked very pretty in a black net dress, embroidered with white floss, very *distinguée*, with scarlet flowers. Mrs. B. wore her violet satin, her boddice adorned with a jet necklace, which Mr. B., who has a taste of his own, considered too like mourning for a time of rejoicing, though he told her confidentially that he admired her toilette very much. Another lady wore a blue silk, trimmed with an Isle-of-Wight-lace tunic and a gold tiara, and a fourth appeared in her wedding dress of plain white silk, with fair hair and blushes for personal ornaments. Mrs. ——, bored at finding herself compelled to live in Shimoga, did not trouble herself to dress her fair locks, but appeared as she rose from her couch, rough as a terrier dog. Being at heart a dear little woman, she cheered up in the genial company, and forgot the four wee children the dear woman had left in the shoe, so worried she did not know what to do. She became the life of the party, and distinguished herself by valiantly killing a scorpion during the absence of the gentlemen, putting her dainty little foot upon it amidst general applause. Then Mrs. —— played the 'Silver Trumpets' so exquisitely that Mrs. B. fancied herself once more in the

Eternal City under the great dome, in presence of ——. This was followed by songs, and then more than one person was observed to yawn, and the party separated after a chorus from the Christy Minstrels.

Coompsee, December 24.

Instead of returning to Bangalore, as originally planned, I have come on with the camp, as everyone said it was a great pity to be within sixty miles of the finest waterfalls in the world, and not to see them.

I am writing in L.'s tent. It is blowing a gale of wind, and we have just had the tent-ropes tightened. The rapid changes of climate in Mysore make the country very trying, and the only way to meet the difficulty and counteract bad effects is to pay great attention to clothing. In the morning, from six to nine o'clock, I can comfortably wear warm woollen stockings, flannel vest, a petticoat, and my wadded velvet jacket. Before breakfast I bathe, and then dispense with several of these articles; and at three, when I take my siesta, I am glad to throw off as much clothing as is compatible with propriety. But, before starting for my evening walk, I wrap myself up again, though not so extensively as in the early morning.

We found the old fort of Coompsee in a very ruinous and filthy condition, uninhabited, and doubtless deserted because it is unhealthy, as it well may be with a moat of stagnant water; and I should have left the place with an unpleasing impression had we not found the town itself very neat and clean. The verandahs in front of the houses are generally painted with broad white and red stripes, and bamboos had been put up here and there, from which they suspended strings of leaves—a simple style of decoration in honor of L.'s visit.

Anantpoor, December 29.

As Mr. C. is coming to the Falls on purpose to drive me, so he says, I was of course consigned to his care; but when it was daylight he gave the reins over to me, and I felt much less nervous driving myself, though it was so cold that my hands were quite benumbed.

The road was very pretty, running through jungle, with a peep, from time to time, of the distant country. The jungle was high, beautiful graceful clumps of bamboos meeting over our heads, and forming natural arches across the road. The latter part of the drive was through a splendid avenue of Dhoopada trees for at least three miles, up to the bungalow; and so lovely was the avenue, that to see it was worth the whole journey. The Dhoopada is a giant, with large deep-green leaves and round foliage, with perfectly scarlet masses here and there—not of flowers, but of leaves just turning. The whole way down the avenue the Amildar had put up bamboos, with strings of green leaves and scarlet flowers across the road, which added to the general effect. All the town had turned out, and we found a great crowd, with a deafening concert of tomtoms, at least half-a-mile from the refuge of the bungalow.

We had a scorching sun and high wind all day rendering the tents unbearable. About three o'clock

L. saw the people of the place, who assembled by hundreds, and heard all they had to say. Many, however, remained squatted near the tents after the rest had gone, waiting to waylay us when we strolled out in the evening, either for the pleasure of staring at us, or to present petitions. There is one peculiarity about the natives, namely, that they never consider a decision as final, and will go on appealing for years. Hundreds of petitions are sent in about matters that have been finally settled years before; and some petitioners have followed us about the whole of this tour, turning up wherever we go, with the old story.

I walked with L. to the old fort, to see a big gun, which had, however, been blown up. The fort is a picturesque ruin, and as we turned to leave it the scene was very striking. On one side the sun was setting in golden glory over the grass-grown walls, and at the same moment the full moon was rising in silvery beauty in a cold blue sky, reflected in a large sheet of water. Altogether it was a lovely scene.

We returned through the town, followed by a large crowd, who were kept at a distance with difficulty. Even the animals seemed astonished at a blue petticoat, and buffaloes and dogs appeared eager for an onslaught.

Saugor, December 30.

Started by moonlight. I drove all the way, directly it was light. The road ran through a jungle of wondrous foliage, and there was an interesting variety of birds—hundreds of small green parrots with long sweeping tails, jungle fowls, jays, paddy birds, and large vultures of different kinds—all looking up their morning meal. We passed a second beautiful avenue of the Dhoopada trees, and found our tents pitched on some rising ground; but it was very hot all day. This is a great place for sandal-wood carvings, and the people brought up some pretty specimens, and presented me with a flower carved in sandal-wood, which, however, I was not allowed to accept. I ordered a plain box for my valuable lace—a thing I really wanted.

A native, who is to accompany L. through the wild country, called, and I was introduced to him. He was a Jain, and a man of property, but had somewhat the air of a savage in his appearance, having nothing on but a linen cloth about his loins, and a green cloth jacket, the worse for wear. Of course I smiled and salaamed, and he left some sugar-canes and sweetmeats. One kind of sweetmeat is very good. It is called 'hulwá,' and is made of camel's milk and almonds, and is brought by native boats from Arabia.

Talgoopa, December 31.

On our road, we passed a dead bullock by the wayside, upon which at least fifty large vultures were feasting. We met large droves of bullocks and buffaloes coming from the coast, laden with sacks of salt and fish; while, on returning, they carry on their backs grain for exportation to the famine-stricken provinces; so that, although the crops were splendid this year in Mysore, prices are expected to be as high as ever.

The view from the new bungalow at Talgoopa is very picturesque. It stands on the top of a rocky hill, looking over a large sheet of water, a deep blue lake in the morning light, on which floated quantities of large white and scarlet water-lilies, with their large green leaves, the red earth of the road, the grey rocks, and the varied shades of green in the dense woods beyond forming an effective contrast; while, in the far distance, the hill ranges near the Gairsoppa Falls peeped out in hazy indistinctness. I spent all the morning in trying to make a sketch, which I pronounced to be a daub. Mr. C. said he would sit and do duty as a foreground. He came, and sat near me, bewailing his hard fate—only twenty-six, and wanting to go home dreadfully, but not being able to accomplish it. The bright side of the picture is that he is one of the most fortunate men in the Commission—with a good appointment, a very pretty wife, and fine children.

Gairsoppa, January 1, 1869.

The Ghát road is a zigzag like the St. Gothard pass on the Italian side, and when we reached it the view was so beautiful down into the valley that I was persuaded to remain in the carriage; and as we walked the horses, with the horse-boys at their heads, there was no danger. Once I was obliged to get out, a bridge over a brook having been made with nothing but a few sticks, and mud plastered over them, and it was so insecure that it bent with the weight of the carriage.

We are now in the Bombay Presidency, out of L.'s

jurisdiction, but the other side of the river belongs to Mysore. We found a very dirty, tumble-down bungalow, with a few tables and chairs, all ailing, the wood being so dense that it was difficult to pitch a tent.

As soon as L. came up, we proceeded to the Falls, the platform on which the bungalow stands being so high that nothing could be seen beyond the river and the wood, but a mighty roar of unseen waters prepared us for what we were to see.

After following a steep descending path through the wood, we came upon some enormous boulders of rock which, during the rainy season, are covered with water, and, scrambling over these for a few yards, found ourselves at the edge of the fearful abyss. I crawled on my hands and knees, L. holding me, and looked over a sheer drop of 820 feet! the waters rushing over to the left of where I lay. Hundreds of pigeons were flying in and out of the clefts in the rocks. It was a fearful precipice to look over, and yet there was a sort of fascination about it. There is not much water now in the river, but one can imagine what it must be in great floods. The people say that the spray is then so great that the pool at the bottom cannot be discerned. There are four Falls, all from the same level, the largest being called the Raja, the next the Roarer, the third the Rocket, and the last the Dame Blanche, but in great floods they are united in one grand stream.

After leaving the rocks, we walked through the wood to a platform a little below the Falls, a rather rough affair made of only a few planks fastened to some trees. From this, you only see the two latter

Falls, but they are certainly wonderfully beautiful in their graceful shoot from the rocks, and the height inspires you with an irresistible feeling of awe. After a few minutes spent in silent admiration, we climbed up again to the bungalow, and enjoyed our breakfast in the verandah, although it was rather a windy repast.

In the cool of the evening, we again descended to the Falls, and peeped once more over the yawning abyss, the gentlemen being very rash, and making me quite nervous by standing so near the edge. We afterwards crossed the Raja fall, a few yards above the actual descent of water, on a rough bridge made of a few logs of trees tied together with bamboos. It was giddy work, but I did not feel afraid, and we then climbed the rocks between the Raja and the Roarer Falls, and, going on our hands and knees, looked over. The view looking down the ravine, with the sunset lights on the hills beyond, was perfectly beautiful, and quite repaid us for the fatigue.

January 2, 3.

Descending through the wood the next morning, we crossed the river above the Falls, scrambling over the great boulders of slippery rocks, which even the gentlemen said was hard work. When we reached the final bridge above the Roarer, my courage gave way, and I declared I could not cross, but, after saying an 'Ave,' I took L.'s hand, and on we went together. There was no real danger, but it looked so very perilous, and the roar of the waters shook one's nerves.

The palankin had been ordered to meet me across the river higher up, but it was not there, so I had to walk, which, as it was cool and shady, was no great exertion.

Mr. C. went out to shoot bison, but returned unsuccessful, though he captured a baby bison, a few days old. It was a good size and made a great row, crying after its mammy, and, although two buffaloes were secured for its maintenance, it refused to be comforted.

We spent all Sunday at the Falls, but how could it be to me a happy day, with the prospect of L. leaving me the next day! I was very miserable, and not at all well, the exertion of the day before having been too much for me, as exposure under an Indian sun tells at once. I was feverish and weak, and L. gave me some quinine. The previous evening, fireworks and torches were flung over the Falls, and the effect was, I believe, beautiful, but I became so faint just as we were starting to descend through the wood, that I had to be dosed with brandy, and L. would not let me go.

We had a great deal to arrange, as carts could not proceed farther, and the camp was divided, bullocks being hired to convey L.'s tents, and coolies to carry provisions, and as there is a difficulty in procuring food in the mulnad, everything eatable that could be spared had to be sent with him. 'Green Jacket,' the native who was to show L. the way, came to see me with his son, and brought me honey tied up in plantain leaves, but, as we could not understand one another's language, an amusing dumb show followed, he salaaming and I smiling alternately.

Tulgoopa, January 4.

L. walked down with me through the wood, and confided me to the care of the other gentlemen, placing me in the mail phaeton, with a warm eider-down quilt over my knees, for, in the deep jungles, it is bitterly cold when the sun does not penetrate them. Good bye! kisssing of hands! handkerchiefs waving (and used!), and away we go up the ghat, with such a view of the valley and Falls, but I only saw it through very dim glasses, and it was hard work to wring from me a note of admiration that morning.

At Talgoopa, a native came up to the bungalow with the skin of a tiger he had shot, on which Mr. C. gave him the usual reward, and presented me with the skin and the claws. His room in the bungalow presented a curious scene, office tables, with piles of papers, being in one corner, the young bison in another, and, as a centre piece, the buffalo, which had been got in to keep the little savage quiet. Its piteous cries made it impossible for me to enjoy my siesta.

The weather has become much hotter, and the air in the evening feels like that of an exotic conservatory. The gentlemen drank milk punch, and grumbled at their lot, in having to pass the best part of their lives in India, while my thoughts wandered over the distant hills to a little tent somewhere, with somebody in it, all alone.

Saugor, January 5.

I am getting quite a crack whip, and drove all the way. After breakfast, the people came with sandal-wood carvings, but everything was very expensive—one box being 30*l.*, and nothing less than 6*l.* It was so hot that when I went to the tent to wash my hands for lunch, it was like an oven, and the towels were quite hot.

Anantpoor, January 6.

Enjoyed another hot day, which is, however, far preferable to the cold east wind, which dries and chafes the skin like frost in England.

We arranged to go a double march to-morrow. I went for a walk, and the air was scented with sweet-smelling creepers. Captain C. rode Fritz, who is so handsome. What a sensation he would create in *the* Row! Small head and ears, wide distended red nostrils, with a long tail just escaping the ground, which he carries like a plume.

Shimoga, January 7.

Such a disturbed morning, and no sleep after three o'clock; dogs barking, horses neighing, and men chattering all round the tent; so I got up, and started at five in the palankin. At the seventh milestone, Mr. C. put me into the mail phaeton, and we nearly had a bad accident. Going down a steep hill, Ruby made a snap at Topaz, and the latter kicked over the bar and Ruby's trace. I thought he must come down on the stony road, and I jumped out; but the horse-boys stopped the horses, and, with the aid of a Silladar, the harness was undone, and Topaz extricated from his difficulty. No harm was done, except that one of the horse-boys was bitten in the arm.

I was so lazy the next day. The first thing I heard was that Major H. and Mr. C. had gone after a tiger, which turned out to be a panther. He came out of the jungle, when Mr. C. fired from a tree, and the animal fell. They got down, thinking it was dead, when it jumped up, and sprang back into the jungle, but charging out again, sprang upon one of the beaters, clawing his head and throat. Major H. thought the man was killed, but the panther again retreated into the jungle, and the man was saved, and brought into the hospital. Natives are very superstitious, and frequently die when bitten by wild animals from fright, and a conviction that they cannot recover. Major H. related to us how all the camp followers, and the friends of the man had crowded round him, saying, 'Your hearth (cooking place, literally) will be desolate! your wife a widow! and your children orphans! You are indeed a man dead!' Major H. boxed one man's ears, but could not help saying that their expressions were very sympathetic. The mother came, and flung herself at his feet, poor thing! The people insisted on his walking between yellow water and black water, a superstitious practice supposed to be beneficial. The poor fellow died, however, and his hearth is indeed desolate.

Bangalore, January 18.

I was so dreading the long journey into Bangalore by myself, when I learnt that Mr. M. was also going in, so that, if anything should happen, he can pick up the pieces. I was really sorry to say, 'Good-bye,' and pretty Mrs. C. looked half envious, as going into Bangalore from the districts is looked upon in the light of a trip to Paris, or a run up to town in England. Well! off we went at last, a motley procession—*Dignity*, in the person of a mounted Silladar, followed by *Necessity*—that is, two torch-bearers in birthday suits—and *Discomfort*, personified by three bullock-coaches. As soon as we were fairly out of the gates, I proceeded to undress, and then began our troubles. The road was not good, and the coach jolted and swayed to and fro in an eccentric manner, so that being at sea was nothing to it, but, alas! there was no steward to bring the needful. I lit my lamp, and tried to read, as we crept slowly up the hills, but oh! the descents! Three men, who ran by the side of the bullocks to keep them on the road, shouted, twisted their tails, and poked them with sticks, the Jehu flogged, and away they tore, full gallop, regardless of everything. It was trying to one's nerves, and the more so, as, if anything did happen, there was nothing for it but to turn out in nightgown and bare feet. After fourteen hours of this misery, we reached Cadoor. Half the night we travelled through jungles, which were all on fire in parts, and they lighted up the sky, while the flames roared like a waterfall. No doubt, the fires were miles off, but they seemed so near that they terrified me.

I don't think I ever enjoyed a cup of tea so much in my life as I did the one given me on arriving at Cadoor. After dinner, we started again for another fourteen hours. The road was worse than the day before, and in the middle of the night I was so worn out that I nearly fainted. On reaching Tipatoor I was dead beat, but the bungalow was a miserable place, and Mr. M. begged me to go on to Toomkoor, so away we went again, such a wearying journey, and sleep impossible. At last, I slept from sheer exhaustion, and awoke to find myself before a palatial residence; and you may imagine how glad I was to find myself in a comfortable bed in a large airy room.

We left the kindly shelter and friendly house of Mr. and Mrs. P. in their carriage drawn by bullocks, and at Nellamungalum my own carriage met me, and, after dinner, I drove into Bangalore.

I am now all right again, Dr. O. having come to see me, and laughed at my bullock-coach experience.

Bangalore, February.

I am very glad we are to run away from the heat this year, for it is setting in early, but Nundidroog, where we are going, must be very much like being on board ship, the space on its summit being so very limited.

All the boxes have arrived at last safely, and nothing is spoilt. I laughed at the remarks attached to each article, but you made a great omission in not telling me which is the front and which the back of the bonnet and the toilettes, all very puzzling to us in these remote regions. The photograph of the Princess of Wales, with her boy on her back, is charming.

Marie is gone to the marriage of Mrs. C.'s nurse, who has deserted her mistress for a gunner in the artillery. M. holds herself high, and said she should see what company she was to be in before she decided to go on to the *dejeuner*. She was greatly pleased at L.'s giving her the carriage, in which she has just driven away, very neatly dressed, the Arabs prancing, and two running horse-boys in scarlet and white, so she will create quite a sensation, and, perhaps, be taken for the bride.

I was up at six, and took a nice ride this morning. Fritz was so fresh, and seemed to think it was a lark to have such a light weight on his back, instead of the heavy Sowar galloping him round the compound, so he danced and frisked about, while Tsar looked at him complacently, as much as to say, 'What a foolish prig you are! see how well I behave!' I really do believe Arabs almost talk.

Nundidroog, February 21.

We were off at five in the light office-carriage, with the little Arabs, the bullock-coach following with the rattletraps. It was quite dark, and the stars did little to enlighten our way, so we had flaming torches, and a very nasty smell as the consequence, till the sun rose, a blood-red ball, behind some hills in the distance. The country was very wild for miles, with gigantic boulders of rocks, tossed about here and there, but, after a time, the soil began to look more fertile, and the little Arabs stepped out famously, coming in quite fresh at the first station, eight miles. Here Black Prince and Erebus took their place, but the former became alarmed at the tomtoms, which the people had brought out, and no sooner was he in the carriage than he began a series of plunges, refusing to go on. At last, with some persuasion, he went off with a rush, which was very trying to my nerves, and continued very cheerful for the rest of the stage, which was very inconsiderate, as the road seemed to me to be constantly on tank embankments, or, in other words, on the top of a wall, and, of course, we met some gipsy tribes just in the most awkward place, with herds of cattle and donkies, bearing small stacks of wood. However, we reached Devanhalli safe, and changed horses, Gay and Melbourne bringing us on to the foot of the Droog. We left the high road, and came along a cross-country track, which was very sandy.

At the bottom of the hill I got into a tonjon, or chair, L. walking up a precipitous flight of steps from the plain to the top of the Droog. The view from the bottom is wonderful, the great rocky mountain rising in a precipitous manner, and its gigantic sides looking ready to fall and crush you. It is a natural fortress, and its strength has been increased by a double wall and bastions, wherever it was capable of ascent, so as to render it quite impregnable. All this time the sun has been getting up, and is blazing, so I was grateful for a hood over the tonjon, from which hangs a scarlet cloth. Eight men lift the pole on their shoulders with a sort of whoop, and, shouting and singing at the top of their voices, away they go. It was a fine study of the human form divine, as they only sported turbans and fig leaves. They went very fast, only stopping to change men from time to time, one man seeming to command the others, and slapping them all round in turns. Here and there we went short cuts, and did the four miles in an hour and a half, very good going, considering the steepness of the ascent, and as we got higher and higher, the air became cooler and cooler. We passed within the two walls, and leaving a pretty woody hollow on the right, arrived at the highest plateau, with the great grey house in front of us. It is fully exposed to the powers of the air, is very substantially built, and is very handsome, having cost Sir M. C. 4,000*l.* We were told it was all so clean! whereas it was deep in dust, the accumulation of years, all the bedding was dropping to pieces, as also the furniture, and everything was in its wrong place. It was an amusement getting it all in order, but the servants object to the Droog entirely, owing to the cold, so there was a general distribution of blankets and coats, but they sit curled up, looking like martyrs, and shiver with great effect whenever I look at them. The thermometer was 62° this morning in doors, while at Bangalore it was 87°.

The rock falls away precipitously from the house, and looking over the wall down on the plain below, you have a grand view. Near the house there is a little postern gate, whence there is a lovely scene, for, from this spot, you see for miles and miles the little villages dotted about, numerous tanks, and hills covered with jungle, lighted up by sun-gleams. There are hundreds of wild roses, and at the house belonging to Captain ——, where pains have been taken with the garden, the flowers are in great profusion. L. is investigating all the nice dangerous paths, and goes out alone, regardless of my remonstrances, being quite delighted when he finds any extra steep place.

We are thirty-five miles from Bangalore, and have two posts a-day, so work goes on all the same. I have a table in the office, which is so (out with it) jolly!

Nundidroog, February 26.

How can I have news of interest for you, living up here as I do, on the top of a hill 4,800 feet above the sea, in an old fort? To-morrow, however, there will be an event in the arrival of our Bishop, and Marie and I have been busy in making an impromptu chapel for him.

I am studying ornithology. The rock abounds in kites, hawks, and eagles, and the other day Marie put the leopard cat, her special pet, outside the house, tied to a chair, when a kite swooped down and caught it up, but, as he could not manage the chair, he had to let go. He returned, however, with five others, so Marie had to rush to the rescue.

Last week the natives killed a panther, and brought it up to show me. Though very small it had killed a cow. Did I tell you that, just before leaving Bangalore, L. killed a cobra which had swallowed a green snake, half its own size, while the latter, on being opened, was found to contain a toad?

We are expecting a succession of visitors, our first being the T.'s, fresh from England. I shall feel inclined to sniff round them like a dog!

Nundidroog, March 7.

I suppose it is the correct thing to begin with the weather, and one cannot but feel compassion for the unfortunate people frizzling down in the plains, as, from our airy position, we contemplate the misty landscape simmering in the heat below.

The house has been brushed up, washed, and dusted, and looks quite smart; children's merry voices make the walls ring again; there is feasting in the dining-room, singing in the drawing-room, and the old days have come back to the musty, fusty, neglected house, the grandeur of which had departed.

The dear good Bishop was carried off in the tonjon by a crowd of naked natives, shouting and singing to their god Ramanoo, and, as the sound of their voices died away down the ghat, that little excitement was over.

Nundidroog, April 2.

I really am ashamed of myself! I, your special correspondent, who promised you a communication once a week! Well! put it down to the atmosphere of the place, which is essentially lazy. The big four-post beds make one snore to look at them, the glare to wink, the gusts of wind to nod, the old-fashioned sofas invite one to lounge, the easy chairs to snooze, the stillness, the monotonous tick-ticking of the clock, and a general buzzing of insects, are so many lullabys to repose. At four o'clock in the afternoon, a stray traveller, coming into the house, might fancy himself in an enchanted castle, and find sleeping beauties or uglies in every corner of the place, save one, into which there is no admittance except on business.

So much, as an excuse. But our distant position makes other people very busy, and the road hence from Bangalore has not been so wide-awake for years, and will require mending before long. Mr. Smith, the hotel-keeper at Bangalore, says his horses and bullocks have never been so worked, what with wagonettes for the Sahibs and Mem-Sahibs, transits for the ayas and children, trollies for the luggage, and palankins or tonjons for the ghât. Then, the fast-running coolies, who do the thirty-five miles every day (the road being divided into five stages, with a man at each), with bread, meat, and vegetables, ice, and letters, while natives from the neighbouring villages scale the rocks, with fresh fish from the tanks, game, poultry, milk, grain, and what not. And, then we sit, and enjoy the good things.

'And who are *we*?' you ask. Well, let me see. There is interesting Mrs. ——, with her small beautifully-shaped head, with thick plaits of rich auburn hair wound about it, with large brown eyes, who is carried about in a tonjon by eight natives with fig leaves, singing their quaint wild chant. She is always so gentle and quiet, and has a sweet low voice, which says, 'Quite well, thank you,' which is anything but true. With her is Miss ——, who is full of life and spirits, trotting about with a stout stick, up and down, or galloping a pony round the hill, and enjoying it 'Oh! so much!' She will sing for you by the hour, with a full rich voice, which it is a pleasure to listen to, and will croquet you to Jericho, if you give her a chance. She and Mrs. ——, with a small child, live in a queer little house, perched on a precipitous rock, half-a-mile down, their nearest neighbours being a colony of monkeys, who look in now and again.

Higher up is Mr. D.'s house, occupied by a host of people, it being a most elastic place. First, there is Mrs. ——, a very sprightly hospitable dame, who may be seen at an early hour in the morning, *à la bergère*, in an undeniably short costume, knowing little hat, locks flying in the wind (mane down her shoulders), looking after her cows with, *on dit*, a silver crook and milk pails. As, however, no very early hour sees the light of my countenance, I cannot say if this is correct.

Then there is tall, graceful Mrs. ——, with a chignon of golden hair, and five little ——s in tow, of various ages. Two fine boys are to be sent shortly to England round the Cape, the thought of which gives poor mamma a heart-ache. Pretty little Cecie, with her lovely dark eyes, sidles up to L. every evening on the croquet ground, and whispers 'Chocolate, please.' The sweet little pet gets carried into the house for some, of course. Then two babies, in the arms of two smart ayahs, with rings in their noses and ears, wrapped in bright cloths.

Higher still, the Nundi house, looking so grey and solemn, and, inside, smelling sweetly of flowers, stolen from a certain garden hard by, belonging to the other house on the droog, which, though taken, still remains unoccupied.

In one corner, on the ground-floor of the house, in a long low room, lives Marie, my factotum, a very busy person, who keeps the native tailor, who sits cross-legged on the floor, busy also, while a half-caste girl, decidedly pretty, but looking, like the atmosphere, lazy, plays with a handsome wild leopard-cat.

All day long this is the way things go on. Peon, from above, 'Mrs. L.! Mrs. S. wants lemonade,' or, 'Mrs. M. wants beef tea,' or, 'Mrs. F. wants chicken-broth for baby,' or butler calls, or cook calls, or Beebee Sahib (self) calls, the cows come up to be milked, or the hens must be fed, or stores are wanted, or wine has to be opened.

In the large room above are two ayahs with a baby, *mater familias* sitting, sipping lemonade and fanning herself. On the opposite side Mrs. M. doing nothing in particular, but beef-tea awaits her attention, whilst she is absorbed in contemplating a toddling little darling, on whom an ayah gazes with fond admiration. A Mahomedan walks backwards and forwards outside the door—a sharp faithful servant, and watchful, but with one eye wide awake to his own interests.

In another room is Mr. G. reading a novel, his arm in a sling, and a big cheroot in his mouth, puffing away like a chimney. Between him and the room opposite two native servants are fast asleep on two mats, where they are to be found all day long in the same intellectual condition. A third, a very old man, sits near them, with a lot of bottles before him, his occupation being that of a cooler.

In the next room, which is cool and dark, there is nobody; but in the sitting-room leading thence, which smells of smoke and is hot, may be seen the big spider hard at work, and sometimes there is a little spider by his side. There is a very official-looking table, with piles of papers and some maps. 'My dear, don't speak to me,' or, 'there's a peon coming,' or, 'now, go away!' but the little spider is refractory, and says, in reply, 'Bother the peons!' and bullies unmercifully the grand official person, who sits at the official table, before the big official papers.

Now, you know *who* we are. As to *what* we do? Well, at nine, prayers, breakfast at half-past, after which chat and disperse, L. to pen and ink, K. to paint and brushes. Tiffin at two, when we all meet; and at three the ladies go napping, to reappear at half-past five, when we walk, or sit on the edge of the rocks, lazily gazing on the lands below us, and revelling in the golden sunsets which illumine them.

Or we play croquet, and as the game goes on, the scene becomes animated. It is fast getting dark, and Captain A. calls Miss B. 'a wretch,' and Mrs. C. calls Mr. D. 'a horror'; and, as it grows darker, and lanterns are called for, you may hear, in mysterious whisper, someone entreated to 'kill Mrs. B.,' or to 'put Mrs. B. out,' and so on, until the bell rings, and there is a general 'Good night.'

After dinner, in the house, bézique and music divide the time, until Mrs. B., being herself overcome with sleep, suggests that 'Dear Mrs. —— looks very tired,' or 'Mrs. ——, you seem very much fatigued;' and so the party breaks up for the night.

Then follow cigars for the gentlemen, and toast and water for the ladies; and people ascend their ladders into the big beds, and sleep till morning, unless there happens to be a chase after a lizard, or a dash at a scorpion in the bath-room—things not pleasant, but which will occur at times in the best regulated families in this part of the world.

Nundidroog, April 14.

Last week we had a great storm, which has cooled our atmosphere. The peculiar smell of the earth gave warning of the coming rain, and it was a curious sight to watch the storm sweeping up, and hiding one peak after another, with sudden bursts of sunshine on the tanks and clusters of trees in the plain below. In one direction we saw a waterspout, and watched it with our opera-glasses, the sun shining on it, and giving it the strangest appearance, like a column of flame. At last the clouds gathered, and swept over the top of the droog, when down came the refreshing rain with a pleasant patter on the stone balcony.

Mrs. M. has had a great deal of trouble with her servants since she came up here. Her ayah and nurse —the latter a half-caste woman—did not like the droog, and pretended to be ill. The apothecary found out that they were both shamming, so they were sent away; but as the half-caste refused to walk down the ghat, she was carried off by two natives in a blanket strung on a pole! Mrs M. has come out of her room for the first time since her late illness, and is lying on the sofa, looking pale and languid, the lovely brown eyes being bigger and browner than ever.

Her husband has arrived. L. and I, perched on a rock, with opera-glasses, employed ourselves, sister Anne fashion, in spying and reporting his progress. It is one of the great amusements of the place to watch people climbing up the ghat, as we can see our friends miles off an hour or two before they can possibly arrive.

We have had the house full all the week, and every one is delighted to get up here for a little air. I was quite sorry to see Mrs. H. and her two fine little boys depart. They were so good, and charming playthings. They came to dessert every evening in their night-gowns and dressing-gowns—such pretty little figures.

Nundidroog, May 29.

We really are on the move. The monsoon has burst, and we have had one tremendous storm. I never heard such loud thunder. It was like parks of artillery, and the lightning was incessant, forking in every direction. The mountain has put on its nightcap of mist, and is anything but agreeable now as a residence.

Marie left yesterday, and the native servants have it all their own wicked way. All the heavy baggage went down the ghat the day before on the bare backs of fifty coolies, and the house is reduced to its pristine state of bareness and discomfort. There are storms of high winds and rain now every evening, so the place is dreary, especially as everything has been marched off, and not a book left; so L. and I have to fall back upon an old pack of cards and an ancient newspaper.

Bangalore, June 4.

We left Nundi at the early hour of four. There was a strong wind and a thick driving mist, so that we could not see a yard from the door. I got into the tonjon, well wrapped up in a plaid, eight men hoisting me on their shoulders, a peon on one side and the Amildar on the other, the latter having politely come up to escort me down. Away we went at full trot down the ghat, and, as the mist cleared off, the descent was very pretty, with peeps at the country below. The Amildar was so civil, running by my side all the way, L. having taken the short cut, that I felt quite ashamed of my want of confidence in not liking to be alone with the natives. Arrived at the bottom of the ghat, we found the carriage, and a crowd of carts, coolies, and beggars. L. mounted the redoubtable Ajax, and rode off across country to Devanhully, Ajax prancing and curvetting like a small war-horse. I got into the carriage, escorted by Silladars, and quite enjoyed the drive to Bangalore, which we reached at eleven. I felt so pleased to be at home, as everything looked green and pretty, and Marie, all smiles, was waiting at the door of the bungalow.

Bangalore, February 4, 1870.

Here I am, writing to you in our dismantled drawing-room, from which all the pictures and ornaments have disappeared. I have just come from the nursery, where I left my Eddie—Marie's 'delicieux tweet,' and the amah's 'chinna Raja' (little king)—laughing and crowing at the flowers on the wall. You would be amused to see the fuss that is made with the little fellow. Marie superintends, and won't move from the nursery, as she says natives are not to be trusted. The ayah sings, dances, and talks to him; the amah considers she does her duty in feeding; old Poochamma is employed all day long in airing and folding; and Rosalie, the half-caste girl, acts as interpreter. In an evening, Marie drives out with him, while the amah sits in front holding a parasol over him. How shall we ever come down to the marrow-bone coach?

On the 1st, the officers of the Commission gave a dinner and dance as a farewell entertainment to L. in the Public Offices, which were most tastefully decorated for the occasion. One room was fitted up as a drawing-room—windows curtained, walls hung with pictures and mirrors, while sofas and settees had taken the place of the official tables and uneasy chairs.

We sat down to dinner upwards of eighty persons in the centre hall of the offices, at four tables, each table being arranged, provendered, and presided over by the wife of an officer in the Commission, each lady displaying her own good taste in the matter. The white walls of the hall were decorated with flags and spears, and the pillars had garlands of a brilliant scarlet creeper just now in flower, which was most effective. After dinner, Mr. K. made a very pretty speech, and did not spare my blushes—never mind, some say they are becoming. Then they drank our healths, and L. replied.

After dinner the hall was cleared, as if by magic, and dancing began, the band of the 16th Lancers playing in one of the galleries. The whole entertainment was got up most handsomely and tastefully.

On the 2nd, L. went to Mysore to take leave of the little Maharaja, whom he visited in class, learning his A, B, C, with his future courtiers, the young Rajbindes. He afterwards saw them all at play, Colonel M. having taken much pains in teaching them English games. In the evening the town was illuminated, and all the different castes—Brahmins, Seths, Komatis, Lingayuts, and Musalmans, presented complimentary addresses. This was followed by a dinner in the Residency, when there was much speechifying, and the evening ended with a display of fireworks.

Guindy, February 8.

On the 7th, addresses were presented to L. at the Public Offices by the Hindoos and Musalmans of Mysore, and by the people of Coorg. The hall was beautifully decorated, and crowded with many hundreds of natives, who came with garlands of flowers and bouquets to present to L. The address of the Hindoos was well composed, and presented in a handsome sandal-wood box, inlaid with a miniature of the little Raja.

That same evening we left Bangalore. The natives had been very busy all day erecting an arch at the gate, and swinging garlands across the road which leads from the house to the station. Just before we started, the servants came and laid their turbans at our feet as a sign of regret at our departure. Most of them had been several years in L.'s service, and we had found them very faithful. I have not lost a single thing since I have been out here, which speaks well, I think, for the honesty of the household.

It was dark as we drove out of the compound, and the crowd was so great all the way to the station that we were forced to drive slowly, with men at the horses' heads, lest they should take fright at the shouting of the people, the colored lights, and the torches. The station was crowded with all our friends, who had come to see us off. Such a shaking of hands, good-bye, and good wishes! It was quite affecting, and the station at last became so full that the doors had to be closed, and it was some little time before the train could be safely moved out. As soon as it did there was a great cheer, and we were off. Farewell for ever! At a cross road, a little higher up the line, another crowd had collected, and gave another cheer. It was too dark to recognise anyone, so I could only flutter a handkerchief out of the window, to show that the kind feeling was appreciated.

Away we went, whizzing and whirling all through the night. When the train stopped anywhere, the Coorg deputation, who have come down to Madras to see the last of us, cheered lustily.

How dusty and tired we were next morning, when the sun got up, and glared at us unmercifully before we reached Madras, where we found Lord N.'s son, who had kindly come to meet us with an escort. We then drove to this charming place, where there is a very large, white, and luxurious house, standing in a wild park, full of fine trees and antelope, with a glimpse of the sea in the distance.

Lady N. is confined to her room, having met with a serious accident. The horses ran away and dashed the carriage against a tree, one of the horses being killed on the spot, and Lady N. being thrown out. She is now suffering from the shock and many bruises, but the wonder is that she was not more hurt.

I am enjoying the visit here as much as is possible, with the prospect of the voyage before me as soon as the gun at Fort St. George announces the arrival of the French steamer.

Galle, February 15.

The gun boomed at last, the French steamer had arrived, and the pleasant visit at Guindy was at an end.

The steamer left Madras on the 12th at midday, so we were well grilled before we got on board. There was the long drive in from Guindy in the heat, the glare and the dust, and then the waiting in the dirty little bureau of the Messagéries Impériales, where the heat was stifling. Knowing what I should have to encounter on the pier, I begged for a little water, and, soaking a handkerchief, put it as a protection under my hat. What a guy I must have looked! but, just then, I was regardless of appearance. Lord N. met us on the pier to say good-bye; and when a Governor does not think it too hot to turn out for an act of courtesy, I suppose inferior mortals ought not to grumble; so I will only give one growl, and say how sorry I felt for myself and everyone else, as I stood in the sun at the top of the ladder at the end of the pier. Then followed the giddy descent, with the waters surging beneath, my heart in my mouth, or my head in my stomach—I don't know which it was. The leap in, and the agonising moments watching Marie descend with the baby, and the feeling of relief when we were all safely in, and the men pulled off to the ship. There is one comfort in being well frightened—that it is an effectual cure for sea-sickness.

The faithful Coorgs came off to the ship, and got on board to see the last of us, bringing me a photograph of themselves, nicely taken in a group, and they gave three cheers when they left.

The 'Godavery' was a small steamer, well appointed, and the Commandant was very civil. The *cuisine* was excellent, but what was food to me at such times! We had a quick run to Pondicherry, which we reached the same day. The heat was very great, but bearable till we anchored in the roads. At night it was suffocating, and waking with a stifled feeling, I called to L., and fainted away. I was dragged into the saloon, where there was more air, or, I believe, I should never have revived. The Commandant was very considerate, and, as there was only one other lady on board, begged I would occupy the ladies' saloon, where I had more space and air.

We reached Point-de-Galle on the 15th, and as the China steamer had not arrived, we landed, and came to the hotel, which is very comfortable, but the noise outside is distressing. 'Madam, buy ring?' 'I got one very good ring.' 'Master want ruby?' 'Sir—sir, buy fan? Very good fan.' 'Madam, buy basket—very cheap.' 'Comb, sir? very good comb;' and so it goes on all day, a crowd of natives, each one shouting at the top of his voice, anxious to sell his wares, and persecuting everyone who goes in or out of the hotel, or appears at a window, or sits in the verandah. It is such a nuisance!

Marseilles, March 13.

The rest of the voyage home has been both interesting and amusing. The 'Hooghly' is a splendid vessel, the largest on the line, and the arrangements and management are perfect.

The evening before we left Galle, the great ship presented a most curious and animated scene. I can only compare it to a beehive or an ants' nest swarming with human beings. As she lay in the harbour at Galle, she was surrounded by crowds of boats and barges, discharging provender, specie, or luggage, while her decks and vast sides were crowded with people.

The passengers were of all nations, and the manners and customs of some were entertaining. L. was very much taken aback the first morning after we sailed, on going on deck, as it is the custom for gentlemen to do on board the P. and O. steamers, to find that ladies, also with bare feet and airy garments, were enjoying the morning air. Some of the costumes were peculiar. One neglected little boy of five years old wore nothing but a pinafore, which had no strings behind, so that it waved over his head like a flag of distress, while several young girls appeared in white calico drawers and blouses—loose and cool, no doubt, but remarkable.

The *cuisine* was excellent, and the attendance very good, all the meals being served *à la Russe.* One arrangement struck me as being very good, that is, that all the luggage was lettered and placed in the hold, so that there was no difficulty in getting at the boxes; and any lady could go down with ease and get anything she might require.

We had a quick and smooth run to Aden, which we reached on February 25, but, on leaving, the wind had freshened, it was rather rough, and the 'Hooghly' began to roll in a way which I thought very dreadful. Visions of a possible shipwreck on a coral reef would present themselves to my mind—not improbable even, seeing that so many steamers have been lost on the reefs in the Red Sea in fair weather, and now it was foul. That night I put everything ready in case of accident, and sat up in my berth ready for an emergency, getting laughed at by L. for my pains; but when I remember how M. was wrecked in the 'Alma,' in the Red Sca, in perfectly calm weather, and landed on a coral reef in nothing but her night gown, I think I was only prudent.

We arrived at Suez a day earlier than we were expected, the Commandant being anxious to see how quickly the voyage could be made by the Canal in fair weather; but imagine his disgust, and our impatience, when we found that we could not enter the Canal, the Superintendent being absent, and his return uncertain. We were advised not to land, but some gentlemen did so, and were left behind in consequence, for next morning it blew a gale, and the little steamer in which they came off could not get alongside of the 'Hooghly.' After a delay of some hours we steamed away to the entrance of the Canal, and then our troubles began. The Commandant did get us out of them, but I think he was a clever man to do so, for the navigation through the Canal of a ship of 2,500 tons, like the 'Hooghly,' was a miracle of skill, and he never left the passerelle from the moment we started till we anchored at night at Kantara.

The Canal work, though wonderful as a piece of engineering, cannot as yet be said to be a perfect success. It is, for the greater part of the way, extremely nar row, and not only does it not admit of two ships passing one another, excepting in a few places, but a ship of the length of the 'Hooghly' has considerable difficulty in navigating the curves. In many places the depth of the water is quite insufficient to admit of the passage of vessels drawing more than 17 feet (though, nominally, it admits those drawing 21 feet), owing no doubt to the silting process which is always going on.

As it was blowing a gale of wind when we entered the Canal, it was found impossible to steam at regulation speed, or the ship would have been blown on to the bank, and to add to the difficulty, dredging machines were at work, and as we could not stop, and they could not get out of the way, we struck against some of them, and in one instance carried away one of our ladders. After losing sight of Suez and the statue of Lieut. Waghorn at the entrance to the Canal, nothing was to be seen but the trackless desert, and there was no vestige of vegetation or habitation, except the huts of the workmen, till we reached the bitter lakes, where the water, being deeper, admits of rapid passage. After leaving these we reached Ismailia, a tolerably large place, and the terminus of a branch of the Cairo railway.

On leaving Ismailia the Canal again narrows, and we touched the bottom three times. Before we arrived at Kantara, the ship suddenly gave a great lurch over, as if she would turn on her side, and there was a rush at once of people, some to the side and some below, when she righted. It was evident, however, that she had stuck fast, and it was long before she moved again, and when she did, we perceived that something had happened to the screw. The excitement on board was intense, everyone on board who was supposed to understand anything of nautical matters being appealed to as to whether it would be safe to proceed on the voyage in the 'Hooghly.' People consulted together and shook their heads and croaked, and nothing else was discussed all day, most people looking at the blackest side. The next morning a young Frenchman dived under the ship, and ascertained that two or three blades of the screw were broken or bent.

We reached Port Saïd at 2 P.M. on the 4th. Though this town is quite of recent origin, it already numbers 10,000 people, being a fast-rising depôt and port for steamers. Its population is a motley rabble of French, Italians, Germans, and Levantines, added to the indigenous Egyptians. It is very dirty, and the streets are simply tracks of heavy sand. Hotels, shops, and cafés are rising up, and there is a church and a convent, but the appearance of the place is anything but attractive.

Divers went down to examine the damaged screw, which was found not to be so much injured as we feared, although it was apprehended that the speed of the ship would be lessened.

We left on the 5th in bad weather, a strong north-west wind having blown for two or three days, raising a considerable sea, but when we sighted Candia it had fallen, and I was less miserable. The view of the island was beautiful, the higher hills being covered with snow. On the 8th, the sea was again rough, and the 'Hooghly' pitched about in a wonderful way. As I struggled across the saloon, I found myself at one moment tumbling down hill and the next struggling up an incline. As we entered the Straits of Messina, the wind fell, and the sea became calm.

The view of the Calabrian coast on one side, and of Sicily, with the frozen summit of Mount Etna, on the other, was glorious, and we had a most enjoyable run close to the former, passing numerous towns and farms, with bright patches of cultivated ground, and, behind, the lofty rugged mountains. The whole scenery of the Messina Straits is grand and striking, and on leaving them we resumed our north-westerly course, passing by the smoking crater of Stromboli and its sister isles.

The wind was so high that the Commandant thought it prudent to avoid the rough weather which we should probably encounter if we passed through the Straits of Bonifaccio, so we steamed along the eastern side of Corsica, and in the morning had a grand view of Bastia and other places near Cape Corse. But the mestral blew fiercely, and on reaching Marseilles it was so rough that the pilot would not take us into harbour, so we steered into the quarantine basin to our great disgust and wrath. We were all ready to land, and many of us knew that warm hearts and dear hands were waiting on the quay to greet us.

The ship, having been built for the tropics, was bitterly cold, the mestral whistling through the persiennes, while we all shivered and grumbled and bemoaned our hard fate for thirty-six long weary hours, at the end of which time, having all lost our tempers, and many of us caught bad colds, we steered towards the Quai Napoleon. The ship seemed herself irate at her cold reception, and took the roof off a warehouse as she lay to.